CLASSIC WRISTWATCHES

2008–2009

The Price Guide

FOR

Vintage Watch Collectors

BY

Stefan Muser

AND

Michael Ph. Horlbeck

ABBEVILLE PRESS PUBLISHERS

New York   London

RGM

WATCH COMPANY

Dear Readers,

Old wristwatches are high on many collectors' lists at the moment, confirmed by the fact that grand Swiss watch brands regularly bring out new editions of their successful past models, taking great care to reproduce designs for these new classics loyal in all details. Research has shown that a majority of watch fans in an age bracket with good purchasing power react positively to shapes and features of wristwatches from the 1950s and '60s where the terms "beauty," "quality," and "reliability" are concerned. The image of a "good watch" from the days of their youth is often evoked by an Omega, Rolex, Longines, or IWC on the wrist of a father, uncle, or teacher—and contemporary watch designers ingeniously change things up with an array of interesting strap lugs, domed dials, and faceted hour markers.

Certainly there is a lot to be said for buying a watch in a store, one that comes with a guarantee and a modern watch movement. But why be satisfied with an ambitious remake when the original can be had in a perfectly restored or even new state at a fraction of the prices that are demanded today? Collecting wristwatches doesn't need to be an expensive hobby: alongside the "secure investments"—if there is such a thing—this publication also shows interesting ways to enter this fascinating world of design and technology—at interesting price points.

Classic Wristwatches paints a portrait of legendary German and Swiss watch brands, introducing the most sought-after wristwatch models of the twentieth century. Each model is presented individually with a picture and with its most important technical information as well as its current estimated market value. Alongside understanding the technical and historical elements of the subject, putting together this publication also demanded a certain propensity for systematic busywork. And, of course, a representative, well-cared-for archive was necessary in order to illustrate these developments and tendencies.

Without the well-filled image archive of the Dr. H. Crott auction house, such an extensive and wide sampling of collectible wristwatches as the one found here would not have been possible, although the authors' greatest problem actually lay in choosing from the immense archive of pictures and information from more than thirty years of auctioneering.

Stefan Muser has been the owner of the Dr. H. Crott watch auction house in Mannheim, Germany, since 1993 and is well-known in Europe's watch scene. Michael Ph. Horlbeck has written an extensive book on alarm wristwatches and contributes regularly to German watch magazine *ArmbandUhren* with interesting articles on collecting. These two authors have created a reference work like no other.

On page 227, you will find that we have put a focus on pilot's watches, which currently enjoy great popularity among collectors. These models have been removed from their corresponding brand chapters and added to the chapter on pilot's watches. We wish you great pleasure in reading this new publication, certain that you will find a great deal of interesting information here.

DIGITAL AGE WATCHWINDING TECHNOLOGY

the TOURBILLON WATCHWINDER

By constantly indexing the rest position of your watch(es) on this winder, any automatic mechanical watch achieves Tourbillon accuracy (patent pending). A lighted LED display indicates actual turns per day and resets to zero at midnight. A second display shows exact time to facilitate watch resetting if necessary. In single, double or triple watch versions. For detailed information, visit www.orbita.com.

GOING ON A TRIP?
Slip your mounted watch in the Voyager leather case with its own powered mini-winder. You can set it up wherever you are.

ORBITA®
WATCHWINDERS

Made and Serviced in the USA by Orbita Corporation
1205 Culbreth Drive, Wilmington, NC 28405
Call Toll Free: 800-800-4436 or visit www.orbita.com

ULYSSE NARDIN
SINCE 1846
LE LOCLE - SUISSE
ANNIVERSARY 160 - 1600-100
SELF-WINDING OFFICIALLY CERTIFIED
CHRONOMETER MOVEMENT.
LIMITED EDITION OF 500 PIECES.

Everything you need to know about how to use *Classic Wristwatches*

Classic Wristwatches is an overview of vintage wristwatches, put together according to the best of the authors' knowledge and ability to give the reader as wide a survey as possible of collectible models of individual brands, but naturally without any ambition of being complete in any way.

If they are not otherwise marked, these examples are wristwatches that have actually been sold at the Dr. H. Crott auction house in Germany within the last few years.

The estimated values of the watches shown and their developmental prognosis are oriented on the market status in Germany at press time and must be taken as a recommendation only. For the sake of comparison, all estimated values and developmental prognoses are valid for very well-maintained, original, functional, complete wristwatches, even if the watch shown and described in detail may not correspond precisely to this standard. Especially well-documented watches offered with original accessories such as boxes, additional bands, sales tags, guarantee certificates, operation instructions, and original sales receipts may sell for much higher prices. The opposite is also true of less-than-perfect examples in need of restoration or with visible damage, which may bring in amounts clearly below those listed here. This publication does not include forgeries, fakes, and *mariages*.

For the purpose of organization, the models within a brand are not ordered in a strictly chronological sense, but rather according to function and style. However, the year of each model's manufacture is clearly printed to allow the reader a quick overview of the time period in question. The little pictograms found above each watch are also there to serve as additional identification and for overview purposes.

The legend for the pictograms is as follows:

- manual winding
- automatic winding
- calendar functions
- chronograph
- certified chronometer
- alarm

Our **"estimated value"** is based upon models in top or near top quality that are original, complete, and functional.

- ↗   Increase in value may be expected
- →   Good investment
- ↘   Probably valued too highly at the moment

Wristwatch Collecting—The Right Way

To enjoy your watch collection for a long time, you should be making some decisions before you even take your wallet out of your pocket. Don't worry: it's not hard to make the right choices, and many roads really do lead to the same place.

by Michael Ph. Horlbeck, Stefan Muser and PeterrBraun

Every watch collection begins with a special watch: the Omega you got at your first communion, the Longines you received from your great uncle, or the Breitling you bought yourself upon landing your first real job. It could just as well have been a Favre-Leuba you got at a flea market (the one with the spots on the dial), the Junghans that didn't make it past your first attempt at repairing it, or the Rolex Prince you got in the antiquities shop next to the Ponte Vecchio on your first business trip to Italy—the one that actually turned out to be an Alpina Gruen with a Rolex dial. These are watches you associate with something, objects that go past pure function, watches that have become part of your personal history.

At some point the moment arrives when such a watch becomes more than just an instrument for reading the time of day. Suddenly the watch feels differently on the wrist, and you just love to look at it again and again even though you don't want to know what time it is. It might just as well not be running.

Once this watch has been liberated from the mundane job of just displaying the time, then it is only a small step before you really start thinking about your own (little) watch collection.

Getting Started

The basis of a watch collection is not what you might think it is: the first watch with the qualities listed above, but rather the watch that comes after that one. The first watch might have been an accidental purchase; the second certainly wasn't. You purposely searched out the second watch—according to criteria that were influenced by the first watch, whether consciously or subconsciously. One thought that hits close to home is the search for a watch to complete something you already have at home that for some reason you just like. This can be a dial or case variation, a similar model by a different brand, a different model of the same brand, or the complete opposite of your "first love"—to wear, for example, the

A rare sight: Rolex movements are shining examples of reliability, though they rarely see the light of day in their hermetically sealed Oyster cases.

other half of the time or to represent the other side of you.

Most of the time it doesn't take long before you have even acquired a third, fourth, and even a fifth watch, chosen according to this criteria, but much more quickly, and not always consistently. Or maybe never consistently.

It is with the purchase of a sixth watch that problems start to crop up. Experienced watch collectors draw the line at this point:

up to here, one is not yet strictly a collector, but rather more of a "gatherer."

This little conglomeration of watches lays in a drawer with no organization, and only with a great deal of imagination is it possible to understand why these timepieces might belong together. Many different watches allow one to reflect a myriad of moods and freshen up the wardrobe, but that does not yet constitute a collection. This point is where it generally gets exciting.

Many Choices

This doesn't mean that a collection can only be thought of as something upwards of seven watches, for it is really all the same whether the six "collected" watches are going to become part of a set or not. In most cases, not all of them are going to be suitable for a collection anyway, as they are usually just far too different from each other. And with certainty, among the

An interesting collecting theme: special automatic movements. Left: a Jaeger-LeCoultre Memovox with pendulum oscillating weight and alarm function; below: two very early automatic watches and a rare Veglia Novix.

timepieces bought in the first wave of euphoria of one's exciting new hobby, there are a few lemons. That doesn't matter, though.

Every collection is valid as long as the collector can recognize why these timepieces should be together. There is no general set of rules for one "real and true" watch collection. The fields of collecting that can be concentrated upon are simply too numerous and too vast: we are talking here of a period in time of one hundred years and a variety of far more than two hundred watch brands. It's hard to fathom how many different wristwatch models were produced by various manufacturers during this time period. There are supposedly more than 100,000 different references catalogued in just Cartier's archives. Striving for completeness is in any case utopian—no matter what one is collecting.

Leap of Faith

Regardless of one's specialization, the first question is always what you want to do with the watches. Do you want to wear them or not? Keep them running or conserve them? And what is more important to you: originality or quality? There are good reasons for every option, and collecting is really dependent upon the quality of a watch as it is worn every day.

Historical diver's watches are not something you necessarily want to take for a swim with you; you really shouldn't wear a perpetual calendar every day to work; and it may not be the best idea to go play drums for an hour wearing an old rectangular watch powered by a shaped movement without shock protection. Those who place more value on originality will be more careful about subjecting their wristwatches to the elements if they are outfitted with leather straps that have become somewhat brittle over the course of time. And some pieces are simply so rare and/or valuable that they are best enjoyed at home among friends and family—possibly in the company of a grand drop to drink.

What's Worth It?

Wristwatches are a much too wonderful and interesting collector's topic to articulate the question in your mouth: what should the collection be worth? Naturally, sensational auction results and calculated profits in comparison to an original retail price sound wonderful to our ears, but in general there is no great or quick profit to be made by selling old wristwatches—unless you really know what you're doing and have not only great contacts but a bit of luck.

Newbies to the topic of watch collecting are better off banning thoughts of a quick buck. It is far more recommendable for new collectors to buy their watches from serious watch traders, even if the prices there are perhaps not as tempting as one has always heard. Meeting an inexperienced seller who doesn't necessarily know what kind of treasure he or she has in hand and sells it too cheaply happens far less frequently than you might think. Most of the time you get what you pay for when you buy from a private seller.

Naturally, everything is a question of relations, but a not-quite-kosher watch or a watch that has been fiddled together "somehow" is not a good situation for a collector, who learns something new every day, and will be too expensive—regardless of the low price asked for it. Not only does a watch like this take up space, it also weighs heavily on the heart.

The longer one occupies oneself with collecting after finding the hobby, the more trust in one's own ability to judge is won, and then—and only then—can one keep an eye out for that unsuspecting seller. Just as there is no hard and fast rule for a "true" watch collection, there are no generally valid recommendations for "guaranteed" increases in value. The market for classic watches is a lively one, and even pros are not safe from surprises—both positive and negative in nature.

What to Collect

Let's take a look at a more joyful subject: the watches. As you've probably gleaned from the long preamble, there are numerous starting points for watch collections. Collecting according to brand is a logical place to begin that contains great potential for development—on the condition that you choose a brand that has been active for a long time, and possibly still is, and has a corresponding number of different models in its evergreen collection. Various possible structures open up within the universe of this brand: such as the chronological collection, which—according to your financial possibilities and space allowed— can be finely tiered. If you like a certain brand and are beginning to show interest in its history, you might soon find out which models have been labeled "milestones" in its development by book authors, journalists, and established collectors. Since most watch brands of the last century have often reacted similarly to fashion and market trends, and technical innovations reached each one of them within a few years of each other (if they're Swiss), a vivid documentation of the development of the wristwatch can be created using such a chronological brand collection.

Depending on the brand chosen, such a didactic collection can become rather expensive, however.

Collecting wristwatches is always a question of how deep one's pockets are— not only regarding the favored brand, but also regarding the type of watches. While a collection of perpetual calendars can demand great financing, a collection of simple manually wound timepieces can be built up for relatively little money—unless you are specialized in fine Genevan manufacture products or award-winning, record-holding observatory chronometers.

Starting Out Slowly

In order to not capitulate in the face of the sheer size of a collecting theme, you should really set a few boundaries. Just collecting automatic watches can soon turn into a nightmare since watches such as a Harwood from the 1930s fall under its auspices as well as an Omega from the 1940s and a Patek Philippe from the 1980s.

Starting with the Harwood mentioned above, you could head in a direction of "early automatic prototypes" and attempt to find a Rolls, an Hâtot, a Wig-Wag, and even an Autorist for your collection. At some point you will have to have the rotor-winding Rolex Oyster Perpetual, and then you will have a didactically demanding collection that includes history and per-spective: the various technical solutions to a bilaterally winding rotor offer such a wide field that they can easily become a collection within a collection.

Or you could take the hammer automatic of the previously mentioned Harwood as the occasion for targeted collecting of other, later hammer automatics that further brands such as Omega and Jaeger-LeCoultre manufactured. An early Rolex Perpetual would also fit in well here, practically as a direct system comparison. Perhaps you can even seek out other automatic specialties, such as movements with a micro rotor, for example. You see that the topic "automatic" alone offers a myriad of themes that can even include specialized directions like "all watches containing Felsa Caliber 690," "all automatic watch models from the year of my birth," or "all automatic movements of the 1970s with a date window." Collecting chronographs is similar since this complication remains one of the most popular additional functions, at least on men's watches. There are more than enough topics: manually wound or automatic; one or two counters; one or two buttons—possibly even buttons in the crown—integrated flat buttons; round; rectangular; oval; sporty or elegant; rotating bezel; tachymeter scale; all Valjoux, Venus, or Landeron calibers; only chronographs with *manufacture* movements, with calendar functions, and/or moon phase displays ... the list is endless.

The more you know about the history and technology of a brand or watch type, the clearer the lines of a potential collecting theme become. Those who have occupied themselves with the special design refinements of an alarm wristwatch will see this especially practical complication with other eyes and not rest until they have collected all the different alarm movements.

You can also collect according to purely aesthetic points of view as well, concentrating on certain dials, case shapes, or materials, possibly sorted according to era, region, or—as previously mentioned—certain brands.

Garbage or Treasure?

Even if a flea market collector might contradict this, you should only collect watches in perfect or at least very good and functional states, otherwise you will own a veritable junk yard within a short amount of time, which will provide joy neither to its owner nor the casual observer. A good piece of advice: if you have a certain budget at your disposal, then it is certainly more practical to invest it in one or two valuable watches in perfect condition than to waste your hard-earned money on many banal, worn out, or even defective watches. When in doubt or if you have the choice, you should reach for the watch in better condition, or as a second resort for a seriously documented or proven restored watch. Defective or incomplete watches can be purchased for parts, even though it is mainly the same parts of a model or type that wear out or get broken.

Only exceptionally valuable watches with fine *manufacture* movements are worth buying as a wreck to be upgraded later by a professional. But you will need a little expert knowledge to estimate how much restoration will be needed and what it will cost. If you can get the watch cheaply, the investment might be worth it: genuine *manufacture* products by Rolex, Patek Philippe, Jaeger-LeCoultre, Vacheron Constantin, Audemars Piguet, and IWC are quite sought-after and expensive in this era of generally high price levels.

Maintenance

Old wristwatches—especially valuable *manufacture* products and complicated calendar watches—should only be worn if they are not subjected to damaging conditions. Simply sweating on a warm day can lead to great damage to the movement of a classic watch without water resistance (especially the crown and buttons) over time. Those who only wear their watches in the evening or on the weekends would do great service to their automatic models with a watch winder, for the constant use of the winding and setting mechanism does more damage than just the simple moving of the gear train when regularly worn. There are also machines for manually wound watches that make at least the periodic pulling out of the crown and setting of the hands after the movement has stopped running superfluous. Even after quiet periods of two or three weeks, this would be less of a strain on the movement.

Collectors whose favorite pieces while away their lives in a safe swear on keeping them in a horizontal position with periodic (approx. every six months) turning 180 degrees since thin watch oil—like all liquids—gravitates toward the center of the earth, making upper surfaces dry over the course of time. Vertical storage would hit the upper sides of the bearing pivots and drillings, while horizontal storage sees the oil evenly distributed—at least theoretically. It can't hurt, however, to have an expert clean and lubricate a watch you have just acquired before you wear it. Old oil has the same effect polishing paste would on bearings, and is just as unhealthy for the movement's mechanics as a dry bearing.

Old, original leather straps should actually be kept in the box with the watch's papers, sales tags, instruction manuals, rate certificates, invoices, and other artifacts if the watch is often worn, for these straps suffer most in any daily routine. The same is also true for old link bracelets, by the way, the quality of which cannot be compared to modern products. Time reveals itself in that which is hidden, and things breaking almost always happens without preamble at the worst possible moment.

As long as the strap has no decisive influence on the appearance of the watch, it should be exchanged for a comparable or better example of current production. This way you have an ace in the hole in your (unworn) original strap if you want to resell the watch later.

The Right Choice

You see: if you contemplate your collection beforehand and know which watches are suitable for what reasons, you will have great joy with your little watch collection. And if you buy the watches using your brains and some instinct, you will put your money into the right thing, for the market development of new watches shows rather clearly that they are truly not getting any cheaper.

Another interesting collecting theme: certified chronometers from the Swiss watchmaking schools.

Alpina

Zentrale der
Alpina
Union Horlogère
A. G.
Unionsgasse 13
Biel / Schweiz

Siège central
Alpina
Union Horlogère
S. A.
13, rue de l'Union
Bienne / Suisse

Individuals with the same interests tend to achieve goals more effectively in a group. Watchmaker Gottlieb Hauser, hailing from Switzerland's Winterthur, discovered this fact for himself in 1883 and founded the Swiss Watchmaker Corporation (Schweizerische Uhrmacher-Corporation) in the same year. This group had the joint goal of purchasing watch components to get better prices and distributing finished products together as a group in order to be able to market them better. The concept quickly found recognition, and within just a short time numerous watchmakers had joined the cooperative. Together with qualified manufacturers, they began to develop their own calibers. Already in 1896 Alpina was registered as a trademark for movements and cases, and in 1901 it was introduced as a trade brand name. From 1890, the group was headquartered in watch metropolis Biel. Right from the beginning, its products were outfitted only with high-quality components such as Breguet balance springs, balances fitted with gold screws, and heavy gold cases.

In order to win over some German watchmakers, the successful cooperative, now called Alpina Union Horlogère, in 1909 founded the Präcisions-Uhrenfabrik Alpina in Glashütte and from then on sustained production workshops in Geneva, Biel, Besançon, and Glashütte. After World War II the name Alpina could no longer be used in Germany by order of the Allies, so Dugena (Deutsche Uhrmacher-Genossenschaft Alpina) was created.

The brand Alpina was purchased several years ago by Aletta and Peter Stas, the active and very successful founders of Frédérique Constant, as a second brand, which provides a very sensible addition to the Geneva-based company's stable with respect to models and design.

10 Super Compressor — 1968

Case: stainless steel, screwed-down case back, leather strap, Ø 36 mm

Movement: nickel-plated movement with lever escapement, automatic winding, Ø 26 mm

Remarks: diver's watch with two crowns for setting decompression times via an internally revolving bezel calibrated for minutes; this watch was originally retailed by Horlogerie van Hattum in The Hague

Estimated value: $600 →

Chronograph — 1940

Case: 14-karat yellow gold, leather strap, Ø 33 mm

Movement: Caliber 943, damascening, nickel-plated, column-wheel control of chronograph, lever escapement with monometallic compensation balance and Breguet balance spring, manual winding, Ø 29 mm

Remarks: chronograph with 30-minute counter; telemeter scale on outside of black dial; inner spiral for tachymeter scale

Estimated value: $5,000 ↗

Alpina-Gruen Cosmopolitan — 1935

Case: 18-karat yellow gold, screw-down case back, leather strap, bipartite, 23 x 44 mm

Movement: 7 1/2''' caliber, rhodium-plated, 15 jewels, lateral lever escapement with a cut bimetallic balance and Breguet balance spring, manual winding, signed "Gruen Guild"

Remarks: offered by Antiquorum with 18-karat yellow gold Rolex buckle and fitted box bearing copper-colored plastic plate inside cover featuring representation of Eiffel Tower and Paris; blued steel hands in Spade and Moderne style

Estimated value: $6,500 →

Alpina-Gruen Enamel Purse Watch — appx. 1930

Case: four part solid, polished outer case with Art Deco motif in enamel, hinged, spring-loaded mechanism to display watch, 31 x 43 mm

Movement: Caliber 763, rhodium-plated, 15 jewels, straight-line lever escapement with a cut bimetallic balance and blued steel flat balance spring, manual winding

Remarks: fine, rare, keyless silver and enamel purse watch with hinged sliding mechanism to transform watch into desk clock; originally retailed by Walser-Wald in Buenos Aires; offered by Antiquorum

Estimated value: $600 →

Alpina Men's Watch — appx. 1930

Case: chrome-plated, polished, tripartite, leather strap, 31 x 31 mm

Movement: Caliber 761, rhodium-plated, 17 jewels, straight-line lever escapement with cut bimetallic balance and flat balance spring, manual winding

Remarks: unusual cushion-shaped men's wristwatch; numbered case and signed movement; subsidiary seconds; skeletonized blued steel Spade-style hands; this watch was offered by Antiquorum

Estimated value: $120 ↗

Alpina Pocket Watch — 1930s

Case: chrome-plated, hinged cuvette case back, leather strap, tripartite bassine case, polished, Ø 51 mm

Movement: 17-line caliber, straight-line lever escapement with monometallic balance and Breguet balance spring, nickel-plated, fausses côtes decoration, 21 jewels, manual winding

Remarks: chronograph with 30-minute counter, recessed subsidiary seconds, and minute register; outer minute and chronograph scales; case back engraved with "M. Artl. 6468"; offered by Antiquorum; made for German forces in the 1930s

Estimated value: $900 ↗

Alpina Glashütte Savonette — 1910

Case: 14-karat rose gold, Lucia case shape, gold cuvette, Ø 34 mm

Movement: Glashütte chronometer bridge movement no. 2132, frosted finish, gold-plated, polished screws, compensation balance with gold screws, blued balance spring, very finely engraved balance cock, index fine adjustment, gold pallets and escape wheel; ruby endstone on balance set in gold chaton

Remarks: very fine Glashütte-made hunter's pocket watch with Louis XV gold hands; enamel dial with Arabic numerals; outer five-minute scale

Estimated value: $2,600 ↗

Alpina Ladies — appx. 1950

Case: bipartite, polished and brushed stainless steel, leather strap, Ø 25 mm

Movement: Caliber 566, rhodium-plated, 15 jewels, straight-line lever escapement with monometallic balance and self-compensating flat balance spring, signed movement

Remarks: unusual ladies' watch in stainless steel; curved lugs; numbered case; blued steel hands; subsidiary seconds dial; this watch was offered by Antiquorum

Estimated value: $100 →

Angelus

Angelus was founded in 1891 by the Stolz brothers in Le Locle, an upwardly mobile city that developed quickly under the influence of the watch metropolis La Chaux-de-Fonds, located only a few kilometers away. Angelus had been making interesting watches right from its inception, a fact that was honored at a Swiss national exhibition: the company was given an award for the quality of its pocket watches and repeater movements in 1914.

The Stolz brothers occupied themselves with the production of wristwatches—especially chronographs—early on in the company's history, and today Angelus's name continues to primarily be associated with these stopwatches. The company conceived its self-developed calibers for use in complicated models such as the Chronodato.

Alongside the classic Chronodato featuring a date hand and displays of the day and the month in two separate windows, Angelus introduced another variation on the theme in 1942: a model featuring a digital date display. Since the watchmakers used two date disks to achieve this, they could fit a relatively large display into a small amount of space.

The Chronodato with its digital date display can well be viewed as one of the predecessors of today's large-date chronographs, and it was a complete success even back then.

Angelus also manufactured the standard three-handed watches a well as watches powered by shaped movements. Most of the time, these were additionally outfitted with a calendar function, a moon phase display, or a large date. In 1957, Angelus decided to develop a very special watch called the Tinkler. This English word described the timepiece's specialty: the automatic watch was outfitted with a repeater movement. The watchmakers chose AS Caliber 1580 as their base, which they proceeded to outfit with a modular repeater mechanism on the dial side since the back was already taken up with the automatic winding mechanism. Angelus's supplier, AS in Grenchen, demanded a production volume of at least 10,000 pieces, however. Since Angelus was not prepared to deal with such a large quantity at one time, the Tinkler remained a small series of 100 in steel cases—watches that remain rarities to this day. Even if the company's experience with the Tinkler was not the best, Angelus tried to once again realize the concept in 1978. The base this time was an ETA caliber for which Dubois Dépraz created a five-minute repeater module, produced by Kelek. At the time, however, Angelus did not have the financial means to successfully introduce this large watch to the market. Since mechanical movements were no longer in demand in the 1970s, and the company had failed to get a jump on quartz watches in a timely manner, it wasn't long before Angelus fell victim to the quartz crisis. Today, all that is left of this manufacturer of excellent chronographs is a large sign featuring the Angelus logo on the old factory in Le Locle.

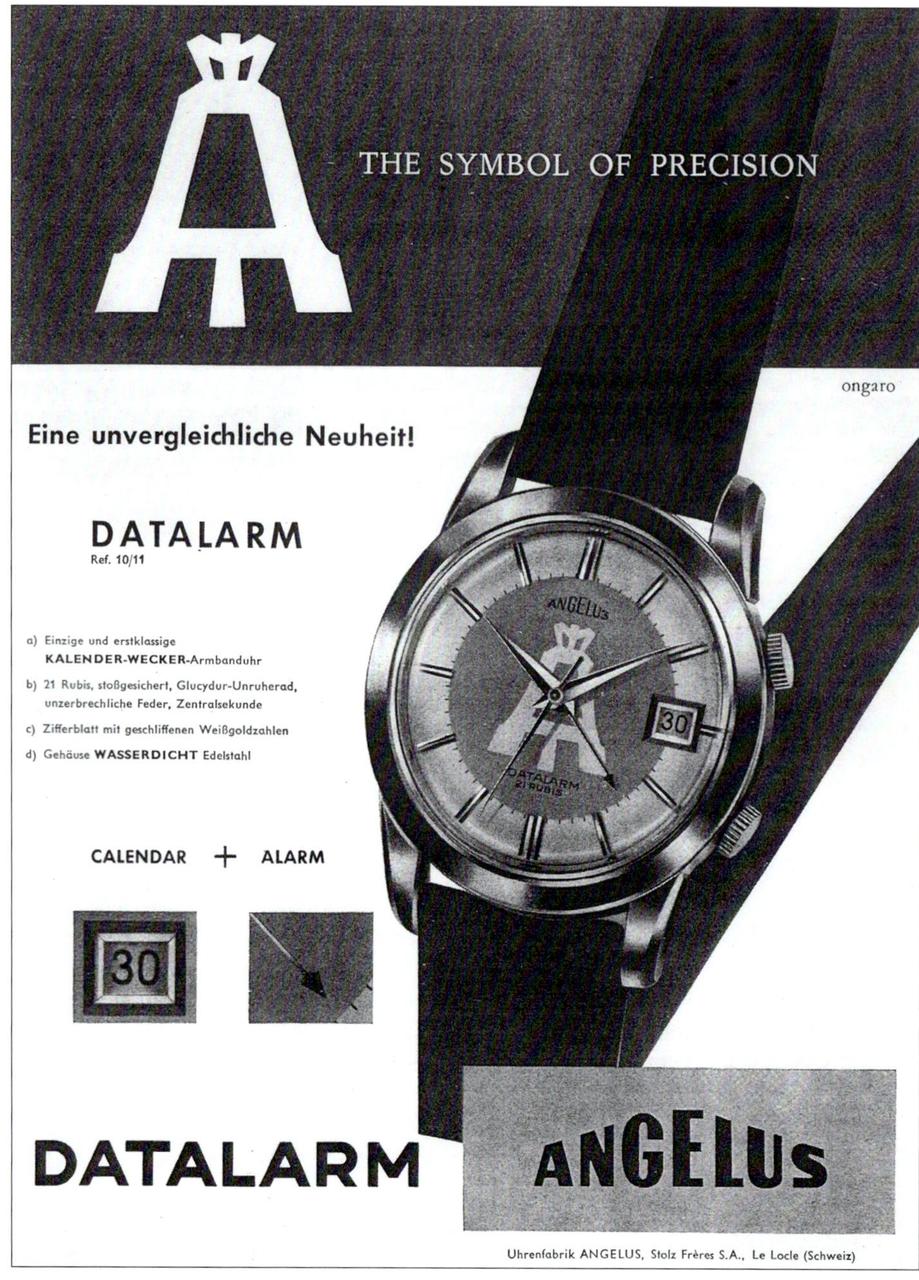

Chronograph — 1945

Case: 18-karat yellow gold, push-down case back, leather strap, Ø 35 mm

Movement: nickel-plated, column-wheel control of chronograph, manual winding

Remarks: chronograph with 45-minute counter

Estimated value: $1,080 →

Chronograph — 1945

Case: 18-karat yellow gold, push-down case back, leather strap, Ø 35 mm

Movement: nickel-plated, côtes de Genève decoration, column-wheel control of chronograph, manual winding

Remarks: chronograph with 45-minute counter

Estimated value: $1,215 →

Chronograph — 1950

Case: stainless steel, screw-down case back, leather strap, Ø 38 mm

Movement: rhodium-plated, column-wheel control of chronograph, manual winding

Remarks: chronograph with 45-minute counter

Estimated value: $1,350 →

Chronodato — 1948

Case: gold-plated, stainless steel push-down case back, leather strap, Ø 38 mm

Movement: nickel-plated, column-wheel control of chronograph, manual winding

Remarks: chronograph with 45-minute counter; complete calendar with display of day, date, and month

Estimated value: $1,350 →

Chronodato — 1942

Case: gold-plated, stainless steel push-down case back, leather strap, Ø 38 mm

Movement: nickel-plated, column-wheel control of chronograph, manual winding

Remarks: chronograph with 45-minute counter; complete calendar

Estimated value: $1,350 →

Chronodato — 1945

Case: stainless steel, push-down case back, leather strap, Ø 38 mm

Movement: rhodium-plated, côtes de Genève decoration, manual winding

Remarks: chronograph with 45-minute counter; complete calendar; date ring different color from dial

Estimated value: $1,620 →

Date Alarm — 1960

Case: stainless steel, strew-down case back, leather strap, Ø 34 mm

Movement: Caliber AS 1568N, nickel-plated, twin spring barrels, 21 jewels, manual winding

Remarks: alarm wristwatch with AS Caliber 1568

Estimated value: $405 →

Tinkler — 1958

Case: 18-karat yellow gold, screw-down case back, leather strap, Ø 36 mm

Movement: Caliber AS 1580, rhodium-plated, automatic winding

Remarks: very rare men's watch with quarter repeater module from a prototype series of 100 watches; button at 9 o'clock activates the repeater

Estimated value: $5,400 →

Audemars Piguet

In Le Brassus in 1875, the youngest of the Grenoble watchmaker family Audemars, Jules-Louis, founded his own workshop in his family's house, where he made complicated movements of the best quality.

Just a short while later, Audemars had actually gotten somewhere: he was getting good contracts, and his watches were in demand in Geneva. In order to avoid delivery problems, he employed various watchmakers from his family and circle of friends in his workshop—among them Edward-Auguste Piguet, someone he already knew from school and choir.

Since Piguet was also dedicated to high-quality watches, the pair decided to found a joint-stock company in 1881: Audemars Piguet SA. From that point on, they no longer made calibers for other companies; they manufactured pocket watches under their own name, most of which were outfitted with additional functions such as repeater mechanisms. Thanks to their success, they were able to open a subsidiary in Geneva in 1889. The brand's headquarters would remain in Le Brassus all the way to the modern day, however.

The pair used the 1889 World's Fair in Paris to introduce a *grande complication* that attracted quite a bit of attention: this was a pocket watch containing a minute repeater, a chronograph, and a perpetual calendar.

The small workshop was no longer large enough for them, and they built a new factory in 1907 that has remained Audemars Piguet's headquarters, though it has been expanded a few times.

In 1918, Audemars passed away, and his partner Piguet followed him one year later. Their sons Paul-Louis Audemars and Paul-Edward Piguet took over the company. Ten years later, the depression hit along with hard times for the company; Audemars Piguet was even at the brink of bankruptcy. The two owners could only save themselves by premiering more reasonably priced watches and going back to the company's roots by once again making watch movements for other brands.

When wristwatches hit the scene, their production was not a challenge for Audemars Piguet since the company had long been manufacturing smaller movements for women's watches. Thus, it was no wonder that Audemars Piguet—known for its complicated mechanisms—made its first wristwatch to contain a minute repeater in 1907.

Audemars Piguet continued to justify its reputation with its wristwatches: alongside high-quality three-handed watches, it was above all the calendar models that were very popular. And the company's reputation would not have been justifiable at all if there had been no perpetual calendar in its program. Jumping digital hour displays and attractive skeletonized watches also belonged to Audemars Piguet's repertoire.

The movements in Audemars Piguet's watches had always been of excellent quality: in 1946, the company introduced a manually wound movement only 1.46 mm in height that continues to be manufactured to this day. As does the slimmest automatic movement of the day, presented in 1967: its height of 2.45 mm also included a rotor on jewel bearings.

The company became absolutely legendary in 1972 with an extremely modern stainless steel watch that accepted no compromise: Audemars Piguet's version of a sports watch was called the Royal Oak, and it featured an octagonal bezel. And even though it was a steel watch, it cost just as much as some other brands' gold models. Its shape and price confused not only customers at first—within the company there were also varying opinions on the new model. Despite these early growing pains, the Royal Oak went on to become the company's flagship model. Audemars Piguet is one of the few brands that has been owned by its founding family uninterruptedly since its establishment—now for more than 130 years.

Royal Oak — 1972

Case: stainless steel, monocoque case, stainless steel link bracelet, Ø 39 mm, water-resistant to 100 m

Movement: Caliber 2121, rhodium-plated, automatic winding

Remarks: first luxury sports watch in stainless steel; early model still with monocoque case; at a retail price of 3,650 Swiss francs in 1972, this was a very expensive watch in its day

Estimated value: $8,775 →

Chronograph — 1949

Case: 18-karat yellow gold, push-down case back, leather strap, Ø 33 mm

Movement: rhodium-plated, côtes de Genève, column-wheel control of chronograph, 21 jewels, regulated in 8 positions, manual winding

Remarks: chronograph with 30-minute counter; this watch has a dedication for a later president of the Coca Cola Corporation engraved on the case back; offered in its original box and with its original certificate

Estimated value: $33,750 ↗

Chronograph with Pulsometer — 1943

Case: platinum, tripartite, push-down case back, leather strap, 38 x 44 mm

Movement: rhodium-plated, fausses côtes decoration, fine matte steel chronograph components, column-wheel control of chronograph

Remarks: elegant doctor's watch in a platinum case with a pulsometer scale on the enamel dial; the chronograph button is integrated into the crown

Estimated value: $54,000 ↗

Chronograph — 1943

Case: 18-karat gold, tripartite, push-down case back, leather strap, Ø 33 mm

Movement: rhodium-plated, fausses côtes decoration, fine matte steel chronograph components, column-wheel control of chronograph, 21 jewels, regulated in 8 positions

Remarks: very rare chronograph with 30-minute counter; this watch was offered with an original Audemars Piguet gold buckle

Estimated value: $27,000 ↗

Chronometer — 1951

Case: 18-karat yellow gold, push-down case back, leather strap, Ø 36 mm

Movement: Caliber VZSS, nickel-plated, côtes de Genève decoration, regulated in 8 positions, manual winding

Remarks: chronometer wristwatch with movement regulated in 8 positions

Estimated value: $5,400 ↗

Men's Watch — 1950

Case: 18-karat yellow gold, push-down case back, leather strap, Ø 31 mm

Movement: rhodium-plated, côtes de Genève decoration, manual winding

Remarks: men's watch with unusually wide bezel

Estimated value: $3,375 ↘

Men's Watch for Cartier — 1955

Case: 18-karat yellow gold, push-down case back, leather strap, Ø 32 mm

Movement: Caliber 2001LEC, rhodium-plated, côtes de Genève decoration, manual winding

Remarks: men's watch signed by both Audemars Piguet and Cartier; made for Cartier

Estimated value: $6,075 →

Men's Watch for Gübelin — 1960

Case: 18-karat yellow gold, push-down case back, leather strap, Ø 32 mm

Movement: Caliber 2001LEL, rhodium-plated, côtes de Genève decoration, manual winding

Remarks: men's watch signed by both Audemars Piguet and Gübelin; made for Gübelin

Estimated value: $3,780 →

Men's Watch — 1948

Case: 18-karat yellow gold, leather strap, 26 x 36 mm

Movement: nickel-plated, côtes de Genève decoration, 18 jewels, regulated in 8 positions, manual winding

Remarks: rare men's watch with rectangular case

Estimated value: $2,700 →

Men's Watch — 1946

Case: platinum, push-down case back, leather strap, 25 x 33 mm

Movement: Caliber 9/10RS, nickel-plated, côtes de Genève decoration, 18 jewels, regulated in 8 positions, manual winding

Remarks: rare platinum men's watch with movement regulated in 8 positions; this watch was offered in its original box and with a certificate from Audemars Piguet

Estimated value: $10,125 ↗

Jump Hour — 1925

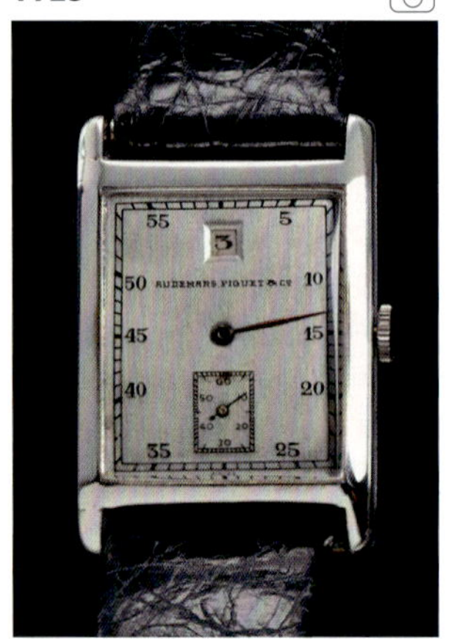

Case: 18-karat white gold, push-down case back, leather strap, 25 x 37 mm

Movement: rhodium-plated, côtes de Genève decoration, 18 jewels, regulated in 8 positions, manual winding

Remarks: extremely rare men's watch with digital jump hour display; regulated in 8 positions

Estimated value: $27,000 ↗

Men's Watch with Digital Display — 1929

Case: 18-karat white gold, push-down case back, leather strap, 27 x 31 mm

Movement: Caliber GHSM, rhodium-plated, côtes de Genève decoration, 17 jewels, regulated in 3 positions, manual winding

Remarks: significant early men's watch with digital display; regulated in 3 positions

Estimated value: $33,750 ↗

Men's Watch — 1942

Case: 18-karat yellow gold, bipartite, push-down case back, leather strap, 23 x 38 mm

Movement: rhodium-plated, fausses côtes decoration, glucydur screw balance, 18 jewels, regulated in 8 positions

Remarks: elegant men's watch with subsidiary seconds in a rectangular case; this watch was offered in box and with a gold buckle

Estimated value: $5,400 ↗

Men's Watch — 1946

Case: 18-karat yellow gold, bipartite, push-down case back, leather strap, 24 x 32 mm

Movement: rhodium-plated, fausses côtes decoration, polished screws, glucydur screw balance, blued balance spring, 18 jewels, regulated in 8 positions

Remarks: rare men's watch in a rectangular case; this watch was offered in box and with a gold buckle

Estimated value: $5,130 →

Men's Watch — 1957

Case: 18-karat yellow gold, push-down case back, leather strap, Ø 35 mm

Movement: Caliber V 7SSC, nickel-plated, côtes de Genève decoration, regulated in 5 positions, manual winding

Remarks: men's watch with movement regulated in 5 positions; this watch was offered in its original box

Estimated value: $3,375 →

Automatic — 1961

Case: 18-karat yellow gold, screw-down case back, leather strap, Ø 35 mm

Movement: Caliber 2072LEC, rhodium-plated, decorated, gold rotor in jewel bearings, 29 jewels, regulated in 5 positions, automatic winding

Remarks: automatic men's watch with date; this watch was offered in box

Estimated value: $6,750 ↗

Automatic — 1956

Case: 18-karat yellow gold, bipartite, screw-down case back, leather strap, Ø 35 mm

Movement: Caliber P2498, rhodium-plated, fausses côtes decoration, gold rotor, polished screws, 21 jewels, regulated in 5 positions

Remarks: classic automatic men's watch with subsidiary seconds; the movement has a gold rotor

Estimated value: $4,050 →

Stop Seconds — 1947

Case: 18-karat gold, tripartite, push-down case back, leather strap, Ø 36 mm

Movement: rhodium-plated, fausses côtes decoration, glucydur screw balance, 18 jewels, regulated in 8 positions

Remarks: elegant men's watch in a yellow gold case; small button at 9 o'clock for halting the balance in order to set the time to the second

Estimated value: $5,400 →

Automatic — 1972

Case: 18-karat white gold, tripartite, leather strap, Ø 32 mm

Movement: Caliber K2120, rhodium-plated, fausses côtes decoration, gold rotor, Gyromax balance, 36 jewels, regulated in 6 positions

Remarks: small men's watch in a white gold case

Estimated value: $3,375 →

Automatic — 1969

Case: 18-karat yellow gold, tripartite, push-down case back, fluted case band, leather strap

Movement: Caliber 2071 LEC, rhodium-plated, fausses côtes decoration, 18-karat gold rotor in jewel bearings, polished screws, 29 jewels, regulated in 5 positions

Remarks: elegant men's watch with 18-karat gold rotor in jewel bearings

Estimated value: $4,725 →

Men's Watch — 1972

Case: 18-karat white gold, push-down case back, leather strap, Ø 33 mm

Movement: rhodium-plated, côtes de Genève decoration, 18 jewels, regulated in 8 positions, manual winding

Remarks: elegant men's watch with movement regulated in 8 positions

Estimated value: $2,700 →

Automatic — 1965

Case: 18-karat white gold, screw-down case back, leather strap, Ø 35 mm

Movement: Caliber K2072, nickel-plated, côtes de Genève decoration, 18-karat gold rotor in jewel bearing, automatic winding

Remarks: automatic men's watch with gold buckle; this watch was offered in its original box

Estimated value: $8,100 ↗

Men's Watch — 1974

Case: 18-karat white gold, push-down case back, leather strap 33 x 34 mm

Movement: Caliber 2003/1, nickel-plated, côtes de Genève decoration, regulated in 8 positions, manual winding

Remarks: rare men's watch with diamond-set hour markers and hands; movement regulated in 8 positions

Estimated value: $2,295 →

Automatic — 1974

Reference number: 5420

Case: 18-karat white gold, push-down case back, leather strap, 32 x 36 mm

Movement: Caliber K2121, rhodium-plated, côtes de Genève decoration, regulated in 5 positions, automatic winding

Remarks: men's watch with movement regulated in 5 positions and 21-karat gold rotor

Estimated value: $2,025 →

Baume & Mercier

This brand's two namesakes, Louis-Victor Baume and Paul Mercier, actually lived a century apart from each other. Louis-Victor Baume (1817–1887) was a watchmaker hailing from the forests north of La Chaux-de-Fonds. Together with his brother Pierre Joseph Célestin, he registered a company called Les Frères Baume in 1830 and invited his younger brothers to join the workshop a few years later. The small company experienced a quick upward swing, especially in England, where in 1851 a flourishing subsidiary was founded under the name Baume Brothers, which was to later become completely independent.

One of the Baume brothers' specialties was precise technical watches: a chronograph with a tourbillon, signed Baume & Co., set a new

record in precision at a chronometry competition organized by the royal observatory in Kiev. The Baume company also took part in all the World's Fairs between 1860 and 1910, wining numerous gold medals with their watches.

William-Adolphe Baume, born in 1885, Louis-Victor's grandson, had already worked in the family business since the days of his youth when, in 1912, he met watchmaker and jeweler Paul Mercier, whose birth name was actually Cherednichenko. His father, an officer of the czar, had met a charming seamstress in Paris and fell in love with her. After the father died in an accident in Russia, Mercier, his mother, and his two sisters moved to Switzerland, where he found work with Genevan chronometer maker Haas. As a creative individual and someone who knew how to enjoy life, Mercier took over the company's commercial management with much success. The serious and rather taciturn William Baume was in charge of technology. Together, they established the brand Baume & Mercier in 1920.

The *manufacture* continued to make precision watches, and in the first year of its new existence it enjoyed a reputation as the Genevan chronometer office's best customer. Trendy wristwatches and reliable chronographs were Baume & Mercier's main sources of turnover.

The founders left the company in the mid-1930s, and new owners Ponti and Gennari, jewelers from Turin, installed Constantin de Gorski as managing director, who in turn thoroughly modernized both the collection and the production equipment. After World War II, Baume & Mercier made a reputation for itself with innovative ladies' watches such as the Marquise model featuring a spring-action bangle (at left) and gained in international importance.

In 1952, Baume & Mercier took over C.H. Meylan Watch SA in Le Brassus, famous for ultra-flat movements, thus gaining additional autonomy. After the death of de Gorski, the brand lost momentum, and the Piaget family, with which the company had cooperated for quite some time, took over the majority in 1964. The two brands blossomed in the shape-obsessed 1970s with avant-garde and innovative timepieces, some outfitted with ultra-flat automatic movements or quartz calibers, before they were purchased by Cartier in 1988, which was later integrated into the Vendôme Group and finally Richemont.

Chronograph — 1945

Case: 18-karat rose gold, monocoque case, leather strap

Movement: Caliber W69, rhodium-plated, Breguet hairspring, 17 jewels, manual winding

Remarks: chronograph with 30-minute counter and tachometer scale

Estimated value: $4,725 →

archive photo

Calendar Watch — 1945

Case: stainless steel, push-down case back, leather strap, 24 x 37 mm

Movement: Caliber ETA 1164, rhodium-plated, 17 jewels, manual winding

Remarks: rare calendar watch (date hand, window display for days and months); corrector on case back

Estimated value: $635 →

archive photo

Men's Watch — 1945

Case: 18-karat yellow gold, monocoque case, leather strap

Movement: Caliber Felsa 690, rhodium-plated, 17 jewels, automatic winding

Remarks: elegant automatic watch with sweep seconds

Estimated value: $540 →

archive photo

Men's Watch — 1948

Case: 18-karat rose gold, push-down case back, leather strap

Movement: Caliber BM 960, rhodium-plated, 15 jewels, manual winding

Remarks: elegant men's watch with subsidiary seconds

Estimated value: $420 →

archive photo

Calendar Chronograph — 1953

Case: 18-karat rose gold, push-down case back, leather strap

Movement: Caliber W72, rhodium-plated, Breguet hairspring, 17 jewels, manual winding

Remarks: chronograph with 30-minute and 12-hour counters; complete calendar with date hand

Estimated value: $2,160 →

archive photo

Chronograph — 1954

Case: 18-karat rose gold, push-down case back, leather strap

Movement: Landeron Caliber 48, nickel-plated, 17 jewels, manual winding

Remarks: chronograph with 30-minute counter and tachometer scale

Estimated value: $1,485 →

archive photo

Ladies' Watch — 1945

Case: stainless steel, push-down case back, gold strap lugs, leather strap

Movement: Caliber AS 1234, rhodium-plated, 17 jewels, manual winding

Remarks: rare ladies' watch in a bipartite, two-tone case

Estimated value: $210 →

archive photo

Ladies' Watch — 1942

Case: 14-karat yellow gold, push-down case back, leather strap, 34 mm

Movement: Caliber AS 1234, rhodium-plated, 17 jewels, manual winding

Remarks: ladies' watch in shaped gold case

Estimated value: $270 →

archive photo

Breitling

Breitling was founded by Léon Breitling in 1884 in La Chaux-de-Fonds. Right from the beginning, this brand specialized in the manu-facture of chronographs, and above all it was the company's wristwatches that were famous for their reliability, proving their survivor qual-ities on the battlefields of World War I. Léon's son Gaston, and later his grandson Willy, made this company into one of the leading chronograph manufacturers based on this reputation. The Breitling name has always stood for quality, robustness, and reliability. Thanks to this reputation, it was Breitling's watches that were the first choice in outfitting the cockpits of the 1930s with the best chronographs. These watches, indispensable for navigation, had to be both precise and robust enough to survive the increasing acceleration powers of modern aviation. Although Breitling didn't manufacture its own movements, the company's assembly

specialists were able to tailor the watches perfectly to the needs of the pilot.

The company introduced a special highlight in 1952, which would from then on be the status symbol and object of desire for pilots all over the world: the Navitimer.

What was so special about it? A slide rule was built into the bezel, making the watch a universal navigation instrument that could take over the calculation of flight time and energy consumption long before computers.

This was also the watch to travel with the first expedition to space on the wrist of astronaut Scott Carpenter on board the *Mercury* capsule. In the late 1960s, Breitling, together with Heuer, Hamilton-Büren, and Dubois Dépraz, heralded the development of the automatic chronograph. After a few years of research, the four com-panies were able to present the fruit of their common labors in 1969: Caliber 11. Together with Calibers 12 and 15, which came later, this was long the only alternative to Zenith's El Primero with regard to automatic chronographs. Despite this exceptional innovation, and even though Breitling had gotten an early start becoming familiar with quartz watches in a changing world market, the company made a crash landing in 1979, going bankrupt. It was bought the same year by Ernest Schneider, a businessman and enthusiastic pilot. At his bidding, the company moved from La Chaux-de-Fonds to Grenchen.

Schneider followed a consistent strategy: although a much less expensive quartz watch measured the time more precisely, the brand never turned its back on mechanical chronographs.

Chronograph — 1935

Reference number: 721

Case: chrome-plated case, tripartite with steel push-down case back, Ø 33 mm

Movement: Venus Caliber 170, nickel-plated, column-wheel control of chronograph, manual winding

Remarks: early manual winding chronograph with 45-minute counter; snail-shaped tachometer scale printed on dial, making it possible to measure speeds as slow as 20km/h

Estimated value: $950 ↗

Chronograph — 1945

Case: stainless steel, bipartite, screw-down case back, Ø 36 mm

Movement: Venus Caliber 170, nickel-plated, column-wheel control of chronograph, manual winding

Remarks: manual winding chronograph with early steel case; fine matte steel components; glucydur screw balance

Estimated value: $950 →

Chronograph — 1940

Reference number: 760

Case: steel case, tripartite, push-down case back, Ø 35 mm

Movement: manual winding

Remarks: early manual winding chronograph with 45-minute counter; the 3, 6, 9 markers are especially accentuated for special legibility of stopped time for long-distance phone calls, which were calculated in three-minute intervals

Estimated value: $810 →

Chronograph — 1945

Reference number: 765

Case: stainless steel, tripartite, push-down case back, Ø 37 mm

Movement: rhodium-plated, fine matte steel chronograph components, column-wheel control of chronograph

Remarks: chronograph with 30-minute and 12-hour counters

Estimated value: $1,620 ↗

Chronograph — 1945

Reference number: 1193

Case: stainless steel, tripartite, push-down case back, Ø 34 mm

Movement: Venus Caliber 188, rhodium-plated, finely polished steel chronograph components

Remarks: chronograph with 30-minute counter; red telemeter and black tachymeter scales

Estimated value: $11,475 →

Antimagnetic — 1945

Case: chrome-plated, tripartite, stainless steel push-down case back, leather strap, Ø 35 mm

Movement: Venus Caliber 188, rhodium-plated, finely finished steel chronograph components

Remarks: chronograph with 30-minute counter; telemeter and tachymeter scales

Estimated value: $1,080 →

Chronograph Datora — 1949

Case: gold-plated case with steel push-down case back, Ø 35 mm

Movement: manual winding

Remarks: calendar chronograph with 30-minute and 12-hour counters; additional date and moon phase displays at 12 o'clock

Estimated value: $2,025 →

Chronograph — 1979

Case: 18-karat yellow gold, tripartite, push-down case back, leather strap, Ø 37 mm

Movement: Caliber 185, rhodium-plated, polished screws, fine matte steel chronograph components, column-wheel control of chronograph, split-seconds function, fine adjustment

Remarks: rare, gold split-seconds chronograph with 30-minute and 12-hour counters; date hand; moon phase at 12 o'clock

Estimated value: $21,600 →

Chronograph Premier

1945

Reference number: 788

Case: stainless steel, tripartite, screw-down case back, leather strap, Ø 35 mm

Movement: rhodium-plated, fine matte steel chronograph components, column-wheel control of chronograph

Remarks: chronograph with 30-minute and 12-hour counters, tachymeter scale

Estimated value: $1,620 →

Chronograph Premier

1945

Reference number: 760

Case: 18-karat gold, tripartite with push-down case back, Ø 35 mm

Movement: manual winding

Remarks: manual winding chronograph with 30-minute counter; fine matte steel components; monometallic screw balance

Estimated value: $1,620 →

Chronograph Premier

1945

Case: steel case with push-down case back, Ø 33 mm

Movement: manual winding

Remarks: simple manual winding chronograph with 45-minute counter; the 3, 6, 9 markers are especially accentuated for special legibility of stopped time for long-distance phone calls, which were calculated in three-minute intervals

Estimated value: $945 →

Chronograph Premier

1945

Case: steel case with push-down case back, Ø 37 mm

Movement: manual winding

Remarks: simple manual winding chronograph with 45-minute counter; the 3, 6, 9 markers are especially accentuated for special legibility of stopped time for long-distance phone calls, which were calculated in three-minute intervals

Estimated value: $945 →

Chronograph Premier

1945

Reference number: 788

Case: 18-karat yellow gold, screw-down case back, faceted, Ø 36 mm

Movement: manual winding

Remarks: simple manual winding chronograph with 30-minute and 12-hour counters, the 3, 6, 9 markers are especially accentuated for special legibility of stopped time for long-distance phone calls, which were calculated in three-minute intervals

Estimated value: $3,510 →

Chronograph Premier

1945

Reference number: 777

Case: 18-karat gold, screw-down case back, faceted, Ø 37 mm

Movement: manual winding

Remarks: simple manual winding chronograph with 45-minute counter

Estimated value: $3,780 ↗

Split-Seconds Chronograph

1950

Reference number: 762

Case: steel case with push-down case back, faceted, Ø 36 mm

Movement: manual winding

Remarks: split-seconds manual winding chronograph with 45-minute counter; the split-seconds function makes it possible to take intermediate times without interrupting the ongoing time

Estimated value: $8,100 →

Split-Seconds Chronograph

1965

Case: 18-karat yellow gold, push-down case back, Ø 36 mm

Movement: manual winding

Remarks: rare manual winding chronograph with 30-minute counter and split-seconds function; the split-seconds function makes it possible to take intermediate times without interrupting the ongoing time

Estimated value: $9,450 ↗

Chronomat — 1945

Case: stainless steel, push-down case back, rotating bezel, faceted, Ø 36 mm
Movement: manual winding
Remarks: manual winding chronograph with 45-minute counter; additional hundredths scale for chronograph seconds
Estimated value: $2,160 →

Chronomat — 1960

Reference number: 808
Case: stainless steel, push-down case back, rotating bezel, Ø 37 mm
Movement: Venus Caliber 175, nickel-plated, column-wheel control of chronograph, manual winding
Remarks: manual winding chronograph with multifunctional bezel including slide rule function; 45-minute counter; Alpha steel hands; this watch came with box and papers
Estimated value: $3,375 →

Navitimer — 1969

Reference number: 806
Case: stainless steel, push-down case back, rotating bezel, Ø 40 mm
Movement: Venus Caliber 178, gold plated, column-wheel control of chronograph, manual winding
Remarks: manual winding chronograph with 30-minute and 12-hour counters; column wheel control of chronograph; glucydur balance; bezel can be used as a slide rule; this watch was offered with original box and papers
Estimated value: $2,970 ↗

Navitimer — 1973

Reference number: 7806
Case: stainless steel, push-down case back, rotating bezel, Ø 40 mm
Movement: Valjoux Caliber 7740, rhodium-plated, fine matte steel components, manual winding
Remarks: manual winding chronograph with 30-minute and 12-hour counters; date window between 4 and 5 o'clock; rotating bezel can be used as slide rule
Estimated value: $2,700 →

Chronomat Automatic Logos — 1975

Reference number: 8808.3
Case: stainless steel, push-down case back, rotating bezel, Ø 41 mm
Movement: Caliber 12, gold-plated, fine matte steel components, eccentric fine adjustment, automatic winding
Remarks: automatic chronograph with 30-minute counter; date at 6 o'clock; rotating bezel can be used as a slide rule
Estimated value: $2,970 ↗

Chronomat — 1963

Reference number: 2110
Case: stainless steel, screw-down case back, rotating bezel, Ø 40 mm
Movement: Caliber 11, nickel-plated, fine matte steel components, automatic winding
Remarks: automatic chronograph with 30-minute and 12-hour counters; 30-miunute scale divided into five blocks for better legibility; additional tachymeter scale
Estimated value: $1,215 →

Chronomat — 1973

Reference number: 7808
Case: stainless steel, tripartite, push-down case back, rotating bezel, Ø 41 mm
Movement: Valjoux Caliber 7740, rhodium-plated, fine matte steel chronograph components
Remarks: large chronograph with 30-minute and 12-hour counters; date window display; rotating bezel can be used as slide rule
Estimated value: $2,835 →

Chronomat — 1973

Reference number: 7808
Case: stainless steel, tripartite, push-down case back, rotating bezel, Ø 40 mm
Movement: Valjoux Caliber 7740, rhodium-plated, fine matte steel chronograph components
Remarks: chronograph with 30-minute and 12-hour counters; rotating bezel can be used as slide rule
Estimated value: $4,050 ↗

Cosmonaute
1975

Reference number: 809.4

Case: gold-plated, stainless steel push-down case back, rotating bezel, Ø 40 mm

Movement: Venus Caliber 178, gold-plated, column-wheel control of chronograph, manual winding

Remarks: manual winding chronograph with 24-hour dial; 30-minute and 12-hour counters; column wheel control of chronograph; glucydur balance; bezel was conceived to be used as a slide rule; this watch was offered with original box and papers

Estimated value: $3,375 →

Cosmonaute
1975

Reference number: 809

Case: stainless steel, screw-down case back, rotating bezel, Ø 41 mm

Movement: Venus Caliber 178, gold-plated, column-wheel control of chronograph, manual winding

Remarks: manual winding chronograph with 24-hour dial; 30-minute and 12-hour counters; rotating bezel can be used as a slide rule

Estimated value: $3,510 →

Chrono-Matic
1969

Reference number: 2130

Case: stainless steel, screw-down case back, rotating bezel, Ø 38 mm

Movement: Caliber 12, nickel-plated, automatic winding

Remarks: automatic chronograph with 30-minute counter; polished steel components; glucydur balance

Estimated value: $1,080 →

Chrono-Matic
1977

Reference number: 2130

Case: stainless steel, screw-down case back, rotating bezel, Ø 38 mm

Movement: Caliber 12, gold-plated, fine matte steel components, automatic winding

Remarks: automatic chronograph with 30-minute counter; polished steel components; glucydur balance

Estimated value: $1,080 →

Super Ocean Regatta
1968

Reference number: 7652

Case: stainless steel, tripartite, screw-down case back, rotating bezel, Ø 48 mm

Movement: Venus Caliber 178, red gold-plated, fine matte steel chronograph components, column-wheel control of chronograph

Remarks: large chronograph with 15-minute and 12-hour counters; the watch is outfitted with double regatta time measurement especially for sailors

Estimated value: $2,160 ↗

Cosmonaute Super Ocean
1975

Reference number: 2105

Case: stainless steel, screw-down case back, rotating bezel, Ø 49 mm

Movement: Caliber 12, rhodium-plated, automatic winding

Remarks: automatic chronograph with 15-minute and 6-hour counters; date window at 6 o'clock; remarkable interval markings on side of watch

Estimated value: $1,890 ↗

Chrono-Matic
1969

Reference number: 2112

Case: stainless steel, screw-down case back, rotating bezel, Ø 39 mm

Movement: Caliber 11, nickel-plated, fine matte steel components, automatic winding

Remarks: automatic chronograph with 30-minute and 12-hour counters; 30-minute scale divided into five blocks for better legibility; additional tachymeter scale

Estimated value: $810 →

Chrono-Matic
1969

Reference number: 2112-15

Case: stainless steel, screw-down case back, rotating bezel, 38 x 44 mm

Movement: Caliber 15, gold-plated, fine matte steel components, automatic winding

Remarks: automatic chronograph with 30-minute counter; Caliber 15, outfitted with a micro rotor, is especially obvious thanks to the subsidiary seconds dial that is slightly raised; date at 6 o'clock; polished steel components; glucydur balance

Estimated value: $945 →

Chronograph AVI

1960

Reference number: 765

Case: steel case, tripartite, screw-down case back, rotating bezel, Ø 41 mm

Movement: Venus Caliber 178, column-wheel control of chronograph, rhodium-plated, manual winding

Remarks: manual winding chronograph; extremely rare variant with 15-minute and 12-hour counters; fine matte steel components

Estimated value: $4,455 ↗

Co-Pilot

1967

Reference number: 765 CP

Case: stainless steel, tripartite, screw-down case back, rotating bezel, leather strap, Ø 40 mm

Movement: Venus Caliber 178, red gold-plated, fine matte steel chronograph components, column-wheel control of chronograph, 17 jewels

Remarks: rare pilot's chronograph with 15-minute and 12-hour counters; a second hour scale is printed onto the rotating bezel

Estimated value: $1,620 →

Chronograph Top Time

1969

Reference number: 815.4

Case: gold-plated, push-down case back, Ø 38 mm

Movement: Valjoux Caliber 7736 TJ, manual winding

Remarks: manual winding chronograph with 30-minute and 12-hour counters; polished steel parts; monometallic balance

Estimated value: $1,350 →

Chronograph Top Time

1969

Reference number: 810

Case: stainless steel, push-down case back, Ø 38 mm

Movement: Venus Caliber 178 TJ, red gold-plated, column-wheel control of chronograph, manual winding

Remarks: manual winding chronograph with 30-minute and 12-hour counters; this watch was offered with original box and papers

Estimated value: $1,620 →

Chronograph Long Playing

1965

Reference number: 7103.3

Case: stainless steel, push-down case back, 40 x 47 mm

Movement: Valjoux Caliber 7740, nickel-plated, manual winding

Remarks: manual winding chronograph with 30-minute and 12-hour counters; date window between 4 and 5 o'clock

Estimated value: $540 →

Chronograph Transocean

1975

Reference number: 7102.3

Case: stainless steel, screw-down case back, 42 x 47 mm

Movement: Valjoux Caliber 7740, manual winding

Remarks: manual winding chronograph with 30-minute and 12-hour counters

Estimated value: $1,890 →

Chronograph Referee Watch

1973

Reference number: 3431

Case: stainless steel, screw-down case back, rotating bezel, Ø 41 mm

Movement: Valjoux Caliber 7731, nickel-plated, manual winding

Remarks: manual winding chronograph with sweep 60-minute counter; minutes are displayed in sweep manner where the chronograph seconds would usually be, making them especially legible; a small window at 6 o'clock displays whether the stop function is activated

Estimated value: $945 →

Chronograph Football

1975

Reference number: 2734.3

Case: stainless steel, push-down case back, rotating bezel, 41 x 47 mm

Movement: Valjoux Caliber 7731, manual winding

Remarks: manual winding chronograph with 60-minute sweep counter; minutes are displayed in sweep manner where the chronograph seconds would usually be, making them especially legible; a small window at 6 o'clock displays whether the stop function is activated

Estimated value: $1,125 →

Chronograph Cadette

1960

Reference number: 1155

Case: steel case, tripartite, push-down case back, Ø 34mm

Movement: Valjoux Caliber 7733, rhodium-plated, manual winding

Remarks: manual winding chronograph with 30-minute counter; polished steel chronograph components; monometallic balance; Incabloc shock protection

Estimated value: $410 →

Chronograph Top Time

1969

Case: gold-plated, tripartite, steel push-down case back, Ø 35 mm

Movement: manual winding

Remarks: simple manual winding chronograph; the chronograph seconds and chronograph minutes are highlighted in orange for better legibility

Estimated value: $810 →

Chronograph Sprint

1975

Reference number: 2018

Case: stainless steel, plastic bezel, 40 x 43 mm

Movement: Valjoux Caliber 7733, nickel-plated, manual winding

Remarks: manual winding chronograph with 30-minute counter; polished steel chronograph components; monometallic balance; Incabloc shock protection

Estimated value: $675 →

Chronograph Top Time

1966

Reference number: 2006

Case: steel case, tripartite, push-down case back, 36 x 36 mm

Movement: Valjoux Caliber 7730, manual winding

Remarks: simple manual winding chronograph

Estimated value: $675 →

Chronograph Datora

1970

Reference number: 2034.3

Case: steel case, tripartite, push-down case back, rotating bezel, Ø 41 mm

Movement: manual winding

Remarks: manual winding chronograph with 45-minute counter; date at 6 o'clock

Estimated value: $1,100 →

Chronograph Pupitre

1975

Reference number: 7101.3

Case: steel case, tripartite, screw-down case back, rotating bezel, Ø 42 mm

Movement: Valjoux Caliber 7740, nickel-plated, manual winding

Remarks: manual winding chronograph with 30-minute and 12-hour counters; so-called Bullhead chronograph: by rotating the movement 90 degrees, the buttons for the chronograph functions were positioned at 11 and 1 o'clock, thus reminiscent of bull horns

Estimated value: $1,890 ↗

Calendar Watch

1950

Case: 18-karat yellow gold, push-down case back, faceted, Ø 36 mm

Movement: Caliber 20, manual winding

Remarks: rare simple watch with date hand and display of weekday and month in two small windows; subsidiary seconds at 6 o'clock

Estimated value: $1,100 →

Men's Watch

1950

Case: gold-plated, stainless steel push-down case back, Ø 33 mm

Movement: Felsa Caliber 4010, manual winding

Remarks: simple three-handed watch

Estimated value: $210 →

STOWA

MADE IN GERMANY. SINCE 1927

STOWA watchmakers take great pride and care when they sit down at their benches to hand made a STOWA watch. They do this since 1927. They only use the finest materials: sapphire crystals, stainless steel cases and mechanical movements. The design of all STOWA watches is simple, legible and understated. When you buy a STOWA, you´re acquiring a piece of esteemed watch history. One that will be with you for a long, long time.

Airman
approx. 1940

Marine
approx. 1942

Antea
approx. 1938

① ② ③

Airman A watch with a famous historical background. During the 1940s, only five companies made the original pilot watches: IWC, A. Lange & Söhne, Laco, Wempe and STOWA. *Relaunch: Airman automatic, since 1997.* **Marine** Inspired by the observation watches once used on navy ships. Used to time navigational maneuvers and coordinate with observation points, the accuracy and legibility of an observation watch were crucial. *Relaunch: Marine Original handwinding, since 2006.* ❸ **Antea** Rooted in time, yet timeless. In the 1930s, STOWA designed a number of watches based on the vocabulary of the Bauhaus movement (1919-1933) *Relaunch: Antea automatic, since 2003*

www.stowa.com · info@stowa.com

Cartier

World War I and their martial appearance, commemorating them with the Tank watch. At the beginning of the 1930s, the Pasha of Marrakesh ordered a watch from Cartier that he wished to take swimming with him. For him Cartier created the Pasha, a water-resistant watch featuring a cabochon on the crown that also seals it. Ensuring that this protective covering couldn't get lost, it was additionally secured with a bow and a chain.

When Louis Cartier passed away on July 23, 1842, the lucky star looking out for the company seemed to lose its twinkle. Cartier fell into a crisis, from which it only recovered at the end of the 1960s. Despite this, the Vendôme Group bought the traditional firm's shares in 1972. Robert Hocq became the company's new president, while his brilliant countryman Alain-Dominique Perrin took over its marketing. With the slogan "Must de Cartier," Cartier embarked upon a comet-like ascension, offering accessories for daily life that were not really all that expensive, but which were of the best taste. And, finally, famous watch models such as the legendary Santos were also resuscitated.

A talented designer, his feel for aesthetics and zeitgeist presented the world with some of its most beautiful watches. His name continues to stand for elegance and luxury to this day: French bon vivant Louis Cartier.

The actual story of the Cartier brand begins with his grandfather, though, Louis-François Cartier, who as a twenty-eight-year-old in 1847, took over the business of his teacher, Adolphe Picard. He made it his company's goal to satisfy even the most unusual demands of his clientele. The watch division of the quickly growing Cartier company was something his son Louis-François-Alfred built, however. From 1893, models marked Cartier were available: they were partially produced by Swiss *manufacture* Vacheron et Constantin.

It was only Alfred's son Louis who would make this brand world-famous, although his marriage to the heiress of the largest Parisian fashion atelier, Andrée-Carolin Worth, may have played an important part. She had the best relationship to the era's high society.

Louis, ever the innovative designer, soon recognized that the future of men's watches was on the wrist, and was able to put this to practical use thanks to his friend Alberto Santos-Dumont. The diminutive Brazilian aviation pioneer literally had his hands full with his self-developed flying machines and could not be bothered to take his pocket watch out of his vest when it was needed. Thus it was for him that Cartier created what was later to become a true design classic: the square Santos, the first pilot's watch in history. From 1911, it was manufactured and sold as a serial product. Other exceptional watches were also created in Louis Cartier's era, some of which can still be found in the line today, at times as shapes that have evolved over the years. Alongside the Tortue (French for "tortoise"), it is above all the Tank that has been such an evergreen. Cartier was impressed by the British tanks built during

Square

Case: 18-karat yellow gold, screw-down case back, leather strap, 28 x 35 mm
Movement: rhodium-plated, côtes de Genève decoration, manual winding
Remarks: gold men's watch with hidden strap lugs
Estimated value: $4,050 →

1970

Coussin

Case: 18-karat yellow gold, screw-down case back, leather strap, 28 x 36 mm
Movement: rhodium-plated, côtes de Genève decoration, manual winding
Remarks: gold men's watch in unusual case; this watch was offered with gold folding clasp
Estimated value: $4,320 →

1970

Square

Case: 18-karat white gold, screw-down case back, leather strap, 38 x 35 mm
Movement: rhodium-plated, côtes de Genève decoration, manual winding
Remarks: white gold men's watch with sapphire cabochon in the crown
Estimated value: $4,320 →

1975

Ellipse

Case: 18-karat yellow gold, screw-down case back, leather strap, 32 x 28 mm
Movement: rhodium-plated, côtes de Genève decoration, manual winding
Remarks: gold men's watch in an unusually styled case
Estimated value: $3,375 →

1970

Baignoire

Case: 18-karat yellow gold, leather strap, 23 x 52 mm
Movement: rhodium-plated, côtes de Genève decoration, manual winding
Remarks: curvex case secured with screws on the side; this watch was offered with a gold folding clasp
Estimated value: $24,300 →

1969

Tank

Case: 18-karat yellow gold, leather strap, 22 x 29 mm
Movement: nickel-plated, côtes de Genève decoration, manual winding
Remarks: gold Tank with faceted emerald in the crown
Estimated value: $8,100 →

1940

Tank St. Elena

Case: 18-karat yellow gold, leather strap, 25 x 38 mm
Movement: nickel-plated, côtes de Genève decoration, manual winding
Remarks: gold men's watch with faceted blue sapphire in the crown; this watch was offered with a gold folding clasp
Estimated value: $4,725 →

1950

Tank Cintrée

Case: 18-karat yellow gold, leather strap, 23 x 46 mm
Movement: nickel-plated, côtes de Genève decoration, 18 jewels, regulated in 8 positions, manual winding
Remarks: gold men's watch with faceted blue sapphire in the crown; this watch was offered with a gold folding clasp
Estimated value: $27,000 →

1925

Tank — 1940

Case: 18-karat yellow gold, yellow gold Milanaise bracelet, 23 x 30 mm

Movement: nickel-plated, côtes de Genève decoration, 18 jewels, manual winding

Remarks: gold Tank with faceted blue sapphire in the crown

Estimated value: $16,200 →

Tank Louis Cartier — 1978

Case: 18-karat yellow gold, leather strap, 24 x 30 mm

Movement: rhodium-plated, côtes de Genève decoration, manual winding

Remarks: gold men's watch secured with screws on the side; blue sapphire in the crown

Estimated value: $3,375 →

Vendôme Carrée — 1930

Case: 18-karat white gold, leather strap, 23 x 23 mm

Movement: nickel-plated, manual winding

Remarks: white gold men's watch; crown set with faceted blue sapphire; enamel dial

Estimated value: $4,860 →

Vendôme Carrée — 1965

Case: 18-karat yellow gold, leather strap 25 x 32 mm

Movement: nickel-plated, côtes de Genève decoration, manual winding

Remarks: rare men's watch with central strap lugs; this watch was offered with a gold folding clasp

Estimated value: $4,725 →

Men's Watch — 1920

Case: 18-karat yellow gold, leather strap, 25 x 31 mm

Movement: nickel-plated, with côtes de Genève, 18 jewels, regulated in 8 positions, manual winding

Remarks: gold men's watch with blue sapphire in the crown; movement regulated in 8 positions; this watch was offered with a gold folding clasp

Estimated value: $13,500 →

Men's Watch — 1925

Case: 18-karat yellow gold, leather strap, 23 x 34 mm

Movement: nickel-plated, côtes de Genève decoration, manual winding

Remarks: gold men's watch with blue sapphire in the crown; this watch was offered with a gold folding clasp

Estimated value: $7,425 →

Santos — 1924

Case: 18-karat yellow gold, yellow gold link bracelet, 25 x 33 mm

Movement: nickel-plated, 18 jewels, regulated in 8 positions, manual winding

Remarks: gold men's watch with blue sapphire in the crown; movement regulated in 8 positions

Estimated value: $10,800 →

Santos — 1925

Case: 18-karat yellow gold, leather strap, 25 x 34 mm

Movement: nickel-plated, 18 jewels, regulated in 8 positions, manual winding

Remarks: early Santos with blue sapphire in the crown; movement regulated in 8 positions; this watch was offered with a gold folding clasp

Estimated value: $5,400 →

Reversible Cabriolet — 1970

Case: 18-karat yellow gold, leather strap, 21 x 32 mm

Movement: nickel-plated, manual winding

Remarks: rare gold watch in reversible case; crown with sapphire cabochon; this watch was offered with a gold folding clasp

Estimated value: $10,125 →

Reverso — 1960

Case: 18-karat yellow gold, leather strap, 22 x 32 mm

Movement: Caliber 838/1, rhodium-plated, côtes de Genève decoration, manual winding

Remarks: rare Cartier with reversible case in Jaeger-LeCoultre's Reverso style

Estimated value: $8,100 →

Escalier Ronde — 1950

Case: 18-karat yellow gold, leather strap, Ø 34 mm

Movement: Caliber 469A, nickel-plated, côtes de Genève decoration, manual winding

Remarks: gold men's watch with recessed crown; this watch was offered with a gold folding clasp

Estimated value: $8,100 →

Vendôme — 1950

Case: 18-karat yellow gold, screw-down case back, leather strap, Ø 33 mm

Movement: nickel-plated, côtes de Genève decoration, manual winding

Remarks: extra-flat men's watch; this watch was offered with a gold folding clasp

Estimated value: $8,775 →

Semi-Mystérieuse — 1960

Case: 18-karat yellow gold, leather strap, Ø 32 mm

Movement: rhodium-plated, côtes de Genève decoration, manual winding

Remarks: semi-mysterious watch with crown hidden on case back; this watch was offered with a gold folding clasp

Estimated value: $6,750 →

Vendôme Ronde — 1940

Case: 18-karat yellow gold, leather strap, Ø 29 mm

Movement: nickel-plated, côtes de Genève decoration, manual winding

Remarks: rare men's watch; this watch was offered with a gold folding clasp

Estimated value: $6,750 →

Alarm Watch — 1952

Case: stainless steel, push-down case back, leather strap, Ø 35 mm

Movement: JLC Caliber 489/1, nickel-plated, twin spring barrels, manual winding

Remarks: early Memovox by Jaeger-LeCoultre made for Cartier

Estimated value: $4,050 →

Men's Watch with Sweep Seconds — 1968

Reference number: 252

Case: 18-karat yellow gold, screw-down case back, leather strap, Ø 34 mm

Movement: gold-plated, decorated, 17 jewels, regulated in two positions, automatic winding

Remarks: gold automatic men's watch regulated in two positions; Cartier gold clasp

Estimated value: $5,400 ↗

Certina

In 1959, Certina surprised the watch world with a new shock protection: not only was the balance shielded from breaking, the entire movement was now safeguarded. The concept was called DS (for "double security") and utilized a rubber ring as a bumper between the movement holder ring and the case. The new Certina DS proved its reliability in 1960 when it survived the 8,222 meter-high climb of Dhaulagiri in the Himalayas by a Swiss expedition. After that, ever newer endurance tests were sought for the DS models. One DS was even put into a hockey puck, where it withstood the extreme shocks of play without the movement being damaged. The DS 2 was used by the crew of the undersea project Sealab II, while the DS 3 was even secured to a submarine tower to prove that it was absolutely water-resistant even at great depths.

The DS principle is certainly the most famous invention of brothers Adolf and Alfred Kurth, who founded the company Kurth Frères in 1888 in Grenchen. In the beginning they only completed movements for other companies, but later their own reliable calibers secured the brand's reputation for robust, sporty watches.

Starting in 1938, this was also mirrored in the company's name. *Certina* is based on the Latin term for "secure" and was legally registered on October 2, 1939.

The little company progressed nicely. Under the management of Hans and Erwin Kurth, the sons of Alfred, Certina finally developed into a large successful company often recognized for its quality.

Early on, the Kurth brothers put their money behind the still young wristwatch, and not only on interesting and very modern cases. Their movements also had no reason to hide within a shell.

Thanks to solid technology and pleasing shapes, Certina became one of the leading brands in the Swiss watch industry. The brand remained with its founding family until 1970 and was managed by Hans as president of the board.

With caliber family 288, Certina introduced its first quickly oscillating movement in 1970. In order to conduct the energy from the mainspring with as little friction as possible, a micro ball bearing was developed for the third wheel of this caliber—a one-of-a-kind technical element.

In 1971, Certina was integrated into ASUAG Holding GWC and later with this group into the Swatch Group. After the quartz crisis was over, only the brand name was left of this once proud *manufacture*, but Certina now has a secure place within the Swatch Group as a producer of extremely robust watches—and so the DS concept lives on.

DS2 Chronolympic

1975

Case: stainless steel, screw-down case back, leather strap, Ø 42 mm,

Movement: Valjoux Caliber 726, rhodium-plated, column wheel control of chronograph, manual winding

Remarks: chronograph with 30-minute and 12-hour counters in the especially robust DS2 case

Estimated value: $410 →

Chronolympic

1975

Case: stainless steel, screw-down case back, leather strap, 40 x 42 mm

Movement: Valjoux Caliber 728, rhodium-plated, column-wheel control of chronograph, manual winding

Remarks: unworn chronograph with sweep 60-minute and 12-hour counters; additional regatta scale

Estimated value: $340 ↘

Automatic DS-3 Super PH 1000 Meters

1975

Case: stainless steel, screw-down case back, rotating bezel, stainless steel link bracelet, 45 x 48 mm

Movement: Caliber 919-1, nickel-plated, automatic winding

Remarks: professional diver's watch in robust DS-3 case; water-resistant to 1000 m

Estimated value: $480 →

DS 288

1970

Case: stainless steel, screw-down case back, leather strap

Movement: Caliber 25-681, rhodium-plated, 27 jewels, automatic winding

Remarks: unusually robust Certina with DS movement holder ring protecting the movement from heavy shocks; Caliber 25-681 has a micro ball bearing third wheel

Estimated value: $210 →

288

1970

Case: stainless steel, screw-down case back, leather strap

Movement: Caliber 25-681, rhodium-plated, 27 jewels, automatic winding

Remarks: automatic men's watch with Certina manufacture Caliber 25-682; micro ball bearing minute pinion

Estimated value: $210 →

DS

1960

Case: gold-plated, stainless steel screw-down case back, leather strap

Movement: Caliber 25-65, automatic winding

Remarks: first Certina DS outfitted with a special movement holder ring (DS) protecting the movement from heavy shocks

Estimated value: $210 →

DS 2

1968

Case: stainless steel, screw-down case back, rotating bezel, leather strap

Movement: Caliber 25-651, automatic winding

Remarks: DS diver's watch with rotating bezel; orange minute hand for better legibility

Estimated value: $675 →

Alarm

1976

Case: stainless steel, screw-down case back, leather strap

Movement: Caliber 681 (base: AS 5007), 25 jewels, automatic winding

Remarks: automatic alarm wristwatch with rare Caliber AS 5007 only displaying the date; the set alarm time is displayed via a reference marker on the center disk

Estimated value: $540 →

Chronoswiss

When Gerd-Rüdiger Lang introduced his first mechanical watches to the market in 1982, industry insiders didn't predict a long run for him. The buzzwords "mechanical boom" had not yet been invented—it was mass-produced wares with electronic insides that were dominating watchmaker and jewelers' stocks.

It would seem that the critics had made up their minds without taking the consumers into consideration, and the spontaneous success of Lang's fine, striking mechanical timekeepers gave him the courage to look around for a bigger factory in Munich relatively quickly.

The brand name Chronoswiss was something Lang invented to display what were for him the two most important components of his com-pany: for one, the Greek word for time, *chronos*, and for another the adjective *Swiss*, symbolizing his relationship to the motherland of mechanical watchmaking. Lang only uses components that were manufactured in Switzerland for his watches—for him a constant symbol of durability in our fast-paced times. In 1988, Chronoswiss became the first wrist-watch manufacturer to use the regulator dial, which was inspired by precision clocks, thus creating a lasting calling card for himself. Model families like Pacific, Hora, Kairos, and Orea were created, among them mechanical treasures such as the Chronograph Rattrapante and specialties like the Grand Régulateur, a combination of pocket and wristwatch. The movements in these early Chronoswiss watches were often remnant and new old stock of vintage movement calibers, which were at least partially modified. A stroke of luck allowed Lang to secure the production rights and tooling of Enicar Caliber 165, which today represents a fine little specialty among modern automatic movements. The watches from the first limited series have long become classics and are still sold on the secondary market for clearly more than their retail prices. "For many people, we are a brand that has been here forever," Chronoswiss's founder Lang says, surprised himself that his brand is mentioned today in the same breath as many traditional Swiss watchmakers, some of which are centuries old.

The Chronoswiss brand has actually been around for twenty-five years. At the time it was founded, the future looked bleak for mechanical watches and therefore for Lang's beloved vocation of watchmaking. However, Lang was even then feeling the "fascination of mech-anics" that has today become his brand's tagline.

The unmistakable appearance of the typical Chronoswiss case with its generous sapphire crystal surface, fluted edges, large onion-shaped crown, and heavy, curved lugs was grinned at twenty years ago by his competitors. But at the beginning of the 1990s, these characteristics were being copied everywhere and are today once again trendy. The case back with its sapphire crystal—Chronoswiss as a bridge-builder between the watchmaking traditions of both the past and modern watch design consistently added this to every one of its models—is today a basic standard.

Régulateur — 1988

Reference number: CH 6321

Case: 18-karat yellow gold/steel, screw-down exhibition case back, leather strap, Ø 38 mm

Movement: Unitas Caliber 6376 Z, swan-neck fine adjustment, modified with off-center display of the hour, 17 jewels, manual winding

Remarks: limited edition of the first regulator (3,000 pieces)

Estimated value: $3,375 →

Hora — 1990

Reference number: CH 1351

Case: 18-karat white gold/yellow gold, screw-down exhibition case back, leather strap

Movement: FHF Caliber 29, shaped movement, modified for digital jump hour display, 15 jewels, manual winding

Remarks: limited edition (700 pieces)

Estimated value: $4,050 →

Régulateur Réctangulaire — 1993

Reference number: CH 1951

Case: 18-karat yellow gold, screw-down exhibition case back, leather strap

Movement: FHF Caliber 29 from 1934, shaped movement, modified with off-center display of the hour, 16 jewels, manual winding

Remarks: limited edition (650 pieces)

Estimated value: $4,725 →

Grand Régulateur — 1995

Reference number: CH 2281

Case: 18-karat yellow gold, screw-down exhibition case back, Ø 47 mm

Movement: Minerva Caliber 17-22 from 1921, Breguet hairspring, finely finished, modified with off-center display of the hour, 15 jewels, manual winding

Remarks: wearable as pocket watch or wristwatch (bayonet clasp); limited edition (300 pieces)

Estimated value: $6,750 →

Kairos Chronograph — 1989

Reference number: CH7221

Case: 18-karat yellow gold, screw-down exhibition case back, leather strap, Ø 38 mm

Movement: Valjoux Caliber 72Z, swan-neck fine adjustment, finely finished, modified with off-center display of time, 17 jewels, manual winding

Remarks: limited edition (500 pieces)

Estimated value: $6,075 →

Kairos Chronograph Skelett — 1990

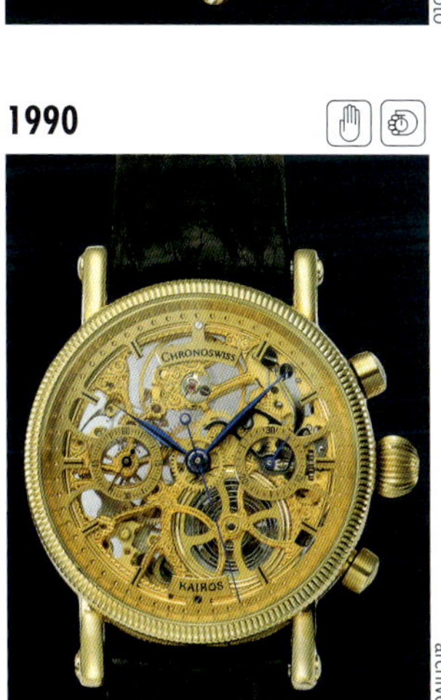

Reference number: CH 2321

Case: 18-karat yellow gold, screw-down exhibition case back, leather strap, Ø 38 mm

Movement: Valjoux Caliber 23, completely skeletonized and engraved, gold-plated, 17 jewels, manual winding

Remarks: limited edition (700 pieces)

Estimated value: $7,425 →

Kelek Répétition — 1988

Case: gold-plated, movable strap lugs, leather strap

Movement: Caliber DK 87 with five-minute repeater module, 21 jewels, automatic winding

Remarks: strikes the hours and five minute intervals that have passed since noon or midnight on demand

Estimated value: $2,565 →

Pacific — 1993

Reference number: CH 2814

Case: stainless steel, screw-down exhibition case back, leather strap, Ø 38.5 mm

Movement: ETA Caliber 2892-A2, 21 jewels, automatic winding

Remarks: sporty men's watch from the first Chronoswiss collection; water-resistant to 100 m

Estimated value: $675 →

Cyma

How could it be possible to make life easier on watch retail shops? How could the watchmakers be helped in working more effectively and quickly, ultimately making their lives much easier?

Cyma, one of Switzerland's biggest watch manufacturers with more than 1,000 employees, was one of the first companies to produce completely exchangeable components for its movements in the 1920s. A sensational development that was only made possible with precise manufacturing processes: hours of finishing and adjustment during repair were no more, for the company's replacement components fit without problem right into the movements.

Cyma, quickly advancing to one of Switzerland's largest watch companies, already had a tempestuous history behind it at this time. Although it was only officially registered in 1903 as Cyma, its roots reach back to 1862. It was founded not on one single company, but was created from several located in various Swiss regions.

Schwob Frères in La Chaux-de-Fonds is generally pronounced the origin of the later *manufacture*. Schwob Frères was apparently also a financial participant in Sandoz & Cie, which was founded in 1871 by Henri Sandoz in Le Locle. Sandoz moved to Tavannes, north of Biel, in 1891 and specialized in the manufacture of exclusive complication watches, repeaters, and chronographs as Tavannes Watch Co. Using the most modern machines, the company—which distributed its products under the brand names Cyma, Cyma-Tavannes, and even just Tavannes—developed into one of the largest watch manufacturers in Switzerland by 1910.

Even simple Cyma models were very precise watches with excellent rate results and were often sold as officially tested chronometers. Ladies watches, on the other hand, were not available from Cyma for a long time. Their small movements were still too imprecise in the 1920s, and thus not good enough for Cyma. Only when their small movements ran precisely and reliably, did Cyma add a ladies' watch line. All Cyma models had simple, elegant shapes. The alarm wristwatch Time-O-Vox, which was in the program for a short time, was one of the most popular models. At this time, Cyma used an in-house development for the balance's shock protection called Cymaflex that was advertised extensively.

Alongside beautiful manually wound watches, Cyma also had two automatic caliber families in its program. While the hammer automatics were chiefly used for winding according to the Harwood principle back then, Cyma developed eccentric winding with a spring-loaded rotor axis for its Autorotor caliber.

Very early on, Cyma turned to the groundbreaking microelectronics ravaging the industry for rate precision: in 1973, the company was already producing electronic watches. Thanks to these early tendencies, Cyma survived the Swiss watch industry's quartz crisis in the 1970s. Today, the company works strictly with quartz watches in the private label sector.

Chronomètre — 1930

Case: chrome-plated, push-down case back, leather strap, 22 x 37 mm
Movement: silver-plated, côtes de Genève decoration, jewels set in chatons, manual winding
Remarks: chronometer wristwatch
Estimated value: $410 →

Chronomètre — 1950

Case: 18-karat yellow gold, push-down case back, leather strap, Ø 33 mm
Movement: rhodium-plated, côtes de Genève decoration, jewels set in chatons, manual winding
Remarks: chronometer wristwatch with original Cyma sales tag
Estimated value: $1,080 →

Chronomètre — 1950

Case: 18-karat yellow gold, push-down case back, leather strap, Ø 34 mm
Movement: nickel-plated, côtes de Genève decoration, jewels set in chatons, manual winding
Remarks: gold chronometer wristwatch
Estimated value: $810 →

Navystar Chronomètre — 1968

Case: 18-karat yellow gold, screw-down case back, leather strap, Ø 35 mm
Movement: Caliber 485.1, nickel-plated, côtes de Genève decoration, 77 jewels, automatic winding
Remarks: gold chronometer wristwatch with Cyma manufacture Caliber 485.1; eccentric rotor
Estimated value: $945 →

Service Watch — 1940

Case: stainless steel, screw-down case back, textile strap, Ø 38 mm
Movement: rhodium-plated, côtes de Genève decoration, jewels set in chatons, manual winding
Remarks: wristwatch for the British military forces (signed "W.W.W.")
Estimated value: $410 →

Service Watch — 1940

Case: stainless steel, screw-down case back, leather strap, Ø 38 mm
Movement: rhodium-plated, côtes de Genève decoration, jewels set in chatons, manual winding
Remarks: nearly new wristwatch for the British military forces (signed "W.W.W.")
Estimated value: $410 →

Chronograph — 1920

Case: silver, push-down case back, leather strap, Ø 34 mm
Movement: silver-plated, côtes de Genève decoration, column-wheel control of chronograph, manual winding
Remarks: rare chronograph with 30-minute counter; enamel dial; signed Tavannes Watch
Estimated value: $2,700 →

Time-O-Vox — 1953

Case: gold-plated stainless steel, push-down case back, leather strap, Ø 34 mm
Movement: Cyma Caliber 464, gold-plated, gong, manual winding
Remarks: extremely rare alarm wristwatch, only about 3,000 pieces manufactured; subsidiary seconds and sweep alarm hand; watch operated via the crown and two small buttons
Estimated value: $2,025 →

archive photo

Doxa

Georges Ducommun of Le Locle, who had just come of age in 1889, was trying to decide how to best spend his future. He had recognized the great need for pocket watches. He wanted to catch this train and therefore founded a workshop for watches at the age of twenty-one. His success said it all, and the small workshop soon grew into a large factory.

The secret of Ducommun's success was the quality of his products: he was known for personally examining every one of the watches to leave his company despite its quick growth. Not only increasing sales numbers showed that he was on the right track; his watches were also awarded several prizes at the exhibitions in Liège in 1905 and Milan in 1906.

In 1908, Ducommun developed an eight-day movement and had it patented right away. It was to be used in timekeepers for the automobile dashboards he had recently added to his program. Since he himself had purchased one of the newfangled iron horses, he was convinced that this invention would be a good sales market for his watch brand as well.

The successful businessman registered the name Doxa in 1910 for a line of his watches that were delivered as chronometers. And in the 1920s, he made the first Doxa wristwatches. Shortly thereafter, Ducommun extended his program again: alongside normal, reasonably priced everyday watches, he also manufactured jewelry watches for ladies and gentlemen. He had so much success with his company that he became rich and purchased the chic Château des Monts, a wonderful manor house high above the city of Le Locle that today houses the city's watch museum.

In 1936, Ducommun passed away, and his brother-in-law Jacques Nardin took over Doxa's management. He also literally had watchmaking in his blood—no wonder, for he was the grandson of Ulysse Nardin, the founder of the *manufacture* of the same name in Le Locle.

Nardin continued to increase the company's program. Alongside normal everyday watches, Doxa now above all manufactured chronographs outfitted with calibers by Valjoux and Venus. There were also unusual watches in the program, among them the 1958 Grafic with its noteworthy shape. The company further introduced a technical specialty in the shape of a simple three-handed watch containing a jump hour display.

The best-known Doxa model to this day remains one that is equally as uncompromising: the Sub 300 introduced in 1967, a large, heavy diver's watch that is water-resistant to 300 meters and outfitted with an obvious orange dial. The dial color is one that the manufacturer chose on purpose: the company's developmental consultants—members of the U.S. Diver's Company—had found out that under water in the twilight of mid-range diving depths, a watch with an orange dial is most easily read. The special elements of the Sub 300 don't stop there. Its rotating bezel has two rows of numbers: the dive time can be read from the inner row, while the outer is a functional de-compression display, an element that lends this timepiece the predicate Professional. Doxa developed an entire family of diver's watches, among others some with black and silver dials. A chronograph also belonged to the program. In 1978, Doxa lost its independence and has since belonged to Aubry Frères SA. Recently, the brand has created some wind with successful remake editions of the diver's watches.

Men's Automatic Watch — 1948

Case: 18-karat yellow gold, push-down case back, leather strap, 31 x 37 mm
Movement: Caliber AS 1361N, nickel-plated, 17 jewels, automatic winding
Remarks: automatic men's watch
Estimated value: $340 →

Antimagnétique — 1940

Case: nickel-plated, push-down case back, leather strap, Ø 38 mm
Movement: nickel-plated, manual winding
Remarks: wristwatch with movable strap lugs
Estimated value: $270 →

Jumping Seconds — 1965

Case: stainless steel, push-down case back, leather strap, Ø 35 mm
Movement: nickel-plated, jumping seconds, manual winding
Remarks: extremely rare wristwatch with added mechanism for jumping seconds display; this watch was offered with original Doxa sales tag
Estimated value: $810 →

Retrograde Hours/Antimagnetic — 1950

Case: 14-karat yellow gold, screw-down case back, leather strap, Ø 35 mm
Movement: Caliber 118, nickel-plated, jumping seconds, retrograde hours, manual winding
Remarks: rare wristwatch with retrograde hours (day/night display) and jumping seconds
Estimated value: $1,080 →

Pilot's Chronograph — 1940

Case: stainless steel, screw-down case back, leather strap Ø 38 mm
Movement: rhodium-plated, côtes de Genève decoration, column-wheel control of chronograph, manual winding
Remarks: rare pilot's watch for the German Air Force
Estimated value: $1,620 →

Anti-Magnetic Chronograph — 1940

Case: stainless steel, push-down case back, leather strap, Ø 37 mm
Movement: nickel-plated, column-wheel control of chronograph, manual winding
Remarks: chronograph with 30-minute counter
Estimated value: $945 →

Chronograph — 1940

Case: stainless steel, push-down case back, leather strap, Ø 35 mm
Movement: nickel-plated, manual winding
Remarks: chronograph with off-center display of the time at 12 o'clock
Estimated value: $410 →

Chronograph with Complete Calendar — 1949

Case: stainless steel, push-down case back, leather strap, Ø 35 mm
Movement: Valjoux Caliber 72C, nickel-plated, column-wheel control of chronograph, manual winding
Remarks: chronograph with 30-minute and 12-hour counters; complete calendar
Estimated value: $1,890 →

Eberhard & Co.

The love of precision and sports time measurement is what led the Eberhard family to make a name for itself in the watch industry. Company founder Georges-Emile Eberhard, born in 1865 in St. Imier, opened his first workshop in La Chaux-de-Fonds in 1887. His watches sold well, likely also because Eberhard often traveled to neighboring countries in order to profit from all the market opportunities there as well. Thanks to his commitment, he expanded the company in 1906. His specialty was precision watches and chronographs.

Early on, Eberhard successfully made timekeepers for automobile competitions. In Italy, one of the hot spots for automobiles, Eberhard was the official timekeeper for almost all motorized sporting events until well into the 1930s.

From 1919, Eberhard's two sons Georges and Maurice took over the company's management. They recognized that the future of watches was on the wrist. And this was especially true of the world of sports, in which precise timekeeping was a must, and in which the main figures generally needed to keep their hands free. Eberhard began developing a chronograph for the wrist, and after just one year of research, the watchmakers introduced the new model: a monopusher chronograph that was to become the brand's flagship model.

Ten years later, Eberhard & Co. became the official watchmaker of the Royal Italian Navy, not in the least because of its contributions to Italian motor sports.

The company continued to consistently develop its sports watches. From 1935, Eberhard & Co.

could for the first time boast two-button chronographs that made addition timekeeping possible. From 1938, the company's collection was enriched by a model featuring a 12-hour counter.

In 1939, Eberhard & Co. offered its first split-seconds chronograph as its program's top model. Now it covered practically every variation of sports timekeeping.

In the 1940s, a new caliber came out: chronograph Caliber 1600, which was based on a Valjoux *ébauche*. Chiefly, this was a column

wheel-controlled monopusher chronograph, but it had a special element: a slide located at 4 o'clock allowed the wearer to interrupt the timing as often as desired and start it up again. Caliber 1600 was therefore vastly suitable for every kind of addition timekeeping.

In 1942, Maurice Eberhard became the sole owner of the company. After the sudden fatal accident of his daughter in 1962, he was a broken man and left the business world, selling the successful company. Today, Eberhard & Co. is owned by Italians, though it continues to do its manufacturing in Switzerland.

Chronograph — 1948

Case: stainless steel, push-down case back, leather strap, Ø 40 mm
Movement: rhodium-plated, column wheel control of chronograph, manual winding
Remarks: large chronograph with 30-minute counter
Estimated value: $1,750 →

Chronograph — 1925

Case: 18-karat yellow gold, leather strap, Ø 39 mm
Movement: nickel-plated, column wheel control of chronograph, manual winding
Remarks: chronograph with 30-minute counter; enamel dial; hinged hunter case back
Estimated value: $2,700 →

Chronograph — 1945

Case: 18-karat yellow gold, push-down case back, leather strap, Ø 39 mm
Movement: nickel-plated, column-wheel control of chronograph, manual winding
Remarks: chronograph with 30-minute counter
Estimated value: $2,160 →

Chronograph Extra-Fort — 1945

Case: stainless steel, 18-karat gold bezel, push-down case back, leather strap, Ø 40 mm
Movement: Valjoux Caliber 65, nickel-plated, column-wheel control of chronograph, manual winding
Remarks: nearly new chronograph with 30-minute counter
Estimated value: $1,625 →

Chronograph Extra-Fort — 1955

Case: 18-karat yellow gold, push-down case back, leather strap, Ø 39 mm
Movement: nickel-plated, column-wheel control of chronograph, manual winding
Remarks: chronograph with 30-minute and 12-hour counters
Estimated value: $2,430 →

Chronograph — 1956

Case: stainless steel, push-down case back, leather strap
Movement: Caliber 1600, nickel-plated, column wheel control of chronograph, manual winding
Remarks: chronograph with 30-minute and 12-hour counters; this chronograph functions as a one-button chronograph; the second button at 4 o'clock is for additional measurements and when pressed this button stops the chronograph, pressing it again allows the measurement to continue
Estimated value: $1,625 →

archive photo

Chronograph with Complete Calendar — 1950

Case: 18-karat yellow gold, push-down case back, leather strap, Ø 35 mm
Movement: rhodium-plated, column wheel control of chronograph, manual winding
Remarks: chronograph with 30-minute and 12-hour counters; complete calendar
Estimated value: $2,700 →

Split-Seconds Chronograph Extra-Fort — 1945

Case: 18-karat yellow gold, push-down case back, leather strap, Ø 40 mm
Movement: rhodium-plated, double column-wheel control of chronograph, manual winding
Remarks: chronograph with 30-minute and 12-hour counters; split-second mechanism for stopping intermediate times
Estimated value: $8,775 →

Enicar

British race car driver Stirling Moss wore an Enicar. So did his colleague Jim Clark. Diving pioneer Hans Hass counted on the reliability of his Enicar watch, something that the company communicated in its advertising of the day. While people might remember these facts, hardly anyone remembers that the company was founded on a little veranda on Rue du Crêt in La Chaux-de-Fonds, or that the name Enicar is the name of its founder spelled backwards: Racine.

Together with his wife Emma, Ariste Racine founded the successful company on October 1, 1913. Their first customer was a Japanese man by the name of Tezohdo. Just one year later, the Racines began doing business in Russia. Their most successful models were 11½-line and 13-line calibers outfitted with an unusual additional function: a little compass at 12 o'clock. Watches bearing the portrait of the political leader of the country they were going to be sold in printed on the dial later became a specialty.

Just two years after its establishment, the company founder had difficulty hiring a qualified workforce in La Chaux-de-Fonds. Thus, he founded a subsidiary in his mother's workshops in Lengnau in 1916 with six employees and called it Longeau Watch. A new chapter in the history of Enicar began in 1918 with the entry of Ariste's brother, Oskar, who was in charge of building up the caliber production. Enicar grew quickly; the Racines increased the size of their company in Lengnau and decided to give up the venue in La Chaux-de-Fonds. The Enicar brand only surfaced in Lengnau in 1932 when Longeau Watch became a joint stock company, though all of the shares remained in the hands of the family—even in 1940 when Ariste Jr., the founder's son, took over the management of the company that was as old as he was.

It was the above all its extremely robust and reliable watches that made the name Enicar famous; they kept on ticking whether under water or high in the Himalayas. An exceptional example of this was the fact that Enicar had outfitted the Swiss Himalaya expedition of 1956 with a new automatic model. The mountain climbers were enthusiastic and loved to compare the endurance and reliability of their watches with their sherpas, the native baggage carriers who accompanied them into the mountains. Thus, this timekeeper became the original member of the Sherpa family, whose very solid, sporty models were remarkable in their extreme robustness. It is no accident that the Sherpas became the Enicar brand's flagship.

The watches were based on Enicar's own caliber series 1120, 1140, and 160. The first caliber family, 1120, was offered in a version called Supertest. These watches were chronometers—models that the company itself had regulated in three positions before selling. In the thirty-jewel automatic version (1125), these models were sometimes even offered with a jewel bearing called Rubyrotor.

Thanks to a solid model policy, it looked as if Enicar would survive the 1970s quartz crisis without damage. But the breakdown of the Asian market hit the company hard and led to Enicar SA's insolvency. It had to declare bankruptcy on July 15, 1987.

Enicar's calibers experienced a somewhat more fortunate destiny: today they continue to tick as the base of many Chronoswiss automatic calibers.

Super Dive Sherpa

1970

Case: stainless steel, screw-down case back, leather strap, Ø 40 mm

Movement: Caliber AR 1145, gold-plated, automatic winding

Remarks: Sherpa diver's watch with rotating inner bezel (flange)

Estimated value: $945 →

Sherpa Guide Worldtime Rubyrotor

1964

Case: stainless steel, bayonet case back, leather strap, Ø 43 mm

Movement: Caliber AR 1126, gold-plated, jewel bearings, 30 jewels, automatic winding

Remarks: Caliber 1126 with jewel bearing rotor, an independent, second time can be set via the reference city ring

Estimated value: $1,220 →

Sherpa Jet Automatic

1969

Case: stainless steel, screw-down case back, leather strap, Ø 36 mm

Movement: nickel-plated, automatic winding

Remarks: sporty wristwatch with two time zones (GMT) and two-tone 24-hour ring

Estimated value: $810 →

Sherpa Jet Automatic

1975

Case: stainless steel, screw-down case back, leather strap, 37 x 41 mm

Movement: Caliber AR 166 (respective 1146), gold-plated, automatic winding

Remarks: Sherpa with second time zone and colorful 24-hour ring

Estimated value: $675 →

Jet Graph

1969

Case: stainless steel, screw-down case back, rotating bezel, leather strap, Ø 41 mm

Movement: Valjoux Caliber, gold-plated, column-wheel control of chronograph, manual winding

Remarks: chronograph with 30-minute and 12-hour counters; second time zone set via the bezel; additional time zone can be set via the rotating small red triangle reference marker

Estimated value: $1,620 →

Jet Graph

1969

Case: stainless steel, screw-down case back, rotating bezel, leather strap, Ø 41 mm

Movement: Valjoux Caliber 724, gold-plated, column-wheel control of chronograph, manual winding

Remarks: chronograph with 30-minute and 12-hour counters; second time zone set via the bezel; additional time zone can be set via the rotating small red triangle reference marker

Estimated value: $1,620 →

Alarm

1975

Case: stainless steel, screw-down case back with membranous gasket, leather strap

Movement: Caliber AS 1931, red gold-plated, twin spring barrels, manual winding

Remarks: wristwatch alarm with date and double sounding board case back according to the Vulcain Cricket principle

Estimated value: $540 →

Memostar

1971

Case: stainless steel, screw-down case back, leather strap, 39 x 44 mm

Movement: Lémania Caliber LWO 2980, nickel-plated, gong, automatic winding

Remarks: rare automatic alarm wristwatch with Lémania caliber outfitted with one single spring barrel

Estimated value: $1,220 →

Eterna

He was a man of action, and his adventurous journeys brought him global fame—of course, we are talking about Norwegian anthropologist Thor Heyerdahl. In 1947, he left Peru on his balsa wood raft called *KonTiki* in order to test whether people could have immigrated to the Polynesian islands in this manner. Three and a half months and almost 5,000 miles later he reached the Tuamotu Islands. His experiment had worked.

An indispensable piece of equipment for him on this trip was a watch manufactured in small series especially developed for the researcher, an indestructible watch whose name was to become a hallmark for its manufacturer: the KonTiki by Eterna.

By this time, the company had already had a turbulent history. In Grenchen, one of the poorest regions of Switzerland, the company was first founded as Watch Manufacture Urs Schild by a school teacher of the same name and Josef Girard, a doctor. Girard had previously established a watchmaker school and had also shipwrecked an *ébauche* factory he had previously founded.

The duo built the new watch *manufacture* inaugurated in 1856 directly on the banks of the city's stream. Thus, they were able to harness the power of its water and use it for their company. Success was not long in coming: in 1870 they already had to expand.

Schild introduced modern machines to the factory. His son Max, who had taken over its management in 1888, was in favor of rationalization. He had studied industrial production in the United States at the Illinois Watch Company and wanted to apply these experiences to his own company. However, the Swiss were afraid of losing their jobs and called a strike. Max was forced out of the company, and his brother Theodor took the rudder. The machine engineer modernized the factory and introduced a new company name in 1906: Eterna-Werke, Gebrüder Schild & Co.

Theodor saw that the future belonged to the wristwatch and reacted correspondingly. In 1914, he introduced a sensation: the first serially manufactured alarm wristwatches in the world. By 1930, Eterna was making the smallest wristwatch produced in series with a baton movement.

Two years later Schild split his company in response to pressure from the industrial association: Eterna AG for assembling watches and ETA AG, specializing in the manufacture of *ébauches*. What joined the two divisions was the fact that all newly developed movements were first put into Eterna watches before they could be sold to other companies.

The movement developed for the KonTiki and Heyerdahl in 1947 already possessed new automatic winding, the rotor of which rolled on five ball bearings, each with a diameter of only 0.65 mm. These five balls were to become the brand's logo, and the system became the standard for the entire watch industry.

In the 1970s, Eterna competed with Japanese companies for the slimmest quartz movement—and won with a height of under one millimeter and a weight of just over one gram.

Then the quartz crisis hit hard and only a fusion within the Swiss watch industry could save Eterna, which became part of ASUAG. Omega and Tissot, part of a group called SSIH, which later became the Swatch Group, took over ETA SA. Eterna AG was sold to the PCW Group in 1984, and nowadays finds itself under the ownership of the F.A. Porsche family.

Eterna-Matic Chronometer — 1965

Case: stainless steel, screw-down case back, Ø 34 mm

Movement: Caliber 1422, nickel-plated, decorated, 21 jewels, automatic winding

Remarks: chronometer wristwatch

Estimated value: $340 →

KonTiki 20 — 1968

Case: stainless steel case, screw-down case back, stainless steel link bracelet, Ø 36.5 mm

Movement: Eterna Caliber 1489K, rhodium-plated, decorated, 21 jewels, automatic winding

Remarks: a typical sporty men's watch, the KonTiki was extremely popular in the 1960s

Estimated value: $410 →

Eterna-Matic Centenaire — 1960

Case: 18-karat yellow gold, push-down case back, yellow gold Milanaise bracelet, Ø 33 mm

Movement: Caliber 1428U, nickel-plated, automatic windng

Remarks: elegant gold watch with gold bracelet

Estimated value: $480 →

Eterna-Matic — 1965

Case: 18-karat yellow gold, leather strap, Ø 38 mm

Movement: Caliber 1253, nickel-plated, automatic winding

Remarks: automatic wristwatch

Estimated value: $270 →

Eterna-Matic 3000 — 1965

Case: 18-karat yellow gold, push-down case back, leather strap, Ø 33 mm

Movement: Caliber 1456, nickel-plated, decorated, 21 jewels, automatic winding

Remarks: elegant men's watch

Estimated value: $340 →

Eterna-Matic Chronometer — 1955

Case: 18-karat yellow gold, screw-down case back, leather strap, Ø 34 mm

Movement: rhodium-plated, decorated, 21 jewels, automatic winding

Remarks: chronometer wristwatch

Estimated value: $810 →

Eterna-Matic Chronometer Centenaire — 1965

Case: 18-karat yellow gold, leather strap, Ø 34 mm

Movement: Caliber 1429U, nickel-plated, automatic winding

Remarks: anniversary chronometer from 1965

Estimated value: $810 →

Eterna-Matic — 1965

Case: 18-karat yellow gold, push-down case back, leather strap, Ø 34 mm

Movement: nickel-plated, decorated, automatic winding

Remarks: fine men's watch with date display

Estimated value: $350 →

Chronograph — 1950

Case: stainless steel, screw-down case back, leather strap, Ø 38mm
Movement: Caliber 703, rhodium-plated, column-wheel control of chronograph, manual winding
Remarks: chronograph with 30-minute counter; telemeter scale and snail shaped tachymeter scale
Estimated value: $540 →

Chronograph — 1938

Case: yellow gold, push-down case back, leather strap, Ø 30mm
Movement: nickel-plated, column wheel control of chronograph, manual winding
Remarks: small chronograph with 30-minute counter
Estimated value: $810 →

Chronograph Doctor's Watch — 1945

Case: stainless steel, push-down case back, leather strap, Ø 33 mm
Movement: nickel-plated, column-wheel control of chronograph, manual winding
Remarks: nearly unworn chronograph with 30-minute counter and pulsometer scale
Estimated value: $540 →

Chronograph Doctor's Watch — 1950

Case: 18-karat yellow gold, screw-down case back, leather strap, Ø 38 mm
Movement: Caliber E 704, nickel-plated, column-wheel control of chronograph, manual winding
Remarks: heavy gold chronograph with 30-minute and 12-hour counters; pulsometer scale
Estimated value: $1,350 →

Chronograph with Complete Calendar — 1945

Case: 18-karat yellow gold, push-down case back, leather strap, Ø 36 mm
Movement: nickel-plated, column-wheel control of chronograph, manual winding
Remarks: chronograph with 30-minute and 12-hour counters; complete calendar
Estimated value: $1,890 →

Calendar Watch — 1945

Case: 14-karat yellow gold, push-down case back, leather strap, Ø 33 mm
Movement: Caliber 1118H, nickel-plated, manual winding
Remarks: rare men's watch with complete calendar (date hand and display windows for weekday and month)
Estimated value: $540 →

Service Watch — 1935

Case: stainless steel, leather strap, 38 x 48 mm
Movement: Caliber 852S, nickel-plated, manual winding
Remarks: early pilot's watch for the German air force
Estimated value: $540 →

Eterna-Matic Anatomic Sevenday — 1975

Case: gold-plated, push-down case back, leather strap, Ø 41 mm
Movement: Caliber K1543, rhodium-plated, automatic winding
Remarks: unworn men's watch with weekday and date displays
Estimated value: $135 ↘

Klassik Sinn.

Excelsior Park

Jules-Frédéric Jeanneret founded his company, later called Excelsior Park, in 1866 in Saint-Imier. He was interested above all in short-term timekeeping and thus, of course, the design of stopwatches. Therefore, the young company was practically predestined to be a chronograph specialist.

Twenty-two years later, in 1888, Jeanneret's sons took over the company. One of them, Albert Jeanneret, registered a patent for a chronograph in 1891. Two years later, he transferred the direction of the company to his sons, Henri and Constant, the founder's grandsons.

These brothers, however, had no consensus about how the company should be run. In 1901, they therefore decided to go their separate ways: Constant left the company and a short time later bought Léonidas, a company that also specialized in manufacturing chronographs.

Henri Jeanneret continued to manage the company, which was now called Jeanneret-Brehm & Cie. Under his leadership, it developed wonderfully. Today, it is no longer possible to discern at which time he began to christen his watches Excelsior Park. This brand name was already to be found on the company's early wristwatches.

In order to fulfill the high demands that Jeanneret had set, Excelsior Park chiefly developed and manufactured its own calibers for its chronographs. The shaped movement Caliber 42, like all other movements by Excelsior Park, was outfitted with an unusual module: the crown wheel was positioned directly above the balance, making it different from most conventional chronograph calibers.

Excelsior Park did not exclusively use its own calibers, however. The company's watchmakers put Venus Caliber 179 containing a split-seconds mechanism, modern Valjoux Caliber 7740, Venus 140 featuring an off-center time display, and various Landeron calibers in their cases. Even if the company specialized in sports chronographs, Excelsior Park also naturally included three-handed watches in its program. Like many other companies, this chronograph specialist also felt the effects of the quartz crisis at the end of the 1970s. Even the most in-expensive quartz watches offered stop functions for very little money—who needed expensive mechanical chronographs? In 1984, Excelsior Park was liquidated. Flume, well-known as a tool supplier to watchmaker workshops, bought the rights to the brand. This Essen, Germany-based company at first tried to resuscitate the brand and manufactured several small series of

chronographs under the name Excelsior Park. The attempt failed, however, and the name

wandered into the annals of watch history in the year 1986.

Chronograph — 1948

Case: stainless steel, screw-down case back, leather strap, Ø 37 mm

Movement: nickel-plated, côtes de Genève decoration, column-wheel control of chronograph, manual winding

Remarks: chronograph with 45-minute counter

Estimated value: $1,080 →

Chronograph Pulsometer — appx. 1950

Case: stainless steel, screw-down case back, leather strap, Ø 37 mm

Movement: nickel-plated, côtes de Genève decoration, manual winding

Remarks: chronograph with 45-minute counter and pulsometer scale

Estimated value: $1,620 →

Limited Edition Chronograph — 1980

Case: 18-karat yellow gold, push-down case back, leather strap, Ø 37 mm

Movement: rhodium-plated, côtes de Genève decoration, manual winding

Remarks: unworn chronograph from a limited edition, no. 7/27; 30-minute counter and off-center display of the time

Estimated value: $4,725 →

Chronograph — 1948

Case: 18-karat rose gold, push-down case back, leather strap, Ø 35 mm

Movement: nickel-plated, côtes de Genève decoration, column-wheel control of chronograph, manual winding

Remarks: chronograph with 45-minute counter

Estimated value: $1,755 →

Excel-O-Graph — 1965

Case: stainless steel, push-down case back, rotating bezel, leather strap, Ø 42 mm

Movement: rhodium-plated, côtes de Genève decoration, column-wheel control of chronograph, manual winding

Remarks: nearly unworn chronograph with 30-minute and 12-hour counters; rotating bezel can be used as slide rule

Estimated value: $1,755 →

Chronograph — ca. 1965

Case: stainless steel, screw-down case back, rotating bezel, leather strap, Ø 39 mm

Movement: Caliber 40-68, rhodium-plated, côtes de Genève decoration, column-wheel control of chronograph, manual winding

Remarks: chronograph with 30-minute and 12-hour counters

Estimated value: $610 →

Chronograph Monte Carlo — 1970

Case: stainless steel, screw-down case back, rotating bezel, leather strap, Ø 43 mm

Movement: Valjoux Caliber 7740, rhodium-plated, manual winding

Remarks: chronograph with 30-minute and 12-hour counters

Estimated value: $1,620 →

Chronograph Monte Carlo — 1975

Case: stainless steel, screw-down case back, rotating bezel, leather strap, Ø 42 mm

Movement: Valjoux Caliber 7740, rhodium-plated, manual winding

Remarks: chronograph with 30-minute and 12-hour counters

Estimated value: $1,620 →

Fortis

When watchmaker Walter Vogt decided to found a collective company for producing watches called Vogt und Rüefli with his partner Alfred Rüefli in 1912, he already knew how important the quality of a watch movement was. Educated as a watchmaker at Eterna, Vogt had the best prerequisites to manufacture reliable timepieces. Since, at this time, movement manufacturers only delivered *ébauches* to be assembled by each watch manufacturer—who also added the escapement and even sometimes jewels and the main-spring—it was up to each of the companies how lavishly the movement was to be finished. For Vogt, it was clearly the precision of the watches that was his priority. By the following year, the brand Fortis had been registered. In 1914, Vogt and Rüefli separated, and the company was renamed Vogt & Co. With the later change to a joint stock company, it finally received its current name: Fortis Uhren AG. Walter Vogt made his most important decision when he elected to manufacture the new

automatic wristwatch developed by Englishman John Harwood in the 1920s. Thanks to his good contacts with movement factory A. Schild, also located in Grenchen, both companies began to perfect Harwood's design, optimizing it for serial production.

Fortis naturally also produced watches under its own name during this time, among them the first chronographs in 1937. Later a specialty of the brand became chronograph movements housed in a water-resistant movement container and pressed into the case from the front.

A new era began in 1948 when Rolf Vogt joined his father's company. Thanks to his clever business sense and feel for new trends, he achieved the establishment of the Fortis brand in many world markets.

Rolf Vogt wanted to give his brand its own face. Thus, a number of exceptional watches such as Eden Roc and Trueline were created, models that are considered design classics today. In 1956, Fortis also had an alarm in its collection, and the Manager introduced two years later was the first water-resistant alarm for the wrist. Proving the quality of the Manager, it was even delivered as an officially certified chronometer. In order to get the best rate results possible during serial production, Fortis's technicians developed a new testing element. BEP, or the Balance Electrotiming Process, allowed Fortis to achieve impressive precision results. The watches tested using this process received a special tag to alert the customer to the timepiece's high quality. The Performance model opened a new dimension—tying the brand to aviation, a relationship that is still current today, and especially military aviation. A collection of pilot's watches and pilot's chronographs was continuously extended, characterizing the brand's new image along with a line of Cosmonaut watches made for space. This brand continues to be headquartered in Grenchen, though it is now German owned.

Wandfluh

1937

archive photo

Reference number: 189 190

Case: stainless steel, screw-down case back, leather strap

Movement: Venus Caliber 152, screw balance, manual winding

Remarks: chronograph with 30-minute and 12-hour counters; rare case design with integrated movement container that is pressed into the case from the front

Estimated value: $1,620 ↗

Chronograph

1940

archive photo

Reference number: 87910

Case: chrome-plated, push-down case back, leather strap, Ø 35 mm

Movement: Venus Caliber 150, column-wheel control of chronograph, manual winding

Remarks: chronograph with 30-minute counter

Estimated value: $475 →

Chronograph

1940

archive photo

Reference number: 39804

Case: 18-karat yellow gold, leather strap

Movement: Valjoux Caliber 22, manual winding

Remarks: chronograph with telemeter and inner tachymeter scales; 30-minute counter

Estimated value: $1,890 →

Chronograph

1947

archive photo

Reference number: 324

Case: 18-karat yellow gold

Movement: Landeron Caliber 48, 17 jewels, manual winding

Remarks: double case back; 30-minute counter; tachymeter

Estimated value: $945 →

Chronograph

1952

archive photo

Case: stainless steel, case container design, push-down case back, leather strap, Ø 36 mm

Movement: Valjoux Caliber 72, Breguet hairspring, rhodium-plated, 17 jewels, manual winding

Remarks: chronograph with 30-minute and 12-hour counters; rare case design with integrated movement container that is pressed into the case from behind

Estimated value: $1,620 →

Chronograph

1960

archive photo

Case: 18-karat yellow gold, push-down case back, leather strap, Ø 35 mm

Movement: Valjoux Caliber 92, column wheel control of chronograph; swing pinion, 17 jewels, manual winding

Remarks: rare chronograph with 30-minute counter; unusual combination of exclusive column wheel control of chronograph and simple swing pinion

Estimated value: $1,620 →

Marinemaster

1972

archive photo

Reference number: 8001

Case: stainless steel, screw-down case back, rotating bezel, leather strap

Movement: Valjoux Caliber 72, 17 jewels, manual winding

Remarks: chronograph with minutes and hours; rotating black diver's bezel

Estimated value: $1,080 →

Marinemaster

1968

archive photo

Reference number: 337462 8-76

Case: stainless steel, screw-down case back, leather strap

Movement: ETA Caliber 2783, 21 jewels, automatic winding

Remarks: diver's watch with rotating decompression scale on the dial; date display; rotating ring underneath the crystal; luminous dial

Estimated value: $1,080 →

Manager

1954

Case: stainless steel, screw-down case back, leather strap,

Movement: Caliber AS 1475, rhodium-plated, twin spring barrels, 21 jewels, manual winding

Remarks: first water-resistant alarm wristwatch; this model was also available as a chronometer

Estimated value: $475 →

Brain matic Alarm

1971

Reference number: 187.80.45

Case: steel

Movement: Caliber AS 5008, 13 1/3 lines, 21 jewels

Remarks: "Dugena" engraved on rotor; antimagnetic; 1,450 Vickers

Estimated value: $1,080 →

Tiffany & Co. by Fortis

1940

Reference number: 328 479

Case: 14-karat gold

Movement: ETA Caliber 735, 7 1/2 x 11 lines, 17 jewels

Remarks: shaped movement engraved with "Fortis"

Estimated value: $675 →

Eden Roc

1950

Reference number: 2220

Case: stainless steel, push-down case back, leather strap, Ø 34 mm

Movement: ETA Caliber 2390, screw balance, 21 jewels, manual winding

Remarks: elegant men's watch, movement electronically regulated (BEP = Balance Electrotiming Process)

Estimated value: $270 →

Stratoliner

1962

Case: stainless steel, push-down case back, rotating bezel with reference markers, leather strap, Ø 36 mm

Movement: Felsa Caliber F 4009, 41 jewels, automatic winding

Remarks: elegant men's watch with display of date and weekday

Estimated value: $410 →

Performance

1965

Reference number: 476.980

Case: 18-karat yellow gold, push-down case back, leather strap, Ø 35 mm

Movement: ETA Caliber 2532, screw balance, 25 jewels, automatic winding

Remarks: sporty elegant men's watch; date display

Estimated value: $340 →

Manual Winding

1967

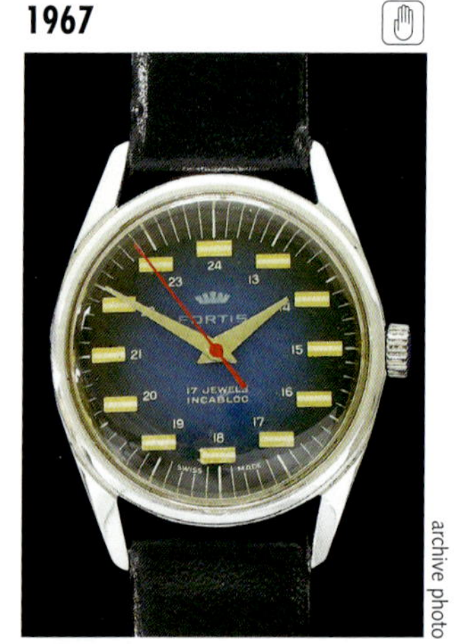

Reference number: 7001

Case: stainless steel, screw-down case back, leather strap

Movement: FHF Caliber Standard 96, 17 jewels, manual winding

Remarks: Incabloc shock protection

Estimated value: $340 →

Easy-Math

ca. 1970

Reference number: 7242

Case: chrome-plated, rotating inner bezel (flange), leather strap, Ø 37 mm

Movement: FHF Caliber 969, rhodium-plated, 17 jewels, manual winding

Remarks: sporty men's watch with compass function and logarithmic calculation scale on the adjustable numeral ring

Estimated value: $810 →

Reach the World with Timezone.com

International Reach

TimeZone.com is the world's largest and most complete online resource for watch enthusiasts and collectors. Launched in 1994, Time Zone has grown from a small group of enthusiasts to over 45,000 registered users today. More impressive is the number of people who visit TimeZone: in 2006 the site was visited by more than 3 million unique visitors* around the world. TimeZone's reach is truly international, TimeZone's 31 moderators are located in 9 countries and offers discussion in English, French and Japanese. The site is viewed by large numbers of enthusiasts in Italy, France, Germany, Hong Kong, Japan, Singapore, Russia, Switzerland, the UK, Canada, the Netherlands, and many more. There is no other source that covers the world of watches like TimeZone.

TimeZone's viewer traffic has increased dramatically in the past few years. The site receives visits from about 330,000 unique visitors* each month, compared with 32,000 per month in 2002. Today TimeZone generates about 9.5 million page views per month, compared with about 250,000 in 2002. TimeZone averages well over 2,000 new message posts each day, and on some days as many as 3,000 new messages are posted. For watch lovers the world over, TimeZone is the place to be.

Resources Attract a Broad and Affluent Community

TimeZone's extensive resources and many special events attract an affluent group of enthusiast and collectors. TimeZone's brand forums serve as home base for online enthusiasts of the leading watch brands, including Patek Philippe, Rolex, Audemars Piguet, Vacheron Constantin, Breguet, Jaeger LeCoultre, Lange & Söhne, Cartier, Panerai, IWC, and many more. TimeZone's Vintage Watch forum is the meeting place for aficionados of timepieces from the golden age. The Watchmaking Forum provides a place for those with technical interests to seek advice and share information. If you want to open a watch and see what makes it tick, TimeZone offers an online watch school taught by a professional watchmaking instructor. One of TimeZone's most visited pages is Industry News – you can get the all the latest updates here with just a click. The Lifestyle, Automotive and Photography forums offer pleasing and informative diversions.

TimeZone matches its strong online offerings with an industry leading line-up of real world events. TimeZoners around the world host collector get togethers (or "GTGs") where enthusiasts meet others who share their passion, and often leading personalities in the world of watches. Each year TimeZone sends reporters to the Basel and Geneva watch shows to post daily reports. TimeZone's Basel/SIHH Forum is the best place to get real time updates on the newest watches from the top brands. TimeZone also hosts annual Collectors' Tours of Switzerland and Germany. These events take up to 20 collectors on private guided tours of the leading manufacturers and museums, including Patek Philippe, Vacheron Constantin, Audemars Piguet, Jaeger LeCoultre, Lange & Söhne, Glashütte Original, Blancpain, and more. Tours often include a special private dinner with leading independent watchmakers such as Philippe Dufour, Vianney Halter, Felix Baumgartner, Kees Engelbarts, and others.

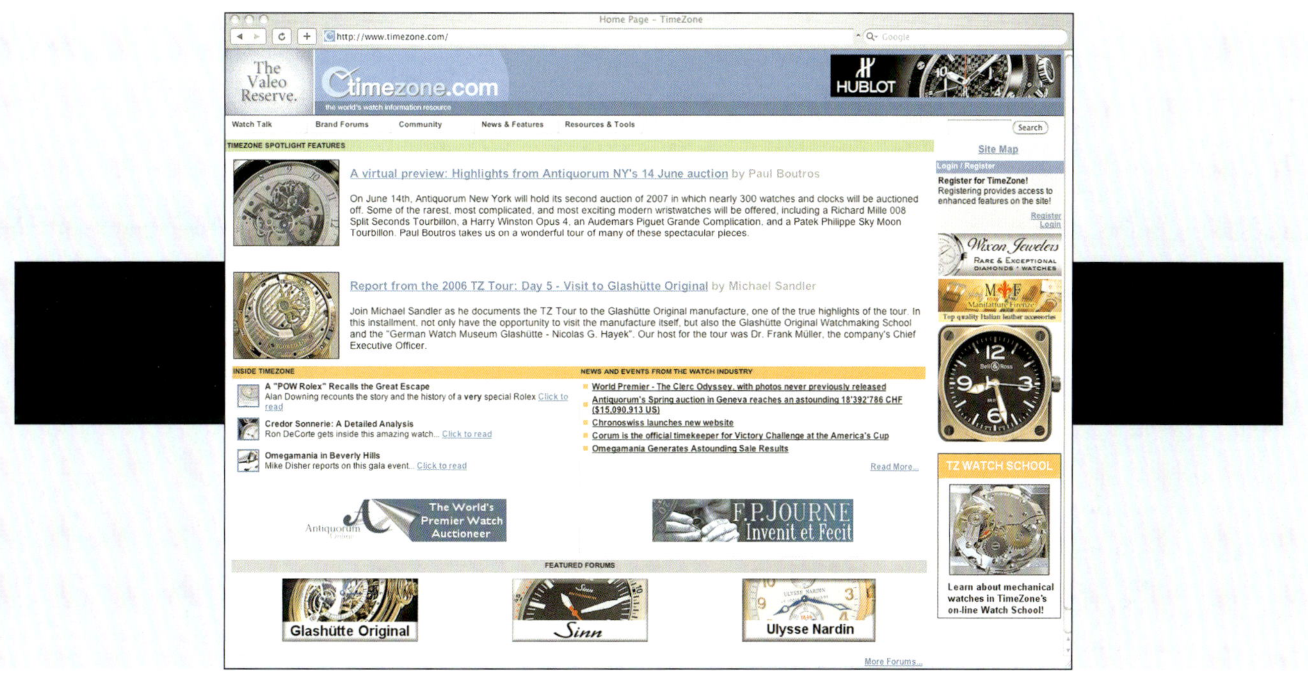

If you are an advertiser who wants to reach watch enthusiasts, TimeZone.com is the place to be. For more information or to obtain a rate sheet, please e-mail us at advertise@timezone.com

** Unique Visitors: The total number of unique visitors during the report period.*
A unique visitor is identified by their IP address or domain name

Girard-Perregaux

The history of the Girard-Perregaux brand officially began with a marriage: in 1854 Constant Girard and Marie Perregaux decided to spend the rest of their lives together. Girard immediately renamed his company, known as Girard & Cie until then.

The roots of the company, however, extend even further back, all the way to the year 1791. At that time watchmaker Jean-François Bautte joined the company of his teacher, J. D. Moulinier. The company developed wonderfully, and it was mainly blue bloods who swore on the timekeepers of Moulinier & Bautte. When Bautte died in 1837, his grandson took over the company and sold it to Felipe Hecht in 1897. It was only in 1905 that his son Juan sold it to the owners of Girard-Perregaux.

Constant Girard dedicated himself to the highest precision for the manufacture of his watches, a plan that his wife Marie, the daughter of a chronometer maker, supported as far as pos-sible. They were also exceptional aesthetes: technical solutions had to be visually pleasing as well. And because Girard had a thing for gold, he even had bridges, wheels, and entire base plates made of the valuable metal. The two could soon harvest the fruits of their labors: they won several chronometer competitions put on by the Neuchâtel Observatory, and by 1889 they had received a total of thirteen gold medals and awards.

The company received the last medals for its most famous timepiece: a tourbillon with three parallel gold bridges. Only twenty pieces of this model, the production of which was extremely difficult, were created over the course of twenty-five years. Its unusual design was rediscovered in the late twentieth century when Girard-Perregaux realized the tourbillon within the framework of a wristwatch.

The *manufacture*'s watches were always known as reliable, something that brought the company a lucrative deal with the German navy in 1879. These models, outfitted with a protective

grille over the sensitive crystal, were made especially for officers and were worn held to the wrist with a leather strap. Thus, this model can be said to be one of the oldest wristwatches known to history.

Although Girard-Perregaux was a standing member of the jury at World's Fairs since 1905, the brand itself went quiet until it was purchased by Graef & Co.

The Olimpico series was one of Girard-Perregaux's most traditional model lines. Every four years the company presented a new model in honor of the Olympic Games.

The automatic watches sold under the name Gyromatic were better known, however. This model received its name from the special elements that allowed the rotor to wind the mainspring in both rotational directions. Small balls called *Gyrotrons* moved in three radially arranged conical slits in the minute wheels.

Today, it is less well-known that Girard-Perregaux was one of the pioneers of quartz technology, even defining the standard frequency of 32,768 Hertz. In 1970, the company brought the first serial quartz wristwatch to the market.

Parallel to this, the company continued working on increasing the precision of mechanical movements: thus, the HF, an automatic watch with an ultra-fast frequency, was born. Its balance beat at 36,000 half-oscillations per hour.

Girard-Perregaux is one of the few companies that has retained its *manufacture* status to the present day, despite the fact that the brand was sold one last time—in 1992 to Turin entrepreneur and former race car driver Dr. Luigi Macaluso, who continues to manage it today.

Men's Watch with Large Date — 1945

Case: stainless steel, push-down case back, leather strap, 24 x 37 mm
Movement: nickel-plated, jewels set in chatons, manual winding
Remarks: rare men's watch with large date; date changed by pushing the crown
Estimated value: $675 →

Men's Watch — 1945

Case: chrome-plated, push-down case back, leather strap, Ø 35 mm
Movement: rhodium-plated, manual winding
Remarks: unworn men's watch
Estimated value: $270 →

Chronometer HF — 1965

Reference number: 8856B
Case: stainless steel, screw-down case back, leather strap, Ø 34 mm
Movement: Caliber 30, nickel-plated, manual winding
Remarks: unworn chronometer with original sales tag
Estimated value: $1,080 ↗

Chronometer GP — 1960

Case: 18-karat yellow gold, screw-down case back, leather strap, Ø 34 mm
Movement: rhodium-plated, regulated in 5 positions, manual winding
Remarks: chronometer with patented fine adjustment; movement regulated in 5 positions
Estimated value: $1,080 ↗

Calendar Watch — 1950

Case: stainless steel, screw-down case back, leather strap, Ø 33 mm
Movement: Caliber 382, nickel-plated, automatic winding
Remarks: men's watch with subsidiary seconds and complete calendar (date hand, display windows for weekday and month)
Estimated value: $410 →

Doctor's Chronograph — 1940

Case: 14-karat yellow gold, push-down case back, leather strap, Ø 31 mm
Movement: Caliber 281, nickel-plated, column-wheel control of chronograph, manual winding
Remarks: so-called doctor's chronograph with scale for easy measurement of the pulse
Estimated value: $1,620 →

Men's Watch — 1970

Case: stainless steel, push-down case back, leather strap, Ø 37 mm
Movement: rhodium-plated, manual winding
Remarks: unworn elegant men's watch with subsidiary seconds
Estimated value: $270 →

Chronograph Olimpico — 1975

Case: stainless steel, screw-down case back, rotating bezel, leather strap, Ø 39 mm
Movement: rhodium-plated, decorated, manual winding
Remarks: chronograph with 30-minute and 12-hour counters
Estimated value: $810 →

Glashütte

If you research the roots of the former combine Glashütter Uhrenbetriebe, you will come across names that read like a *Who's Who* of the German watch industry.

The conglomerate's direct predecessor was Deutsche Präzisions-Uhren-Fabrik Glashütte GmbH, founded in 1918. Due to economic problems, this company was split in two in 1925: into Uhren-Rohwerke-Fabrikation Glashütte AG (Urofa) and Glashütter Uhren-fabrik AG (Ufag). Glashütter Uhrenbetriebe was later created for the most part from these two firms in the German Democratic Republic.

Ufag sold its watches under the brand name Tutima, while Urofa only made movements like

Unser Fertigungsprogramm:

Damenarmbanduhren · Herrenarmbanduhr
Armbanduhrstopper · Datumuhren
Marinechronometer · Schiffswanduhren
Beobachtungsuhren

the famed Caliber 59 from about 1941, a 13-line chronograph movement with flyback function.

The best-known brand to be found within the Glashütter Uhrenbetriebe was that of the A. Lange & Söhne *manufacture*. Its founder, Ferdinand Adolph Lange, was the one to bring watchmaking to the economically weak Erzgebirge region, making Glashütte the most important German center of the watchmaking industry at the time. Glashütte also had him to thank for the many small companies that found their home in the region including suppliers, assemblers, and other specialists. Among the most important of those were Adolf Schneider, Moritz Grossmann, Ludwig Strasser and Gustav Rohde, along with Julius Assmann with his Union watch factory. The Mühle manufactory, which was well-known for its marine chronometers, was also later integrated into the Glashütter Uhrenbetriebe.

After World War II, Glashütte's production workshops were dismantled for reparations to the Soviet Union and shipped to the east. But by 1946, Glashütte was once again manufacturing watches—and these were not to be sneezed at: the calibers were offered in various quality levels, with Q1 being the highest.

The real history of the GUB began in 1951 when in the German Democratic Republic's Glashütte brands were put together to form VEB Glashütter Uhrenbetriebe. One of

Glashütte's specialties became the rare chronograph Caliber 64. Several manually wound and automatic movements were also made there.

In the 1960s, the GUB delivered many of the so-called catalogue watches for West German mail-order companies such as Quelle. These watches—outfitted with Spezichron and Spezimatic calibers that were driven by automatic winding or quartz movements and were 100-percent Glashütte design and manufacture—were an important source of Western currency in the GDR.

With the end of the German Democratic Republic in 1989, the GUB also had to be restructured. The basis of the East's upswing was privatization, and the now-privatized company founded a new brand called Glashütte Original, which based its production on the newly developed automatic Caliber 10-30 that came about shortly before the fall of the Berlin Wall.

The Glashütte watchmakers left in the current incarnation of the company now continually conceive and manufacture new complications that prove the talent of its new-old *manufacture*. In 2000, Glashütter Uhrenbetriebe was sold to Switzerland's Swatch Group.

Men's Watch Q1 — 1955

Case: gold-plated, stainless steel push-down case back, leather strap, Ø 33 mm
Movement: Caliber 60.3, nickel-plated, manual winding
Remarks: Quality 1 men's watch
Estimated value: $340 →

Men's Watch — ca. 1950

Case: gold-plated stainless steel, push-down case back, leather strap, Ø 33 mm
Movement: nickel-plated, manual winding
Remarks: elegant men's watch in a gold-plated case
Estimated value: $210 →

Men's Watch — ca. 1950

Case: gold-plated, stainless steel push-down case back, leather strap, Ø 33 mm
Movement: nickel-plated, manual winding
Remarks: simple men's watch
Estimated value: $210 →

Men's Watch Q1 — 1950

Case: 14-karat yellow gold, leather strap, Ø 33 mm
Movement: Caliber 28, gold-plated, frosted finish, manual winding
Remarks: rare yellow gold Quality 1 men's watch
Estimated value: $2,970 →

Men's Watch with Sweep Seconds — 1960

Case: gold-plated, stainless steel push-down case back, leather strap, Ø 34 mm
Movement: Caliber 70.1, nickel-plated, manual winding
Remarks: flat men's watch
Estimated value: $270 →

Men's Watch with Sweep Seconds — 1960

Case: gold-plated, stainless steel push-down case back, leather strap, Ø 33 mm
Movement: Caliber 70.1, nickel-plated, manual winding
Remarks: flat men's watch
Estimated value: $270 →

Men's Watch — 1950

Case: chrome-plated, stainless steel push-down case back, leather strap, Ø 33 mm
Movement: Caliber 60, nickel-plated, manual winding
Remarks: simple men's watch
Estimated value: $210 →

Men's Watch Q1 — 1950

Case: gold-plated, stainless steel screw-down case back, leather strap, Ø 33 mm
Movement: gold-plated, frosted finish, manual winding
Remarks: Quality 1 men's watch
Estimated value: $340 →

Urofa Men's Watch — 1945

Case: chrome-plated, stainless steel push-down case back, leather strap, Ø 35 mm

Movement: Caliber 611, nickel-plated, manual winding

Remarks: rare Urofa men's watch

Estimated value: $210 →

Tutima Men's Watch — 1937

Case: gold-plated, stainless steel push-down case back, leather strap

Movement: Caliber 58, 16 jewels, manual winding

Remarks: Tutima men's watch with shaped movement developed by Urofa in 1935 and available in different sizes

Estimated value: $675 →

archive photo

Tutima Chronograph — 1942

Case: chrome-plated, push-down case back, leather strap

Movement: Caliber 59, nickel-plated, column-wheel control of chronograph, 17 jewels, manual winding

Remarks: so-called German army chronograph outfitted with Urofa Caliber 59 (official supply watch)

Estimated value: $4,725 →

archive photo

Chronograph — 1960

Case: gold-plated, stainless steel screw-down case back, leather strap, Ø 36 mm

Movement: Caliber 64, nickel-plated, column-wheel control of chronograph, manual winding

Remarks: extremely rare chronograph with 30-minute counter; this design is based on the so-called German army chronograph, Caliber 59, and has a much smaller diameter

Estimated value: $2,050 ↗

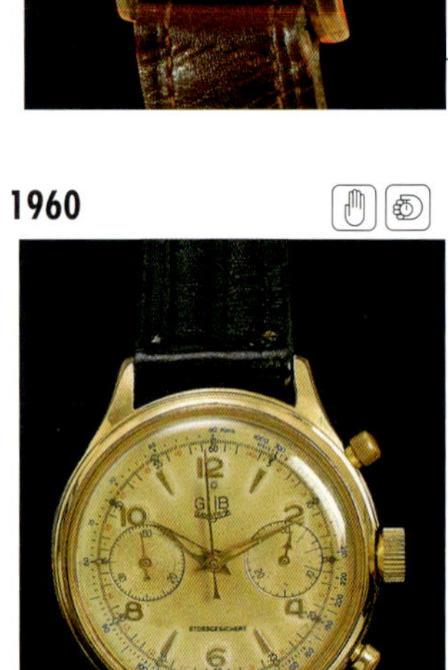

Men's Watch with Date/Weekday — 1955

Case: gold-plated, stainless steel screw-down case back, leather strap, Ø 37 mm

Movement: Caliber 56.1, nickel-plated, manual winding

Remarks: rare men's watch with display of weekday and date

Estimated value: $410 →

Men's Watch Q1 — 1950

Case: gold-plated, stainless steel screw-down case back, leather strap, Ø 33 mm

Movement: Caliber 28, gold-plated, frosted finish, manual winding

Remarks: Quality 1 men's watch

Estimated value: $1,100 →

Men's Watch — 1960

Case: gold-plated, stainless steel screw-down case back, leather strap, Ø 35 mm

Movement: Caliber 60.1, nickel-plated, manual winding

Remarks: flat men's watch

Estimated value: $270 →

Men's Watch Q1 — 1960

Case: gold-plated, stainless steel push-down case back, Ø 33 mm

Movement: Caliber 60.3, nickel-plated, manual winding

Remarks: Quality 1 men's watch

Estimated value: $270 →

Men's Watch — 1960

Case: gold-plated, screw-down case back, leather strap, Ø 35 mm

Movement: Caliber 60.1, nickel-plated, manual winding

Remarks: flat men's watch with large, applied hour markers

Estimated value: $270 →

Men's Watch Q1 — 1948

Case: gold-plated, stainless steel screw-down case back, leather strap, Ø 33 mm

Movement: Caliber 28, gold-plated, frosted finish, manual winding

Remarks: Quality 1 men's watch

Estimated value: $1,100 →

Spezimatic — 1955

Case: yellow gold, push-down case back, leather strap, Ø 34 mm

Movement: Caliber 662, rhodium-plated, automatic winding

Remarks: rare gold automatic watch

Estimated value: $1,900 ↗

Spezimatic — ca. 1960

Case: gold-plated, stainless steel push-down case back, leather strap, Ø 35 mm

Movement: nickel-plated, 26 jewels, automatic winding

Remarks: automatic watch with date

Estimated value: $210 →

Chronometer Q1 — ca. 1955

Case: gold-plated, stainless steel push-down case back, leather strap, Ø 36 mm

Movement: Caliber 70.3, nickel-plated, manual winding

Remarks: rare wristwatch chronometer with Quality 1 movement

Estimated value: $10,800 →

Spezimatic — 1955

Case: 14-karat yellow gold, push-down case back, leather strap, Ø 34 mm

Movement: Caliber 661, rhodium-plated, 26 jewels, automatic winding

Remarks: rare gold automatic watch with date

Estimated value: $1,080 →

Spezimatic — ca. 1957

Case: gold-plated, stainless steel push-down case back, leather strap, Ø 36 mm

Movement: nickel-plated, 26 jewels, automatic winding

Remarks: flat automatic watch with date

Estimated value: $230 →

Spezimatic — ca. 1970

Case: gold-plated, stainless steel push-down case back, leather strap, Ø 42 mm

Movement: nickel-plated, 26 jewels, automatic winding

Remarks: large and fashionable automatic watch with date, never worn

Estimated value: $210 →

Hamilton

Select design paired with unusual precision made Hamilton Watch Company a first choice in the United States, and also all over the world, for those in search of both precise timing and fashionable statements.

This company founded in 1892 in Lancaster, Pennsylvania, manufactured high-quality watches in relatively small numbers. Because of their above-average precision, Hamilton was also called the Patek Philippe of America. And thus it should come as no surprise that by the year 1900 more than 55 percent of all American railway engineers relied on a Hamilton—as did General Pershing and his advisors during World War I and Admiral Byrd, who journeyed to Antarctica in 1928. Hamilton watches not only belonged to the official equipment of American airmail pilots, the crews of most of the U.S. airlines also trusted the precision of these timepieces. The company also supplied the American navy and air force starting in 1937. Hamilton decided early on in the history of wristwatches to manufacture the newfangled timepieces. Their design made them very different from the models of other brands. Seen from today's point of view, Hamilton could almost be called the first designed watch brand. At the end of the 1920s, the Hamilton's watches were strongly characterized by the contemporary Art Deco style. Combinations of contrary shapes on the cases actually made for harmonious mixes—such as on the famous Piping Rock, whose round case was held in a tonneau-shaped frame. Wristwatches with bezels made of black enamel were another specialty of the brand.

In 1929, Hamilton Watch bought the Illinois Watch Company, which only continued to be manufactured in Springfield for another four years. The brand name Illinois Watch, however, was kept until the mid-1950s.

During World War II, Hamilton had to discontinue the production of civilian watches for a while: large military demands occupied the company's entire capacity. Among other things, Hamilton manufactured chronometers for the U.S. Navy.

The company began developing its first electro-mechanical movements directly after the end of the war. What came about was the first real innovation in 477 years: the Hamilton Electric, which was conceived in conjunction with the German company Epperlein. The movements—in a way predecessors of the quartz technology to come—weren't especially reliable, but they stimulated the clientele's belief in progress and were also used in American design icons such as the Savitar, Spectra, Vega, and above all, the Ventura models. The latter made a comeback in the 1990s in the Hollywood movie *Men in Black*.

Hamilton's Fontainebleau was yet another watch created with an exceptional shape, this time housing an automatic chronograph.

In 1966, Hamilton merged with Switzerland's Büren Watch to become Hamilton-Büren. This union was spearheaded by Büren's New York importer Roland Gsell, who had a financial interest in the Swiss company. For this reason, the automatic chronograph caliber that Büren developed together with Breitling, Heuer, and Dubois Dépraz was also known as Hamilton Caliber 11.

After 1966 most of Hamilton's watches were made in Switzerland by Büren until the headquarters in Lancaster closed all foreign subsidiaries due to the poor economic situation. The brand name Hamilton was eventually sold to the SSIH subsidiary Aetos in Geneva. Today, this brand belongs to the Swatch Group, the direct successor of the SSIH.

Men's Watch — 1940

Case: platinum, push-down case back, white gold Milanaise bracelet, 21 x 41 mm

Movement: Caliber 982, nickel-plated, côtes de Genève, manual winding

Remarks: rare rectangular platinum men's watch with diamond-set dial

Estimated value: $2,430 →

Men's Watch — 1940

Case: 14-karat white gold, leather strap 21 x 41 mm

Movement: Caliber 980, nickel-plated, jewels set in chatons, shaped movement, manual winding

Remarks: men's watch with diamond-set dial

Estimated value: $1,350 →

Piping Rock — 1945

Case: 14-karat yellow gold, leather strap, 28 x 42 mm

Movement: Caliber 747, nickel-plated, manual winding

Remarks: design men's watch with movable strap lugs

Estimated value: $2,300 ↗

Cambridge — 1935

Case: platinum, push-down case back, leather strap, 21 x 38 mm

Movement: Caliber 982, rhodium-plated, côtes de Genève, jewels set in chatons, 19 jewels, manual winding

Remarks: extremely rare platinum men's watch with white gold buckle; this watch was offered in its original box with certificate and transport box

Estimated value: $2,100 ↗

Royal Air Force Service Watch — 1965

Case: stainless steel, screw-down case back, leather strap, Ø 36 mm

Movement: Caliber H 75, rhodium-plated, manual winding

Remarks: British Royal Air Force pilot's watch

Estimated value: $810 ↗

General Service Watch — 1973

Case: stainless steel, leather strap, 35 x 41 mm

Movement: rhodium-plated, manual winding

Remarks: service wristwatch of the British armed forces

Estimated value: $475 →

Royal Air Force Chronograph — 1969

Case: stainless steel, screw-down case back, leather strap, Ø 39 mm

Movement: Caliber Valjoux 7733, nickel-plated, manual winding

Remarks: British Royal Air Force pilot's chronograph with 30-minute counter; the right side of the case was created as integrated crown and button protection

Estimated value: $945 ↗

Ventura (Electric) — 1957

Case: 14-karat yellow gold, push-down case back, leather strap, 31 x 50 mm

Movement: Caliber 505, rhodium-plated, decorated, electromechanical energy

Remarks: design classic by Hamilton with the first serially manufactured electromechanical movement (Epperlein System)

Estimated value: $3,375 ↗

Hanhart

Whether it was during gym class at school or a sports competition, almost every European kid has had to rely on what a Hanhart stopwatch has said about his or her athletic skills. This company hailing from Gütenbach in the Black Forest was long one of the most reputable and biggest manufacturers of mechanical and electronic stopwatches. Its roots extend almost 125 years back into the past—and into Switzerland.

There—or, more precisely, in Diessenhofen—is where Adolf Hanhart opened his first watch and jewelry shop in 1882. Twenty years later, he moved to Schwenningen in the Black Forest.

Upon joining the company in 1920, his son Wilhelm Julius (Willy) recognized an opportunity and invested in the design of a reasonably priced stopwatch. Four years later, he laid the cornerstone for an exceptional career in the world of sports and began his tenure as the world's best-known and most important stopwatch producer.

From 1932 on, his company dedicated itself solely to the manufacture of watches. The first autonomous pocket and wristwatch calibers were quickly developed, including stopwatch Caliber 57 with its ultra-fast frequencies of 180,000 and 360,000 vph. This watch made precision measurements of up to one-hundredth of a second possible.

The most famous model of the Black Forest company was created in 1939: a pilot's chronograph with flyback function. The resetting of the chronograph "on the fly" with immediate restarting made it possible for pilots to keep precise time while navigating. During World War II, the Hanhart chronograph was chosen as official equipment for German pilots. Hanhart paid the price for this honor after the war: in 1945 the company was dismantled. Willy Hanhart himself was threatened with incarceration, despite his being a Swiss citizen. He fled to his country of birth in 1947, where he remained until 1949.

During this upheaval, his wife reorganized the company in Gütenbach. Hanhart once again had an extensive program containing pocket and wristwatches, even continuing to make the famous pilot's watch until 1962.

In 1951, the company introduced another of its own developments: the Sans-Souci alarm wristwatch powered by Caliber 301. At the same time, the company began to offer a civilian version of the famous chronograph. In the 1950s, there was a large selection of different wristwatches in the collection.

Hanhart survived the quartz crisis more or less thanks to its stopwatches, but ran into trouble at the beginning of the 1990s. In 1992, a group of Munich investors purchased the traditional company.

Today, alongside stopwatches, replicas of the old pilot's chronographs are the main items associated with the name Hanhart. Both the one-button version and the variation with two buttons asymmetrically arranged with regard to the crown are once again being produced, though these days they house modern movements.

German Air Force Chronograph — 1935

Case: stainless steel, screw-down case back, leather strap, Ø 41 mm

Movement: nickel-plated, column-wheel control of chronograph, manual winding

Remarks: rare German pilot's chronograph with an unusual dial

Estimated value: $2,700 →

German Air Force Chronograph — 1935

Case: chrome-plated, screw-down case back, leather strap, Ø 41 mm

Movement: nickel-plated, column-wheel control of chronograph, manual winding

Remarks: one-button pilot's chronograph of the early German air force with 30-minute counter

Estimated value: $2,050 →

German Air Force Chronograph — 1936

Case: nickel-plated, screw-down case back, rotating bezel, leather strap, Ø 39 mm

Movement: nickel-plated, column-wheel control of chronograph, manual winding

Remarks: one-button chronograph of the early German air force

Estimated value: $2,430 →

German Air Force Chronograph — 1942

Case: nickel-plated, screw-down case back, leather strap, Ø 39 mm

Movement: nickel-plated, column-wheel control of chronograph, manual winding

Remarks: rare one-button pilot chronograph of the German air force; rotating bezel

Estimated value: $2,430 →

German Navy Chronograph — 1940

Case: nickel-plated, screw-down case back, rotating bezel, leather strap, Ø 39 mm

Movement: nickel-plated, column-wheel control of chronograph, manual winding

Remarks: rare one-button chronograph of the German navy with stamped eagle and navy number (KM185)

Estimated value: $4,050 →

German Air Force Chronograph — 1945

Case: stainless steel, screw-down case back, rotating bezel, leather strap, Ø 38 mm

Movement: nickel-plated, column-wheel control of chronograph, manual winding

Remarks: stainless steel pilot's chronograph with 30-minute counter

Estimated value: $2,025 →

Sans-Souci — 1952

Case: chrome-plated, stainless steel push-down case back, rotating bezel, leather strap, Ø 36 mm

Movement: Hanhart Caliber 301, nickel-plated, 17 jewels, manual winding

Remarks: wristwatch alarm with one spring barrel; this watch was owned by watch designer Malonek who developed Caliber 301 into Caliber 302 for Hanhart; Malonek wore this watch for testing purposes as well as on private trips

Estimated value: $405 →

Sans-Souci — 1952

Case: gold-plated, stainless steel push-down case back, rotating bezel, link bracelet, Ø 36 mm

Movement: Hanhart Caliber 301, nickel-plated, manual winding

Remarks: wristwatch alarm with one spring barrel; this watch is of the second series and has a slide to turn off the alarm function at 9 o'clock

Estimated value: $405 →

Heuer

In 1860, twenty-year-old Edouard Heuer founded a watch workshop. His company developed so well that only four years later he needed to look for larger facilities, which he found in Biel. In 1880, Heuer produced his first serial chronographs. When Edouard Heuer passed away in 1892, his watchmakers were already considered specialists in chronographs of every kind.

His sons Jules and Charles managed the company starting in 1902. They presented a so-called doctor's chronograph in 1910 with which doctors could calculate their patients' pulse frequencies within just a few seconds. The brand's first wristwatches left the factory after 1913—at first, however, they were just ladies' models. In 1916 Heuer patented a sensation: the Microsplit, a stopwatch that could measure the time precisely to the hundredth of a second. The chronograph business developed into the main source of income for Heuer in the ensuing years. The company bought movements, encased them, and gave them additional functions such as slide rules and tide indicators. In the mid-1960s, Heuer was one of the main forces behind the development of the first automatic chronograph caliber—legendary Caliber 11—created in conjunction with Breitling, Hamilton-Büren, and Dubois Dépraz.

Heuer maintained a large selection of different watch types. An army pilot's chronograph, the Monaco, and the Autavia are of course some of the better-known models. One of Heuer's greatest competitors was Léonidas SA in Saint-Imier, a company that also made chronographs. Julien Bourquin founded this company in 1841, choosing the legendary Spartan king Leonidas, who in antiquity fought against the Persians and then died on the battlefield, as its patron. At the beginning Léonidas produced simple pocket watches, though Bourquin soon specialized in the manufacture of stopwatches and chronographs. His customers included various foreign ministries which he supplied with pilot's chronographs and service watches. Alongside that, Léonidas also produced civilian chronographs with calendar functions, three-handed watches with moon phase displays, and alarm wristwatches. Additionally, the company also manufactured board clocks for airplanes and automobiles. The most famous of Léonidas's watches, however, remains the pilot's flyback chronograph containing Valjoux Caliber 222. Only 250 of these were made.

On January 1, 1964, Heuer forced the irksome competitor into a merger and at first produced different models under both names. The Léonidas name quickly disappeared from the dials, however.

In order to guarantee continued existence of the Heuer brand during the quartz crisis, Jack W. Heuer was forced to sell his company to Lémania and a few other stockholders, including the Piaget family. In 1985, Heuer-Léonidas was purchased by the high-tech concern Techniques d'Avant-Garde (TAG), and its name was changed to TAG Heuer.

In 1999, the luxury goods concern LVMH (Louis Vuitton Moet & Hennessy) purchased the brand, though it continues to be called TAG Heuer—even if various very successful reissued classics at first only carried a simple Heuer on their dial.

"

Chronograph — 1935

Case: chrome-plated, tripartite, stainless steel push-down case back, leather strap, Ø 32 mm
Movement: rhodium-plated, fausses côtes decoratino, column-wheel control of chronograph, fine matte steel chronograph components
Remarks: chronograph with 30-minute counter; luminous numerals printed on dial for better legibility; hands inlaid with luminous substance
Estimated value: $810 →

Chronograph — 1940

Case: 18-karat yellow gold, push-down case back, leather strap Ø 35 mm
Movement: nickel-plated, column-wheel control of chronograph, manual winding
Remarks: fine chronograph with 30-minute counter
Estimated value: $2,295 ↗

Chronograph — 1945

Case: gold-plated, stainless steel push-down case back, leather strap, Ø 35 mm
Movement: Landeron Caliber 248, manual winding
Remarks: chronograph with 30-minute counter
Estimated value: $405 →

Chronograph — 1945

Case: stainless steel, push-down case back, leather strap, Ø 32 mm
Movement: nickel-plated, column-wheel control of chronograph, manual winding
Remarks: nearly new chronograph with 30-minute counter
Estimated value: $1,080 ↗

Chronograph — 1943

Case: stainless steel, push-down case back, leather strap, Ø 34 mm
Movement: nickel-plated, manual winding
Remarks: chronograph with 30-minute counter
Estimated value: $810 ↗

Chronograph — 1950

Case: 14-karat yellow gold, push-down case back, leather strap, Ø 35 mm
Movement: Landeron Caliber 48, nickel-plated, manual winding
Remarks: chronograph with 30-minute counter
Estimated value: $1,890 ↗

Chronograph — 1950

Case: stainless steel, screw-down case back, leather strap, Ø 35 mm
Movement: nickel-plated, column-wheel control of chronograph, manual winding
Remarks: chronograph with 30-minute counter
Estimated value: $1,220 ↗

Chronograph — 1952

Case: 18-karat yellow gold, push-down case back, leather strap, Ø 35 mm
Movement: nickel-plated, column-wheel control of chronograph, manual winding
Remarks: elegant chronograph
Estimated value: $2,025 ↗

Chronograph Complete Calendar Moon Phase

Case: stainless steel, push-down case back, leather strap, Ø 36mm

Movement: Valjoux Caliber 730, gold-plated, column-wheel control of chronograph, manual winding

Remarks: chronograph with complete calendar and moon phase

Estimated value: $4,050 →

1950

Chronograph with Complete Calendar

Case: 18-karat red gold, push-down case back, leather strap, Ø 37 mm

Movement: nickel-plated, column-wheel control of chronograph, manual winding

Remarks: chronograph with complete calendar

Estimated value: $3,375 →

1945

Chronograph with Complete Calendar

Case: 14-karat yellow gold, push-down case back, leather strap, Ø 35 mm

Movement: Caliber 72C, nickel-plated, column-wheel control of chronograph, manual winding

Remarks: chronograph with complete calendar

Estimated value: $2,700 →

1945

Chronograph with Complete Calendar

Case: stainless steel, push-down case back, leather strap, Ø 35 mm

Movement: rhodium-plated, column-wheel control of chronograph, manual winding

Remarks: chronograph with complete calendar

Estimated value: $2,025 →

1940

Chronograph with Complete Calendar

Case: stainless steel, screw-down case back, leather strap, Ø 37 mm

Movement: rhodium-plated, column-wheel control of chronograph, manual winding

Remarks: chronograph with complete calendar

Estimated value: $2,025 →

1945

Chronograph with Complete Calendar

Case: 14-karat yellow gold, push-down case back, leather strap, Ø 35 mm

Movement: nickel-plated, column-wheel control of chronograph, manual winding

Remarks: chronograph with complete calendar

Estimated value: $2,970 ↗

1948

Chronograph Complete Calendar Moon Phase

Case: 14-karat gold, push-down steel case back, leather strap, Ø 34 mm

Movement: Valjoux Caliber 88, nickel-plated, column-wheel control of chronograph, 17 jewels, manual winding

Remarks: gold chronograph with complete calendar and the moon phase

Estimated value: $4,050 →

1950

Chronograph with Complete Calendar

Case: stainless steel, push-down case back, leather strap, Ø 35 mm

Movement: nickel-plated, column-wheel control of chronograph, manual winding

Remarks: chronograph with complete calendar

Estimated value: $2,160 ↗

1948

Chronograph · 1960

Case: stainless steel, screw-down case back, leather strap, Ø 37 mm

Movement: Valjoux Caliber 72, nickel-plated, column-wheel control of chronograph, manual winding

Remarks: chronograph with 30-minute and 12-hour counters

Estimated value: $1,890 →

Chronograph · 1960

Case: 14-karat yellow gold, bipartite, screw-down case back, leather strap

Movement: rhodium-plated, column-wheel control of chronograph, fine matte steel chronograph components

Remarks: chronograph with 30-minute and 12-hour counters; printed telemeter (red) and tachymeter (blue) scales; this watch was made by Heuer for Abercrombie & Fitch, London

Estimated value: $3,510 →

Heuer Solunar/Abercrombie & Fitch · 1948

Case: stainless steel, screw-down case back, leather strap, Ø 36 mm

Movement: nickel-plated, manual winding

Remarks: rare men's watch; Solunar model with additional tide display at 6 o'clock

Estimated value: $1,350 ↗

Chronograph · 1970

Case: gold-plated, stainless steel screw-down case back, leather strap, Ø 36 mm

Movement: Valjoux Caliber 72, rhodium-plated, column-wheel control of chronograph, manual winding

Remarks: chronograph with 30-minute and 12-hour counters

Estimated value: $1,890 ↗

Chronograph Carrera · 1955

Case: gold-plated, screw-down case back, leather strap, Ø 36 mm

Movement: Valjoux Caliber 72, nickel-plated, column-wheel control of chronograph, manual winding

Remarks: nearly new chronograph with 30-minute and 12-hour counters

Estimated value: $1,755 ↗

Chronograph Carrera · 1970

Case: stainless steel, screw-down case back, leather strap, Ø 35 mm

Movement: Landeron Caliber 189, nickel-plated, manual winding

Remarks: stainless steel chronograph with 45-minute counter; date at 12 o'clock

Estimated value: $1,620 →

Calendar Carrera · 1975

Case: stainless steel, screw-down case back, leather strap, Ø 35 mm

Movement: Valjoux Caliber 7730, nickel-plated, manual winding

Remarks: simple sports chronograph; reference number 7753

Estimated value: $1,620 ↗

Carrera · 1965

Reference number: 2447

Case: stainless steel, bipartite, screw-down case back, leather strap, Ø 36 mm

Movement: Valjoux Caliber 72, rhodium-plated, column-wheel control of chronograph, fine matte steel chronograph components

Remarks: Carrera chronograph with 30-minute and 12-hour counters; red tachymeter scale printed around the perimeter of the dial with region from 50 to 200

Estimated value: $1,620 →

Chronograph Montreal — 1975

Case: stainless steel, screw-down case back, stainless steel link bracelet, 42 x 48 mm

Movement: Caliber 12, red gold-plated, micro rotor, automatic winding

Remarks: heavy automatic chronograph with 30-minute and 12-hour counters; date window at 6 o'clock

Estimated value: $1,350 →

Chronograph Autavia — 1975

Case: stainless steel, screw-down case back, rotating bezel, leather strap, 42 x 47 mm

Movement: Caliber 11, nickel-plated, micro rotor, automatic winding

Remarks: heavy automatic chronograph with 30-minute and 12-hour counters; date window at 6 o'clock

Estimated value: $1,890 ↗

Chronograph Autavia — 1975

Case: stainless steel, screw-down case back, rotating bezel, leather strap, 42 x 48 mm

Movement: Caliber 12, gold-plated, micro rotor, automatic winding

Remarks: heavy automatic chronograph with 30-minute and 12-hour counters; date window at 6 o'clock

Estimated value: $1,755 ↗

Chronograph Autavia Manual Winding — 1978

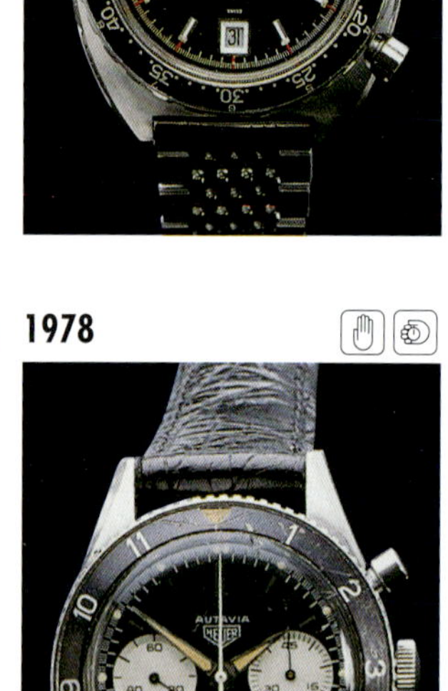

Case: stainless steel, screw-down case back, rotating bezel, leather strap, Ø 39 mm

Movement: Valjoux Caliber 92, nickel-plated, with column-wheel control of chronograph, manual winding

Remarks: early Autavia chronograph with 45-minute counter; the movement combines an exclusive column wheel with a simple vibrating pinion

Estimated value: $1,620 →

Chronograph Calculator — 1970

Case: stainless steel, screw-down case back, rotating bezel, leather strap, 46 x 43 mm

Movement: Caliber 12, gold-plated, micro rotor, automatic winding

Remarks: automatic chronograph with slide rule function integrated into the rotating bezel

Estimated value: $2,025 ↗

Autavia — 1970

Case: stainless steel, tripartite, screw-down case back, rotating bezel, leather strap, Ø 41 mm

Movement: Valjoux Caliber 7733, nickel-plated; slideway control of chronograph; mirror-polished chronograph components

Remarks: large chronograph with 30-minute counter whose 5-minute intervals are highlighted; additional minute scale on the rotating bezel

Estimated value: $1,890 →

Chronograph Autavia GMT — 1975

Case: stainless steel, screw-down case back, rotating bezel, stainless steel link bracelet, Ø 42 mm

Movement: Caliber 11, gold-plated, micro rotor, 17 jewels, automatic winding

Remarks: automatic chronograph with 30- minute and 12-hour counters; additional 24-hour display

Estimated value: $2,160 ↗

Chronograph Autavia GMT — 1970

Case: stainless steel, push-down case back, rotating bezel, leather strap, Ø 41 mm

Movement: Valjoux Caliber 724, nickel-plated, column-wheel control of chronograph, manual winding

Remarks: heavy chronograph with additional 24-hour display

Estimated value: $945 →

Chronograph Monaco Manual Winding — 1975

Case: stainless steel, push-down case back, leather strap, 40 x 45 mm
Movement: nickel-plated, manual winding
Remarks: chronograph with 30-minute and 12-hour counters
Estimated value: $4,725 →

Chronograph Monaco — 1975

Case: stainless steel, leather strap, 40 x 45 mm
Movement: Caliber 12, gold-plated, micro rotor, automatic winding
Remarks: heavy automatic chronograph with 30-minute counter and date window
Estimated value: $4,725 →

Chronograph Tides — 1975

Case: stainless steel, push-down case back, rotating bezel, Ø 41 mm
Movement: Valjoux Caliber 721, rhodium-plated, column-wheel control of chronograph, manual winding
Remarks: large chronograph with additional tide display at 9 o'clock
Estimated value: $2,025 ↗

Chronograph Autavia Manual Winding — 1960

Case: stainless steel, screw-down case back, rotating bezel, Ø 40 mm
Movement: Valjoux Caliber 72, nickel-plated, manual winding
Remarks: sporty stainless steel chronograph
Estimated value: $1,890 →

Chronograph Carrera — 1975

Case: stainless steel, screw-down case back, stainless steel link bracelet, Ø 39 mm
Movement: Caliber 12, gold-plated, micro rotor, automatic winding
Remarks: heavy automatic chronograph with 30-minute and 12-hour counters
Estimated value: $1,350 →

Chronograph — 1973

Case: stainless-steel, screw-down case back, leather strap, 41 x 46 mm
Movement: Valjoux Caliber 7734, nickel-plated, manual winding
Remarks: orange anodized chronograph with 30-minute counter and date
Estimated value: $1,080 →

Chronograph — 1975

Case: stainless steel, bipartite, screw-down case back, leather strap
Movement: Valjoux Caliber 7734, nickel-plated, slideway control of chronograph; mirror-polished chronograph components, 17 jewels
Remarks: large, sporty chronograph with 30-minute counter and date window at 6 o'clock; tachymeter scale printed on flange; this watch was offered with its original buckle
Estimated value: $1,080 →

Chronograph Carrera — 1975

Case: gold-plated, screw-down case back, leather strap, Ø 38 mm
Movement: Caliber 12, gold-plated, micro rotor, automatic winding
Remarks: automatic chronograph with 30-minute and 12-hour counters
Estimated value: $1,080 →

IWC

When the twenty-seven-year-old American engineer Florentine Ariosto Jones, hailing from Boston, founded the International Watch Company in Switzerland, he didn't do it simply because Switzerland had become a land of low wages in comparison to the United States in the mid-nineteenth century. The American method of manufacturing watches with strongly automated processes had just about reached the boundaries of its capacity at home, and on searching out a new production location, he found that Switzerland offered itself perfectly with its horological know-how and low wages. In the Swiss Jura region, where most watchmakers made their homes, no one wanted to listen to anything about automated machine production—a method of production for which only a few workers were needed. But Jones received an offer from the city of Schaffhausen, and one potential business partner was a certain Johann Heinrich Moser. This man had invented a new system for industrially harnessing the power of the Rhine's flowing water. Gear wheels and transmission ropes were powered by water wheels, which in turn gave their energy to machines. Thanks to Moser's invention, the new IWC could receive its energy practically free. Jones saw the wisdom of this, and Moser became one of the founders of the International Watch Company in 1869. Just one year later IWC produced 10,000 watches—all of them for the American market.

These exports began to bottleneck in 1874, however, when the United States started to

demand 25 percent protective duty on foreign goods. The powers that be turned IWC into a joint stock company. Jones returned to Boston, and IWC was bought by the Schaffhausen Handelsbank.

Four years later, the entrepreneurial Rauschenbach family took over the helm. They opened new markets for IWC—most especially in neighboring Germany where the watches were high in demand thanks to their excellent quality. The company soon recognized the importance of aviation and offered pilots precision watches that they could also wear over their thick pilot's jackets. The tradition of IWC pilot's watches, which began here, is something that the Schaffhausen-based company has kept alive to this day.

It would, however, be unjustified to reduce IWC to the production of pilot's watches alone.

IWC's movements were known as exceptionally solid in design and technically well thought out—not only in collector's circles. IWC also walked down its own path in terms of cases. The Ingenieur was launched in 1954: a soft iron core within its case protected the movement from the influence of magnetic fields which would normally impact rate precision. The basic three-handed models of the Schaffhausen *manufacture* were also famous, embodying the simple understatement of these high-quality watches.

In the 1970s, IWC was sold to the VDO/ Mannesmann concern together with Jaeger-LeCoultre, finally ending up under the umbrella of the Richemont Group in the new millennium.

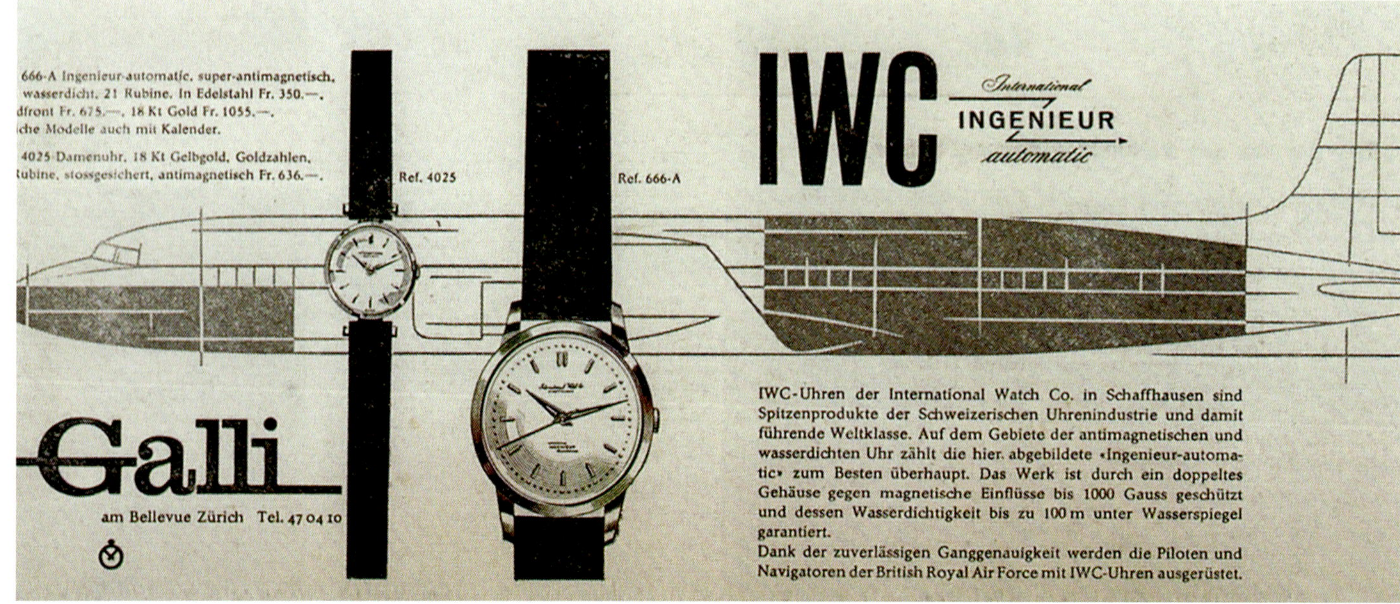

Men's Watch — 1930

Case: 14-karat yellow gold, push-down case back, leather strap, 21 x 37mm
Movement: manual winding
Remarks: very early IWC wristwatch in rectangular gold case; the strap lugs of this watch are simple, soldered gold wires
Estimated value: $2,160 ↗

Men's Watch — 1918

Case: silver, push-down case back, leather strap, 29 x 35 mm
Movement: gold-plated, frosted finish, manual winding
Remarks: very early IWC wristwatch in a cushion-shaped silver case with soldered strap lugs
Estimated value: $1,620 ↗

Men's Watch — 1938

Case: stainless steel, push-down case back, leather strap, 24 x 40 mm
Movement: IWC Caliber 87, nickel-plated, côtes de Genève, manual winding
Remarks: early rectangular IWC men's watch with subsidiary seconds; shaped movement
Estimated value: $2,970 ↗

Men's Watch — 1937

Case: stainless steel, push-down case back, leather strap, 21 x 44 mm
Movement: IWC Caliber 87, rhodium-plated, côtes de Genève, jewels set in chatons, manual winding
Remarks: early wristwatch in rectangular stainless steel case
Estimated value: $3,240 ↗

Men's Watch — 1935

Case: 14-karat yellow gold, bipartite, push-down case back, leather strap, 22 x 36 mm
Movement: IWC Caliber 87, rhodium-plated, fausses côtes decoration, jewels set in chatons, polished screws
Remarks: men's watch in rectangular stainless steel case
Estimated value: $3,375 →

Men's Watch — 1927

Case: 18-karat yellow gold, bipartite, push-down case back, leather strap, 23 x 38 mm
Movement: rhodium-plated, fausses côtes decoration, jewels set in chatons
Remarks: rare men's watch in rectangular stainless steel case
Estimated value: $3,375 →

Men's Watch — 1920

Case: 18-karat yellow gold, tripartite, push-down case back, leather strap, 23 x 35 mm
Movement: gold-plated, frosted finish, jewels set in chatons
Remarks: extremely rare early men's watch in a gold Art Deco case; obvious asymmetrical arrangement of the movement, which was pushed toward the 6 o'clock position; the upper part of the case is decorated with a black Art Deco motif
Estimated value: $3,375 →

Men's Watch — 1927

Case: 14-karat yellow gold, bipartite, push-down case back, leather strap, 24 x 35 mm
Movement: Caliber 84, gold-plated, frosted finish, jewels set in chatons, polished screws
Remarks: fine men's watch in a rectangular Art Deco case; the slanted surfaces of the case are finely guilloché; this watch was offered with an IWC buckle
Estimated value: $2,970 →

Men's Watch — 1941

Case: 14-karat yellow gold, push-down case back, leather strap, Ø 36 mm

Movement: IWC Caliber 83, rhodium-plated, côtes de Genève, jewels set in chatons, manual winding

Remarks: men's watch in yellow gold case

Estimated value: $1,890 →

Men's Watch — 1942

Case: 14-karat yellow gold, push-down case back, leather strap, Ø 35 mm

Movement: IWC Caliber 83, rhodium-plated, côtes de Genève, jewels set in chatons, manual winding

Remarks: men's watch that visually looks bigger than it is thanks to its strap lugs, which give the watch a youthful appeal

Estimated value: $1,350 ↘

Men's Watch — 1943

Case: stainless steel, push-down case back, leather strap, Ø 35 mm

Movement: IWC Caliber 83, rhodium-plated, côtes de Genève, manual winding

Remarks: simple men's watch with subsidiary seconds; applied hour numerals are highlighted with a light-colored ring

Estimated value: $1,350 →

Men's Watch — 1942

Case: stainless steel, push-down case back, leather strap, Ø 35 mm

Movement: IWC Caliber 83, rhodium-plated, côtes de Genève, jewels set in chatons, manual winding

Remarks: simple men's watch with subsidiary seconds and teardrop-shaped strap lugs

Estimated value: $1,485 →

Men's Watch — 1941

Case: 18-karat yellow gold, push-down case back, leather strap, Ø 35 mm

Movement: IWC Caliber 8, rhodium-plated, côtes de Genève, manual winding

Remarks: simple men's watch with subsidiary seconds

Estimated value: $1,620 →

Men's Watch — 1956

Case: 18-karat yellow gold, push-down case back, leather strap, Ø 33 mm

Movement: IWC Caliber 89, rhodium-plated, côtes de Genève, jewels set in chatons, manual winding

Remarks: simple men's watch with strongly accentuated strap lugs

Estimated value: $1,620 →

Men's Watch — 1928

Case: stainless steel, push-down steel case back, leather strap, Ø 35 mm

Movement: gold-plated, frosted finish, manual winding

Remarks: very early wristwatch in what was an exclusive stainless steel case for the time

Estimated value: $1,620 →

Men's Watch — 1947

Case: 18-karat yellow gold, push-down case back, leather strap, Ø 35 mm

Movement: IWC Caliber 88, rhodium-plated, côtes de Genève jewels set in chatons, manual winding

Remarks: simple men's watch with highly noticeable shaped strap lugs

Estimated value: $1,620 →

Men's Watch — 1954

Case: 18-karat yellow gold, push-down case back, leather strap, Ø 37 mm

Movement: IWC Caliber 89, rhodium-plated, côtes de Genève, jewels set in chatons, manual winding

Remarks: elegant men's watch in yellow gold case with highly noticeable shaped strap lugs

Estimated value: $2,295 →

Men's Watch — 1957

Case: 18-yellow gold, push-down case back, leather strap, Ø 35 mm

Movement: IWC Caliber 89, rhodium-plated, côtes de Genève, jewels set in chatons, manual winding

Remarks: elegant, classic men's watch

Estimated value: $1,890 →

Men's Watch — 1952

Case: 18-karat yellow gold, push-down case back, leather strap, Ø 36 mm

Movement: IWC Caliber 89, rhodium-plated, côtes de Genève, jewels set in chatons, manual winding

Remarks: elegant men's watch in yellow gold case

Estimated value: $1,620 →

Men's Watch — 1947

Case: 18-karat yellow gold, push-down case back, leather strap, Ø 35 mm

Movement: IWC Caliber 89, rhodium-plated, côtes de Genève, manual winding

Remarks: very flat men's watch with highly noticeable strap lugs

Estimated value: $1,755 ↗

Men's Watch — 1960

Case: stainless steel, push-down case back, leather strap, Ø 33 mm

Movement: IWC Caliber 401, rhodium-plated, côtes de Genève, jewels set in chatons, manual winding

Remarks: simple men's watch

Estimated value: $1,080 ↗

Men's Watch — 1949

Case: 18-karat yellow gold, push-down case back, leather strap, Ø 36 mm

Movement: IWC Caliber 89, rhodium-plated, côtes de Genève, manual winding

Remarks: simple men's watch with fan-shaped strap lugs

Estimated value: $1,350 →

Men's Watch — 1957

Case: stainless steel, push-down case back, leather strap, Ø 35 mm

Movement: IWC Caliber 89, rhodium-plated, côtes de Genève, manual winding

Remarks: simple men's watch

Estimated value: $1,080 →

Men's Watch — 1954

Case: 18-karat yellow gold, push-down case back, leather strap, Ø 35 mm

Movement: IWC Caliber 89, rhodium-plated, côtes de Genève, jewels set in chatons, manual winding

Remarks: elegant men's watch in gold case with curved strap lugs

Estimated value: $1,350 →

Men's Watch — 1936

Case: 14-karat yellow gold, push-down case back, leather strap, Ø 30 mm

Movement: IWC Caliber 83, nickel-plated, côtes de Genève, manual winding

Remarks: early IWC men's watch with subsidiary seconds and highly noticeable shaped strap lugs

Estimated value: $2,025 →

Men's Watch — 1940

Case: 18-karat red gold, push-down case back, leather strap Ø 32 mm

Movement: IWC Caliber 62, rhodium-plated, côtes de Genève, jewels set in chatons, manual winding

Remarks: elegant men's watch in a red gold case with highly noticeable shaped strap lugs

Estimated value: $1,620 →

Men's Watch — 1941

Case: stainless steel, push-down case back, leather strap, Ø 35 mm

Movement: IWC Caliber 83, nickel-plated, côtes de Genève, manual winding

Remarks: rare, early IWC men's watch

Estimated value: $1,755 ↗

Men's Watch — 1941

Case: stainless steel, push-down case back, leather strap, Ø 35 mm

Movement: IWC Caliber 83, nickel-plated, côtes de Genève, manual winding

Remarks: early IWC men's watch with subsidiary seconds

Estimated value: $1,620 ↗

Automatic — 1960

Case: 18-karat rose gold, tripartite, push-down case back, leather strap, Ø 36 mm

Movement: Caliber 89, rhodium-plated, fausses côtes decoration, automatic winding

Remarks: elegant men's watch in rose gold case

Estimated value: $1,350 ↘

Men's Watch — 1970

Case: 18-karat yellow gold, monocoque, Ø 34 mm

Movement: rhodium-plated, fausses côtes decoration

Remarks: elegant men's watch; this timepiece was offered in its original box

Estimated value: $1,080 →

Men's Watch — 1946

Case: 14-karat yellow gold, bipartite, push-down case back, gold link bracelet with folding clasp, Ø 31 mm

Movement: Caliber 62, rhodium-plated, fausses côtes decoration, jewels set in chatons, 17 jewels, regulated in three positions

Remarks: gold men's watch in a typical gold case made for the American market; this watch was offered with a gold link bracelet and folding clasp

Estimated value: $2,025 →

Automatic — 1952

Case: stainless steel, bipartite, push-down case back, leather strap, Ø 34 mm

Movement: Caliber 852, rhodium-plated, fausses côtes decoration, automatic winding, 21 jewels

Remarks: elegant men's watch in a stainless steel case; visually dominant strap lugs

Estimated value: $1,080 →

Portuguese — 1975

Case: stainless steel, push-down case back, Ø 42 mm

Movement: IWC Caliber 982, rhodium-plated, côtes de Genève, jewels set in chatons, manual winding

Remarks: first new edition of the legendary Portuguese series; this watch was offered in its original box with papers

Estimated value: $22,950 →

Portuguese — 1941

Case: stainless steel, tripartite, push-down case back, leather strap, Ø 42 mm

Movement: Caliber 74, gold-plated, frosted finish, jewels set in chatons, polished screws, index fine adjustment

Remarks: rare original Portuguese; this watch was sold on September 6, 1941; between 1939 and 1952 only 304 Portuguese models were manufactured and delivered with Caliber 74; this watch was offered with an IWC master registry certificate and documentation

Estimated value: $24,300 →

Automatic — 1955

Case: 18-karat yellow gold, tripartite, push-down case back, leather strap, Ø 35 mm

Movement: Caliber 8521, rhodium-plated, fausses côtes decoration, index fine adjustment, automatic winding, 21 jewels

Remarks: elegant gold men's watch

Estimated value: $1,620 →

Automatic — 1951

Case: 18-karat yellow gold, bipartite, push-down case back, leather strap, 32 x 44 mm

Movement: Caliber 85, rhodium-plated, fausses côtes decoration, automatic winding, 21 jewels

Remarks: gold IWC in square case with noticeable strap lugs

Estimated value: $4,050 ↗

Automatic — 1969

Case: stainless steel, push-down case back, leather strap, Ø 35 mm

Movement: Caliber IWC 8541, rhodium-plated, côtes de Genève, 23 jewels, automatic winding

Remarks: this IWC movement was regulated in 5 positions; date window at 3 o'clock

Estimated value: $2,700 ↗

Automatic De Luxe — 1961

Case: yellow gold, push-down case back, gold link bracelet, Ø 35 mm

Movement: IWC Caliber 8531, nickel-plated, côtes de Genève, 21 jewels, automatic winding

Remarks: rarely worn heavy gold watch with original IWC gold bracelet and original certificate; date window at 3 o'clock

Estimated value: $6,075 →

Automatic — 1961

Case: stainless steel, tripartite, push-down case back, gold link bracelet, Ø 34 mm

Movement: Caliber 853, rhodium-plated, fausses côtes decoration, automatic winding, index fine adjustment, 21 jewels

Remarks: simple men's watch with noticeable second hand

Estimated value: $1,890 →

Automatic — 1968

Reference: R1160AD

Case: 18-karat yellow gold, bipartite, push-down case back, gold link bracelet, 30 x 30 mm

Movement: Caliber 8541, rhodium-plated, côtes de Genève, polished screws, automatic winding

Remarks: gold men's watch in square case

Estimated value: $1,620 ↘

Automatic — 1963

Case: 18-karat yellow gold, push-down case back, leather strap, 31 x 40 mm

Movement: IWC Caliber 853, rhodium-plated, côtes de Genève, automatic winding

Remarks: men's watch with unusual and very solid-looking square case; date window at 3 o'clock

Estimated value: $4,050 ↗

Automatic — 1965

Case: 18-karat yellow gold, push-down case back, leather strap, 30 x 39 mm

Movement: IWC Caliber 8541, nickel-plated, côtes de Genève, date, automatic winding

Remarks: automatic wristwatch with famous IWC eccentric automatic winding in rectangular case; date window at 3 o'clock

Estimated value: $2,430 →

Automatic — 1953

Case: 18-karat yellow gold, push-down case back, leather strap, Ø 33 mm

Movement: IWC Caliber 8521, nickel-plated, côtes de Genève, 21 jewels, automatic winding

Remarks: automatic wristwatch with famous IWC eccentric automatic winding; date window at 3 o'clock

Estimated value: $2,430 ↗

Automatic/Türler — 1959

Case: 18-karat yellow gold, push-down case back, leather strap, Ø 34 mm

Movement: IWC Caliber 8531, rhodium-plated, côtes de Genève, automatic winding

Remarks: a special edition for Swiss jeweler Türler, this model has a double signature on the dial; date window at 3 o'clock

Estimated value: $2,160 →

Automatic — 1967

Case: 18-karat yellow gold, push-down case back, leather strap, Ø 35 mm

Movement: IWC Caliber 8541, nickel-plated, côtes de Genève, date, 25 jewels, automatic winding

Remarks: automatic wristwatch with famous IWC eccentric automatic winding; date window at 3 o'clock

Estimated value: $2,025 →

Automatic — 1963

Case: stainless-steel, push-down case back, stainless steel link bracelet, Ø 35 mm

Movement: IWC Caliber 8531, 21 jewels, automatic winding

Remarks: simple stainless steel men's watch; date window at 3 o'clock

Estimated value: $2,430 ↗

Automatic — 1960

Case: 18-karat yellow gold, push-down case back, leather strap, Ø 35 mm

Movement: IWC Caliber 853, rhodium-plated, côtes de Genève, 21 jewels, automatic winding

Remarks: simple automatic men's watch

Estimated value: $2,025 →

Automatic — 1952

Case: stainless steel, leather strap, Ø 35 mm

Movement: IWC Caliber 852, rhodium-plated, côtes de Genève, automatic winding

Remarks: high-quality automatic men's watch with highly noticeable double-faceted strap lugs

Estimated value: $2,430 ↗

30 ATM Aquatimer Automatic — 1971

Case: stainless steel, screw-down case back, rotating inner diver's bezel, leather strap, Ø 40 mm

Movement: IWC Caliber 8541B, nickel-plated, automatic winding

Remarks: water-resistant to 300 meters; date window at 3 o'clock

Estimated value: $3,780 →

Aquatimer Automatic — 1971

Case: stainless steel, bipartite, screw-down case back, leather strap, Ø 37 mm

Movement: Caliber 8541B, rhodium-plated, fausses côtes decoration, automatic winding, 21 jewels

Remarks: nearly new diver's watch; the dive time is set on the rotating flange using the second crown

Estimated value: $9,450 →

Aquatimer Automatic — 1976

Case: stainless steel with rotating inner bezel, screw-down case back, Tropic strap, Ø 40 mm

Movement: IWC Caliber 8541, rhodium-plated, côtes de Genève, automatic winding

Remarks: original Tropic textile strap; the second crown at 2 o'clock is used to set the dive time on the inner rotating ring; 14-point bezel; date window at 3 o'clock

Estimated value: $3,780 →

Yacht Club — 1974

Case: stainless steel, bipartite, screw-down case back, leather strap, Ø 36 mm

Movement: rhodium plated, fausses côtes decoration, jewels set in chatons, 17 jewels, regulated in 3 positions

Remarks: automatic Yacht Club

Estimated value: $1,890 →

Yacht Club — 1972

Case: 18-karat yellow gold, screw-down case back, leather strap, Ø 36 mm

Movement: IWC Caliber 8541B, rhodium-plated, côtes de Genève, automatic winding

Remarks: nearly new and rare sporty Yacht Club automatic watch in a modern, very robust-looking yellow gold case; date window at 3 o'clock,

Estimated value: $4,050 ↗

Yacht Club — 1969

Case: stainless steel, screw-down case back, leather strap, Ø 36 mm

Movement: IWC Caliber 8541B, nickel-plated, date, 23 jewels, automatic winding

Remarks: sporty automatic watch in modern stainless steel case

Estimated value: $2,160 ↗

Yacht Club II — 1976

Case: stainless steel, screw-down case back, stainless steel link bracelet, Ø 38 mm

Movement: IWC Caliber 3254, rhodium-plated, côtes de Genève, automatic winding

Remarks: remarkable octagonal bezel

Estimated value: $2,430 →

Yacht Club — 1964

Case: stainless steel, bipartite, screw-down case back, leather strap, Ø 31 mm

Movement: Caliber 8541, côtes de Genève, polished screws, index fine adjustment

Remarks: automatic Yacht Club in a small case

Estimated value: $1,890 →

Ingenieur — 1959

Case: 18-karat red gold, tripartite, screw-down case back, leather strap, Ø 36 mm

Movement: Caliber 8531, rhodium-plated, fausses côtes decoration, automatic winding, index fine regulation, 21 jewels

Remarks: elegant gold Ingenieur model

Estimated value: $8,775 →

Ingenieur — 1963

Case: stainless steel, tripartite, screw-down case back, leather strap, Ø 36 mm

Movement: Caliber 8531, rhodium-plated, fausses côtes decoration, automatic winding, index fine adjustment, 21 jewels

Remarks: sporty Ingenieur model

Estimated value: $4,725 ↗

Ingenieur — 1963

Case: stainless steel, tripartite, screw-down case back, leather strap, Ø 36 mm

Movement: Caliber 853, rhodium-plated, fausses côtes decoration, automatic winding, index fine adjustment, 21 jewels

Remarks: elegant gold men's watch

Estimated value: $4,050 →

Ingenieur — 1960

Case: 18-karat yellow gold, tripartite, screw-down case back, leather strap, Ø 36 mm

Movement: Caliber 8531, rhodium-plated, fausses côtes decoration, automatic winding, index fine adjustment, 21 jewels

Remarks: elegant gold men's watch

Estimated value: $6,750 →

Ingenieur — 1953

Case: stainless steel, tripartite, screw-down case back, leather strap, Ø 36 mm

Movement: Caliber 852, rhodium-plated, fausses côtes decoration, automatic winding, 21 jewels

Remarks: sporty Ingenieur model

Estimated value: $4,050 →

Ingenieur — 1963

Reference number: 666A

Case: 18-karat yellow gold, tripartite, screw-down case back, leather strap, Ø 36 mm

Movement: Caliber 8531, rhodium-plated, fausses côtes decoration, automatic winding, index fine adjustment, 17 jewels

Remarks: gold Ingenieur; sold to Blech in Copenhagen on October 26, 1963; this watch was offered with a certificate from IWC's master registry

Estimated value: $8,775 ↗

Ingenieur — 1960

Case: 18-karat yellow gold, screw-down case back, leather strap, Ø 36 mm

Movement: Caliber 8531, rhodium-plated, côtes de Genève, 21 jewels, regulated in 8 positions, automatic winding

Remarks: rare, gold men's watch with date window at 3 o'clock; movement protected from magnetic fields

Estimated value: $7,425 ↗

Ingenieur — 1960

Case: stainless steel, screw-down case back, stainless steel link bracelet, Ø 36 mm

Movement: IWC Caliber 8531, rhodium-plated, decorated, automatic winding

Remarks: extremely rare Ingenieur with special dial; only 250 pieces of this model were manufactured with this dial

Estimated value: $6,075 ↗

Ingenieur — 1960

Case: stainless steel, tripartite, screw-down case back, stainless steel link bracelet, Ø 36 mm

Movement: Caliber 8531, rhodium-plated, fausses côtes decoration, automatic winding, index fine adjustment, 17 jewels

Remarks: men's watch with remarkable stainless steel link bracelet

Estimated value: $4,725 →

Ingenieur — 1963

Case: stainless steel, tripartite, screw-down case back, leather strap, Ø 37 mm

Movement: Caliber 8531, rhodium-plated, fausses côtes decoration, automatic winding, index fine adjustment, 21 jewels

Remarks: automatic Ingenieur with date display

Estimated value: $3,915 →

Ingenieur — 1980

Case: 18-karat yellow gold, tripartite, screw-down case back, stainless steel link bracelet, 34 x 33 mm

Movement: Caliber 375, rhodium-plated, decorated, automatic winding, 22 jewels, regulated in 5 positions

Remarks: heavy gold Ingenieur model; dial, bezel, and bracelet links are diamond-set

Estimated value: $10,800 →

Ingenieur — 1980

Case: stainless steel, tripartite, screw-down case back, gold bezel, stainless steel link bracelet, Ø 34 mm

Movement: Caliber 37521, gold-plated, decorated, automatic winding, 21 jewels, regulated in 5 positions

Remarks: Ingenieur with gold bezel and stainless steel link bracelet

Estimated value: $3,375 →

Ingenieur SL Automatic — 1978

Reference number: 1832

Case: stainless steel, tripartite, screw-down case back, stainless steel link bracelet, Ø 40 mm

Movement: Caliber 8541, rhodium-plated, decorated, polished screws

Remarks: large, heavy Ingenieur model with stainless steel link bracelet; this watch was offered in its original box, with original certificate and guarantee, and a certificate from IWC's master registry

Estimated value: $12,150 →

Ingenieur SL — 1973

Case: 18-karat yellow gold, screw-down case back, 18-karat gold link bracelet, Ø 40 mm

Movement: Caliber IWC 8541B, rhodium-plated, côtes de Genève, automatic winding

Remarks: especially heavy (260 grams) gold watch; like all Ingenieurs, this one is especially protected from magnetic fields

Estimated value: $14,850 ↗

Ingenieur SL Automatic — 1980

Case: 18-karat yellow gold, tripartite, screw-down case back, gold link bracelet, Ø 34 mm

Movement: Caliber 375, rhodium-plated, finely finished, polished screws, automatic winding, 22 jewels, regulated in 8 positions

Remarks: rare small Ingenieur in a heavy gold case with an original IWC gold link bracelet

Estimated value: $8,100 →

IWC Porsche Design — 1990

Case: black anodized aluminum, case made of several parts, screw-down case back, metal link bracelet, Ø 39 mm

Movement: rhodium-plated, polished screws, automatic winding

Remarks: rare automatic IWC Porsche Design in a black anodized aluminum case; the top part of the watch can be opened so that the compass integrated into the case underneath can be seen

Estimated value: $3,375 ↗

Jaeger-LeCoultre

become damaged. The famous Atmos clock followed in 1928, a timepiece that gets its energy from the differences in temperature in its environment. To this day, it remains the official Swiss gift to foreign state guests. In 1929, Caliber 101 was added to the repertoire, the smallest mechanical movement ever serially manufactured. And, finally, in 1931 the famous Reverso model followed, whose easily rotated case served to protect the sensitive crystal on the front. According to legend, the inspiration for the exceptional case design came from British polo players stationed in India. Jaeger-LeCoultre soon enjoyed an excellent reputation as a *manufacture* to watch. Its specialties, then and now, counted calendar watches with moon phases, perpetual calendars, and alarm watches among them. In 1948, after the death of Jacques-David LeCoultre, the company was purchased by SAPIC Holding. It then passed through a number of hands until it finally found a home within the VDO/ Mannesmann concern at the end of the 1970s. Just about twenty years later, the company sold its entire watch holdings (called Les Manufactures Horlogères and included Jaeger-LeCoultre, IWC, and A. Lange & Söhne) to the Richemont Group.

The name of this company should actually be switched, for the history of Jaeger-LeCoultre began with Antoine LeCoultre, born in 1803 in Le Sentier, located in the Vallée de Joux, Switzerland's "watch valley," where the roots of his family extend back to the sixteenth century. At the age of thirty he founded a factory for movement components in his hometown, the place where Jaeger-LeCoultre continues to operate to this very day.

Antoine LeCoultre was a very imaginative man. In 1844, he invented the millionometer, an instrument that made it possible to take measurements with the precision of a thousandth of a millimeter (or a millionth of a meter—hence the name). Even the double function of a crown for winding and setting, which may seem so natural to us today, is one of LeCoultre's inventions, which made key winding superfluous. Antoine LeCoultre registered many patents, and after his death, the *manufacture* LeCoultre & Compagnie specialized in producing fine, complicated watch movements.

The second part of this company's history began in 1925 with the introduction of Alsatian engineer Edmond Jaeger (born in 1850), who had previously supplied both Cartier and the French navy, among others, with movements. The *manufacture*'s double name gave him the opportunity to develop and produce not only movements, but also entire wristwatches. The Duoplan was created in 1926 with a bipartite baguette movement that could be easily exchanged in just a few minutes should it

Reverso   1935

Case: stainless steel, push-down case back, leather strap, 23 x 38 mm

Movement: gold-plated, côtes de Genève, manual winding

Remarks: one of the first Reversos in the famous reversible case with sweep seconds

Estimated value: $4,725 →

Reverso/Favre-Leuba   1930

Case: stainless steel, push-down case back, leather strap, 21 x 38 mm

Movement: rhodium-plated, côtes de Genève, manual winding

Remarks: rare early Reverso in the famous reversible case with sweep seconds; signed by both Jaeger-LeCoultre and Favre-Leuba

Estimated value: $4,725 →

Reverso   1930

Case: 18-karat yellow gold, push-down case back, leather strap, 21 x 39 mm

Movement: gold plated, côtes de Genève, manual winding

Remarks: extremely rare Reverso in the famous reversible case; this watch has an engraved polo player on its case back

Estimated value: $9,450 →

Reverso Sawaiman Guards   1935

Case: stainless steel, push-down case back, leather strap

Movement: rhodium-plated, fausses côtes decoration, 15 jewels, manual winding

Remarks: extremely rare Reverso with engraved and enameled coat of arms of the Sawaiman Guards, the personal body guards of Maharaja Sawaiman of Jaipur

Estimated value: $8,100 ↗

Reverso   1940

Case: stainless steel, push-down case back, leather strap

Movement: rhodium-plated, fausses côtes decoration, manual winding

Remarks: early rare Reverso with sweep seconds in the famous reversible case

Estimated value: $5,400 →

Reverso   1935

Case: 18-karat yellow gold, push-down case back, leather strap

Movement: rhodium-plated, fausses côtes decoration, 15 jewels, regulated in two positions, manual winding

Remarks: early rare Reverso with sweep seconds; this watch has an engraved and enameled coat of arms on the case back

Estimated value: $13,500 ↗

Reverso   1940

Case: 9-karat yellow gold, push-down case back, leather strap

Movement: rhodium-plated, fausses côtes decoration, manual winding

Remarks: early rare Reverso with sweep seconds in the famous reversible case; this watch has a hand-engraved coat of arms on the case back

Estimated value: $6,750 →

Reverso Maharani   1935

Case: 18-karat yellow gold, push-down case back, leather strap

Movement: rhodium-plated, fausses côtes decoration, manual winding

Remarks: only a few pieces of the Reverso Maharani were produced, and these were presumed missing up to now; this watch was made for the Maharaja of Karputala, who had his wife perpetuated on its case back thanks to a lavish enamel technique

Estimated value: $94,500 ↗

Reverso — 1940

Case: stainless steel, push-down case back, leather strap, 22 x 38 mm

Movement: Caliber 437, gold-plated, côtes de Genève, manual winding

Remarks: early Reverso with sweep seconds

Estimated value: $4,725 →

Reverso Luxe/Meister, Rio de Janeiro — 1950

Case: stainless steel, leather strap, 23 x 38 mm

Movement: rhodium-plated, jewels set in chatons, shaped movement, manual winding

Remarks: rare Reverso with sweep seconds; dial printed with "Meister, Rio de Janeiro"

Estimated value: $5,400 →

Calendar Watch — 1950

Case: stainless steel, push-down case back, leather strap, 24 x 40 mm

Movement: shaped movement, nickel-plated, côtes de Genève, manual winding

Remarks: rectangular men's watch with calendar, sweep date hand, weekday in the window at 12 o'clock, and subsidiary seconds

Estimated value: $2,700 →

Calendar Watch — 1945

Case: gold-plated, push-down case back, leather strap, 24 x 40 mm

Movement: Caliber 806/AW, rhodium-plated, côtes de Genève, manual winding

Remarks: rare rectangular men's watch with complete calendar and moon phase; sweep date hand; weekday and month in window display

Estimated value: $3,375 ↗

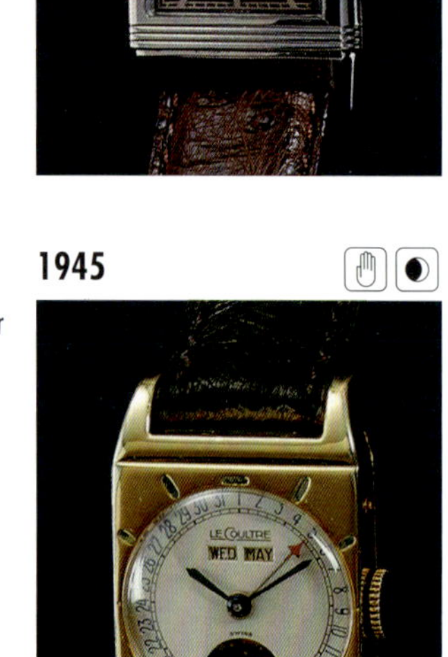

Calendar Watch — 1950

Case: 18-karat yellow gold, push-down case back, leather strap, 24 x 40 mm

Movement: shaped movement, nickel-plated, côtes de Genève, manual winding

Remarks: rectangular men's watch with calendar, sweep date hand, weekday in window display at 12 o'clock, subsidiary seconds

Estimated value: $6,075 ↗

Men's Watch with Digital Display — 1950

Case: 18-karat rose gold, push-down case back, leather strap, 27 x 35 mm

Movement: Caliber 480/CW, nickel-plated, côtes de Genève, manual winding

Remarks: rare men's watch with digital display of the time

Estimated value: $3,375 →

Men's Watch — 1945

Case: 10-karat rolled gold, push-down steel case back, leather strap, 27 x 39 mm

Movement: Caliber 438/4CW, nickel-plated, côtes de Genève, manual winding

Remarks: rare men's watch in an unusual design case

Estimated value: $1,350 →

Men's Watch — 1945

Case: stainless steel, push-down case back, leather strap, 28 x 36 mm

Movement: gold-plated, côtes de Genève, manual winding

Remarks: men's wristwatch in rectangular case

Estimated value: $675 →

Men's Watch — 1950

Case: stainless steel, push-down case back, leather strap, Ø 33 mm
Movement: Caliber P478, gold-plated, manual winding
Remarks: simple men's watch
Estimated value: $270 ↗

General Service Watch — 1940

Case: chrome-plated, push-down case back, leather strap, Ø 32 mm
Movement: Caliber 470, gold-plated, côtes de Genève, manual winding
Remarks: military wristwatch of the British armed forces
Estimated value: $405 →

Men's Watch — 1945

Case: 14-karat yellow gold, push-down case back, leather strap, Ø 32 mm
Movement: Caliber 463, gold-plated, frosted finish, manual winding
Remarks: small men's watch with luminous numerals
Estimated value: $1,220 →

Men's Watch — 1940

Case: stainless steel, push-down case back, leather strap, Ø 30 mm
Movement: shaped movement, nickel-plated, côtes de Genève, manual winding
Remarks: rare wristwatch with calendar, sweep date hand, weekday in window display at 12 o'clock
Estimated value: $1,620 →

Memovox — 1951

Case: stainless steel, push-down case back, leather strap, Ø 35 mm
Movement: Caliber 489/1, rhodium-plated, manual winding
Remarks: very early alarm wristwatch; a reference marker on the inner disk displays the alarm time
Estimated value: $1,620 →

Men's Watch — 1950

Case: 18-karat yellow gold, push-down case back, leather strap, Ø 33 mm
Movement: Caliber 450 2A, gold-plated, côtes de Genève, manual winding
Remarks: simple men's watch
Estimated value: $945 →

Club Automatic — 1975

Case: stainless steel, screw-down case back, leather strap, 38 x 43 mm
Movement: nickel-plated, automatic winding
Remarks: automatic men's watch with day and date display in the window at 3 o'clock
Estimated value: $540 →

Chronometer Geomatic — 1980

Case: stainless steel, screw-down case back, leather strap, Ø 36 mm
Movement: Caliber K881G, nickel-plated, côtes de Genève, 23 jewels, regulated in 6 positions, automatic winding
Remarks: nearly new steel chronometer with date window at 3 o'clock; officially certified chronometer; the movement was regulated in 6 positions; this watch was offered in its original box with papers
Estimated value: $2,970 ↗

Mystérieuse — 1950

Case: 14-karat white gold, push-down case back, leather strap, Ø 33 mm

Movement: Caliber 918/2, nickel-plated, manual winding

Remarks: rare white gold men's watch with diamond-set dial; two diamonds serve as the hands, which appear to move freely

Estimated value: $2,025 →

Mystérieuse — 1950

Case: 14-karat white gold, screw-down case back, leather strap, Ø 33 mm

Movement: Caliber K812, rhodium-plated, côtes de Genève, hammer automatic

Remarks: rare white gold men's watch with diamond-set dial; two diamonds serve as the hands, which appear to move freely

Estimated value: $2,160 →

Semi-Mystérieuse — 1950

Case: 18-karat yellow gold, push-down case back, leather strap, Ø 32 mm

Movement: rhodium-plated, côtes de Genève, manual winding

Remarks: rare watch with semi-mysterious time display; the crown is hidden on the case back; this watch was offered in its original box

Estimated value: $4,725 →

Calendar Watch — 1948

Case: 18-karat red gold, push-down case back, leather strap, Ø 36 mm

Movement: Caliber 484/A, gold-plated, côtes de Genève, manual winding

Remarks: elegant men's watch with complete calendar in red gold case; sweep date hand; window display of weekday and month

Estimated value: $4,725 →

Calendar Watch — 1950

Case: gold-filled, push-down case back, leather strap, Ø 35 mm

Movement: Caliber 486/AW, rhodium-plated, côtes de Genève, manual winding

Remarks: simple men's watch with complete calendar and moon phase; sweep date hand; window display of weekday and month; moon phase in small subsidiary dial at 6 o'clock; this watch was only signed "LeCoultre" and sold in the United States

Estimated value: $2,025 →

Calendar Watch — 1950

Case: 18-karat red gold, push-down case back, leather strap, Ø 35 mm

Movement: Caliber 494/A, gold-plated, côtes de Genève, manual winding

Remarks: elegant red gold men's watch with complete calendar and moon phase; sweep date hand; window display of weekday and month; moon phase in small subsidiary dial at 6 o'clock

Estimated value: $5,400 →

Calendar Watch — 1945

Case: stainless steel, gold bezel, push-down case back, leather strap, Ø 33 mm

Movement: Caliber 494/1, rhodium-plated, côtes de Genève, manual winding

Remarks: elegant men's watch with complete calendar and moon phase in a two-tone case; sweep date hand; window display of weekday and month; moon phase in the small subsidiary dial at 6 o'clock

Estimated value: $5,400 →

Calendar Watch — 1949

Case: stainless steel, push-down case back, leather strap Ø 35 mm

Movement: Caliber 464/A, gold-plated, côtes de Genève, manual winding

Remarks: rare steel men's watch with calendar; sweep date hand; window display of weekday and month

Estimated value: $3,375 →

Futurematic — 1948

Case: plated, push-down case back, leather strap, Ø 35 mm

Movement: Caliber 497, nickel-plated, côtes de Genève, 17 jewels, automatic winding

Remarks: automatic men's watch with hammer automatic winding and power reserve indicator; the crown is hidden on the case back to visually underscore that the watch is self-winding when worn

Estimated value: $1,620 →

Automatic with Power Reserve — 1955

Case: gold-plated, screw-down case back, leather strap, Ø 34 mm

Movement: Caliber 481, nickel-plated, côtes de Genève, automatic winding

Remarks: unusual men's watch with hammer automatic and power reserve indicator at 12 o'clock; this watch is only signed "LeCoultre" and was sold in the United States

Estimated value: $1,080 →

Automatic with Power Reserve — 1945

Case: gold-plated, screw-down case back, leather strap, Ø 34 mm

Movement: Caliber 481, rhodium-plated, côtes de Genève, automatic winding

Remarks: elegant automatic men's watch (hammer automatic); power reserve indicator at 12 o'clock

Estimated value: $945 →

Automatic with Power Reserve — 1945

Case: yellow gold, push-down case back, leather strap, Ø 35 mm

Movement: Caliber 481, rhodium-plated, côtes de Genève, automatic winding

Remarks: elegant men's watch (hammer automatic); power reserve indicator at 12 o'clock; crown is recessed in the case

Estimated value: $1,620 →

Futurematic — 1950

Case: gold-plated, push-down case back, leather strap, Ø 35 mm

Movement: Caliber 497, rhodium-plated, côtes de Genève, automatic winding

Remarks: automatic men's watch with hammer automatic and power reserve indicator at 9 o'clock; the crown is hidden on the case back to visually underscore that the watch is self-winding when worn

Estimated value: $1,350 →

Futurematic — 1940

Case: 14-karat yellow gold, push-down case back, leather strap, Ø 35 mm

Movement: Caliber 497, rhodium-plated, côtes de Genève, automatic winding

Remarks: automatic men's watch with hammer automatic and power reserve indicator at 9 o'clock; the crown is hidden on the case back to visually underscore that the watch is self-winding when worn; this watch is only signed "LeCoultre"

Estimated value: $1,755 →

Futurematic — 1950

Case: gold-plated, push-down case back, leather strap, Ø 35 mm

Movement: Caliber 497, rhodium-plated, côtes de Genève, automatic winding

Remarks: automatic men's watch with hammer automatic and power reserve indicator at 9 o'clock; crown on case back; only signed "LeCoultre"

Estimated value: $1,080 →

Futurematic — 1951

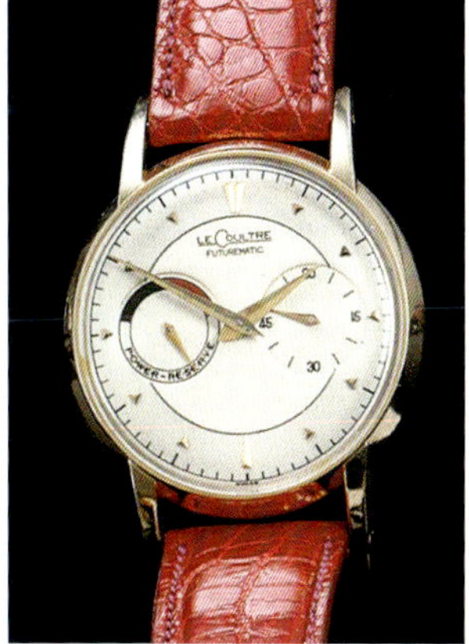

Case: gold-plated, push-down case back, leather strap, Ø 35 mm

Movement: Caliber 497/1, nickel-plated, côtes de Genève, automatic winding

Remarks: men's watch with hammer automatic and power reserve indicator at 9 o'clock; crown on the case back

Estimated value: $1,080 →

Chronograph — 1950

Case: stainless steel, screw-down case back, leather strap, Ø 35 mm

Movement: Valjoux Caliber 72, nickel-plated, column-wheel control of chronograph functions, manual winding

Remarks: simple chronograph with 30-minute and 12-hour counters; only signed "LeCoultre"

Estimated value: $1,890 →

Chronograph — 1950

Case: 18-karat yellow gold, screw-down case back, leather strap, Ø 35 mm

Movement: Valjoux Caliber 72, rhodium-plated, column-wheel control of chronograph functions, manual winding

Remarks: chronograph with 30-minute and 12-hour counters; this watch was offered in its box with a LeCoultre sales tag and papers

Estimated value: $4,725 ↗

Chronograph — 1960

Case: stainless steel, screw-down case back, leather strap, Ø 35 mm

Movement: Valjoux Caliber 72, rhodium-plated, column-wheel control of chronograph, manual winding

Remarks: simple chronograph with 30-minute and 12-hour counters; only signed "LeCoultre"

Estimated value: $1,890 →

Chronograph — 1970

Case: stainless steel, screw-down case back, rotating bezel, leather strap, Ø 40 mm

Movement: Valjoux Caliber 72, rhodium-plated, column-wheel control of chronograph, manual winding

Remarks: sporty chronograph with 30-minute and 12-hour counters in heavy steel case with a rotating bezel; only signed "LeCoultre"

Estimated value: $2,295 ↗

Chronograph — 1940

Case: yellow gold, push-down case back, leather strap, Ø 35 mm

Movement: nickel-plated, column-wheel control of chronograph, manual winding

Remarks: simple chronograph with 30-minute counter; only signed "Jaeger"

Estimated value: $2,295 →

Chronograph — 1950

Case: 18-karat yellow gold, push-down case back, leather strap, Ø 36 mm

Movement: Caliber 285, nickel-plated, column-wheel control of chronograph, manual winding

Remarks: rare simple chronograph with 45-minute counter

Estimated value: $3,105 →

Chronograph — 1950

Case: stainless steel, screw-down case back, rotating bezel, leather strap, Ø 38 mm

Movement: Valjoux Caliber 726, gold-plated, column-wheel control of chronograph, manual winding

Remarks: sporty chronograph with 30-minute and 12-hour counters; only signed "Jaeger"

Estimated value: $1,620 ↗

Chronograph — 1934

Case: stainless steel, push-down case back, leather strap, Ø 35 mm

Movement: Caliber 285, nickel-plated, column-wheel control of chronograph, manual winding

Remarks: early wristwatch chronograph with 30-minute counter; tachymeter scale and movable strap lugs; twin signatures: Jaeger and Hausmann & Co.

Estimated value: $1,080 →

Memovox — 1951

Case: stainless steel, push-down case back, leather strap, Ø 35 mm

Movement: Caliber 489/1, rhodium-plated, manual winding

Remarks: very early Memovox with alarm function

Estimated value: $2,025 ↗

Wrist Alarm — 1951

Case: gold-plated, push-down case back, leather strap, Ø 32 mm

Movement: Caliber 489/1, nickel-plated, manual winding

Remarks: early alarm wristwatch; a reference marker displays the set alarm time on the inner disk; this watch was made for the American market and only signed "LeCoultre"

Estimated value: $1,080 →

Memovox — 1960

Case: yellow gold, push-down case back, leather strap, Ø 35 mm

Movement: Caliber 814, rhodium-plated, manual winding

Remarks: rare parking meter alarm wristwatch; to conveniently be reminded of the parking meter running, its time is shown in half-hour increments on the inner disk

Estimated value: $2,025 ↗

Wrist Alarm — 1956

Case: gold-plated, push-down case back, leather strap, Ø 32 mm

Movement: Caliber 814, rhodium-plated, manual winding

Remarks: early alarm wristwatch; a reference marker displays the set alarm time on the inner disk; this watch was made for the American market and only signed "LeCoultre"

Estimated value: $1,350 ↗

Wrist Alarm — 1951

Case: gold-plated, push-down case back, leather strap, Ø 34 mm

Movement: Caliber 814, rhodium-plated, manual winding

Remarks: early alarm wristwatch; a reference marker displays the set alarm time on the inner disk; this watch was made for the American market and only signed "LeCoultre"; automobile brand Ford logo is found at 12 o'clock

Estimated value: $1,350 ↗

Memovox — 1951

Case: 18-karat yellow gold, leather strap, Ø 35 mm

Movement: Caliber P489/1, nickel-plated, manual winding

Remarks: alarm wristwatch in gold case; a reference marker displays the set alarm time on the inner disk

Estimated value: $2,430 →

Memovox — 1960

Case: stainless steel, 18-karat yellow gold bezel, push-down case back, leather strap, Ø 35 mm

Movement: rhodium-plated, manual winding

Remarks: nearly unworn alarm wristwatch in unusual two-tone case with fluted bezel

Estimated value: $1,890 ↗

Memovox — 1960

Case: gold-plated, push-down case back, leather strap, Ø 34 mm

Movement: Caliber 814, rhodium-plated, manual winding

Remarks: elegant alarm wristwatch with a company logo on the dial

Estimated value: $1,350 →

Memovox Automatic — 1967

Case: 18-karat yellow gold, screw-down case back, leather strap, Ø 37 mm

Movement: Caliber 916, rhodium-plated, automatic winding

Remarks: gold alarm wristwatch with rotor automatic movement

Estimated value: $3,375 ↗

Memovox Automatic — 1957

Case: gold-plated, push-down case back, leather strap, Ø 38 mm

Movement: Caliber 825, nickel-plated, côtes de Genève, automatic winding

Remarks: alarm wristwatch with hammer automatic movement and date window at 3 o'clock; a reference marker displays the set alarm time on the inner disk

Estimated value: $1,755 →

Memovox Automatic — 1967

Case: stainless steel, screw-down case back, leather strap, Ø 37 mm

Movement: Caliber 916, rhodium-plated, automatic winding

Remarks: discrete alarm wristwatch with automatic movement

Estimated value: $1,755 →

Memovox Automatic — 1958

Case: 18-karat yellow gold, screw-down case back, leather strap, Ø 37 mm

Movement: Caliber 825, rhodium-plated, automatic winding

Remarks: elegant alarm wristwatch with the first automatic alarm caliber (hammer automatic); date window at 3 o'clock

Estimated value: $3,375 ↗

Memovox — 1951

Case: 18-karat red gold, push-down case back, leather strap, Ø 35 mm

Movement: Caliber 489/1, rhodium-plated, manual winding

Remarks: simple alarm wristwatch

Estimated value: $3,645 ↗

Memovox Polaris — 1966

Case: stainless steel, push-down case back, leather strap, Ø 42 mm

Movement: Caliber 425, rhodium-plated, 17 jewel, automatic winding

Remarks: rare alarm wristwatch with automatic winding (hammer automatic) for divers; water-resistant to 300 m; diving time set with rotating inner bezel (flange)

Estimated value: $13,500 ↗

Memovox Automatic Snowdrop — 1975

Case: stainless steel, screw bezel, leather strap, Ø 43 mm

Movement: Caliber 916, rhodium-plated, automatic winding

Remarks: Snowdrop alarm wristwatch in design case; monocoque case closed via the bezel; date window at 3 o'clock

Estimated value: $1,080 →

Memovox Automatic — 1975

Case: stainless steel, screw-down case back, stainless steel link bracelet, 38 x 45 mm

Movement: Caliber 916, rhodium-plated, automatic winding

Remarks: automatic alarm wristwatch with very solid case and stainless steel link bracelet

Estimated value: $945 →

Junghans

More than one hundred years ago, this company was the largest watch manufacturer in the world. During its heyday, 12,000 watches emerged from the workshops daily—and more than 5,000 employees were picked up with a significant logistical effort and brought to Schramberg in the Black Forest's every day to work.

Today, a workforce of about one hundred is dwarfed by the giant factory building, which used to house one of Europe's most modern production parks. The company's history, the acme of which coincided with the advent of conveyor belt production and the later developed radio-controlled watch technology, mirrors the ups and downs of the German watch industry in its entirety.

The American production style was in high in demand in the 1880s, allowing the clock company Junghans to finally compete with overseas suppliers of cheap clocks. The Black Forest-based company had manufactured cuckoo clocks since 1865, with Erhard Junghans progressively using the force of water for the efficient production of components made of brass, wood, and bronze. His brother Franz-Xaver had previously returned from the United States with modern machines and tools in tow. The consistent introduction of "American" production methods and the study of the superior watch technology of the large series producers across the ocean helped Junghans to develop the company's first alarm clock, the famed Caliber 10. It became a milestone of cost-effective, simple design and was manufactured from 1885 to 1930.

An especially clever idea by Erhard's son Arthur in 1907 literally shed light on the subject. He mixed zinc sulfide with radium and applied the radioactively luminescent mixture to hands and dials so that they could be read the whole night through. What an innovation: one no longer needed to light a candle to see the time!

In 1903, Junghans launched its first pocket watch movement, and twenty-five years later its first wristwatch, thus entering a product segment that would continue to be extended in the ensuing years.

The company was partially dismantled by the Allies after World War II, but soon thereafter Junghans once again began developing and producing chronograph Caliber J88 and Minivox Caliber J89, which was patented in 1949.

Alongside chronographs and alarm wristwatches, Junghans manufactured above all simple watches outfitted with manually wound and automatic movements that were famous for the precision of their rates. In the 1950s, this company was the third largest producer of chronometers after Rolex and Omega.

After the Diehl concern from Nuremberg took over the majority of its stock in 1956, Junghans was divided into two departments: watches and precision engineering. During the quartz crisis of the 1970s, this proud name slipped into anonymity until the development of radio-controlled technology showed it the way out of its misery and secured the future of the brand. In 2000, Diehl sold Junghans's watch division to Egana-Goldpfeil Holding, headquartered in Hong Kong.

German Army Pilot's Chronograph — 1950

Case: chrome-plated, screw-down case back, leather strap, Ø 38 mm

Movement: Caliber 88, gold-plated, frosted finish, column-wheel control of chronograph, manual winding

Remarks: rare first edition of the German army pilot's chronograph featuring a fluted bezel; engraved with air force number 6645-12-120-9351/88-0110

Estimated value: $2,970 ↗

German Army Pilot's Chronograph — 1955

Case: matte finish, stainless steel screw-down case back, rotating bezel, leather strap, Ø 38 mm

Movement: Caliber 88, gold-plated, frosted finish, column-wheel control of chronograph, manual winding

Remarks: pilot's chronograph of the German army; engraved with following inscription: "Bundeseigentum Nr.12-124-8591" ("property of the government" and number)

Estimated value: $1,890 ↗

Chronograph — 1950

Case: chrome-plated, stainless steel push-down case back, leather strap, Ø 36 mm

Movement: Caliber 88, gold-plated, frosted finish, column-wheel control of chronograph, manual winding

Remarks: chronograph with 30-minute counter

Estimated value: $810 →

Chronograph — 1945

Case: stainless steel, screw-down case back, leather strap, Ø 38 mm

Movement: Caliber 88, gold-plated, frosted finish, column-wheel control of chronograph, manual winding

Remarks: chronograph with 30-minute counter

Estimated value: $1,080 →

Chronograph — 1945

Case: chrome-plated, exhibition window case back, leather strap, Ø 36 mm

Movement: Caliber 88, gold-plated, frosted finish, column-wheel control of chronograph, manual winding

Remarks: chronograph with 30-minute counter and transparent case back

Estimated value: $1,080 →

Chronograph — 1950

Case: stainless steel, push-down case back, leather strap, Ø 36 mm

Movement: Caliber 88, gold-plated, frosted finish, column-wheel control of chronograph, manual winding

Remarks: chronograph with 30-minute counter

Estimated value: $1,620 →

Minivox — 1960

Case: stainless steel, push-down case back, leather strap, Ø 35 mm

Movement: Caliber 89, nickel-plated, 20 jewels, manual winding

Remarks: alarm wristwatch with gong on case back; this watch was offered in its original box with certificate

Estimated value: $1,755 →

Automatic with Power Reserve Indicator — 1960

Case: stainless steel, push-down case back, leather strap, Ø 35 mm

Movement: Caliber 80.12, nickel-plated, 22 jewels, automatic winding

Remarks: rare men's watch with power reserve indicator

Estimated value: $810 →

Chronometer

1960

Case: stainless steel push-down case back, leather strap, Ø 34mm
Movement: Caliber 62.1, gold-plated, manual winding
Remarks: chronometer
Estimated value: $810 →

Chronometer

1960

Case: 14-karat yellow gold, push-down case back, leather strap, Ø 35 mm
Movement: Caliber 82.1, gold-plated, manual winding
Remarks: chronometer
Estimated value: $1,485 →

Chronometer Automatic

1955

Case: 14-karat yellow gold, push-down case back, leather strap, Ø 36 mm
Movement: Caliber 83, gold-plated, automatic winding
Remarks: chronometer in gold case
Estimated value: $1,620 →

Chronometer Automatic

1960

Case: gold-plated, stainless steel push-down case back, leather strap, Ø 34 mm
Movement: Caliber 83, gold-plated, 29 jewels, automatic winding
Remarks: chronometer
Estimated value: $1,080 →

Chronometer

1960

Case: gold-plated, stainless steel push-down case back, leather strap, Ø 34 mm
Movement: Caliber 82.1, gold-plated, manual winding
Remarks: chronometer
Estimated value: $675 →

Chronometer

1955

Case: stainless steel, push-down case back, leather strap, Ø 33 mm
Movement: Caliber 82.1, gold-plated, manual winding
Remarks: chronometer
Estimated value: $810 →

German Army Service Watch

1938

Case: chrome-plated, stainless steel push-down case back, leather strap, Ø 36 mm
Movement: Caliber 80, nickel-plated, manual winding
Remarks: service wristwatch for the army's medical corps
Estimated value: $475 →

Men's Watch

1945

Case: stainless steel, push-down case back, 22 x 38 mm
Movement: Caliber 79/1, nickel-plated, manual winding
Remarks: rectangular men's watch
Estimated value: $220 →

A. Lange & Söhne

High watchmaking in Germany is securely tied to one name: Ferdinand Adolph Lange. Without him, the little town of Glashütte would never have experienced the well-being it has starting in the nineteenth century, making it the epicenter of fine watchmaking north of Switzerland for several generations.

Lange was born in 1815 in Dresden. After completing his education with watchmaker to the royalty Johann Christian Friedrich Gutkaes, he went to Paris for more at the side of Thaddäus Winnerl, a student of the great Abraham-Louis Breguet and the most talented watchmaker of his time. Lange remained in Paris for four years before returning to Dresden, marrying the daughter of his former teacher, and becoming his partner.

The reason for Lange's interest in poor little Glashütte was actually logical: in 1843 Saxony's government called for experts to help alleviate poverty in the Erzgebirge region. They were to found companies there with the help of state start-up financing, thus industrializing the region. After several letters, Lange received a loan from the state with which he could hire fifteen youths and train them as watchmakers. Thus, he moved to Glashütte in 1845.

His apprentices had to obligate themselves to work for Lange for another five years after their education ended. Beyond that, however, Lange encouraged them to go into business for themselves and train more craftsmen. Success came quickly with this concept, and Lange was

so popular in Glashütte that he was voted mayor and even later member of Saxony's parliament.

After Lange's passing in 1875, his sons Richard and Emil took over the company. Richard Lange, however, had to retire from daily business in 1886 for health reasons, and from 1919 on grandsons Otto and Rudolf Lange managed the company.

A. Lange & Söhne manufactured wristwatches in the 1920s, though most of them had Swiss *ébauches* as their base. Before and during World War II, the company mainly manufactured pilot's and observation watches alongside their marine chronometers. Lange pocket watch movements ticked within the stately 55 mm cases. The Lange chronometer, manufactured in conjunction with Hamburg Chronometer Works (today Wempe), made the company famous. The sensationally low rate deviation of the marine chronometer was only one second every three days.

Production was revived in the dismantled factory after the end of the war. Lange's watchmakers succeeded in setting up the machines for manufacturing Caliber 28 by 1948. In the same year, however, the family was expropriated, and the company A. Lange & Söhne was integrated into the newly created combine Glashütter Uhrenbetriebe.

Only with Germany's reunification in 1989 was the founder's great-grandson Walter Lange able to resuscitate A. Lange & Söhne with the help of Mannesmann. Remaining true to the original spirit of the company's founder, he turned the company into a special *manufacture*. Lange Uhren GmbH meanwhile belongs to the Richemont Group.

Men's Watch — 1940

Case: 14-karat yellow gold, push-down case back, leather strap, Ø 35 mm

Movement: rhodium-plated, côtes de Genève, manual winding

Remarks: rare Lange wristwatch in Bauhaus design

Estimated value: $9,450 ↗

Men's Watch — 1944

Case: 14-karat yellow gold, push-down case back, leather strap, Ø 36 mm

Movement: 10 1/2 line caliber, nickel-plated, côtes de Genève, manual winding

Remarks: extremely rare men's watch in Bauhaus style with original box and certificate

Estimated value: $12,150 ↗

Men's Watch — 1942

Case: 14-karat yellow gold, push-down case back, leather strap, Ø 36 mm

Movement: 10 1/2 line caliber, rhodium-plated, côtes de Genève, manual winding

Remarks: fine Glashütte men's watch

Estimated value: $8,775 ↗

Men's Watch with Lange Caliber — 1939

Case: 14-karat yellow gold, push-down case back, leather strap, Ø 35 mm

Movement: Caliber 31, gold-plated, frosted finish, jewels set in chatons, manual winding

Remarks: this watch was offered with certification from A. Lange & Söhne's master registry to verify its authenticity

Estimated value: $17,550 →

Men's Watch — 1928

Case: 14-karat yellow gold, push-down case back, leather strap, 23 x 38 mm

Movement: rhodium-plated, côtes de Genève, 16 jewels, regulated in 5 positions, manual winding

Remarks: one of A. Lange & Söhne's first tonneau-shaped gold wristwatches; regulated in 5 positions; dial signature: "A. Lange & Söhne Genf" (Geneva)

Estimated value: $8,100 ↗

Men's Watch — 1932

Case: 14-karat yellow gold, push-down case back, leather strap, 22 x 38 mm

Movement: gold-plated, frosted finish, manual winding

Remarks: Glashütte men's watch in a rectangular case

Estimated value: $4,725 ↗

Men's Watch — 1940

Case: 14-karat yellow gold, push-down case back, leather strap, 21 x 36 mm

Movement: Caliber 8.3/4x12''', rhodium-plated, côtes de Genève, manual winding

Remarks: rare men's watch

Estimated value: $4,725 →

Men's Watch — 1936

Case: 14-karat yellow gold, push-down case back, leather strap, 21 x 38 mm

Movement: 8 3/4 line caliber, nickel-plated, côtes de Genève, shaped movement, manual winding

Remarks: fine Glashütte men's watch

Estimated value: $4,725 →

Lémania

A certain Alfred Lugrin rented a small work-shop in Le Sentier in 1883. The self-taught watchmaker, who had worked his way up from assistant mechanic at Jaeger-LeCoultre to chronograph specialist, began to add chronograph mechanisms to purchased *ebauches* together with three colleagues. By 1885, Lugrin's company was already making complications like repeaters and chronographs; by 1890, the company had grown so much that a generous factory in L'Orient had to be built, which today remains the heart of the oft-annexed modern factory. It was around 1900 that the production of complete watches under the company's own name began.

After Lugrin passed away, his son-in-law Marius Meylan took over managing the company. In 1930, an especially successful caliber inspired him to make its moniker that of the company: Lémania after Lac Léman, which is French for Lake Geneva. In 1932, just two years later, Lémania was integrated into the SSIH along with the brands Omega and Tissot. As a result, it was especially for top brand Omega that Lémania created numerous new movements. Caliber 321 was exceptional, especially since it made it all the way to the moon inside the Speedmaster. In the 1970s, Lémania developed automatic chronograph calibers 1340, 1341, and 5100, which became true classics. The very robust Caliber 5100 remains for many the most reliable chronograph caliber ever created. The development of alarm wristwatch Caliber 980—a variation of which exclusive to Omega including setting the alarm time to the minute—was precisely within this time frame.

In 1981, the SSIH sold Lémania, and after a management buyout, the traditional company was relaunched as Nouvelle Lémania SA. Its journey was not to end here, however, for in 1992 the resuscitated watch brand Breguet, searching for a movement manufacturer, purchased and integrated it. It was from then on that the most complicated Breguet timepieces were created in the Nouvelle Lémania workshops. In the summer of 1999, the complete Breguet group, including Lémania, was purchased by the Swatch Group and restructured under the new name Breguet Manufacture. The Lémania name has now disappeared from the market.

To the ears of a wristwatch collector, the name Lémania stands for first-class pilot's chronographs, though the Lémania brand also brought forth many interesting automatic men's watches and even rare alarm wristwatches.

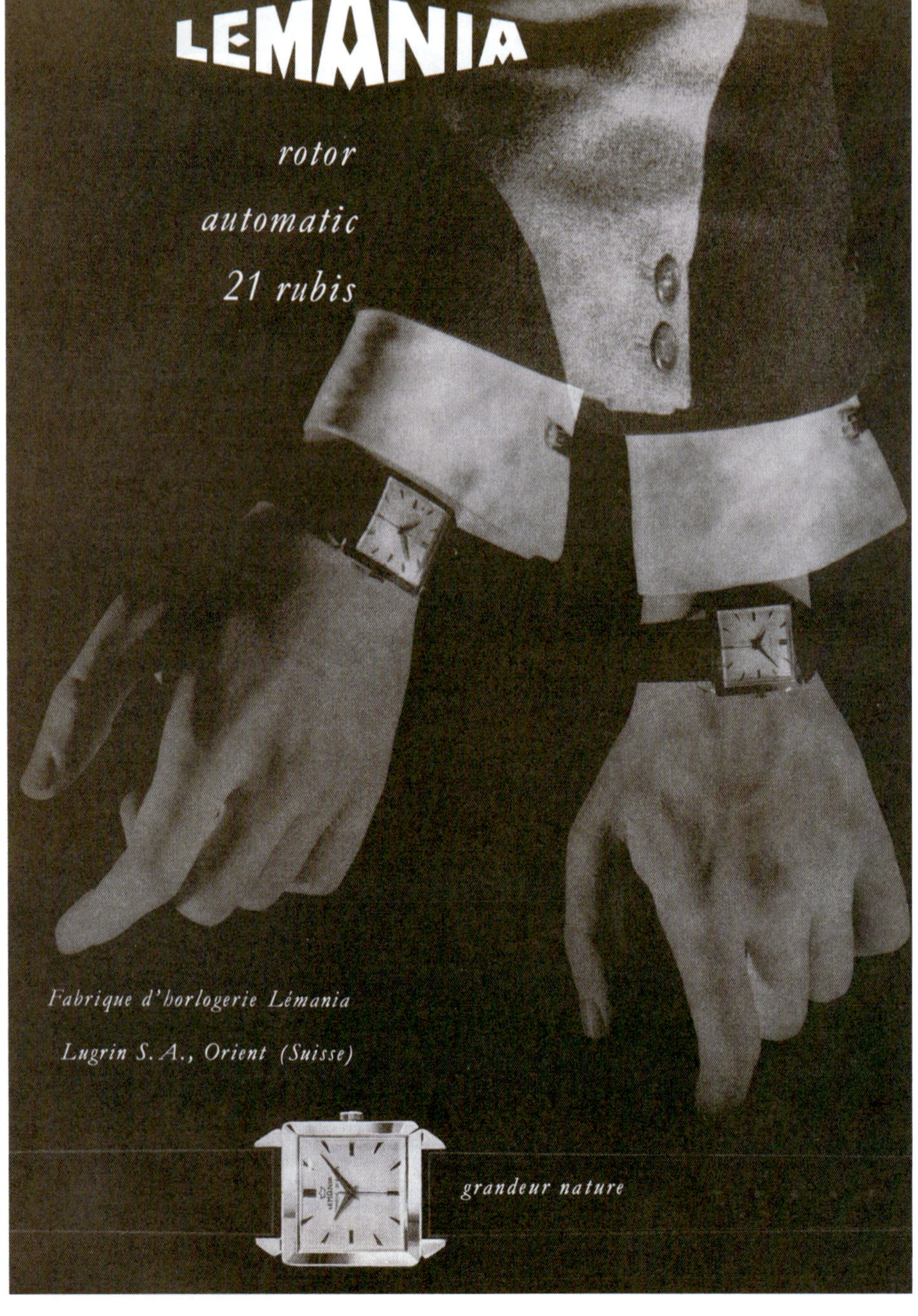

Chronograph — 1935

Case: stainless steel, push-down case back, leather strap, Ø 37 mm
Movement: gold-plated, frosted finish, column-wheel control of chronograph, manual winding
Remarks: chronograph with 30-minute counter
Estimated value: $1,080 →

Chronograph — 1940

Case: stainless steel, push-down case back, leather strap, Ø 37 mm
Movement: gold-plated, frosted finish, column-wheel control of chronograph, manual winding
Remarks: steel chronograph with telemeter scale and additional tachymeter scale
Estimated value: $1,080 →

Chronograph — 1950

Case: stainless steel, push-down case back, leather strap, Ø 34 mm
Movement: column-wheel control of chronograph, manual winding
Remarks: chronograph with 30-minute and 12-hour counters
Estimated value: $675 →

Chronograph — 1940

Case: stainless steel, screw-down case back, leather strap, Ø 35 mm
Movement: nickel-plated, column-wheel control of chronograph, manual winding
Remarks: rare chronograph with 30-minute and 12-hour counters
Estimated value: $1,220 →

Chronograph — 1950

Case: 18-karat yellow gold, push-down case back, leather strap, Ø 32 mm
Movement: nickel-plated, column-wheel control of chronograph, manual winding
Remarks: delicate chronograph in gold case
Estimated value: $1,220 →

Chronograph — 1955

Case: stainless steel, push-down case back, leather strap, Ø 34 mm
Movement: rhodium-plated, column-wheel control of chronograph, manual winding
Remarks: elegant chronograph with 30-minute and 12-hour counters
Estimated value: $945 →

Chronograph — 1940

Case: stainless steel, push-down case back, leather strap, Ø 37 mm
Movement: gold-plated, frosted finish, column-wheel control of chronograph, manual winding
Remarks: early steel chronograph with 30-minute counter
Estimated value: $810 →

Chronograph — 1950

Case: stainless steel, bipartite, screw-down case back, leather strap, Ø 35 mm
Movement: rhodium-plated, column-wheel control of chronograph, fine matte steel chronograph components
Remarks: sporty, elegant chronograph with 30-minute counter; two-tone dial with luminous numerals; minute scale underscored by a black ring; telemeter scale on outer perimeter
Estimated value: $1,080 →

Chronograph — 1950

Case: chrome-plated, bipartite, stainless steel push-down case back, leather strap, Ø 38 mm

Movement: rhodium-plated, finely finished steel chronograph components

Remarks: elegant chronograph with 30-minute counter; tachymeter scale on outer perimeter of dial

Estimated value: $810 →

Chronograph — 1950

Case: stainless steel, tripartite, push-down case back, leather strap

Movement: rhodium-plated, column-wheel control of chronograph, fine matte steel chronograph components, 17 jewels

Remarks: sporty chronograph with 30-minute counter; telemeter and tachymeter scales on outer perimeter of dial

Estimated value: $1,350 →

Chronograph — 1940

Case: stainless steel, tripartite, push-down case back, leather strap, Ø 37 mm

Movement: gold-plated, column-wheel control of chronograph, fine matte steel chronograph components

Remarks: sporty chronograph with 30-minute counter; telemeter scale on outer perimeter of dial; tachymeter scale in snail form in the middle of dial; navette-shaped chronograph buttons

Estimated value: $1,350 ↗

Chronograph — 1975

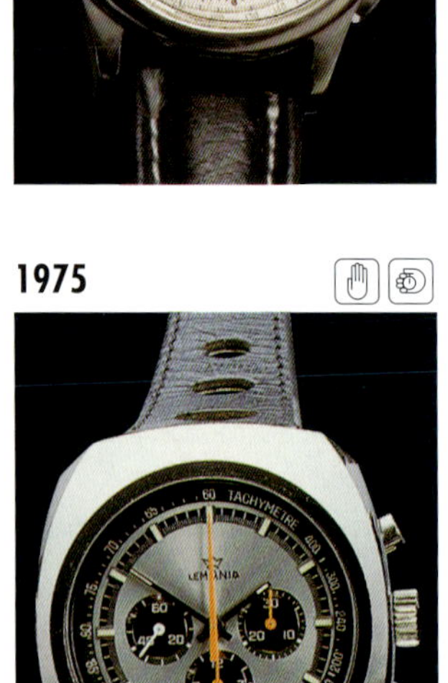

Case: stainless steel, screw-down case back, leather strap, Ø 43 mm

Movement: Caliber 1873, nickel-plated, manual winding

Remarks: chronograph with 30-minute and 12-hour counters

Estimated value: $810 →

Alarm Wristwatch — 1971

Case: gold-plated, bipartite, stainless steel screw-down case back, leather strap, 34 x 43 mm

Movement: Lémania Caliber LWO2980, rhodium-plated, automatic winding

Remarks: automatic alarm wristwatch with integrated gong; this movement has only one mainspring, which also provides the energy for the alarm

Estimated value: $425 →

archive photo

Alarm Wristwatch — 1971

Case: stainless steel, screw-down case back, leather strap, 44 x 38.6 mm

Movement: Lémania Caliber LWO 2980, nickel-plated, 19 jewels, automatic winding

Remarks: automatic alarm wristwatch in stainless steel case; alarm time can be set in either direction

Estimated value: $1,080 →

Alarm Wristwatch — 1971

Case: gold-plated, stainless steel screw-down case back, leather strap, 42.6 x 40 mm

Movement: Lémania Caliber LWO 2980, nickel-plated, 19 jewels, automatic winding

Remarks: automatic alarm wristwatch in original Omega Memomatic case; the case has the Omega stamp between the strap lugs at 6 o'clock

Estimated value: $1,080 →

archive photo

Longines

Longines actually gets its name from the natural setting surrounding the factory: the building is located in Saint-Imier on fields that abut a little river called Les Longines. The company was founded as Agassiz & Cie. in 1832 by Auguste Agassiz and his friends Henri Raiguel and Florian Morel. It began its career as an *établisseur*, assembling purchased components to make complete watches. The production was completed mainly by workers operating out of their homes; Agassiz & Cie. specialized in distribution.

In 1852, Agassiz passed the company's management on to his nephew, Ernest Francillon, who recognized that at this time it was especially robust, reasonably priced watches that were in demand. For Francillon, that primarily meant that he had to rationalize his watch production. In 1866, he purchased the above-mentioned piece of property on the banks of the Schüss in Saint-Imier and promptly made the term *Les Longines* the brand name for his watches. Because the little river delivered free energy, Francillon was able to develop a machine-supported production process in the new factory, which consistently delivered reasonably priced movements and watches with high quality. Francillon was soon exporting his watches all over the world.

Longines became a synonym for professional pilot's watches thanks to the U.S. postal pilot Charles A. Lindbergh, who became the first man to fly across the Atlantic alone on May 21, 1927. Lindbergh had sketched his idea for a practical pilot's watch with navigational aid and sent it to John P.V. Heinmüller, then-director of Longines Wittnauer Watch Co. in the United States. Heinmüller was also president of the International Federation of Aviation and was himself an enthusiastic pilot, and thus recognized the value of Lindbergh's idea. Heinmüller contacted Longines in Switzerland, where the Lindbergh Hour Angle Watch was brought to serial maturity.

Ensuingly, the watches from Saint-Imier became the preferred equipment of pilots and adventurers. Aviation pioneers like Amelia Earhart, Howard Hughes, and Richard Evelyn Byrd trusted their Longines timekeepers.

Longines hit the high point of its fame in the 1950s, when the company even had a television show called *The Longines Chronoscope*. On this show, scientific topics and new technical developments were explained and discussed with guests.

In 1912, Longines introduced an electromechanical system for starting and stopping chronographs. This system qualified the company to become the official timekeeper for big sports events and the Olympic Games.

Good craftsmanship and high rate precision also characterized Longines wristwatches. The company's watchmakers often developed unusual solutions such as Caliber 340 whose rotor revolved on a toothed gear, keeping the movement very flat. Longines's automatic Caliber 980 with twin spring barrels was so technically demanding that it continues to be manufactured by Lémania today—in a modified shape and under another caliber number—for various Swatch Group brands.

Longines chronographs were also technical gems: just look at Caliber 13 ZN, the first chronograph with flyback function—a great step forward for pilots who didn't always have the time to push buttons for stopping and starting while they were navigating.

Like many other brands, Longines lost its independence during the quartz crisis. At first, the brand joined ASUAG along with many other smaller brands; then, via other mergers and buyouts, it became part of the Swatch Group.

Men's Watch — 1915

Case: silver, push-down case back, leather strap, Ø 31 mm

Movement: Caliber 13.34, gold-plated, frosted finish, manual winding

Remarks: early men's watch with enamel dial

Estimated value: $675 →

Men's Watch — 1936

Case: 14-karat yellow gold, push-down case back, leather strap, Ø 32 mm

Movement: Caliber 27.0, gold-plated, frosted finish, jewels set in chatons, manual winding

Remarks: gold men's watch with enamel dial

Estimated value: $1,620 →

Men's Watch — 1947

Case: 14-karat yellow gold, push-down case back, leather strap, Ø 29 mm

Movement: Caliber 9LN, rhodium-plated, jewels set in chatons, manual winding

Remarks: early men's watch with white gold, diamond-set bezel

Estimated value: $1,755 →

Men's Watch — 1953

Case: 14-karat yellow gold, leather strap, 30 x 35 mm

Movement: Caliber 237, rhodium-plated, jewels set in chatons, manual winding

Remarks: unusual men's watch

Estimated value: $810 →

Men's Watch — 1936

Case: stainless steel, push-down case back, leather strap, 22 x 38 mm

Movement: Caliber 25.17, rhodium-plated, côtes de Genève, jewels set in chatons, manual winding

Remarks: early men's watch with sweep seconds; this watch was offered with the original Longines sales tag

Estimated value: $1,220 ↗

Doctor's Watch — 1931

Case: stainless steel, push-down case back, leather strap, 20 x 30 mm

Movement: Caliber 9.32, rhodium-plated, côtes de Genève, jewels set in chatons, shaped movement, manual winding

Remarks: early men's watch in rectangular case; the large subsidiary seconds dial made pulse-taking easier

Estimated value: $2,025 ↗

Hour Glass — 1948

Case: 14-karat red gold, push-down case back, leather strap, 25 x 40 mm

Movement: Caliber 9 LT, nickel-plated, jewels set in chatons, manual winding

Remarks: red gold men's watch in a fitted, shaped case reminiscent of an hourglass

Estimated value: $1,600 ↗

Men's Watch — 1940

Case: 14-karat yellow gold, leather strap, 20 x 42 mm

Movement: Caliber 9L, rhodium-plated, jewels set in chatons, shaped movement, manual winding

Remarks: gold men's watch with striking strap lugs

Estimated value: $1,350 →

Hour Glass — 1954

Case: gold-plated, push-down case back, leather strap, 25 x 40 mm

Movement: Caliber 9 LT, nickel-plated, jewels set in chatons, manual winding

Remarks: gold men's watch in a fitted, shaped case reminiscent of an hourglass

Estimated value: $1,350 →

Men's Watch — 1925

Case: 18-karat yellow gold, push-down case back, leather strap, 24 x 45 mm

Movement: Caliber 10.39, nickel-plated, côtes de Genève, manual winding

Remarks: large men's watch in a rectangular case

Estimated value: $2,000 →

Men's Watch — 1942

Case: 14-karat yellow gold, push-down case back, leather strap, 20 x 42 mm

Movement: Caliber 92, nickel-plated, jewels set chatons, manual winding

Remarks: men's watch with faceted crystal

Estimated value: $1,350 ↗

Men's Watch — 1956

Case: 18-karat yellow gold, push-down case back, leather strap, 26 x 39 mm

Movement: Caliber 9 LT, nickel-plated, jewels set in chatons, shaped movement, manual winding

Remarks: gold men's watch with shaped lugs

Estimated value: $6,100 →

Automatic — 1954

Case: 18-karat yellow gold, push-down case back, leather strap, 31 x 43 mm

Movement: Caliber 22A, nickel-plated, jewels set in chatons, automatic winding

Remarks: elegant men's watch with domed square case

Estimated value: $1,100 →

Men's Watch — 1956

Case: 14-karat yellow gold, leather strap, 25 x 33 mm

Movement: Caliber 19.4, nickel-plated, jewels set in chatons, manual winding

Remarks: rare men's watch in a striking cutaway case design

Estimated value: $1,100 →

Men's Watch — 1947

Case: 18-karat yellow gold, push-down steel case back, leather strap, 25 x 38 mm

Movement: Caliber 10L, rhodium-plated, jewels set in chatons, manual winding

Remarks: extravagant men's watch with accentuated strap lugs

Estimated value: $950 →

Men's Watch — 1953

Case: 14-karat yellow gold, push-down case back, leather strap, 27 x 41 mm

Movement: Caliber 9LT, rhodium-plated, jewels set in chatons, shaped movement, manual winding

Remarks: elegant men's wristwatch with striking shaped strap lugs; this watch was offered in its original box

Estimated value: $1,100 →

Conquest Automatic — 1954

Case: 18-karat yellow gold, screw-down case back, leather strap, Ø 35 mm
Movement: Caliber 19AS, nickel-plated, jewels set in chatons, automatic winding
Remarks: elegant automatic watch
Estimated value: $1,200 →

Conquest Calendar Automatic — 1955

Case: 18-karat yellow gold, screw-down case back, leather strap, Ø 35 mm
Movement: Caliber 19ASD, rhodium-plated, jewels set in chatons, 19 jewels, automatic winding
Remarks: automatic men's watch with date display; this watch was offered in its original box
Estimated value: $1,350 →

Conquest Automatic Power Reserve — 1960

Reference number: 9032
Case: stainless steel, screw-down case back, leather strap, Ø 35 mm
Movement: Caliber 294, nickel-plated, 24 jewels, automatic winding
Remarks: extremely rare automatic jewel bearing, rotor-driven timepiece; central 45-hour power reserve indicator; date
Estimated value: $1,900 ↗

Conquest Automatic — 1954

Case: 18-karat yellow gold, screw-down case back, leather strap, Ø 35 mm
Movement: Caliber 19AS, nickel-plated, jewels set in chatons, 19 jewels, automatic winding
Remarks: heavy gold men's watch in original box
Estimated value: $1,100 →

Flagship Automatic — 1960

Reference number: 3503
Case: yellow gold, push-down case back, leather strap, Ø 35 mm
Movement: Caliber 340, gold-plated, 17 jewels, automatic winding
Remarks: automatic men's watch with unusual winding mechanism utilizing a toothed rim underneath the rotor
Estimated value: $950 →

Grand Prize Automatic — 1965

Case: 14-karat yellow gold, screw-down case back, leather strap, Ø 34 mm
Movement: Caliber 340, rhodium-plated, automatic winding
Remarks: automatic men's watch with applied, faceted gold markers; unusual winding mechanism utilizing a toothed rim underneath the rotor
Estimated value: $800 →

Admiral Automatic — 1968

Case: gold-plated, leather strap, Ø 35 mm
Movement: Caliber 501, nickel-plated, automatic winding
Remarks: automatic watch with rare black dial
Estimated value: $300 →

Mystérieuse — 1957

Case: 18-karat white gold, push-down case back, leather strap, Ø 32 mm
Movement: Caliber 237, rhodium-plated, jewels set in chatons, manual winding
Remarks: white gold men's watch with diamond-set bezel; hour hand moves with a rotating center disk
Estimated value: $2,100 ↗

Doctor's Chronograph — 1930

Case: 14-karat yellow gold, gold cuvette, leather strap, Ø 35 mm

Movement: Caliber 13.33, gold-plated, frosted finish, column-wheel control of chronograph, manual winding

Remarks: early chronograph with 30-minute counter; enamel dial; central strap lugs

Estimated value: $8,800 ↗

Chronograph — 1930

Case: yellow gold, leather strap, Ø 33 mm

Movement: nickel-plated, column-wheel control of chronograph, manual winding

Remarks: early chronograph with 30-minute counter; enamel dial

Estimated value: $10,100 ↗

Chronograph — 1925

Case: silver, silver cuvette, leather strap, Ø 35 mm

Movement: Caliber 13.33, nickel-plated, côtes de Genève, column-wheel control of chronograph, manual winding

Remarks: early chronograph with 30-minute counter; enamel dial

Estimated value: $6,100 ↗

Chronograph — 1925

Case: 18-karat yellow gold, with gold cuvette, leather strap, Ø 35 mm

Movement: Caliber 13.33, gold-plated, frosted finish, column-wheel control of chronograph, manual winding

Remarks: early chronograph with 30-minute counter; enamel dial

Estimated value: $8,800 ↗

Chronograph — 1925

Case: nickel, leather strap, Ø 40 mm

Movement: nickel-plated, côtes de Genève, column-wheel control of chronograph, manual winding

Remarks: early chronograph with 30-minute counter; enamel dial

Estimated value: $4,700 ↗

Chronograph — 1930

Case: 18-karat yellow gold, gold cuvette, leather strap, Ø 36 mm

Movement: Caliber 13.33, nickel-plated, côtes de Genève, column-wheel control of chronograph, manual winding

Remarks: early chronograph with 30-minute counter; enamel dial

Estimated value: $8,800 ↗

Chronograph — 1936

Case: silver, gold-plated, push-down case back, leather strap, Ø 34 mm

Movement: nickel-plated, côtes de Genève, column-wheel control of chronograph, manual winding

Remarks: chronograph with 30-minute counter; enamel dial

Estimated value: $6,100 ↗

Chronograph — 1934

Case: 18-karat yellow gold, push-down case back, leather strap, Ø 34 mm

Movement: Caliber 13.33, gold-plated, frosted finish, column-wheel control of chronograph, manual winding

Remarks: chronograph with 30-minute counter; dial later replaced by Longines

Estimated value: $6,100 ↗

Chronograph — 1937

Case: 18-karat yellow gold, tripartite, push-down case back, leather strap

Movement: Caliber 13ZN, gold-plated, frosted finish, column-wheel control of chronograph, matte chronograph steel components

Remarks: rare simple chronograph with 30-minute counter

Estimated value: $7,400 ↗

Chronograph — 1930

Case: 14-karat red gold, Ø 35 mm, tripartite, push-down case back, leather strap

Movement: Caliber 13.33, gold-plated, frosted finish, column-wheel control of chronograph, finest matte chronograph steel components

Remarks: fine one-button red gold chronograph with movable strap lugs and 30-minute counter; chronograph button integrated in the crown; time set by pushing the small button

Estimated value: $6,100 ↗

Chronograph — 1957

Case: 18-karat yellow gold, Ø 38 mm, bipartite, screw-down case back, gold link bracelet

Movement: Caliber 30CH, rhodium-plated, jewels set in chatons, column-wheel control of chronograph, finest matte steel components

Remarks: very rare chronograph with 30-minute counter and blue tachymeter scale; this watch was offered on a gold link bracelet

Estimated value: $8,800 ↗

Chronograph — 1934

Case: stainless steel, Ø 47 mm, tripartite, push-down case back, leather strap

Movement: Caliber 13ZN, gold-plated, frosted finish, column-wheel control of chronograph, matte steel components

Remarks: early chronograph with 30-minute counter; blue tachymeter and red telemeter scales

Estimated value: $6,800 ↗

Chronograph — 1946

Case: stainless steel, Ø 37 mm, tripartite, push-down case back, leather strap

Movement: Caliber 1268Z, rhodium-plated, finely finished steel components

Remarks: one-button chronometer with central 60-minute counter; extra-large minute chapter ring printed on dial

Estimated value: $3,250 ↗

Chronograph — 1959

Case: 18-karat yellow gold, push-down case back, leather strap, Ø 36 mm

Movement: Caliber 30CH, rhodium-plated, jewels set in chatons, column-wheel control of chronograph, 18 jewels, manual winding

Remarks: fine chronograph with 30-minute counter

Estimated value: $6,800 ↗

Chronograph — 1937

Case: stainless steel, Ø 37 mm, tripartite, push-down case back, leather strap

Movement: Caliber 13ZN, rhodium-plated, fausses côtes decoration, column-wheel control of chronograph, fine matte chronograph steel components, 18 jewels

Remarks: chronograph with 30-minute counter; this watch was sold on April 22, 1937, in Peru

Estimated value: $6,800 ↗

Chronograph — 1936

Case: stainless steel, Ø 36 mm, push-down case back, leather strap

Movement: Caliber 13ZN, rhodium-plated, fausses côtes decoration, column-wheel control of chronograph, fine matte chronograph steel components

Remarks: rare chronograph with 30-minute counter and minute chapter ring on dial perimeter; this watch was delivered to Longines, France

Estimated value: $8,100 ↗

Chronograph — 1940

Case: stainless steel, Ø 34 mm, tripartite, push-down case back, leather strap

Movement: Caliber 13ZN, rhodium-plated, fausses côtes decoration, column-wheel control of chronograph, fine matte chronograph steel components

Remarks: chronograph with 30-minute counter; telemeter scale on perimeter of dial and central tachymeter scale

Estimated value: $5,400 ↗

Chronograph — 1943

Case: stainless steel, Ø 36 mm, tripartite, push-down case back, leather strap

Movement: Caliber 13ZN, rhodium-plated, fausses côtes decoration, column-wheel control of chronograph, fine matte chronograph steel components

Remarks: chronograph with 30-minute counter; blue tachymeter and telemeter scales

Estimated value: $6,800 ↗

Chronograph — 1945

Case: stainless steel, Ø 39 mm, bipartite, screw-down case back, leather strap

Movement: Caliber 13ZN, rhodium-plated, fausses côtes decoration, column-wheel control of chronograph, fine matte chronograph steel components, 17 jewels

Remarks: extremely rare chronograph with central 60-minute counter and small 12-hour counter at 3 o'clock; chronograph minute hand in red

Estimated value: $13,500 ↗

Chronograph — 1942

Reference number: 92

Case: stainless steel, Ø 36 mm, tripartite, push-down case back, leather strap

Movement: Caliber 13ZN, rhodium-plated, fausses côtes decoration, column-wheel control of chronograph, fine matte chronograph steel components, 17 jewels

Remarks: early chronograph with 30-minute counter

Estimated value: $6,100 ↗

Chronograph — 1952

Case: 18-karat rose gold, Ø 37 mm, tripartite, push-down case back, leather strap

Movement: Caliber 30CH, rhodium-plated, fausses côtes decoration, jewels set in chatons, column-wheel control of chronograph, finest matte chronograph steel components

Remarks: rare chronograph with 30-minute counter and blue tachymeter scale; the case has especially striking strap lugs

Estimated value: $8,100 ↗

Chronograph — 1947

Case: stainless steel, Ø 38 mm, tripartite, screw-down case back, leather strap

Movement: Caliber 30CH, rhodium-plated, jewels set in chatons, column-wheel control of chronograph, finest matte chronograph steel components, 18 jewels

Remarks: chronograph with 30-minute counter; blue tachymeter scale; black telemeter scale

Estimated value: $6,800 ↗

Chronograph — 1957

Case: 18-karat red gold, Ø 37 mm, tripartite, push-down case back, leather strap

Movement: Caliber 30CH, rhodium-plated, jewels set in chatons, column-wheel control of chronograph, finest matte chronograph steel components, 18 jewels

Remarks: elegant chronograph with 30-minute counter and tachymeter scale; the strap lugs are very noticeable due to their shape

Estimated value: $8,100 ↗

Chronograph — 1950

Case: 18-karat yellow gold, Ø 37 mm, tripartite, push-down case back, leather strap

Movement: Caliber 13ZN, gold-plated, frosted finish, column-wheel control of chronograph, matte chronograph steel components

Remarks: gold chronograph with 30-minute counter and tachymeter scale

Estimated value: $6,100 ↗

Chronograph — 1942

Case: stainless steel, Ø 36 mm, tripartite, push-down case back, leather strap
Movement: Caliber 13ZN, gold-plated, frosted finish, column-wheel control of chronograph, matte chronograph steel components
Remarks: chronograph with 30-minute counter; two-tone dial; blue tachymeter scale; red telemeter scale
Estimated value: $6,800 ↗

Doctor's Chronograph — 1943

Case: stainless steel, push-down case back, leather strap, Ø 37 mm
Movement: Caliber 13ZN, gold-plated, frosted finish, column-wheel control of chronograph, manual winding
Remarks: chronograph with added pulsometer scale for easier pulse-taking
Estimated value: $7,500 ↗

Chronograph — 1948

Case: 14-karat yellow gold, Ø 35 mm, tripartite, push-down case back, leather strap
Movement: Caliber 30CH, rhodium-plated, jewels set in chatons, column-wheel control of chronograph, finest matte chronograph components, 17 jewels
Remarks: elegant chronograph with 30-minute counter and tachymeter scale
Estimated value: $7,500 ↗

Chronograph — 1944

Case: stainless steel, push-down case back, leather strap, Ø 35 mm
Movement: Caliber 13ZN, rhodium-plated, côtes de Genève, column-wheel control of chronograph, manual winding
Remarks: heavy chronograph with 30-minute counter; this watch was offered in its original box and with papers
Estimated value: $8,800 ↗

Military Chronograph — 1941

Case: stainless steel, screw-down case back, leather strap, Ø 37 mm
Movement: Caliber 13ZN, gold-plated, frosted finish, column-wheel control of chronograph, manual winding
Remarks: rare military pilot's chronograph with 30-minute counter
Estimated value: $10,800 ↗

Chronograph — 1945

Case: 18-karat yellow gold, push-down case back, leather strap, Ø 38 mm
Movement: Caliber 13ZN, rhodium-plated, côtes de Genève, column-wheel control of chronograph, manual winding
Remarks: chronograph with 30-minute counter
Estimated value: $7,500 ↗

Chronograph — 1939

Case: stainless steel, screw-down case back, leather strap, Ø 35 mm
Movement: Caliber 13ZN, gold-plated, frosted finish, column-wheel control of chronograph, manual winding
Remarks: chronograph with 30-minute counter; this watch was offered in its original box
Estimated value: $9,500 ↗

Chronograph — 1944

Case: 18-karat yellow gold, push-down case back, leather strap, Ø 38 mm
Movement: Caliber 13ZN, gold-plated, frosted finish, column-wheel control of chronograph, manual winding
Remarks: rare chronograph
Estimated value: $6,800 ↗

Men's Watch with Stop-Seconds

1951

Case: gold-plated, push-down case back, leather strap, Ø 31 mm

Movement: Caliber 12.68Z, rhodium-plated, manual winding

Remarks: rare men's watch with permanent re-settable chronograph seconds and sweep minute counter

Estimated value: $1,600 →

Chronograph

1951

Case: stainless steel, Ø 38 mm, bipartite, screw-down case back, leather strap

Movement: Caliber 30CH, rhodium-plated, jewels set in chatons, column-wheel control of chronograph, finest matte chronograph steel components, 18 jewels

Remarks: chronograph with 30-minute counter; blue tachymeter and red telemeter scales

Estimated value: $6,000 ↗

Men's Watch with Stop-Seconds and Flyback

1950

Case: stainless steel, push-down case back, leather strap, Ø 37 mm

Movement: Caliber 12.68Z, rhodium-plated, jewels set in chatons, manual winding

Remarks: extremely rare men's watch; sweep seconds; flyback function; central 60-minute counter

Estimated value: $10,100 ↗

Antimagnetic Chronograph

1951

Case: stainless steel, push-down case back, leather strap, Ø 37 mm

Movement: Caliber 30CH, nickel-plated, côtes de Genève, column-wheel control of chronograph, manual winding

Remarks: chronograph with 30-minute counter and restored dial

Estimated value: $6,800 ↗

Chronograph

1952

Case: 14-karat yellow gold, push-down case back, leather strap, Ø 35 mm

Movement: Caliber 30CH, nickel-plated, côtes de Genève, column-wheel control of chronograph, manual winding

Remarks: gold chronograph with 30-minute counter

Estimated value: $8,800 ↗

Doctor's Chronograph

1956

Case: stainless steel, push-down case back, leather strap, Ø 38 mm

Movement: Caliber 30CH, nickel-plated, jewels set in chatons, column-wheel control of chronograph, manual winding

Remarks: chronograph with added pulsometer scale for easier pulse-taking

Estimated value: $9,500 ↗

Doctor's Chronograph

1951

Case: 18-karat yellow gold, push-down case back, leather strap, Ø 35 mm

Movement: Caliber 30CH, rhodium-plated, jewels set in chatons, column-wheel control of chronograph, manual winding

Remarks: chronograph with added pulsometer scale for easier pulse-taking

Estimated value: $7,500 ↗

Chronograph

1966

Case: stainless steel, Ø 36 mm, tripartite, push-down case back, leather strap

Movement: Caliber 30CH, rhodium-plated, jewels set in chatons, column-wheel control of chronograph, finest matte chronograph steel components, 18 jewels

Remarks: chronograph with 30-minute counter; the watch has an added pulsometer scale for easier pulse-taking

Estimated value: $3,400 ↗

Vernier Chronograph — 1968

Case: stainless steel, screw-down case back, leather strap, 43 x 44 mm

Movement: Caliber 30CH, nickel-plated, jewels set in chatons, column-wheel control of chronograph, manual winding

Remarks: very rare chronograph with vernier hand for measuring tenths of a second

Estimated value: $3,400 ↗

Chronograph — 1970

Case: stainless steel, screw-down case back, leather strap, 44 x 44mm

Movement: Valjoux Caliber 726, nickel-plated, column-wheel control of chronograph, manual winding

Remarks: heavy chronograph with 30-minute and 12-hour counters

Estimated value: $1,900 →

Comet — 1975

Case: stainless steel, screw-down case back, stainless steel link bracelet, 34 x 41 mm

Movement: Caliber 702, rhodium-plated, manual winding

Remarks: rare men's watch with time displayed on rotating disks

Estimated value: $475 →

Ultra-Chron — 1978

Case: stainless steel, screw-down case back, stainless steel link bracelet, Ø 43 mm

Movement: Caliber 431, nickel-plated, automatic winding

Remarks: diver's watch with rotating inner bezel (flange)

Estimated value: $900 →

Chronograph — 1960

Case: stainless steel, push-down case back, leather strap, Ø 34 mm

Movement: Caliber 332, nickel-plated, column-wheel control of chronograph, 17 jewels, manual winding

Remarks: chronograph with 30-minute and 12-hour counters

Estimated value: $1,900 ↗

Diver's Automatic — 1965

Case: stainless steel, screw-down case back, leather strap, Ø 42 mm

Movement: Caliber 290, nickel-plated, automatic winding

Remarks: automatic diver's watch with rotating inner bezel (flange)

Estimated value: $2,000 ↗

Conquest XX Olympic Games 1972 — 1972

Case: stainless steel, screw-down case back, leather strap, Ø 36 mm

Movement: Caliber 334, nickel-plated, column-wheel control of chronograph, manual winding

Remarks: one-button chronograph; special model for the Olympic Games 1972 in Munich; Olympic engraving on case back

Estimated value: $800 →

Conquest Automatic — 1975

Case: stainless steel, screw-down case back, leather strap, Ø 43 mm

Movement: Caliber 431, nickel-plated, automatic winding

Remarks: diver's watch with rotating inner bezel (flange); ultra-fast frequency of 36,000 vph

Estimated value: $1,100 →

Mido

It took a great deal of courage and vision to found a watchmaker's workshop precisely in 1918, the final year of World War I. Watch technician Georges Schaeren must have possessed a little of both, for the watches he manufactured in the 1920s distinctly fit the zeitgeist of the era.

He created delicate ladies' watches with cases geometrically decorated in enamel and China lacquer or embellished with floral patterns. For the world of men, he had a great selection of unusually designed watches. The shapes of these watches were inspired by the striking radiator grills of the most well-known automobiles of his time. Thus, the wearer of a Mido was already expressing his or her preference for certain brands back then.

Schaeren and his brother made Mido a joint stock company in 1925, the latter taking over the business side. Thanks to a large demand for these unusual, modern watches, the company continued to grow. Soon, Mido was selling its watches in sixty-five countries spanning the globe and had to build a new factory. The brothers chose to do so in Biel, which remained the brand's headquarters until just a few years ago. Schaeren not only manufactured contemporary watches; he also brought a number of remarkable new developments to the market. In 1934 he presented to the world the Multifort, an automatic wristwatch that not only stayed water-resistant to 30 meters, but whose movement was also antimagnetic and protected by shock protection.

In 1936, the Permadur came to the market with its unbreakable mainspring. Three years later, Mido presented its Radiotime, a wristwatch that could be synchronized with the time signal emanating from the radio just by pressing a button.

One of Mido's most important inventions was the Aquadura gasket system, which the company had introduced in the 1930s. Thanks to special gasket rings made of cork, the watches remained evenly water-resistant for a long time. Even the steam of a hot sauna couldn't touch them. Another advantage of the Aquadura gaskets was that the watches could be made small enough to fit the fashion of that era. The system needed much less room than conventional gaskets.

The Multicenter chronograph was also unusual. It displayed not only chronograph seconds, but also minutes thanks to a sweep hand. The basis for this development was provided by a chronograph caliber made by Valjoux. Minerva calibers were also used in the chronographs.

The best-known Mido watch to this day is without a doubt the Ocean Star. Its monocoque case saw the movement being added through the dial side, with the crystal actually closing the case. This way, the watch did not need a screw-down case back.

Until 1971, Mido remained within the family. At that point it was taken over by General Watch Co., the brand conglomerate of the ASUAG-SSIH. This is how the brand also found its way to its current owner, the Swatch Group.

Multicenterchrono — 1950

Case: stainless-steel, screw-down case back, Ø 35 mm
Movement: gold-plated, manual winding
Remarks: chronograph with central 60-minute counter
Estimated value: $2,000 →

Multicenterchrono — 1950

Case: stainless steel case, gold-plated, screw-down case back, leather strap, Ø 34 mm
Movement: gold-plated, column-wheel control of chronograph, manual winding
Remarks: elegant chronograph with central 60-minute counter
Estimated value: $1,800 →

Multifort Superautomatic — 1950

Case: stainless steel, screw-down case back, stainless steel link bracelet, Ø 31 mm
Movement: Caliber 917P, nickel-plated, automatic winding
Remarks: early rotor automatic; this watch was offered in box and with sales tag
Estimated value: $550 →

Multicenterchrono — 1950

Case: stainless steel, screw-down case back, leather strap, Ø 35 mm
Movement: gold plated, column-wheel control of chronograph, manual winding
Remarks: chronograph with central 60-minute counter
Estimated value: $1,900 →

Multifort Datometer Super Automatic — 1948

Case: stainless steel, screw-down case back, leather strap, Ø 34 mm
Movement: Caliber D91713, rhodium-plated, automatic winding
Remarks: men's watch with hammer automatic; date
Estimated value: $550 ↘

Multicenterchrono — 1950

Case: stainless steel, screw-down case back, leather strap Ø 35 mm
Movement: gold-plated, column-wheel control of chronograph, manual winding
Remarks: chronometer with sweep minute counter
Estimated value: $1,900 →

Multifort Super Automatic — 1953

Case: stainless steel, screw-down case back, leather strap, Ø 29 mm
Movement: Caliber 717, rhodium-plated, 17 jewels, automatic winding
Remarks: small Mido hammer automatic in a water-resistant case
Estimated value: $200 →

Multicenterchrono — 1950

Case: stainless steel, screw-down case back, leather strap, Ø 35 mm
Movement: gold-plated, column-wheel control of chronograph, manual winding
Remarks: chronograph with sweep minute counter; buttons have star-shaped grooves for better handling
Estimated value: $1,900 →

archive photo

Minerva

Minerva, the Roman goddess of the arts and crafts, is who the owners of this company chose to name their business for. They envisioned the goddess holding her hands over their small company, one that would soon create a good reputation for itself with excellent chronograph movements.

But long before these owners asked the Roman goddess for her aid, the company had been founded in 1858 in Villeret by the brothers Charles-Yvan and Hippolyte Robert as a small factory for assembling movements. The *ébauches* were purchased from the factory known as FHF in Fontainemelon. Twenty years later, Charles and Georges Robert took over the management of this *établisseur* factory, and in 1885 their brother Yvan-Robert joined them as the third manager. The three chose an arrow-shaped version of the letters RF for Robert Frères as their logo and had it registered in 1887.

Around the turn of the century, they even dared to manufacture their own calibers for pocket watches. In 1908, the Robert brothers presented their first movement to include a chronograph function, Caliber 9CH. With this, they laid the cornerstone for their future development, the manufacture of high-quality chronograph calibers.

The aforementioned moniker Minerva was one they only chose to use starting in 1923, one of the most important years in the company's history for a number of reasons. First, the company's owners changed its name to Fabrique Minerva, Robert Frères SA, and second, they presented their first chronograph caliber for wristwatches, Caliber 13-20 CH. The watches that they outfitted with this new movement became the new top models of the small *manufacture*.

In the 1930s it might have appeared that the goddess Minerva had turned her back on the company—it bore the full brunt of the world economic crisis, which was in full swing. The founding family left the company and sold it to watch technician Jacques Pelot and mechanic Charles Haussener. The pair fought with all their might for the company's survival and developed numerous new calibers. Under their management, Minerva specialized more and more in chronographs. In 1940, Pelot's nephew, André Frey, entered the company and soon bought the whole thing. Under his management, one of the most important Minerva movements was developed, Caliber 48 featuring subsidiary seconds. Frey passed away in September 2004, four years after the sale of the company to an Italian investor group who planned a great comeback.

In late 2006, Richemont took over, and today Minerva exclusively makes movements for the group's Montblanc brand.

One-Button Chronograph

1930

Case: stainless steel, push-down case back, leather strap, Ø 42 mm

Movement: rhodium-plated, côtes de Genève, column-wheel control of chronograph, manual winding

Remarks: chronograph with 30-minute counter

Estimated value: $4,700 ↗

Chronograph

1935

Case: stainless steel, Ø 42 mm, tripartite, push-down case back, leather strap

Movement: rhodium-plated, fausses côtes decoration, column-wheel control of chronograph, fine matte chronograph steel components, manual winding

Remarks: early large one-button chronograph with 30-minute counter and tachymeter scale

Estimated value: $3,800 →

German Air Force Chronograph

1940

Case: stainless steel, screw-down case back, leather strap

Movement: frosted finish, gold-plated, manual winding, column-wheel control of chronograph

Remarks: rare pilot's chronograph of the German air force with 30-minute counter and tachymeter scale

Estimated value: $3,100 ↗

Chronograph

1940

Reference number: VB712

Case: stainless steel, Ø 31 mm, bipartite, screw-down case back, leather strap

Movement: rhodium-plated, column-wheel control of chronograph, finely finished steel chronograph components

Remarks: small chronograph with 30-minute counter

Estimated value: $3,400 →

Chronographe Antimagnétique

1940

Case: stainless steel, push-down case back, leather strap, Ø 35 mm

Movement: nickel-plated, column-wheel control of chronograph, manual winding

Remarks: chronograph with 30-minute and 12-hour counters

Estimated value: $2,000 →

Antimagnetic Chronograph

1940

Case: 18-karart yellow gold, push-down case back, leather strap, Ø 33 mm

Movement: gold-plated, frosted finish, column-wheel control of chronograph, manual winding

Remarks: fine gold chronograph with 30-minute counter

Estimated value: $3,400 →

Chronograph

1940

Case: stainless steel, Ø 36 mm, bipartite, screw-down case back, leather strap

Movement: rhodium-plated, fausses côtes decoration, column-wheel control of chronograph, fine matte steel chronograph components

Remarks: sporty chronograph with 30-minute and 12-hour counters; complete calendar with date hand; window display for weekdays and months

Estimated value: $4,100 →

Split-Seconds Chronograph

1943

Case: stainless steel, push-down case back, leather strap, Ø 43 mm

Movement: nickel-plated, côtes de Genève, double column-wheel control of chronograph, manual winding

Remarks: rare pilot's chronograph with split-seconds function, 30-minute counter; luminous numerals

Estimated value: $16,000 ↗

Chronograph — 1945

Reference number: 1335

Case: stainless steel, screw-down case back, leather strap, Ø 35mm

Movement: nickel-plated, column-wheel control of chronograph, manual winding

Remarks: chronograph with 30-minute counter

Estimated value: $2,300 →

Chronograph — 1945

Case: 18-karat yellow gold, Ø 34 mm, tripartite, push-down case back, leather strap

Movement: rhodium-plated, fine matte steel chronograph components, polished screws

Remarks: elegant gold chronograph with 30-minute counter

Estimated value: $3,100 →

Chronograph — 1945

Case: stainless steel, Ø 35 mm, bipartite, screw-down case back, leather strap

Movement: rhodium-plated, column-wheel control of chronograph, finely finished steel chronograph components

Remarks: sporty chronograph with 30-minute counter; additional decimal scale on the dial

Estimated value: $2,450 →

Chronograph — 1945

Reference number: 1335

Case: stainless steel, Ø 35 mm, bipartite, screw-down case back, leather strap

Movement: Caliber 13.20, gold-plated, frosted finish, column-wheel control of chronograph, finely finished steel chronograph components, polished screws, 17 jewels

Remarks: chronograph with 30-minute counter and tachymeter scale

Estimated value: $2,450 →

Chronograph — 1948

Case: stainless steel, Ø 35 mm, bipartite, screw-down case back, leather strap

Movement: rhodium-plated, fausses côtes decorations, column-wheel control of chronograph, fine matte steel chronograph components

Remarks: chronograph with 30-minute counter

Estimated value: $2,450 →

Chronograph with Complete Calendar — 1955

Case: stainless steel, screw-down case back, leather strap, Ø 36 mm

Movement: Valjoux Caliber 723, nickel-plated, column-wheel control of chronograph, 17 jewels, manual winding

Remarks: chronometer with 30-minute and 12-hour counters; complete calendar

Estimated value: $3,375 ↗

Chronograph — 1965

Case: stainless steel, Ø 36 mm, tripartite, screw-down case back, leather strap

Movement: Valjoux Caliber 72, rhodium-plated, decorated, column-wheel control of chronograph, fine matte steel chronograph components

Remarks: sporty chronograph with 30-minute and 12-hour counters

Estimated value: $2,450 →

Chronograph — 1970

Case: stainless steel, screw-down case back, leather strap, Ø 38 mm

Movement: Valjoux Caliber 72, rhodium-plated, column-wheel control of chronograph, manual winding

Remarks: fine chronograph with 30-minute and 12-hour counters

Estimated value: $1,350 →

Wine: From Grape to Glass

"The ultimate gift for any wine lover." —*Touring & Tasting Magazine*

Tailor-made for the contemporary wine consumer who drinks what he or she likes, this vividly illustrated text discusses not only awe-inspiring vintages, but also unknown wines from countries only recently included on the wine maps of the world. Half the book is devoted to the wine-making process itself; the other half examines the best wines of the world, country by country, and guides the reader to an understanding of the intricacies of wine tasting and appreciation.

By Jens Priewe
1,000 full-color illustrations
256 pages · 9 x 11⅞ in. · Hardcover
ISBN-13: 978- 0-7892-0917-7
$45.00

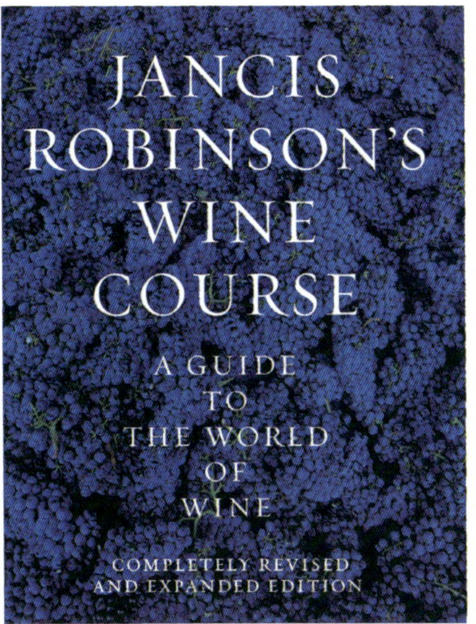

Jancis Robinson's Wine Course: A Guide to the World of Wine

"She has an encyclopedic grasp of her subject and doesn't put a foot wrong… a splendid introduction to the world of wine." —Stephen Brook, *Decanter Magazine*

"Witty, brilliant, authoritative." —Robert M. Parker, Jr., *The Wine Advocate*

Dedicated to ensuring that you get the most out of every glass, Jancis Robinson's Wine Course explains how to taste and store wine, what to serve on special occasions at home, and how to order the best value from a restaurant wine list. Robinson also describes the distinctive characteristics of hundreds of different grape varieties and studies the traditional and innovative methods employed in the creation of great wines.

By Jancis Robinson
170 full-color illustrations
352 pages · 8 x 11 in. · Paperback
ISBN-13: 978-0-7892-0883-5
$29.95

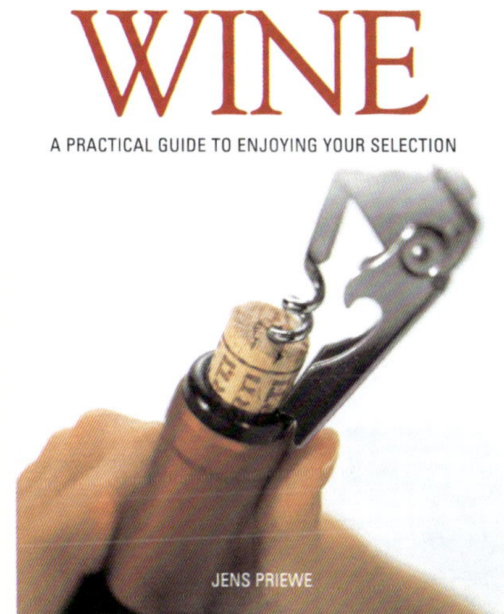

Wine: A Practical Guide to Enjoying Your Selection

Following the success of the author's *Wine: From Grape to Glass*, this new book offers a treasury of invaluable information for the contemporary wine consumer who would like to know more about caring for wine and serving it properly. In this essential guide, internationally acclaimed expert Jens Priewe fully describes, with lively text and striking photographs, the correct way to handle wine, from uncorking and tasting to serving and storing.

By Jens Priewe
200 full-color illustrations
128 pages · 7¾ x 10 in. · Hardcover
ISBN-13: 978-0-7892-0745-6
$32.50

Published by ABBEVILLE PRESS
137 Varick Street, New York, NY 10013
1-800-ARTBOOK (in U.S. only)
Also available wherever fine books are sold
Visit us at www.abbeville.com

Movado

usual 30-minute totalizer, the movement was outfitted with a 60-minute counter at 3 o'clock. The new chronograph, presented in 1939, gave birth to an evolution, Caliber 95M, which featured an additional 12-hour counter.
In 1969, Movado lost its entrepreneurial independence and had to merge with Zenith, and in 1984, the brand was sold to the North Amer-ican Watch Corporation, a company that also owns the brand Concord.

Without a doubt the Museum Watch is the best-known of all Movado's models: it owes its name to the fact that it has a permanent spot in the Museum of Modern Art in New York. The simple watch, the dial of which is only decorated by a so-called sun dot at 12 o'clock, was created by American designer Nathan George Horwitt in 1947. Collectors also still search out the ergonomically domed Polyplan watches with shaped movements and a crown at 12 o'clock.

Movado was founded in 1881 in Le Chaux-de-Fonds by Alsatian Achille Ditisheim, who began with the manufacture of pocket watches in his little workshop. Convinced of their brother's quick success, Léopold and Isidor soon joined him. The three of them founded L.A.I. Ditisheim. For purposes of recognition, they had different names registered to sell their watches. The most successful of these names came to the fore in 1903: Movado. This word was taken from the artificial world language Esperanto and means "always in motion." The greatest advantage of this name was the easy pronunciation in various languages, lending it high recognition.

When in 1905 the fourth brother, Isaac, entered the company, it was renamed Ditisheim & Frères. Seemingly inspired by the name Movado, the company also tried to go down new paths with its movements and watches. Attention to detail was visible especially on the movements. Thus, all bridges and cocks were designed in either a strict geometrical manner or flowing harmoniously. In 1912, the Polyplan was presented, the shaped movement of which had a base plate that was rounded on both sides. The mechanism's curved shape ensured that it perfectly fit the strongly domed watch case. In 1914, Movado presented a trench watch that featured an additional grille over the sensitive crystal. The grille could be raised by a button located on the case at 6 o'clock so that the soldier could more easily read the time.

Before Movado attacked the development of a true chronograph, the Chronoplan was introduced in 1937, a short-term timer precise to the minute with a double rotating bezel. Outfitted with two reference markers, one was turned to the position of the hour hand and the other to the minute hand's position. Thus, longer measurements of time could easily be read using the watch's normal hands.

In developing its own chronograph caliber, Movado also went its own way. Instead of making a completely new movement, the developers took a tried-and-tested manually wound caliber and built a chronograph module for it, which was positioned on the back of the slightly altered mechanism. Caliber 90M's special element lay in its counter: instead of the

Chronomètre — 1920

Case: Sterling silver, push-down case back, leather strap, 26 x 45 mm

Movement: rhodium-plated, côtes des Genève, jewels set in chatons, 15 jewels, manual winding

Remarks: very early wristwatch (appx. 1920) in navette-shaped case; two soldered silver wires serve as the strap lugs

Estimated value: $800 →

Polyplan — 1930

Case: 18-karat white gold, hinged case back, leather strap, 22 x 56 mm

Movement: Movado Caliber 400, nickel-plated, decorated, manual winding

Remarks: interesting men's watch in a strongly domed rectangular case; the crown is located between the lugs at 12 o'clock to give the case's shape a more elongated appearance

Estimated value: $7,500 →

Chronomètre — 1925

Case: 18-karat white gold, push-down case back, leather strap, 27 x 29 mm

Movement: nickel-plated, côtes de Genève, jewels set in chatons, 17 jewels, manual winding

Remarks: early white gold wristwatch in Art Deco design; subsidiary seconds; chronometer; movement adjusted in four positions

Estimated value: $1,600 →

Pilot's Watch Chronomètre — 1935

Case: stainless steel, push-down case back, rotating bezel, Ø 38 mm

Movement: Movado Caliber 75, rhodium-plated, jewels set in chatons, 15 jewels, manual winding

Remarks: extremely rare early pilot's watch; certified chronometer; movement adjusted in four positions

Estimated value: $2,100 →

Men's Watch — 1940

Case: 9-karat yellow gold, push-down case back, leather strap, 25 x 37 mm

Movement: Movado Caliber 510, nickel-plated, côtes de Genève, jewels set in chatons, manual winding

Remarks: men's watch in rectangular case; movement adjusted in four positions

Estimated value: $300 →

Curvex — 1945

Case: stainless steel, leather strap, 23 x 41 mm

Movement: nickel -plated, côtes de Genève, jewels set in gold chatons, 15 jewels, manual winding

Remarks: rare men's watch in a domed Curvex case; double signature Huber/Movado leads to the assumption that this watch is a special edition for Munich retailer Huber; movement adjusted in four positions

Estimated value: $950 →

Polygraf — 1960

Case: stainless steel, push-down case back, leather strap, Ø 36 mm

Movement: nickel-plated, manual winding

Remarks: extremely rare men's watch with world time display (two-tone 24-hour ring and additional 24-hour hand); this watch was offered with the original Movado sales tag

Estimated value: $2,700 →

Men's Watch — 1945

Case: stainless steel, screw-down case back, leather strap, Ø 32 mm

Movement: Movado Caliber 261, nickel-plated, jewels set in chatons, manual winding

Remarks: exceptional wristwatch with unusual two-tone hour display: the light-colored ring shows the hours from 7 to 18, while the dark ring shows them from 1 to 6 and 19 to 24; numerals on the dark hour ring are printed with luminous substance

Estimated value: $340 ↘

Tempomatic — 1945

Case: stainless steel, push-down case back, leather strap, Ø 37 mm

Movement: Movado Caliber 226, nickel-plated, automatic winding

Remarks: men's watch with hammer automatic; this watch was offered in its original box

Estimated value: $800 →

Chronomètre — 1940

Case: stainless steel, push-down case back, leather strap, Ø 31 mm

Movement: Movado Caliber 75, rhodium-plated, côtes de Genève, jewels set in chatons, 15 jewels, manual winding

Remarks: simple wristwatch chronometer regulated in 4 positions

Estimated value: $400 →

Automatic — 1950

Case: gold-plated stainless steel, screw-down case back, leather strap, Ø 35 mm

Movement: Movado Caliber 221A, nickel-plated, automatic winding

Remarks: simple men's watch with hammer automatic movement

Estimated value: $400 ↘

Men's Watch — 1950

Case: 18-karat red gold, push-down case back, leather strap, Ø 34 mm

Movement: nickel-plated, polished edges, jewels set in chatons, manual winding

Remarks: simple men's watch with subsidiary seconds

Estimated value: $550 ↘

Automatic — 1955

Case: stainless steel, screw-down case back, leather strap, Ø 33 mm

Movement: Movado Caliber 202, nickel-plated, automatic winding

Remarks: simple steel watch with exceptional date display; both the date and the weekday are displayed in the subsidiary seconds dial at 6 o'clock; hammer automatic movement

Estimated value: $700 ↘

Calendoscope — 1950

Case: gold-plated, stainless steel push-down case back, leather strap, Ø 34 mm

Movement: Movado Caliber 123, rhodium-plated, 15 jewels, manual winding

Remarks: simple men's watch with date window at 3 o'clock

Estimated value: $200 ↘

Automatic — 1955

Case: 18-karat yellow gold, screw-down case back, leather strap, Ø 33 mm

Movement: Movado Caliber 115, rhodium-plated, automatic winding

Remarks: simple men's watch with hammer automatic and subsidiary seconds

Estimated value: $550 ↘

Antimagnetic — 1945

Case: stainless steel, screw-down case back, leather strap, Ø 35 mm

Movement: Movado Caliber 75, rhodium-plated, jewels set in chatons, manual winding

Remarks: simple men's watch with subsidiary seconds

Estimated value: $400 ↘

Calendar Watch   1948

Case: 18-karat red gold, push-down case back, leather strap, Ø 34 mm

Movement: nickel-plated, jewels set in chatons, manual winding

Remarks: simple red gold watch with subsidiary seconds and complete calendar; sweep date hand; window displays for weekday (9 o'clock) and month (3 o'clock)

Estimated value: $1,900 →

Calendar Watch   1950

Case: 18-karat yellow gold, push-down case back, leather strap, Ø 32 mm

Movement: Movado Caliber 470, nickel-plated, jewels set in chatons, manual winding

Remarks: men's watch with complete calendar; sweep date hand; window displays for weekday (9 o'clock) and month (3 o'clock); red stones replace eight hour markers

Estimated value: $1,600 →

Calendar Watch with Moon Phase   1948

Case: 18-karat rose gold, screw-down case back, leather strap, Ø 34 mm

Movement: Movado Caliber 473, nickel-plated, manual winding

Remarks: men's watch with subsidiary seconds, complete calendar and moon phase; sweep date hand; window displays for weekday and month; moon phase display located in subsidiary seconds dial

Estimated value: $3,000 →

Sport Calendomatic   1940

Case: gold-plated stainless steel, screw-down case back, leather strap, Ø 34 mm

Movement: Movado Caliber 223, nickel-plated, decorated, automatic winding

Remarks: simple men's watch with hammer automatic movement; complete calendar; sweep date hand; window displays for day and month

Estimated value: $1,800 →

Chronograph   1950

Case: stainless steel, push-down case back, leather strap, Ø 36 mm

Movement: Movado Caliber C95M, nickel-plated, with column-wheel control of chronograph, manual winding

Remarks: simple chronograph with 60-minute and 12-hour counters; tachymeter scale

Estimated value: $2,700 →

Chronograph   1945

Case: stainless steel, push-down case back, leather strap, Ø 35 mm

Movement: Movado Caliber 90, rhodium-plated, column-wheel control of chronograph, manual winding

Remarks: simple wristwatch chronograph with off-center 60-minute counter and tachymeter scale

Estimated value: $3,400 →

Chronograph   1945

Case: stainless steel, screw-down case back, leather strap, Ø 33 mm

Movement: Movado Caliber 90, nickel-plated, decorated, column-wheel control of chronograph, manual winding

Remarks: men's chronograph with off-center 60-minute counter, unusual for a chronograph

Estimated value: $3,000 →

Doctor's Watch   1948

Case: 14-karat yellow gold, screw-down case back, leather strap, Ø 33 mm

Movement: Movado Caliber 470, nickel-plated, manual winding

Remarks: rare so-called doctor's chronograph: simple hacking mechanism with reset possibility; pulsometer for easier pulse-taking

Estimated value: $3,400 →

Automatic — 1955

Case: 18-karat yellow gold, push-down case back, leather strap, Ø 35 mm

Movement: Movado Caliber 115, silver-plated, automatic winding

Remarks: simple men's watch with hammer automatic and subsidiary seconds; unusual dial with guilloché zone in the center

Estimated value: $1,100 ↘

Men's Watch — 1950

Case: gold-plated, push-down case back, leather strap, Ø 34 mm

Movement: Movado Caliber 365, nickel-plated, jewels set in chatons, manual winding

Remarks: remarkably designed dial

Estimated value: $300 ↘

Chronograph — 1950

Case: stainless steel, screw-down case back, leather strap, Ø 34 mm

Movement: Movado Caliber 95, nickel-plated, decorated, column-wheel control of chronograph, manual winding

Remarks: wristwatch chronograph with off-center 60-minute and 12-hour counters

Estimated value: $2,300 →

Chronograph Super Sub Sea — 1965

Case: stainless steel, screw-down case back, rotating bezel, leather strap, Ø 41 mm

Movement: Movado Caliber 146H, rhodium-plated, frosted finish, manual winding

Remarks: chronograph with 30-minute and 12-hour counters; light-colored subdials; all 12 numerals printed on subdials; additional tachymeter scale

Estimated value: $1,600- →

Chronograph Datron HS 360 — 1975

Case: stainless steel, screw-down case back, leather strap, Ø 37 mm

Movement: Movado Caliber 3019PHC, nickel-plated, column-wheel control of chronograph, automatic winding

Remarks: heavy automatic chronograph outfitted with the legendary Zenith El Primero beating at 36,000 vph; unusual arrangement of date window at 12 o'clock

Estimated value: $945 →

Super Sub Sea/Datron HS360 — 1975

Case: stainless steel, screw-down case back, rotating bezel, leather strap, Ø 42 mm

Movement: Movado Caliber 3019PHC, nickel-plated, column-wheel control of chronograph, automatic winding

Remarks: heavy automatic chronograph outfitted with the legendary Zenith El Primero beating at 36,000 vph; unusual arrangement of date window at 12 o'clock

Estimated value: $2,000 →

Chronograph Astronic — 1975

Case: stainless steel, screw-down case back, stainless steel link bracelet, 38 x 45 mm

Movement: Movado Caliber 3019PHF, rhodium-plated, column-wheel control of chronograph, automatic winding

Remarks: chronograph (Caliber El Primero) with 30-minute and 12-hour counters; complete calendar and moon phase

Estimated value: $2,000 →

Chronograph Datron HS360 — 1975

Case: stainless steel, screw-down case back, stainless steel link bracelet, Ø 43 mm

Movement: Movado Caliber 3019PHC, nickel-plated, column-wheel control of chronograph, automatic winding

Remarks: heavy automatic chronograph outfitted with the legendary Zenith El Primero beating at 36,000 vph; unusual arrangement of date window at 12 o'clock

Estimated value: $1,500 →

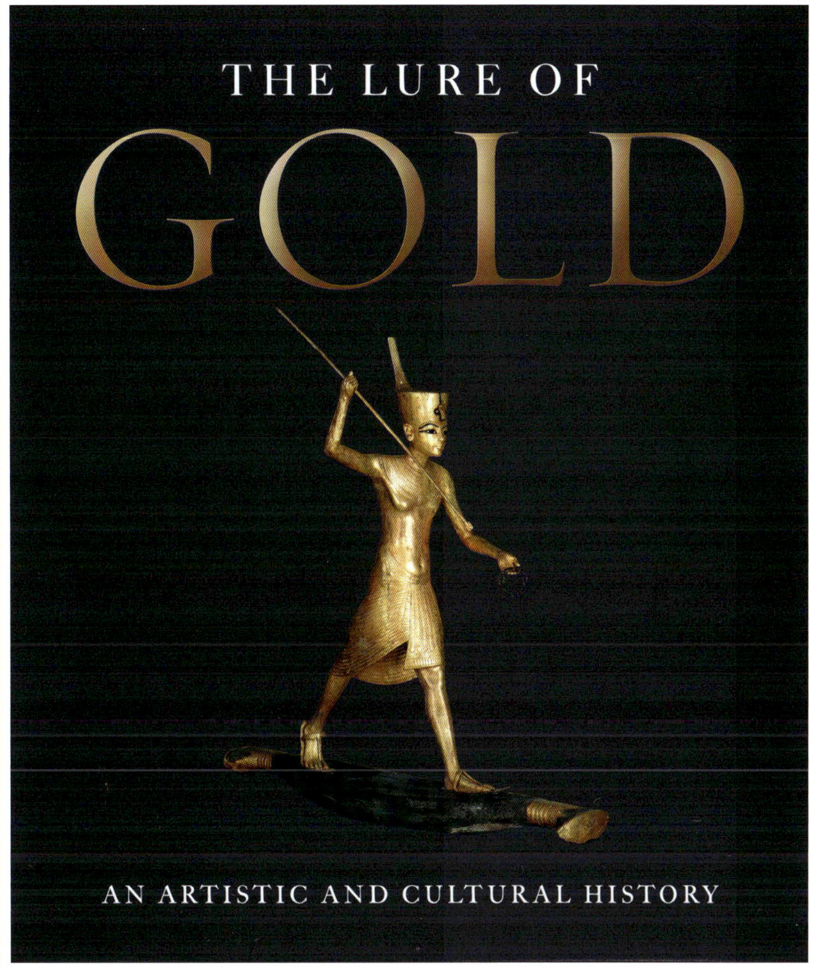

The Lure of Gold: An Artistic and Cultural History

The richly illustrated story of how gold, the world's most beautiful element, has influenced the art, economy, and society of every civilization, this beautiful volume explains how people throughout time have mined and refined gold (creating jewelry, religious objects, and diverse works of art) and used

By Hans-Gert Bachmann
285 full-color illustrations
280 pages · 10½ x 11¹³⁄₁₆ in.
Cloth · ISBN-13: 978-0-7892-0900-9
$75.00

Published by ABBEVILLE PRESS
137 Varick Street, New York, NY 10013
1-800-ARTBOOK (in U.S. only)
Also available wherever fine books are sold
Visit us at www.abbeville.com

Ulysse Nardin

Today, he would be called a young entrepreneur: at the age of nineteen, the highly gifted watchmaker Ulysse Nardin founded his own company in Le Locle. His first watches were delivered to Piguet Frères, who were at the time among the world's best chronometer manufacturers. After his apprenticeship, young Nardin used the opportunity to educate himself further in the presence of reputable masters William Dubois and Louis Richard. His father, also a watchmaker, had at first given him the capital to found his watch company and later even got a job as an employee of his son. From 1846 on, Ulysse Nardin made and sold watches under his own name. His repeaters and pocket chronometers were especially popular in South America, Mexico, and the United States. After Ulysse Nardin's death at the age of fifty-three, his only son Paul-David took over the company. In 1860, Ulysse and Paul-David Nardin made their first marine chronometer, an object that would become the great specialty of the brand

Ulysse Nardin (1823 - 1876)

for years to come. The anchor in the company's logo originated in this marine chronometer. Marine chronometers by Ulysse Nardin were always among the most precise watches of their time.

Early on, Ulysse Nardin had also begun to manufacture wristwatches. Alongside normal three-handed watches, these were above all chronographs. To make them, the company used purchased movements, mainly Valjoux and Venus calibers.

After the death of Paul-David in 1920, his sons Alfred, Ernest, and Gaston took over the company's management and turned it into a joint stock company. The Ulysse Nardin brand survived both world wars and the world economic crisis without problem, but the introduction of the quartz marine chronometer in the 1960s broke the company's back. The beginning of the 1970s saw the end of the more than 100-year-old family tradition. Only the name and the run-down headquarters in Le Locle remained of the once proud company.

These last bits of Ulysse Nardin were purchased in 1983 by Rolf Schnyder, who was able to resuscitate the brand. In a certain way, history repeated itself, for an exceptional watchmaking talent once again heavily contributed to the renewed success: Dr. Ludwig Oechslin. Schnyder discovered him as a young apprentice watchmaker in Lucerne. Today, the multitalented Oechslin has completed doctorates in several subjects and is the curator of the watch museum in La Chaux-de-Fonds.

Pilot's Chronograph A.R.A. Navigacion — 1925

Case: silver, silver cuvette, leather strap, Ø 39 mm

Movement: nickel-plated, côtes des Genève, column-wheel control of chronograph, manual winding

Remarks: very early crown-button chronograph with 30-minute counter; enamel dial with obvious origins in pocket watch; numerals inlaid with luminous substance; two soldered silver wires serve as strap lugs; hinged case back

Estimated value: $6,100 ↗

Chronograph — 1920

Case: 18-karat yellow gold, gold cuvette, leather strap, Ø 38 mm

Movement: nickel-plated, côtes de Genève, column-wheel control of chronograph, manual winding

Remarks: very early crown-button chronograph with 30-minute counter; enamel dial; hinged case back; two pocket watch bows serve as strap lugs

Estimated value: $5,400 ↗

Chronograph — 1930

Case: yellow gold, gold cuvette, leather strap, Ø 34 mm

Movement: nickel-plated, côtes de Genève, column-wheel control of chronograph, manual winding

Remarks: very early crown-button chronograph with 30-minute counter and double tachymeter scale; outer tachymeter scale covers speeds down to 60 km/h; scale in center of enamel dial covers speed measured down to 10 km/h

Estimated value: $4,700 ↗

Chronograph — 1925

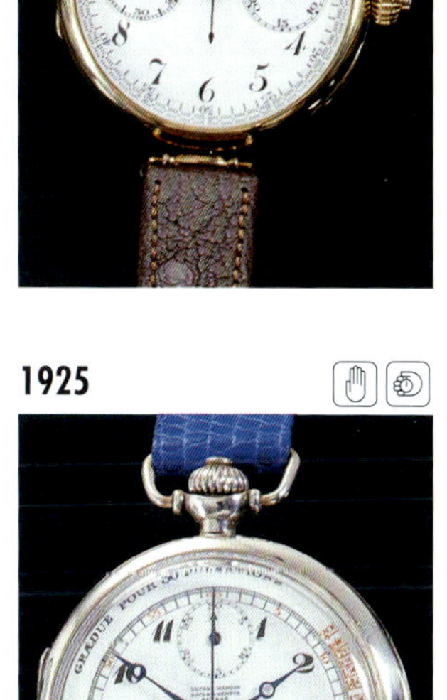

Case: silver, silver cuvette, leather strap, Ø 38 mm

Movement: nickel-plated, column-wheel control of chronograph, manual winding

Remarks: very early wristwatch chronograph with 30-minute counter; enamel dial; the button for the chronograph functions is integrated into the crown; across from the crown is a second bow used for lugs; hinged case back

Estimated value: $4,700 ↗

Chronograph — 1925

Case: 18-karat yellow gold, hinged case back, leather strap, Ø 37 mm

Movement: nickel-plated, côtes de Genève, with column-wheel control of chronograph, manual winding

Remarks: early one-button chronograph with 30-minute counter and double tachymeter scale; soldered gold bows serve as lugs

Estimated value: $4,700 ↗

Chronograph — 1925

Case: 18-karat yellow gold, push-down case back, leather strap, Ø 37 mm

Movement: gold-plated, frosted finish, column-wheel control of chronograph, manual winding

Remarks: early crown button chronograph with 30-minute counter and tachymeter scale; tachymeter scale snail on perimeter of enamel dial allows speed measurements down to 20 km/h

Estimated value: $7,500 ↗

Chronograph — 1925

Case: 18-karat yellow gold, push-down case back, leather strap, Ø 34 mm

Movement: nickel-plated, column-wheel control of chronograph, manual winding

Remarks: elegant one-button chronograph with 30-minute counter and additional pulsometer scale for easier pulse-reading; enamel dial; comparatively small subdials

Estimated value: $6,700 ↗

Chronograph — 1930

Case: 18-karat yellow gold, push-down case back, leather strap, Ø 33 mm

Movement: nickel-plated, column-wheel control of chronograph, manual winding

Remarks: early one-button chronograph with 30-minute scale and tachymeter scale; tachymeter scale snail on perimeter of enamel dial allows speed measurements down to 40 km/h

Estimated value: $6,000 ↗

Chronograph — 1930

Case: stainless steel, push-down case back, leather strap, 35 x 41 mm

Movement: nickel-plated, column-wheel control of chronograph, manual winding

Remarks: fine, early one-button chronograph with 30-minute counter at 3 o'clock; cushion-shaped stainless steel case; enamel dial

Estimated value: $4,700 ↗

Chrongrafo Medical — 1925

Case: stainless steel, push-down case back, leather strap, Ø 37 mm

Movement: nickel-plated, column-wheel control of chronograph, manual winding

Remarks: early one-button chronograph with 30-minute counter and pulsometer scale; enamel dial; movable lugs

Estimated value: $6,000- ↗

Doctor's Chronograph — 1930

Case: 18-karat yellow gold, push-down case back, leather strap, 32 x 41 mm

Movement: rhodium-plated, côtes de Genève, column-wheel control of chronograph, manual winding

Remarks: fine Doctor's Chronograph with 30-minute counter and pulsometer scale

Estimated value: $9,500 ↗

Chronograph — 1940

Case: 18-karat yellow gold, push-down case back, leather strap, 32 x 37 mm

Movement: nickel-plated, column-wheel control of chronograph, manual winding

Remarks: elegant one-button chronograph with 30-minute counter in cushion-shaped gold case

Estimated value: $6,700 ↗

Chronograph — 1945

Case: stainless steel, push-down case back, leather strap, Ø 38 mm

Movement: rhodium-plated, côtes de Genève, column-wheel control of chronograph, manual winding

Remarks: chronograph with 30-minute and 12-hour counters

Estimated value: $2,700 →

Chronograph — 1925

Case: 18-karat yellow gold, push-down case back, leather strap, Ø 35 mm

Movement: rhodium-plated, côtes de Genève, column-wheel control of chronograph, manual winding

Remarks: very elegant one-button chronograph with 30-minute counter; tachymeter and telemeter scales; gold case with covered lugs

Estimated value: $7,500 ↗

Chronograph — 1938

Case: 18-karat yellow gold, push-down case back, leather strap, Ø 37 mm

Movement: nickel-plated, column-wheel control of chronograph, manual winding

Remarks: chronograph with 30-minute counter at 3 o'clock; for South American market; moveable lugs are especially striking

Estimated value: $4,700 ↗

Chronograph — 1945

Case: 18-karat red gold, push-down case back, leather strap, Ø 33 mm

Movement: nickel-plated, manual winding

Remarks: simple chronograph with 30-minute counter

Estimated value: $3,400 ↗

Doctor's Chronograph — 1945

Case: 18-karat yellow gold, push-down case back, leather strap, Ø 37 mm

Movement: rhodium-plated, column-wheel control of chronograph, manual winding

Remarks: elegant one-button chronograph with 30-minute counter; pulsometer and tachymeter scales; covered lugs

Estimated value: $3,400 ↗

Chronograph — 1945

Case: 18-karat yellow gold, Ø 34 mm, tripartite, push-down case back, leather strap

Movement: rhodium-plated, finely finished, column-wheel control of chronograph, finely finished steel chronograph components

Remarks: fine chronograph with 30-minute counter; telemeter scale; tachymeter scale in center of dial

Estimated value: $6,000 →

Chronograph — 1945

Case: 18-karat red gold, push-down case back, leather strap, Ø 37 mm

Movement: rhodium-plated, côtes de Genève, column-wheel control of chronograph, manual winding

Remarks: simple gold chronograph with 30-minute counter; this watch was offered in original box

Estimated value: $3,400 ↗

Chronograph — 1945

Case: 18-karat yellow gold, Ø 36 mm, tripartite, push-down case back, leather strap

Movement: rhodium-plated, column-wheel control of chronograph, fine matte steel chronograph components, polished screws, 17 jewels, regulated in one position

Remarks: gold chronograph with 30-minute counter; complete calendar with date hand; weekday and month in window displays

Estimated value: $3,500 →

Chronograph — 1945

Case: stainless steel, Ø 35 mm, bipartite, screw-down case back, leather strap

Movement: rhodium-plated, column-wheel control of chronograph, fine matte steel chronograph components

Remarks: elegant chronograph with 30-minute and 12-hour counters

Estimated value: $4,700 →

Chronograph — 1945

Case: stainless steel, push-down case back, leather strap, Ø 35 mm

Movement: nickel-plated, column-wheel control of chronograph, manual winding

Remarks: simple chronograph with 45-minute counter

Estimated value: $2,400 →

Chronograph — 1945

Case: stainless steel, 35 mm, bipartite, screw-down case back, leather strap

Movement: rhodium-plated, column-wheel control of chronograph, fine matte steel chronograph components

Remarks: sporty chronograph with 30-minute counter and three-color dial; tachymeter and telemeter scales

Estimated value: $3,500 →

Chronograph

Case: 18-karat yellow gold, Ø 34 mm, tripartite, push-down case back, leather strap

Movement: rhodium-plated, finely finished, column-wheel control of chronograph, mirror-polished screws

Remarks: fine gold men's chronograph with 30-minute counter; telemeter scale and additional tachymeter scale snail

Estimated value: $5,400

Chronograph — 1948

Case: stainless steel, screw-down case back, leather strap, Ø 35 mm

Movement: nickel-plated, column-wheel control of chronograph, manual winding

Remarks: chronograph with 30-minute counter at 3 o'clock; numerals inlaid with luminous substance for better legibility

Estimated value: $4,700 ↗

Chronograph — 1948

Case: stainless steel, screw-down case back, leather strap, Ø 29 mm

Movement: nickel-plated, column-wheel control of chronograph, manual winding

Remarks: very small chronograph with 30-minute counter and polished escapement

Estimated value: $2,700 →

Chronograph with Complete Calendar — 1960

Case: stainless steel, screw-down case back, leather strap, Ø 36 mm

Movement: Caliber N13HQ, nickel-plated, côtes de Genève, column-wheel control of chronograph, manual winding

Remarks: chronograph with 30-minute and 12-hour counters; complete calendar; sweep date hand; window displays for weekday and month

Estimated value: $3,700 ↗

Chronograph with Complete Calendar — 1950

Case: 18-karat red gold, Ø 35 mm, tripartite, push-down case back, leather strap

Movement: red gold-plated, column-wheel control of chronograph, finely finished steel chronograph components

Remarks: fine red gold chronograph with 30-minute and 12-hour counters; complete calendar with date hand; window displays for weekday and month

Estimated value: $3,700 →

Chronograph — 1970

Case: stainless steel, screw-down case back, leather strap, Ø 38 mm

Movement: Caliber N13B, gold-plated, côtes de Genève, column-wheel control of chronograph, manual winding

Remarks: heavy chronograph with 30-minute and 12-hour counters; tachymeter scale on bezel

Estimated value: $2,700 ↗

Complete Calendar — 1965

Case: 18-karat yellow gold, Ø 27 mm, push-down case back, leather strap

Movement: Caliber 31.3.071, gold-plated, fausses côtes decoration, mirror-polished screws

Remarks: small gold ladies' watch with complete calendar; hand displays for date, weekday, and month; moon phase display in window at 12 o'clock

Estimated value: $2,000 →

Chronograph with Complete Calendar — 1980

Case: 18-karat yellow gold, Ø 39 mm, tripartite, exhibition case back, leather strap

Movement: Valjoux Caliber 88, gold-plated, fausses côtes decorations, column-wheel control of chronograph, highly polished screws, fine matte steel chronograph components

Remarks: fine gold chronograph with 30-minute and 12-hour counters; complete calendar with date hand; window displays for weekday and month; moon phase display at 6 o'clock; the movement can been seen through the exhibition case back

Estimated value: $4,000 →

Automatic Chronometer — 1980

Case: stainless steel, screw-down case back, leather strap, Ø 36 mm

Movement: Caliber NB1100, nickel-plated, 25 jewels, automatic winding

Remarks: wristwatch chronometer with ultra-fast frequency of 36,000 vph; date window at 3 o'clock; this watch was offered with a small chronometer certificate

Estimated value: $1,600 ↗

Nivada

Founded in 1925, this company was officially called Wüllmann Schneider, Nivada SA. Nivada remained a so-called *établisseur*: instead of investing in the development of its own movements, it relied on robust purchased technology. Thus, in most of Nivada's watches it was contemporary ETA calibers that did the work. Despite less exclusivity, these mechanisms achieved very precise rates. Even the movements bought from Phénix SA in Porrentruy were convincing in their precision.

Thanks to this business relationship, there were often exceptionally interesting calibers in Nivada watches that are among the most sought-after classics. An example of this would be the Nivada Rollamatic (some of the watches were also known as the Rollador), outfitted with Phénix Caliber 200 with its rolling bearing in the rotor.

A milestone in the history of Nivada was the presentation of the Reglavit, the only water-resistant watch model whose rate could be regulated by a screw on the case back. The advantage of this was that the case didn't have to be opened to regulate the watch, and water resistance was not endangered since the gaskets remained untouched.

The Antarctic model developed for an expedition headed for the ice attained world fame thanks to the similarity of the bearded man in the company's advertising to Cuban revolutionary leader Fidel Castro. The advertisement was immediately banned and all printed matter confiscated on the Caribbean island, which was still under the Batista regime's rule. Naturally, that made the watch even more interesting… Nivada's extremely robust watches wrote their own chapter in the industry's history. Whether diver's watches like the thousand-meter water-resistant Depthmaster whose case looked like the Panerai Luminor's or the Depthomatic outfitted with a depth gauge—those searching for watches for extreme use always found what they needed at Nivada.

Various alarm wristwatches were also included in Nivada's program. Alongside models outfitted with AS calibers, Nivada also had exclusive alarms powered by Lémania movements. Since Nivada was a big customer of MSR subsidiary Phénix, the company was also allowed to offer the legendary Vulcain Cricket alarm under its own name. A slightly different variation, the Wanderer, was also produced for the American brand Croton.

Croton Watch Co. was Nivada's American distribution partner, known as Horowitz & Son in New York. These two companies worked so closely together that Nivada in America was not only distributed under its own name and Croton's name, but also at times under the double moniker Croton Nivada.

Nivada remained a family business for its entire duration. Schneider's son Max successfully took over the management of the company, and the fiftieth anniversary of Nivada in 1976 was honored with a special catalogue. Nivada went bankrupt during the quartz crisis, however, and the rights to its name were sold.

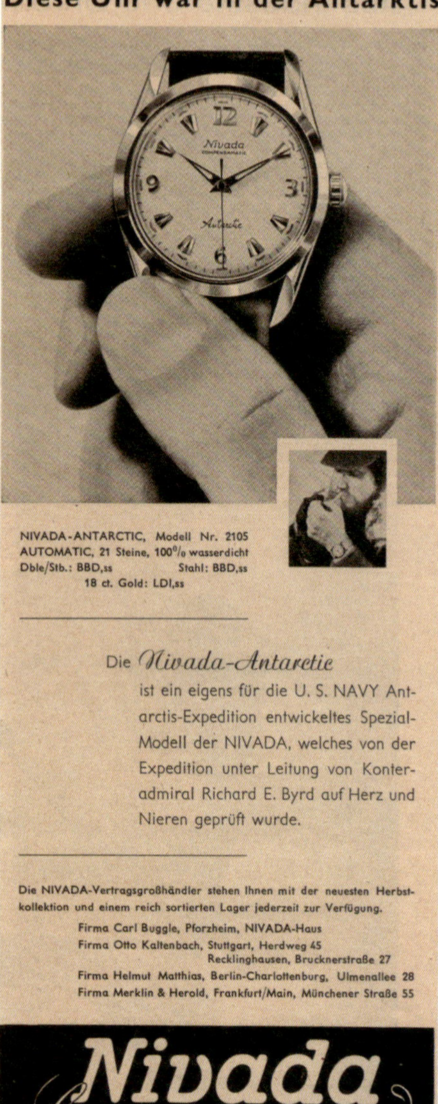

Visualmatic — 1948

Case: 18-karat yellow gold, screw-down case back, leather strap, Ø 35 mm

Movement: Caliber AS 1382N, rhodium-plated, automatic winding

Remarks: rare automatic men's watch with power reserve indicator (36 hours) at 12 o'clock

Estimated value: $1,600 →

Men's Watch — 1950

Case: 18-karat white gold, push-down case back, leather strap, Ø 33 mm

Movement: Caliber R 34, red gold-plated, manual winding

Remarks: white gold men's watch with diamond-set dial; this watch carries the double signature "Croton Nivada" of the brand's U.S. distribution

Estimated value: $475 →

Antarctic Chronometer — 1960

Case: 18-karat yellow gold, screw-down case back, leather strap, Ø 34 mm

Movement: ETA Caliber 2452, red gold-plated, 17 jewels, regulated in 4 positions, automatic winding

Remarks: gold chronometer regulated in 4 positions

Estimated value: $1,100 →

Chronomaster Aviator Sea Diver — 1969

Case: stainless steel, screw-down case back, rotating bezel, leather strap, Ø 38 mm

Movement: Valjoux Caliber 23, nickel-plated, column-wheel control of chronograph, manual winding

Remarks: sporty chronograph with 30-minute counter

Estimated value: $550 →

Chronomaster Aviator Sea Diver — 1969

Case: stainless steel, screw-down case back, rotating bezel, leather strap, Ø 38 mm

Movement: Valjoux Caliber 23, nickel-plated, column-wheel control of chronograph, manual winding

Remarks: chronograph with 30-minute counter; this watch bears the signature "Croton" for the brand's U.S. distribution

Estimated value: $550 →

Chronomaster Aviator Sea Diver — 1969

Case: stainless steel, screw-down case back, rotating bezel, leather strap, Ø 40 mm

Movement: Landeron Caliber 248, nickel-plated, manual winding

Remarks: large chronograph with 30-minute counter; added regatta scale on the rotating bezel

Estimated value: $475 →

Alertamatic — 1971

Case: gold-plated, stainless steel screw-down case back, leather strap, 44 x 38.6 mm

Movement: Lémania Caliber 2980, rhodium-plated, 19 jewels, automatic winding

Remarks: automatic alarm wristwatch; this movement is the same as Omega Caliber 980 (Memomatic)

Estimated value: $800 →

archive photo

Depthomatic — 1969

Case: stainless steel, screw-down case back, leather strap, Ø 45 mm

Movement: ETA Caliber 2472, rhodium-plated, 25 jewels, automatic winding

Remarks: rare diver's watch with integrated depth gauge; the display is triggered by water filling a hose encircling the dial, which creates a thin colored strip (like on a thermometer); maximum depth shown is 200 meters

Estimated value: $1,100 →

archive photo

Omega

Today it may be hard to believe, but the watch giant Omega began its career as a one-man operation. In 1848, twenty-three-year-old Louis Brandt founded a so-called *comptoir d'établissage* in La Chaux-de-Fonds, a workshop for the assembly of watch components with a distribution and sales department. The success of Brandt's watches was not long in coming thanks to their attractive appearance and high quality. These timekeepers were in demand even in foreign countries, and Brandt spent long weeks traveling through Europe to ensure delivery. Brandt's sons Louis Paul and César continued the active distribution policy of their father and moved the company headquarters to Biel in 1880. One of the reasons for the move was the city's better travel options. Additionally, the city's canals offered water power free of charge, something that was of great importance to a mechanical workshop at the time. Finally, the Brandt brothers planned to manufacture their own watches with their own movements. They successfully realized this plan, and by 1889 their company was the largest watch factory in Switzerland.

Although the Brandts joined forces with other manufacturers now and then for individual

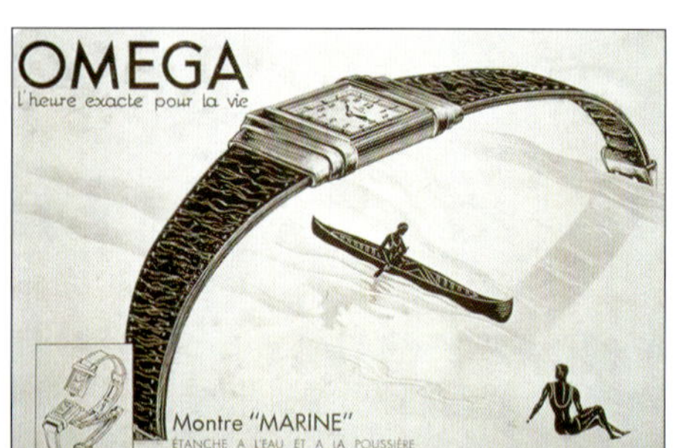

models, the focus of the company was the development of autonomous watches and movements. In 1894, an especially successful caliber, which was far ahead of most of its competitor products thanks to its simple design and the exchangeability of all components, lent the company the name it would carry to the present day: Omega, the last letter of the Greek alphabet. By 1903, all other brand names used by the company up to that point had been given up, and Paul-Emile Brandt took over the management of Omega, retaining control for fifty years.

Paul-Emile Brandt's top priority was always precision. For this reason, in 1917 the British air force took an Omega on as the official service watch, and one year later the American army followed suit. In 1919, an Omega won the precision competition of the Neuchâtel Observatory for the first—but not the last—time. This success became the basis for a new watch line, the Constellation Chronometer, which for many years gave Omega the top position in the number of chronometers tested. In 1967, Omega received its millionth official rate certificate for a chronometer. The numerous models containing the legendary 30-millimeter caliber are a chapter in and of themselves and were sold for decades in various incarnations. They dominated the official chronometer competitions at observatories for a long time.

The most famous of all Omega models is surely the Speedmaster. This somewhat reserved looking chronograph actually became the official equipment of NASA astronauts thanks to its robustness and precision and was thus already a legend before taking part in the first moon landing. Even in the area of sports timing, this brand made a name for itself. Omega was and is still the official timekeeper for important sporting events such as the Olympic Games. Omega has covered just about every niche with its watches. An automatic alarm wristwatch that could set the wake-up time precisely to the minute was even in the program: Memomatic. The Biel-based company did not shy away from the world of water, either, and created a diver's watch line with the tell-all name Seamaster. The most professional of the Omega diver's watches is model 600, also called Ploprof (for *plongeur professionel*, or "pro diver"). This watch proved itself on the wrists of professional divers employed by Comex in 252-meter depths. Even more popular is the Seamaster Professional, which can even boast a film and television career. In the 1920s, the company merged with Tissot to become SSIH (Société Suisse de l'Industrie Horlogère). Combining this with ASUAG (which also owned Longines), under the leadership of Nicolas G. Hayek, the SMH (Société Suisse de Microélectronique et Horlogerie) was created, which later became the Swatch Group.

Men's Watch — 1936

Case: 18-karat yellow gold, push-down case back, leather strap, Ø 38 mm

Movement: Caliber 30 T2, red gold-plated, manual winding

Remarks: fine men's watch

Estimated value: $800 →

Men's Watch — 1945

Case: stainless steel, push-down case back, leather strap, Ø 35 mm

Movement: Caliber 30 T2, nickel-plated, manual winding

Remarks: simple men's watch

Estimated value: $300 →

Seamaster Automatic — 1953

Case: gold-plated stainless steel, push-down case back, leather strap, Ø 35 mm

Movement: Caliber 354, red gold plated, automatic winding

Remarks: hammer automatic; gold-plated case with hidden strap lugs

Estimated value: $475 →

Men's Watch — 1935

Case: stainless steel, push-down case back, leather strap, 31 x 35 mm

Movement: Caliber 26.5 SOB T2, silver plated, manual winding

Remarks: rare fine men's watch in a light shaped case

Estimated value: $550 →

Men's Watch — 1940

Case: stainless steel, push-down case back, leather strap, Ø 35 mm

Movement: Caliber 30 T2, silver-plated, manual winding

Remarks: elegant men's watch with unusual hour hand

Estimated value: $550 →

Seamaster XVI — 1956

Case: 18-karat red gold, push-down case back, leather strap, Ø 34 mm

Movement: Caliber 471, red gold-plated, automatic winding

Remarks: rare red gold Seamaster XVI in honor of the sixteenth Olympic Games in Melbourne; engraved Olympic cross on case back

Estimated value: $3,400 ↗

Men's Watch — 1925

Case: stainless steel, push-down case back, leather strap, Ø 30 mm

Movement: Caliber 26.5 SOB T2, silver-plated, manual winding

Remarks: early small men's watch with sports car motif on dial

Estimated value: $1,100 →

Men's Watch Automatic — 1945

Case: stainless steel, push-down case back, leather strap, Ø 35 mm

Movement: Caliber 30.10 RA PC, red gold-plated, automatic winding

Remarks: early hammer automatic

Estimated value: $550 →

Men's Watch — 1955

Case: 18-karat yellow gold, push-down case back, leather strap, 24 x 37 mm

Movement: Caliber 302, red gold-plated, manual winding

Remarks: fine men's watch

Estimated value: $800 →

Men's Watch Automatic — 1943

Case: 14-karat yellow gold, push-down case back, leather strap, 31 x 40 mm

Movement: Caliber 342, red gold-plated, automatic winding

Remarks: gold shaped watch with hammer automatic movement

Estimated value: $1,900 ↗

Men's Watch — 1947

Case: gold-plated, push-down case back, leather strap, 27 x 40 mm

Movement: Caliber 470, red gold-plated, 17 jewels, automatic winding

Remarks: rare men's watch with automatic movement

Estimated value: $300 →

Men's Watch Automatic — 1959

Case: 18-karat yellow gold, push-down case back, leather strap, 27 x 35 mm

Movement: Caliber 571, red gold-plated, 24 jewels, regulated in 2 positions, automatic winding

Remarks: fine men's watch; regulated twice

Estimated value: $900 →

Men's Design Watch — 1952

Reference number: 6532

Case: 14-karat yellow gold, push-down case back, leather strap, 25 x 36 mm

Movement: Caliber 302, red gold-plated, 17 jewels, manual winding

Remarks: extremely rare men's watch with extravagant design case

Estimated value: $2,200 →

Marine — 1930

Case: stainless steel, push-down case back, leather strap, 24 x 34 mm

Movement: Caliber 19.4 T2, silver-plated, manual winding

Remarks: rare early water-resistant men's watch with double case

Estimated value: $4,100 ↗

Men's Watch — 1934

Case: stainless steel, push-down steel case back, leather strap, 25 x 39 mm

Movement: Caliber T17, nickel-plated, shaped movement, manual winding

Remarks: early Omega men's watch

Estimated value: $550 →

Men's Watch — 1927

Case: 14-karat yellow gold, leather strap, 21 x 37 mm

Movement: Caliber T17, nickel-plated, shaped movement, manual winding

Remarks: rare men's watch

Estimated value: $675 →

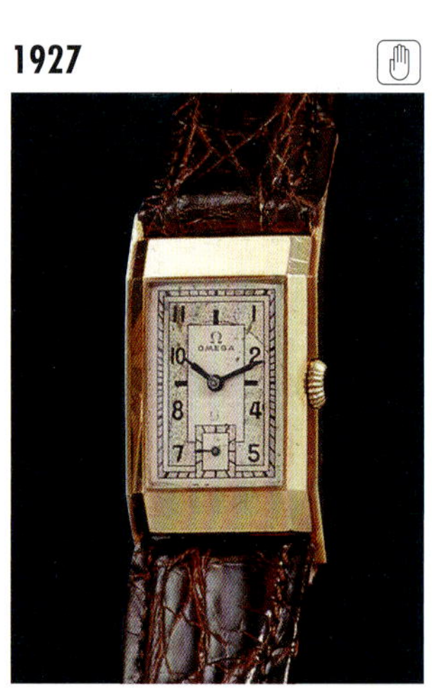

Men's Watch — 1927

Case: steel, 22 x 39 mm, tripartite, push-down case back, leather strap

Movement: nickel-plated, finely finished, polished screws, 15 jewels

Remarks: rare early wristwatch in an asymmetrical case

Estimated value: $1,500 →

Marine — 1930

Case: 14-karat yellow gold, 36 x 23 mm, tripartite, leather strap

Movement: rhodium-plated, finely finished, polished screws, 15 jewels

Remarks: rare wristwatch in Omega's patented marine case; this watch was produced with the signature "Udall & Ballou" for the jeweler of the same name in New York

Estimated value: $6,800 ↗

Men's Watch — 1954

Case: stainless steel, 31 x 40 mm, bipartite, push-down case back, leather strap

Movement: Caliber 344, red gold plated, pendulum oscillating weight, index fine adjustment

Remarks: automatic watch in gold design case

Estimated value: $1,800 ↗

Men's Watch — 1952

Case: 14-karat yellow gold, 31 x 40 mm, bipartite, push-down case back, leather strap

Movement: Caliber 344, red gold-plated, pendulum oscillating weight, index fine adjustment

Remarks: automatic watch in design case

Estimated value: $2,200 ↗

Cosmic — 1935

Case: 18-karat yellow gold, push-down case back, leather strap, Ø 34 mm

Movement: Caliber 27 DL PC, gold-plated, manual winding

Remarks: men's watch with complete calendar and moon phase

Estimated value: $4,100 ↗

Cosmic — 1938

Case: stainless steel push-down case back, leather strap, Ø 35 mm

Movement: Caliber 27DL PC, red gold-plated, manual winding

Remarks: men's watch with complete calendar and moon phase

Estimated value: $4,100 ↗

Cosmic — 1940

Case: 18-karat red gold, push-down case back, leather strap, Ø 35 mm

Movement: Caliber 381, red gold-plated, manual winding

Remarks: men's watch with complete calendar and moon phase

Estimated value: $4,750 ↗

Cosmic — 1948

Case: 18-karat yellow gold, push-down case back, leather strap, Ø 34 mm

Movement: Caliber 381, red gold-plated, manual winding

Remarks: men's watch with complete calendar and moon phase; this watch was offered in its original box and with certificate

Estimated value: $4,100 ↗

Cosmic — 1946

Reference number: 2473

Case: 14-karat yellow gold, Ø 34 mm, tripartite, push-down case back

Movement: Caliber 27DLPC, red gold-plated, polished screws, 17 jewels

Remarks: rare beautiful calendar watch with complete calendar, date hand, display of weekday and month in window; subsidiary seconds and moon phase display at 6 o'clock

Estimated value: $3,800 ↗

Cosmic — 1946

Reference number: 2471/1

Case: stainless steel, Ø 35 mm, tripartite, push-down case back, leather strap

Movement: Caliber 27DLPC, red gold-plated, polished screws, 17 jewels

Remarks: steel calendar watch with complete calendar, date hand, display of weekday and month in window; subsidiary seconds and moon phase display at 6 o'clock

Estimated value: $4,750 ↗

Cosmic — 1950

Reference number: 2471

Case: stainless steel, Ø 35 mm, tripartite, push-down case back, leather strap

Movement: Caliber 381, red gold-plated

Remarks: Cosmic model with complete calendar, date hand, display of weekday and month in window; moon phase at 6 o'clock

Estimated value: $3,800 ↗

Cosmic — 1953

Case: 18-karat yellow gold, Ø 35 mm, tripartite, push-down case back, leather strap

Movement: Caliber 381, red gold-plated

Remarks: fine gold Cosmic model with complete calendar, date hand, display of weekday and month in window; subsidiary seconds and moon phase display at 6 o'clock

Estimated value: $3,900 ↗

Cosmic — 1950

Case: 14-karat rose gold, 32 x 44 mm, bipartite, push-down case back, leather strap

Movement: Caliber 381, gold-plated, polished screws

Remarks: rare Cosmic model with complete calendar, date hand, display of weekday and month in window; subsidiary seconds and moon phase display at 6 o'clock

Estimated value: $5,400 ↗

Men's Watch — 1936

Case: 18-karat red gold, push-down case back, leather strap, Ø 37 mm

Movement: Caliber 30 T2 PC, red gold-plated, manual winding

Remarks: elegant men's watch

Estimated value: $3,400 ↗

Chronomètre — 1942

Case: stainless steel, push-down case back, leather strap, Ø 36 mm

Movement: Caliber 30 T2 SC RG, red-plated, manual winding

Remarks: extremely rare wristwatch chronometer with Guillaume balance

Estimated value: $3,500 →

Automatic Chronometer Centenaire — 1945

Case: 18-karat yellow gold, push-down case back, yellow gold Milanaise bracelet, Ø 34 mm

Movement: Caliber 30.10 RA PC JUB, red gold-plated, automatic winding

Remarks: extremely rare anniversary chronometer with hammer automatic movement in celebration of Omega SA's 100th anniversary

Estimated value: $6,100 →

Centenaire — 1948

Reference number: OT 2500
Case: 18-karat yellow gold, push-down case back, leather strap, Ø 35 mm
Movement: Caliber 30.10 RA PC, red gold-plated, automatic winding
Remarks: extremely rare anniversary model with hammer automatic movement in celebration of Omega SA's 100th anniversary
Estimated value: $4,700 ↗

Constellation Automatic Chronometer — 1952

Case: 18-karat yellow gold, screw-down case back, yellow gold Milanaise bracelet, Ø 35 mm
Movement: Caliber 354, red gold-plated, regulated in 6 positions, automatic winding
Remarks: heavy gold chronometer with hammer automatic movement regulated in six positions
Estimated value: $3,000 →

Seamaster Automatic Chronometer — 1951

Case: stainless steel, screw-down case back, leather strap, Ø 34 mm
Movement: Caliber 342, red gold-plated, regulated in 6 positions, automatic winding
Remarks: chronometer with hammer automatic movement regulated in six positions
Estimated value: $2,500 →

Seamaster Automatic Chronometer — 1943

Case: stainless steel, screw-down case back, leather strap, Ø 34 mm
Movement: Caliber 352, red gold-plated, regulated in 6 positions, automatic winding
Remarks: unworn rare wristwatch chronometer; this watch was offered in its original box
Estimated value: $2,300 →

Seamaster Automatic Chronometer — 1950

Case: 14-karat yellow gold, screw-down case back, leather strap, Ø 34 mm
Movement: Caliber 352, red gold-plated, automatic winding
Remarks: men's watch with hammer automatic and chronometer certificate
Estimated value: $2,200 →

Cloisonné — 1963

Case: 18-karat yellow gold, Ø 34 mm, tripartite, push-down case back, leather strap
Movement: Caliber 285, red gold-plated, polished screws, 17 jewels
Remarks: rare gold men's watch with 30 mm caliber; cloisonné-technique enamel dial; this watch was offered with an original Omega gold buckle
Estimated value: $13,500 ↗

Superlative Chronometer — 1933

Reference number: 2562
Case: 14-karat yellow gold, push-down case back, leather strap, Ø 37 mm
Movement: Caliber 30 T2 SC RG, manual winding
Remarks: gold wristwatch chronometer
Estimated value: $2,700 ↗

Seamaster Chronometer for Türler — 1950

Reference number: 2577/2520
Case: 18-karat yellow gold, screw-down case back, leather strap, Ø 34 mm
Movement: Caliber 352, red gold-plated, 17 jewels, regulated in 6 positions, automatic winding
Remarks: rare automatic men's chronometer with signature of Swiss jeweler Türler
Estimated value: $2,100 →

Chronomètre — 1946

Case: 18-karat yellow gold, Ø 33 mm, tripartite, push-down case back, leather strap
Movement: Caliber 30 T2 RG, red gold-plated, 17 jewels, regulated in 6 positions
Remarks: gold chronometer with 30 mm caliber
Estimated value: $4,100 ↗

Chronomètre — 1949

Reference number: 2517-2
Case: stainless steel, Ø 35 mm, tripartite, push-down case back, leather strap
Movement: Caliber 352, red gold-plated, polished screws, pendulum oscillating weight, index fine adjustment, 17 jewels, regulated in 6 positions
Remarks: rare automatic chronometer in stainless steel case
Estimated value: $2,300 ↗

Seamaster Automatic Chronometer — 1950

Reference number: 2577/2520 SC
Case: 18-karat yellow gold, Ø 34 mm, bipartite, screw-down case back, leather strap
Movement: Caliber 352, red gold-plated, polished screws, pendulum oscillating weight, index fine adjustment, 17 jewels
Remarks: gold Constellation chronometer
Estimated value: $2,200 ↗

Chronometer — 1947

Reference number: 30 T2 SCRG
Case: 18-karat yellow gold, Ø 35 mm, tripartite, push-down case back, leather strap
Movement: Caliber 30 T2 SCRG, red gold-plated, mirror-polished screws, gold screw compensation balance, fine adjustment, 16 jewels
Remarks: elegant chronometer with 30 mm caliber
Estimated value: $3,400 ↗

Constellation Automatic Chronometer — 1962

Case: 18-karat red gold, screw-down case back, leather strap, Ø 35 mm
Movement: Caliber 551, red gold-plated, automatic winding
Remarks: rare wristwatch chronometer; this watch was offered in its original box and with its original gold buckle
Estimated value: $4,700 ↗

Model — 1946

Case: 18-karat yellow gold, Ø 33 mm, tripartite, push-down case back, leather strap
Movement: Caliber 30 T2 RG, red gold-plated
Remarks: gold wristwatch chronometer with 30 mm caliber
Estimated value: $3,400 ↗

Automatic Chronometer Constellation — 1958

Case: stainless steel, push-down case back, leather strap, Ø 35 mm
Movement: Caliber 505, gold-plated, automatic winding
Remarks: Constellation chronometer model
Estimated value: $950 →

Automatic Chronometer Constellation — 1963

Case: 18-karat yellow gold, screw-down case back, leather strap, Ø 34 mm
Movement: Caliber 551, red gold-plated, 24 jewels, regulated in 6 positions, automatic winding
Remarks: chronometer with movement regulated in six positions; this watch was offered in its original box and with its original buckle
Estimated value: $3,400 →

Constellation Automatic Chronometer 1975

Case: gold plated stainless steel, screw-down case back, leather strap, Ø 35 mm
Movement: Caliber 751, red gold-plated, 24 jewels, regulated in 6 positions, automatic winding
Remarks: chronometer with movement regulated in six positions
Estimated value: $1,100 →

Constellation Automatic Chronometer 1970

Case: gold-plated, stainless steel push-down case back, leather strap, Ø 38 mm
Movement: Caliber 751, red gold-plated, 24 jewels, regulated in 6 positions, automatic winding
Remarks: extra-large Constellation chronometer model with movement regulated in six positions
Estimated value: $1,100 ↗

Automatic Chronometer Constellation 1968

Case: 18-karat yellow gold, screw-down case back, gold link bracelet, Ø 35 mm
Movement: Caliber 564, gold-plated, automatic winding
Remarks: Constellation chronometer model; this watch was offered with original box and certificate
Estimated value: $3,500 ↗

Constellation Automatic Chronometer 1966

Case: yellow gold, screw-down case back, leather strap, Ø 35 mm
Movement: Caliber 561, gold plated, automatic winding
Remarks: Constellation chronometer model
Estimated value: $2,000 →

Constellation Automatic Chronometer 1967

Case: 18-karat yellow gold, screw-down case back, yellow gold Milanaise bracelet, Ø 35 mm
Movement: Caliber 564, red gold-plated, 24 jewels, regulated in 6 positions, automatic winding
Remarks: men's watch with movement regulated in six positions; this watch was offered in original box and with original papers
Estimated value: $3,500 ↗

Constellation De Luxe 1963
Automatic Chronometer

Case: 18-karat yellow gold, screw-down case back, leather strap, Ø 34 mm
Movement: Caliber 561, red gold-plated, 24 jewels, regulated in 6 positions, automatic winding
Remarks: Constellation chronometer model with movement regulated in six positions
Estimated value: $2,400 →

Constellation 1966

Case: 18-karat yellow gold, Ø 34 mm, tripartite, screw-down case back, leather strap
Movement: Caliber 564, red gold-plated, polished screws, winding rotor, 24 jewels, regulated in 6 positions
Remarks: gold Constellation chronometer model with date window at 3 o'clock
Estimated value: $2,100 ↗

Constellation 1966

Case: 18-karat yellow gold, Ø 35 mm, tripartite, screw-down case back, gold bracelet
Movement: Caliber 561, red gold-plated, polished screws, winding rotor, index fine adjustment, 24 jewels, regulated in 6 positions
Remarks: elegant gold men's watch with crown recessed in case; this watch was offered with its original gold bracelet
Estimated value: $3,400 ↗

Constellation
1961

Case: stainless steel, gold plated, Ø 34 mm, tripartite, screw-down case back, leather strap

Movement: Caliber 551, red gold-plated, polished screws, winding rotor, index fine adjustment, 24 jewels, regulated in 6 positions

Remarks: Constellation chronometer model in gold-plated stainless steel case

Estimated value: $1,200 ↗

Seamaster Automatic Chronometer
1953

Reference number: 2520 SC

Case: 18-karat yellow gold, bipartite, screw-down case back, leather strap

Movement: Caliber 351, red gold-plated, pendulum oscillating weight, fine adjustment, 17 jewels

Remarks: gold Seamaster chronometer model; this watch was manufactured on August 13, 1953 and sold in the United States

Estimated value: $950 ↗

Seamaster Automatic Chronometer
1967

Reference number: ST 168.022

Case: stainless steel, tripartite, screw-down case back, stainless steel link bracelet

Movement: Caliber 564, red gold-plated, polished screws, winding rotor

Remarks: stainless steel chronometer; this watch was manufactured on October 3, 1967, and sold in Italy

Estimated value: $1,600 ↗

Seamaster Automatic Chronometer Officially Certified
1971

Case: 18-karat yellow gold, screw-down case back, yellow gold link bracelet, Ø 37 mm

Movement: red gold-plated, automatic winding

Remarks: extremely rare chronometer; this watch was offered in an Omega box

Estimated value: $4,700 ↗

Seamaster Automatic Chronometer
1967

Reference number: CD 168.022

Case: stainless steel / 14-karat gold-plated, tripartite, screw-down case back, leather strap

Movement: Caliber 564, red gold-plated, polished screws, winding rotor

Remarks: Seamaster chronometer model in a gold-plated stainless steel case; date window at 3 o'clock; this watch was sold on December 21, 1967, in the United States

Estimated value: $1,350 ↗

Ranchero
1959

Case: stainless steel, push-down case back, leather strap, Ø 36 mm

Movement: Caliber 267, red gold-plated, manual winding

Remarks: rare men's watch with manually wound movement

Estimated value: $3,400 ↗

Ranchero
1957

Case: 18-karat yellow gold, push-down case back, leather strap, Ø 35 mm

Movement: Caliber 267, red gold-plated, manual winding

Remarks: rare Omega Ranchero in yellow gold with a white dial

Estimated value: $3,000 ↗

Railmaster
1956

Reference number: 2914-1 SC

Case: stainless steel, screw-down case back, leather strap, Ø 38 mm

Movement: Caliber 284, red gold-plated, 17 jewels, manual winding

Remarks: anti-magnetic men's watch with extra-thick dial

Estimated value: $4,100 ↗

Chronograph — 1928

Case: stainless steel, push-down case back, leather strap, Ø 38 mm

Movement: Caliber 33.3 CHRO, red gold-plated, frosted finish, column-wheel control of chronograph, manual winding

Remarks: early one-button chronograph with 30-minute counter

Estimated value: $6,800 ↗

Chronograph — 1928

Case: 18-karat yellow gold, push-down case back, leather strap, Ø 38 mm

Movement: Caliber 33.3 CHRO, red gold-plated, frosted finish, column-wheel control of chronograph, manual winding

Remarks: early one-button chronograph with 30-minute counter

Estimated value: $8,100 ↗

Chronograph — 1975

Case: stainless steel, leather strap, Ø 38 mm

Movement: Caliber 33.3 CHRO, red gold-plated, frosted finish, column-wheel control of chronograph, manual winding

Remarks: one-button chronograph with 30-minute counter

Estimated value: $6,800 ↗

Chronograph — 1928

Case: stainless steel, Ø 33 mm

Movement: gold-plated, frosted finish, column-wheel control of chronograph, manual winding

Remarks: one-button chronograph with 30-minute counter in stainless steel case

Estimated value: $6,100 ↗

Chronograph — 1928

Case: 18-karat yellow gold, push-down case back, leather strap, Ø 37 mm

Movement: Caliber 33.3 CHRO, nickel-plated, column-wheel control of chronograph, manual winding

Remarks: gold chronograph with 30-minute counter

Estimated value: $4,700 ↗

Chronograph — 1939

Case: 14-karat yellow gold, push-down case back, leather strap, 32 x 40 mm

Movement: Caliber 28.1 CHRO T1, nickel-plated, column-wheel control of chronograph, manual winding

Remarks: one-button chronograph with 30-minute counter in shaped case

Estimated value: $4,700 ↗

Chronograph — 1935

Case: stainless steel, push-down case back, leather strap, Ø 37 mm

Movement: Caliber 33.3 CHRO T3, rhodium-plated, column-wheel control of chronograph, manual winding

Remarks: one-button chronograph with 30-minute counter

Estimated value: $4,100 ↗

Chronograph — 1930

Case: stainless steel, push-down case back, leather strap, Ø 37 mm

Movement: nickel-plated, column-wheel control of chronograph, manual winding

Remarks: early chronograph with 30-minute counter and movable strap lugs

Estimated value: $3,400 →

Chronograph — 1941

Case: stainless steel, push-down case back, leather strap, Ø 38 mm

Movement: Caliber 33.3 CHRO, nickel-plated, column-wheel control of chronograph, manual winding

Remarks: nearly unworn early chronograph with 30-minute counter

Estimated value: $3,400 ↗

Chronograph — 1940

Case: 18-karat red gold, push-down case back, leather strap, Ø 35 mm

Movement: Caliber 27 CHRO C12, nickel-plated, column-wheel control of chronograph, manual winding

Remarks: chronograph with 30-minute and 12-hour counters

Estimated value: $3,800 ↗

Chronograph — 1931

Case: 18-karat yellow gold, push-down case back, leather strap, Ø 35 mm

Movement: Caliber 27 CHRO T1 PC, rhodium-plated, column-wheel control of chronograph, manual winding

Remarks: chronograph with 30-minute counter

Estimated value: $3,400 ↗

Chronograph — 1946

Case: 14-karat red gold, push-down case back, leather strap, Ø 35 mm

Movement: Caliber 27 CHRO C12 T2 PC, manual winding

Remarks: early red gold chronograph with 30-minute and 12-hour counters

Estimated value: $3,800 ↗

Chronograph — 1933

Case: 18-karat yellow gold, push-down case back, leather strap, Ø 36 mm

Movement: Caliber 33.3 CHRO, silver-plated, column-wheel control of chronograph, manual winding

Remarks: chronograph with 30-minute counter

Estimated value: $3,800 ↗

Chronograph — 1938

Case: stainless steel, screw-down case back, leather strap, Ø 38 mm

Movement: Caliber 33.3 CHRO T6, nickel-plated, column-wheel control of chronograph, manual winding

Remarks: early chronograph in rare stainless steel case

Estimated value: $4,700 ↗

Seamaster Chronograph — 1950

Case: gold plated stainless steel, push-down case back, leather strap, Ø 34 mm

Movement: Caliber 321, gold-plated, column-wheel control of chronograph, manual winding

Remarks: chronograph with 30-minute and 12-hour counters

Estimated value: $2,700 ↗

Seamaster Chronograph — 1958

Case: stainless steel, push-down case back, leather strap, Ø 35 mm

Movement: Caliber 321, red gold-plated, column-wheel control of chronograph, manual winding

Remarks: chronograph with 30-miunute and 12-hour counters

Estimated value: $3,400 ↗

Chronograph — 1958

Case: 18-karat rose gold, Ø 34 mm, tripartite, push-down case back, leather strap
Movement: Caliber 320, gold-plated, column-wheel control of chronograph, finely finished steel chronograph components, mirror-polished screws, 17 jewels
Remarks: gold chronograph with 30-minute counter and tachymeter scale
Estimated value: $4,100 ↗

De Ville Chronograph — 1969

Reference number: 145018
Case: stainless steel, 35 mm, bipartite, screw-down case back, leather strap
Movement: Caliber 861, red gold-plated, fine matte steel components, 17 jewels
Remarks: elegant De Ville chronograph model with 30-minute and 12-hour counters; tachymeter scale
Estimated value: $3,000 ↗

De Ville Chronograph — 1967

Case: 18-karat yellow gold, push-down case back, leather strap, Ø 35 mm
Movement: Caliber 320, gold-plated, column-wheel control of chronograph, manual winding
Remarks: chronograph with 30-minute counter
Estimated value: $3,400 ↗

De Ville Chronograph — 1975

Case: stainless steel, screw-down case back, leather strap, Ø 35 mm
Movement: Caliber 930, red gold-plated, manual winding
Remarks: chronograph with 30-minute counter and date
Estimated value: $3,500 ↗

Chronograph — 1940

Case: stainless steel, Ø 38 mm, bipartite, screw-down case back, leather strap
Movement: Caliber 33.3, rhodium-plated, column-wheel control of chronograph, fine matte steel chronograph components
Remarks: discrete chronograph with 30-minute counter and tachymeter scale
Estimated value: $4,100 ↗

Chronograph — 1958

Case: 18-karat red gold, Ø 35 mm tripartite, push-down case back, leather strap
Movement: Caliber 321, red gold-plated, column-wheel control of chronograph, fine matte steel chronograph components
Remarks: sporty, elegant chronograph with 30-minute and 12-hour counters; tachymeter scale; red gold case
Estimated value: $3,800 ↗

Seamaster Automatic Chronograph — 1977

Case: 18-karat yellow gold, screw-down case back, leather strap, 38 x 43 mm
Movement: Caliber 1040, gold-plated, automatic winding
Remarks: automatic chronograph with sweep minute counter; 12-hour counter; 24-hour display; according to engraving, this watch was a gift from Lémania to an employee: "Lémania à Albert Piguet 1934-1977"
Estimated value: $5,400 ↗

Speedmaster Professional — 1970

Reference number: 145022
Case: 18-karat yellow gold, screw-down case back, yellow gold link bracelet, Ø 42 mm
Movement: Caliber 861, red gold-plated, manual winding
Remarks: gold Speedmaster chronograph model; limited to 1,014 pieces (this watch is engraved with number 347/1014); solid gold
Estimated value: $10,800 ↗

Seamaster Chronograph — 1970

Case: blackened stainless steel, screw-down case back, leather strap, 44 x 46 mm

Movement: Caliber 861, red gold-plated, manual winding

Remarks: chronograph with black case; 30-minute and 12-hour counters

Estimated value: $2,000 ↗

Speedmaster Professional — 1973

Case: stainless steel, screw-down case back, stainless steel link bracelet, 45 x 51 mm

Movement: Caliber 861, red gold-plated, manual winding

Remarks: heavy chronograph with 30-minute and 12-hour counters

Estimated value: $2,000 ↗

Seamaster Chronograph — 1963

Reference: 145.006-66

Case: stainless steel, screw-down case back, leather strap, 38 x 43 mm

Movement: Caliber 321, red gold-plated, column-wheel control of chronograph, manual winding

Remarks: Seamaster chronograph model with 30-minute and 12-hour counters

Estimated value: $2,400 ↗

Seamaster Chronograph — 1977

Case: stainless steel, screw-down case back, leather strap, Ø 40 mm

Movement: Caliber 861, red gold-plated, manual winding

Remarks: chronograph with 30-minute and 12-hour counters; subsidiary dial scale additionally extended to 45 minutes

Estimated value: $2,100 →

Seamaster Chronograph — 1968

Case: 18-karat yellow gold, screw-down case back, leather strap, Ø 37 mm

Movement: Caliber 321, gold-plated, column-wheel control of chronograph, manual winding

Remarks: rare gold chronograph with 30-minute and 12-hour counters

Estimated value: $8,100 ↗

Chronostop — 1968

Case: stainless steel, screw-down case back, leather strap, 35 x 39 mm

Movement: Caliber 865, red gold-plated, manual winding

Remarks: simple chronograph with second counter

Estimated value: $1,100 ↗

Speedmaster Professional Chronograph — 1963

Broad Arrow

Case: stainless steel, screw-down case back, leather strap, Ø 40 mm

Movement: Caliber 321, red gold-plated, column-wheel control of chronograph, manual winding

Remarks: Speedmaster chronograph model with 30-minute and 12-hour counters; additional transparent case back

Estimated value: $20,300 ↗

Speedmaster Professional Chronograph — 1968

Case: stainless steel, screw-down case back, leather strap, Ø 42 mm

Movement: Caliber 321, red gold-plated, column-wheel control of chronograph, manual winding

Remarks: Speedmaster chronograph model with 30-minute and 12-hour counters; additional transparent case back

Estimated value: $3,400 ↗

Speedmaster Professional Chronograph

1980

Case: stainless steel, screw-down case back, leather strap, Ø 42 mm

Movement: Caliber 861, red gold-plated, manual winding

Remarks: chronograph with 30-minute and 12-hour counters

Estimated value: $3,000 ↗

Speedmaster Professional Chronograph

1980

Case: stainless steel, screw-down case back, leather strap, Ø 42 mm

Movement: Caliber 866, red gold-plated, manual winding

Remarks: chronograph with 30-minute and 12-hour counters; moon phase and date

Estimated value: $5,400 ↗

Seamaster Chronograph

1971

Case: stainless steel, screw-down case back, leather strap, 41 x 46 mm

Movement: Caliber 861, red gold-plated, manual winding

Remarks: chronograph with 30-minute and 12-hour counters; subsidiary dial scale additionally extended to 45 minutes

Estimated value: $2,400 ↗

Seamaster Chronostop

1970

Case: stainless steel, screw-down case back, leather strap, 41 x 47 mm

Movement: Caliber 865, red gold-plated, manual winding

Remarks: simple chronograph with rotating inner bezel (flange)

Estimated value: $2,200 ↗

Speedmaster Professional Mk V

1968

Case: stainless steel, stainless steel link bracelet, Ø 43 mm

Movement: Caliber 1045, red gold-plated, automatic winding

Remarks: heavy automatic chronograph with sweep minute counter; 12-hour counter; 24-hour display

Estimated value: $2,400 ↗

Speedmaster Chronograph Automatic

1978

Case: stainless steel, screw-down case back, steel link bracelet, Ø 40 mm

Movement: Caliber 1045, red gold-plated, automatic winding

Remarks: automatic chronograph with sweep minute counter; 12-hour counter; 24-hour display

Estimated value: $1,500 ↗

Seamaster Chronograph Automatic

1975

Case: stainless steel, screw-down case back, leather strap, 41 x 48 mm

Movement: Caliber 1040, red gold-plated, automatic winding

Remarks: large automatic chronograph with sweep minute counter; 12-hour counter; 24-hour display

Estimated value: $1,350 →

Automatic Chronograph FIFA

1970

Case: stainless steel, screw-down case back, leather strap, 40 x 43 mm

Movement: Caliber 1045, red gold-plated, automatic winding

Remarks: special edition chronograph for world soccer organization FIFA

Estimated value: $3,500 ↗

Speedmaster Professional Mk IV — 1975

Case: stainless steel, screw-down case back, stainless steel link bracelet, Ø 42 mm

Movement: Caliber 1041, red gold-plated, automatic winding

Remarks: heavy automatic chronograph with sweep minute counter; 12-hour counter; 24-hour display

Estimated value: $1,500 →

Speedmaster Professional Mk II — 1968

Case: stainless steel, screw-down case back, stainless steel link bracelet, Ø 42 mm

Movement: Caliber 861, red gold-plated, manual winding

Remarks: heavy chronograph with 30-minute and 12-hour counters

Estimated value: $1,800 ↗

Seamaster Chronograph Automatic — 1975

Case: stainless steel, screw-down case back, stainless steel link bracelet, 42 x 48 mm

Movement: Caliber 1040, red gold-plated, automatic winding

Remarks: heavy automatic chronograph with sweep minute counter; 12-hour counter; 24-hour display

Estimated value: $1,500 ↗

Speedmaster 125 — 1977

Case: stainless steel, screw-down case back, stainless steel link bracelet, 42 x 51 mm

Movement: Caliber 1041, red gold-plated, 22 jewels, regulated in 6 positions, automatic winding

Remarks: special edition model for Omega's 125th anniversary; chronograph with sweep minute counter; 12-hour counter; 24-hour display

Estimated value: $2,200 ↗

Flightmaster — 1969

Case: 18-karat yellow gold, 43 x 52 mm, bipartite, screw-down case back, gold link bracelet

Movement: Caliber 910, red gold-plated, fine matte steel chronograph components

Remarks: extremely rare, heavy Flightmaster in a solid gold case (217 grams); 30-minute and 12-hour counters; 24-hour and second time zone displays; this watch was offered with its original gold link bracelet

Estimated value: $11,500 ↗

Flightmaster — 1969

Case: stainless steel, screw-down case back, stainless steel link bracelet, Ø 43 mm

Movement: Caliber 911, red gold-plated, manual winding

Remarks: chronograph with 30-minute and 12-hour counters; second time zone; inner rotating bezel (flange)

Estimated value: $3,400 ↗

Seamaster Automatic — 1978

Case: stainless steel, screw-down case back, rotating bezel, stainless steel link bracelet, Ø 40 mm

Movement: Caliber 1010, red gold-plated, automatic winding

Remarks: heavy men's watch with rotating bezel

Estimated value: $800 ↗

Automatic Seamaster 300 — 1969

Case: stainless steel, screw-down case back, rotating bezel, leather strap, Ø 42 mm

Movement: Caliber 565, red gold-plated, automatic winding

Remarks: Seamaster with additional transparent case back

Estimated value: $1,600 ↗

Seamaster Memomatic — 1971

Case: stainless steel, screw-down case back, leather strap, Ø 40 mm

Movement: Caliber 980, red gold-plated, gong, automatic winding

Remarks: alarm wristwatch that can be set to the minute; Flightmaster case

Estimated value: $1,600 ↗

Seamaster Memomatic — 1969

Case: stainless steel, screw-down case back, leather strap, 40 x 43 mm

Movement: Caliber 980, red gold-plated, gong, automatic winding

Remarks: alarm wristwatch that can be set to the minute; Seamaster case

Estimated value: $1,800 ↗

Seamaster Memomatic — 1975

Case: stainless steel, screw-down case back, leather strap, Ø 40 mm

Movement: Caliber 980, red gold-plated, gong, automatic winding

Remarks: unworn Memomatic alarm wristwatch; can be set to the minute; Series II Seamaster case

Estimated value: $2,000 ↗

Memomatic VIP — 1971

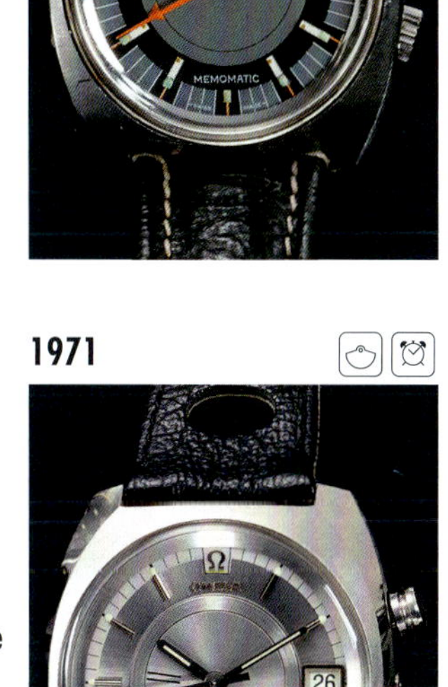

Case: stainless steel, screw-down case back, leather strap, 40 x 43 mm

Movement: Caliber 980, red gold plated, gong, 19 jewels, automatic winding

Remarks: unworn alarm wristwatch; can be set to the minute; Series II Seamaster case; very rare special VIP edition

Estimated value: $2,200 ↗

Seamaster Automatic 600m/2000ft Professional Ploprof — 1972

Case: stainless steel, monocoque, rotating bezel, stainless steel link bracelet, 56 x 45 mm

Movement: Caliber 1002, red gold-plated, automatic winding

Remarks: professional deep-sea diver's watch; water-resistant to 600 meters; French organization for deep-sea research utilized various Ploprof models at a depth of 253 meters in 1972

Estimated value: $10,800 ↗

Seamaster 200 — 1973

Case: stainless steel, 41 x 52 mm, bipartite, screw-down case back, rotating bezel, stainless steel link bracelet

Movement: Caliber 1002, red gold-plated, decorated, automatic winding

Remarks: diver's watch with rotating bezel in Flightmaster case

Estimated value: $1,350 ↗

Stardust Constellation — 1972

Case: 18-karat yellow gold, 32 x 48 mm, bipartite, screw-down case back, leather strap

Movement: Megaquartz Caliber 1510, electromechanical

Remarks: extremely rare heavy Constellation with precision quartz movement Megaquartz f 2,4 MHz; dial crafted in aventurine to look like starry sky; this watch is number 409 from a special series of only 1,000 pieces

Estimated value: $3,400 ↗

Marine Chronometer Constellation — 1975

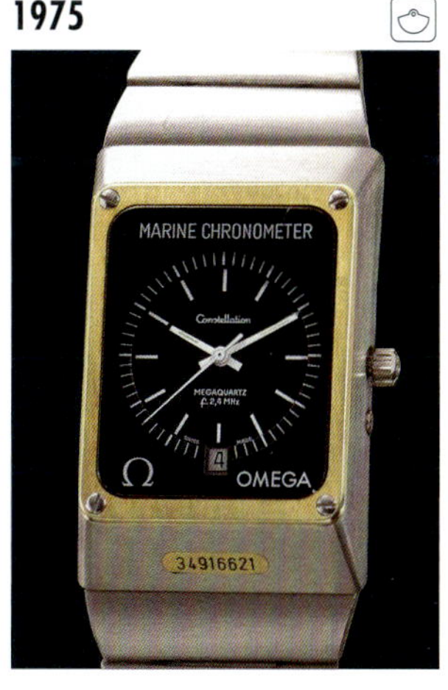

Reference number: 1980074

Case: stainless steel / yellow gold, 32 x 49 mm, tripartite, screw-down case back, stainless steel link bracelet

Movement: Megaquartz Caliber 1511, red gold-plated, polished screws, 13 jewels

Remarks: the Marine Chronometer was the first wristwatch to fulfill all demands of a certified marine chronometer; this watch was offered with a chronometer certificate and a bulletin de marche (rate report) of the Besançon observatory

Estimated value: $2,700 ↗

Officine Panerai

When Giovanni Panerai founded his little workshop in 1860 in a building on the Ponte alle Grazie, a bridge lined with buildings in Florence, he laid the cornerstone for one of the most exceptional watch companies. Orologeria Svizzeria (Swiss Watchmaking), as Panerai named his shop, sold and repaired watches imported from Switzerland. Underneath the same roof, clearly separated from the retail shop, Panerai began to manufacture precision instruments.

The rise of Officine Panerai (literally: "Panerai's workshop") to a highly specialized supplier of the Italian navy took place under Giovanni's grandson Guido. He placed special attention on good rates, and thanks to this, Panerai was soon supplying both the Italian railways and officers of the Royal Navy.

After that, the company became the most important supplier of the Italian navy, but not as one might expect for watches, but rather for depth gauges and marine compasses for the wrist as well as other equipment.

Thanks to the luminous substance Radiomir invented in 1914—a mixture of zinc sulfate and radium bromide—the Panerai dials were especially legible deep under water and at night. Panerai also used this to advantage for the company's watches, and thus Guido was contracted to produce of the first wristwatches for combat divers also called the Radiomir. The first prototypes were produced by Rolex, though the following watches housed in cases according to the Oyster principle were made by Panerai. Thanks to the minimal number of movements needed, Panerai purchased them from Aegler, Rolex Manufacture in Biel, and Angelus.

In 1936, when the first ten watches were delivered, the Panerai Radiomir became a secret piece of navy equipment. The Radiomir was followed by the Mare Nostrum chronograph, which hardly made it past the prototype stage, and the Luminor with its striking crown protection. Only long after World War II was over, in 1955, did Panerai patent this invention. Its easy-to-use bar presses the crown into a cork gasket, ensuring absolute water resistance up to 200 meters. The bar is simple to remove, and a nonsecured crown is immediately recognized by it being off the crown.

After World War II, the Radiomir and the Luminor continued to be manufactured practically unchanged, at first for the armed services and then, starting in 1993, in a limited edition of about 1,000 pieces for the civilian market. This included a Slytech edition for the American actor Sylvester (Sly) Stallone.

The striking visuals of the professional diving instruments, their early tie to the cult brand Rolex, their inclusion of technology related to Rolex's, and the fact that between 1938 and 1994 only about 350 Panerai watches were manufactured, secured the brand complete success at its relaunch under the auspices of the Richemont Luxury Group in 1997. Vintage Panerais from the early days are also profiting from these assets.

Radiomir

1945

Case: stainless steel, screw-down case back,
45 x 52 mm

Movement: rhodium-plated, côtes de Genève,
manual winding

Remarks: rare Radiomir made by Rolex; for
German combat divers; screw-in crown; engraving
on case back "Einsatzgruppe Keller-
Kampfschwimmer 1945" (Keller's unit-combat
divers 1945); this watch was offered with
certificate and complete documentation

Estimated value: $54,000 ↗

Radiomir

1945

Case: stainless steel, screw-down case back,
45 x 52 mm

Movement: rhodium-plated, côtes de Genève,
manual winding

Remarks: rare Radiomir made by Rolex; for
German combat divers; screw-in crown;

Estimated value: $60,750 ↗

Radiomir

1943

Reference number: 3646

Case: stainless steel, screw-down case back,
leather strap, Ø 47 mm

Movement: rhodium-plated, côtes de Genève,
jewels set in chatons, signed by Rolex, 17 jewels,
manual winding

Remarks: important combat diver's watch of the
Italian navy; this watch was offered with its
original leather strap

Estimated value: $60,750 ↗

Radiomir Brevettato

1938

Reference number: 3646

Case: stainless steel, screw-down case back,
leather strap, Ø 47 mm

Movement: rhodium-plated, côtes de Genève,
jewels set in chatons, manual winding

Remarks: important combat diver's watch of the
Italian navy; this watch is a prototype only made
for presentation purposes; case back signed
"Oyster Watch Geneva Swiss"

Estimated value: $94,500 ↗

Luminor

ca. 1950

Case: stainless steel, screw-down case back,
leather strap, Ø 47 mm

Movement: rhodium-plated, côtes de Genève,
jewels set in chatons, manual winding

Remarks: combat diver's watch of the Italian
navy; typical crown protection

Estimated value: $54,000 ↗

archive photo

Luminor

ca. 1950

Case: stainless steel, screw-down case back,
leather strap, Ø 47 mm

Movement: rhodium-plated, côtes de Genève,
jewels set in chatons, manual winding

Remarks: combat diver's watch of the Italian
navy; typical crown protection

Estimated value: $43,200 ↗

archive photo

Luminor Marina Militare

ca. 1950

Case: stainless steel, screw-down case back,
leather strap, Ø 47 mm

Movement: rhodium-plated, côtes de Genève,
jewels set in chatons, manual winding

Remarks: combat diver's watch of the Italian
navy with rare words "Marina Militare" printed
on dial

Estimated value: $64,800 ↗

archive photo

Luminor Egittica

ca. 1956

Case: stainless steel, rotating bezel, screw-down
case back, leather strap, Ø 47 mm

Movement: Angelus 8-day movement, rhodium-
plated, manual winding

Remarks: combat diver's watch for the Egyptian
navy with eight-day movement and rotating
bezel; only about 50 pieces produced

Estimated value: $67,5000 ↗

archive photo

Patek Philippe

The history of Patek Philippe began with a Polish count, Antoine Norbert de Patek (1812–1877) who spent time in political exile in Geneva, thereby discovering a love for fine watchmaking. Together with countryman François Czapek, a talented watchmaker, the former officer founded Patek, Czapek und Cie in 1839.

With the aid of six employees they produced about 200 watches per year. The aesthetic and technical qualities of these watches secured them an enviable reputation right from the beginning of the young company's history. Patek first heard of a watchmaker named Jean-Adrien Philippe (1815–1894) at an exhibition in Paris where he was offering his wares. This watchmaker had made a flat pocket watch that could be both set and wound by the crown—an improvement of barely imaginable dimensions today.

Since Patek's contract with Czapek had run out, he offered Philippe a partnership, and on May 15, 1845, he renamed his company Patek & Co. Since the success of his watches could be attributed to the genius-like watchmaker Philippe, he then added his name to the company. Starting in 1851, the new name was Patek Philippe & Co.

The sights of both these men were set high: they wanted to make the best watches in the world. The duo had great influence on the development of the watch industry. Philippe turned out to be a creative visionary, pushing the industrialization and construction of new tooling forward. He also understood how to introduce his complicated watches to a wide audience, presenting his products at numerous exhibitions. In London in 1851, Queen Victoria purchased a gold pocket watch with Philippe's famous crown winding. Many crowned heads and grand personalities followed her example. Patek Philippe created its first wristwatch in 1868 for the Hungarian Countess Kocewicz—this may well have also been the very first wristwatch in the history of Swiss watchmaking. The passing of Antoine de Patek in March 1877 did not slow Jean-Adrien Philippe's need to innovate. In 1889 he designed a watch movement containing a "perpetual" date, the display of which needed no correction whatsoever, either for the differing lengths of the months or for the leap years. When in 1894 Philippe also passed away, his son-in-law Joseph-Antoine Benassy-Philippe took over the management of the company and turned it into a joint stock company seven years later.

Even though the Philippe family had to sell the Patek Philippe *manufacture* as a result of the great economic crisis of 1929, today the company is still in the hands of a single family: the Stern brothers, until that point the exclusive dial suppliers to Patek Philippe, purchased the *manufacture* in 1932 and took it to a new level. Under their aegis, the finest wristwatches that have ever been seen were made in Geneva, containing many horological complications—from the perpetual calendar to the chronograph and the tourbillon. The brand's simple, timeless models of extraordinarily exquisite creation from this era also enjoy a very special place in the world of collecting. The most expensive watch ever to be sold at auction in Germany is—naturally—a Patek Philippe.

CONTROLE OFFICIEL SUISSE DES CHRONOMETRES
Bureau de Genève

REPUBLIQUE ET CANTON DE GENEVE

POST TENEBRAS LUX

Epreuves pour montres-Bracelet Genre I – Prüfungen für Armbanduhren Uhrenart I
Pruebas para relojes de pulsera Género I – Tests for Wristlet-watches Type I

Bulletin de marche
Gangschein
Boletín de marcha
Watch rate certificate
N° 3776061

Mouvement
Werk
Máquina
Movement
N° 1851610

RÉSERVÉ EXCLUSIVEMENT AUX MONTRES PORTANT LE POINÇON DE GENÈVE
RESERVIERT AUSSCHLIESSLICH DIE UHREN WELCHE DEN STEMPEL VON GENF TRAGEN
RESERVADO EXCLUSIVAMENTE A LOS RELOJES QUE ILEVAN EL CUÑO DE GINEBRA
EXCLUSIVELY RESERVED FOR WATCHES BEARING THE HALL-MARK OF GENEVA

Catégorie / Kategorie / Categoría / Category: I/1

Particularités / Besonderheiten / Particularidades / Watchspecialities: bal.Gyromax

Diamètre du mouvement / Werkdurchmesser / Diámetro de la máquina / Diameter of movement: 21.50 mm

Hauteur / Höhe / Espesor / Thickness: 2.55 mm

PATEK PHILIPPE
GENEVE

Jours / Tage / Dias / Days	Températures [°C]	Positions / Lagen / Posiciones / Positions		Marches journalières [s/d]		Variations des marches journalières [s/d]	
1	23	6H	Verticale, Vertikal, las 6 arriba / 6 heures en haut, 6 Uhr oben, 6 o'clock up	M₁	-2.0		
2	23			M₂	-2.0	V₁	0.0
3	23	3H	Verticale, Vertikal, las 3 arriba / 3 heures en haut, 3 Uhr oben, 3 o'clock up	M₃	-5.1		
4	23			M₄	-5.2	V₃	0.0
5	23	9H	Verticale, Vertikal, las 3 arriba / 3 heures en haut, 3 Uhr oben, 3 o'clock up	M₅	0.0		
6	23			M₆	-1.0	V₅	1.0
7	23	FH	Horizontale, Horizontal, estera abajo / cadran en bas, Zifferblatt unten, dial down	M₇	-1.0		
8	23			M₈	0.0	V₇	1.0
9	23	CH	Horizontale, Horizontal, estera arriba / cadran haut, Zifferblatt oben, dial up	M₉	-1.0		
10	23			M₁₀	-1.0	V₉	0.0
11	8	CH	Horizontale, Horizontal, estera arriba / cadran en haut, Zifferblatt oben, dial up	M₁₁	-5.8		
12	23			M₁₂	-1.0		
13	38			M₁₃	1.0		
14	23	6H	Verticale, Vertikal, las 6 arriba / 6 heures en haut, 6 Uhr oben, 6 o'clock up	M₁₄	-1.0		
15	23			M₁₅	-2.0		

Date de la fin des épreuves – Prüfungen wurden abgeschlossen am – Fecha del fin de las pruebas – Testing complete

Résultats – Ergebnisse – Resultados – Summary

Marche journalière moyenne dans les différentes positions
Mittlerer täglicher Gang in den verschiedenen Lagen
Marcha diara media en las distintas posiciones
Mean daily rate in the different positions — $\overline{M}$ [s/d] — -1.8

Variation moyenne
Mittlere Gangabweichung
Diferencia media
Mean variation — $\overline{V}$ [s/d]

Plus grande variation
Grösste Abweichung
Máxima diferencia
Maximum variation — Vm [s/d]

Différence du plat au pendu
Differenz zwischen liegend unf hängend
Diferencia entre las posiciones horizontal y vertical
Difference between flat and hanging positions — D [s/d]

Plus grande différence ... et l'une ... — P [s/d] — 3.4

... pro Grad Celsius ... grado centigrado ... rate per 1° centigrade — C [s/d°C] — 0.23

... marche ... ahme des Ganges ... inuación de la marcha — Rate-resumption — R [s/d] — 0.0

GENEVE, le — 14/02/199...

CONTROLE OFFICIEL SUISSE DES CHRONOMETRES
Bureau de Genève
Le Directeur :

Copyright by CONTROLE OFFICIEL SUISSE DES CHRONOMETRES - BUREAU DE GENEVE, Switzerland

Chronograph Perpetual Calendar — 1942

Reference number: 1518

Case: stainless steel, push-down case back, leather strap, Ø 35 mm

Movement: rhodium-plated, côtes de Genève, column-wheel control of chronograph, 23 jewels, regulated in 8 positions, manual winding

Remarks: extremely rare chronograph with 30-minute counter, perpetual calendar, and moon phase; only two of these models were ever manufactured in stainless steel; most expensive wristwatch ever auctioned in Germany

Estimated value: $1,890,000 ↗

Chronograph Perpetual Calendar — 1945

Reference number: 1518

Case: 18-karat yellow gold, push-down case back, leather strap, Ø 35 mm

Movement: rhodium-plated, côtes de Genève, column-wheel control of chronograph, 23 jewels, regulated in 8 positions, manual winding

Remarks: extremely rare chronograph with 30-minute counter, perpetual calendar, and moon phase; this watch is from the first series of a total of only 281 ever made

Estimated value: $405,000 ↗

Chronograph Perpetual Calendar — 1960

Reference number: 2499

Case: 18-karat yellow gold, push-down case back, leather strap, Ø 35 mm

Movement: Caliber 13-130, rhodium-plated, côtes de Genève, column-wheel control of chronograph, Seal of Geneva, 23 jewels, regulated in 8 positions, manual winding

Remarks: extremely rare chronograph (from 1951 to 1985 only 349 pieces made); 30-minute counter, complete calendar, moon phase; offered with additional strap of braided elephant hair and a gold buckle in its original mahogany box

Estimated value: $473,000 ↗

Chronograph Perpetual Calendar — 1993

Reference number: 3970E

Case: 18-karat red gold, screw-down case back, leather strap, Ø 36 mm

Movement: Caliber CH27-700, rhodium-plated, côtes de Genève, column-wheel control of chronograph, Seal of Geneva, 24 jewels, regulated in 8 positions, manual winding

Remarks: rare chronograph with 30-minute counter, 24-hour display, complete calendar, moon phases, and display of leap years; this watch was offered with a gold buckle in its original mahogany box and with a certificate

Estimated value: $135,000 ↗

Perpetual Calendar — 1980

Reference number: 3450

Case: 18-karat yellow gold, push-down case back, leather strap, Ø 38 mm

Movement: Caliber 27-460Q, rhodium-plated, côtes de Genève, 18-karat gold rotor, Seal of Geneva, automatic winding

Remarks: extremely rare men's watch with perpetual calendar and moon phase; this model was only manufactured 244 times; this watch was offered in its original mahogany box and with an original certificate

Estimated value: $230,000 ↗

Perpetual Calendar — 1963

Reference number: 3448

Case: 18-karat white gold, push-down case back, leather strap, Ø 37 mm

Movement: Caliber 27-460Q, rhodium-plated, côtes de Genève, Seal of Geneva, 37 jewels, regulated in 8 positions, automatic winding

Remarks: extremely rare men's watch with perpetual calendar and moon phase that was only manufacture 586 times between 1962 and 1982, only a few of which were made in white gold; this watch was offered in its original mahogany box and with an original certificate

Estimated value: $230,000 ↗

Perpetual Calendar — 1970

Reference number: 3448

Case: 18-karat yellow gold, tripartite, push-down case back, leather strap, Ø 37 mm

Movement: Caliber 27-60Q, rhodium-plated, fausses côtes decorations, 18-karat gold rotor, Seal of Geneva, 37 jewels, regulated in 8 positions

Remarks: extremely rare men's watch with perpetual calendar; small date hand at 6 o'clock; window display of weekday and month; moon phase display at 6 o'clock

Estimated value: $135,000 ↗

Sensa Luna — 1979

Reference number: 3448

Case: 18-karat white gold, tripartite, 18-karat white gold link bracelet, Ø 37 mm

Movement: Caliber 27-60Q, rhodium-plated, fausses côtes decorations, 18-karat gold rotor, Seal of Geneva, 37 jewels, regulated in 8 positions

Remarks: extremely rare perpetual calendar with small date hand; window display of weekday and month; only 586 pieces of Ref. 3448 were manufactured between 1962 and 1982; there are only six known of the version shown here without moon phase display, two of which are in white gold

Estimated value: $338,000 →

Perpetual Calendar — 1947

Reference number: 1526

Case: 18-karat yellow gold, tripartite, push-down case back, leather strap

Movement: Caliber 12'''-120 QP, rhodium-plated, fausses côtes decorations, mirror-polished screws, 18 jewels, regulated in 8 positions

Remarks: the first serially manufactured Patek Philippe men's watch with perpetual calendar and moon phase; between 1941 and 1952 only 210 pieces of this reference were manufactured; this watch was offered with an excerpt from the Patek Philippe master registry

Estimated value: $121,500 ↗

Perpetual Calendar Retrograde — 1995

Reference number: 5050

Case: 18-karat white gold, sapphire crystal case back, leather strap, Ø 35 mm

Movement: Caliber 315/136, rhodium-plated, côtes de Genève, gold rotor, Seal of Geneva, 31 jewels, regulated in 8 positions, automatic winding

Remarks: men's watch with perpetual calendar with retrograde date display; window displays of weekday, month and leap year; moon phase at 6 o'clock; small quantity manufactured

Estimated value: $108,000 ↗

Perpetual Calendar — 1993

Reference number: 5040

Case: 18-karat yellow gold, push-down case back with sapphire crystal, leather strap, 35 x 43 mm

Movement: Caliber 240, rhodium-plated, côtes de Genève, 27 jewels, regulated in 8 positions, automatic winding

Remarks: automatic men's watch with perpetual calendar, moon phase, and 24-hour display; small quantity manufactured

Estimated value: $40,500 →

Split-Seconds Chronograph — 1939

Reference number: 1436

Case: 18-karat yellow gold, tripartite, push-down case back, leather strap, Ø 33 mm

Movement: rhodium-plated, fausses côtes decoration, column-wheel control of chronograph, polished screws, finely finished beveled steel chronograph components, Seal of Geneva, 25 jewels, regulated in 8 positions

Remarks: extremely rare chronograph with 30-minute counter and split-seconds; only 38 pieces were made in yellow gold with silver dial, 13 of which with applied Breguet numerals

Estimated value: $270,000 ↗

One-Button Chronograph — 1936

Reference number: 130

Case: 18-karat yellow gold, tripartite, push-down case back, leather strap, Ø 33 mm

Movement: 13''' caliber, rhodium-plated, fausses côtes decoration, mirror-polished screws, column-wheel control of chronograph, finely finished beveled chronograph components

Remarks: chronograph with 30-minute counter and tachymeter scale; chronograph button integrated into crown; first chronograph with a reference number; offered with original Patek Philippe gold buckle and excerpt from master registry

Estimated value: $540,000 →

Chronograph Waterproof — 1949

Reference number: 1463

Case: stainless steel, screw-down case back, leather strap, Ø 35 mm

Movement: Caliber 13-130, rhodium-plated, côtes de Genève, column-wheel control of chronograph, Seal of Geneva, 23 jewels, regulated in 8 positions, manual winding

Remarks: extremely rare stainless steel chronograph with 30-minute counter and tachymeter scale

Estimated value: $202,500 →

Chronograph Waterproof — 1953

Reference number: 1463

Case: 18-karat rose gold, screw-down steel case back, leather strap, Ø 35 mm

Movement: Caliber 13-130, rhodium-plated, côtes de Genève, column-wheel control of chronograph, Seal of Geneva, 23 jewels, regulated in 8 positions, manual winding

Remarks: chronograph with 30-minute counter and tachymeter scale; this watch was offered with in its original box with an excerpt from the master registry

Estimated value: $175,500 →

Chronograph — 1940

Reference number: 591

Case: 18-karat yellow gold, push-down case back, leather strap, Ø 34 mm

Movement: Caliber 13, rhodium-plated, côtes de Genève, column-wheel control of chronograph, 23 jewels, regulated in 8 positions, manual winding

Remarks: chronograph with 30-minute counter and tachymeter scale; this watch was offered with certificate, leather strap, and gold buckle

Estimated value: $67,500 ↗

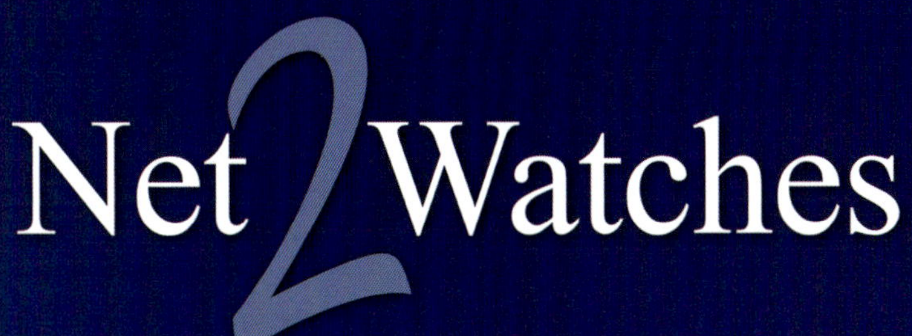

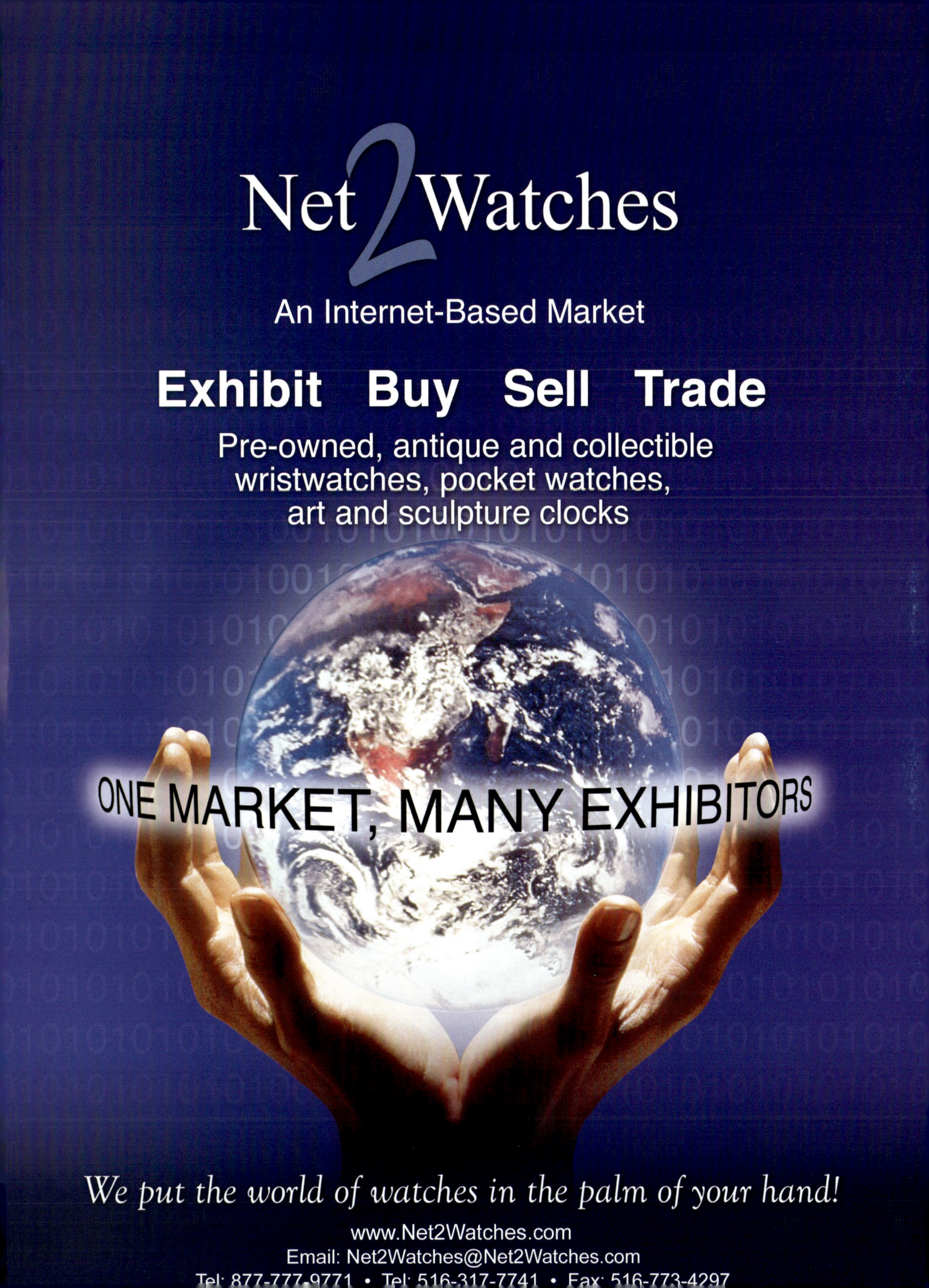
Net2Watches
An Internet-Based Market
Exhibit Buy Sell Trade
Pre-owned, antique and collectible wristwatches, pocket watches, art and sculpture clocks
ONE MARKET, MANY EXHIBITORS
We put the world of watches in the palm of your hand!
www.Net2Watches.com
Email: Net2Watches@Net2Watches.com
Tel: 877-777-9771 • Tel: 516-317-7741 • Fax: 516-773-4297

Chronograph — 1960

Reference number: 1579

Case: 18-karat yellow gold, push-down case back, leather strap, Ø 36 mm

Movement: Caliber 13-130, rhodium-plated, côtes de Genève, column-wheel control of chronograph, manual winding

Remarks: elegant chronograph with 30-minute counter; this watch was offered in its original box

Estimated value: $61,000 ↗

Chronograph — 1938

Case: 18-karat yellow gold, tripartite, push-down case back, leather strap, Ø 33 mm

Movement: Caliber 13'''-130, rhodium-plated, fausses côtes decoration, column-wheel control of chronograph, finely finished, beveled steel chronograph components, mirror-polished screws, 23 jewels, regulated in 6 positions

Remarks: important chronograph with 30-minute counter and tachymeter scale; two-tone dial; this watch was sold to Astrua in Torino, Italy; this watch was offered in its original box and with certificate

Estimated value: $67,500 →

Chronograph — 1945

Reference number: 130

Case: stainless steel, push-down case back, leather strap, Ø 34 mm

Movement: Caliber 13, rhodium-plated, côtes de Genève, column-wheel control of chronograph, 23 jewels, regulated in 8 positions, manual winding

Remarks: extremely rare chronograph in stainless steel with 30-minute counter; stainless steel chronographs were only manufactured in small quantities by Patek Philippe; this watch was offered with an excerpt from the Patek Philippe archives

Estimated value: $94,500 ↗

Chronograph — 1959

Reference number: 130

Case: 18-karat yellow gold, push-down case back, leather strap, Ø 33 mm

Movement: Caliber 13, rhodium-plated, côtes de Genève, column-wheel control of chronograph, 23 jewels, regulated in 8 positions, manual winding

Remarks: chronograph with 30-minute counter; double signature by Patek Philippe and Beyer on dial; this watch was offered in its original box with gold buckle and certificate

Estimated value: $54,000 ↗

Chronograph — 1954

Reference number: 530

Case: 18-karat yellow gold, push-down case back, leather strap, Ø 33 mm

Movement: Caliber 13L, rhodium-plated, finely gold-plated wheels, column-wheel control of chronograph, 23 jewels, regulated in 8 positions, manual winding

Remarks: chronograph with 30-minute counter

Estimated value: $54,000 ↗

World Time — 1949

Reference number: 1415 HU

Case: 18-karat yellow gold, push-down case back, rotating knurled bezel, leather strap, Ø 31 mm

Movement: Caliber 12-200, rhodium-plated, côtes de Genève, 18 jewels, regulated in 8 positions, manual winding

Remarks: wristwatch with world time display; reference cities located on rotating bezel, which can be coordinated with the 24-hour ring

Estimated value: $88,000 ↗

Men's Watch Art Deco — 1928

Case: 18-karat white gold, push-down case back, leather strap, 25 x 40 mm

Movement: Caliber 10, rhodium-plated, côtes de Genève, "moustache" compensating pallets, 18 jewels, regulated in 8 positions, manual winding

Remarks: rare Art Deco men's watch in a rectangular case; hand-engraved case

Estimated value: $27,000 ↗

Men's Watch — 1927

Case: 18-karat white gold, push-down case back with hinge, leather strap, 26 x 35 mm

Movement: frosted finish, gold-plated, "moustache" compensating pallets, manual winding

Remarks: early men's watch; "moustache" compensating pallets

Estimated value: $13,500 ↗

Men's Watch — 1920

Case: 18-karat yellow gold, push-down case back, leather strap, 26 x 43 mm

Movement: Caliber 10, frosted finish, gold-plated, "moustache" compensating pallets, manual winding

Remarks: one of Patek Philippe's earliest wristwatches from 1920; exceptional case with guilloché dial; this watch was offered with gold buckle and certificate

Estimated value: $17,600 ↗

Men's Watch — 1932

Case: 18-karat yellow gold, push-down case back, leather strap, 26 x 44 mm

Movement: frosted finish, gold-plated, manual winding

Remarks: extremely rare men's watch in Curvex case; this watch was offered with gold buckle and Patek Philippe certificate

Estimated value: $24,500 ↗

Chronometro Gondolo — 1913

Case: 18-karat yellow gold, push-down case back, leather strap, 26 x 44 mm

Movement: Caliber 10, frosted finish, gold-plated, "moustache" compensating pallets, manual winding

Remarks: one of Patek Philippe's earliest wristwatches from 1913; this watch was offered with a Patek Philippe certificate

Estimated value: $57,000 ↗

Chronometro Gondolo — 1918

Case: 18-karat yellow gold, push-down case back, leather strap, 31 x 48 mm

Movement: Caliber 12, gold-plated, "moustache" compensating pallets, manual winding

Remarks: one of Patek Philippe's earliest wristwatches from 1918; tonneau-shaped case; this watch was offered with gold buckle and a Patek Philippe certificate

Estimated value: $47,500 ↗

Tiffany & Co. — 1942

Reference number: 431

Case: 18-karat yellow gold, bipartite, push-down case back with hinge, leather strap, 26 x 45 mm

Movement: Caliber 9'''-90, rhodium-plated, fausses côtes decoration, mirror-polished screws, shaped movement, 18 jewels, regulated in 8 positions

Remarks: extremely rare rectangular men's watch; this watch was sold under "Tiffany & Co." by the jeweler of the same name; this watch was offered in its original box with an excerpt from the Patek Philippe master registry

Estimated value: $40,500 ↗

Men's Watch — 1928

Case: 18-karat white gold, push-down case back, leather strap, 24 x 38 mm

Movement: gold-plated, manual winding

Remarks: elegant white gold men's watch in rectangular case

Estimated value: $19,000 ↗

Men's Watch — 1913

Case: 18-karat yellow gold, push-down case back, leather strap, 25 x 41 mm

Movement: rhodium-plated, côtes de Genève, 18 jewels, regulated in 8 positions, manual winding

Remarks: one of the earliest existing men's watches by Patek Philippe; this watch was offered with a gold clasp

Estimated value: $34,000 ↗

Men's Watch — 1936

Reference number: 417

Case: platinum, bipartite, push-down case back, leather strap, 20 x 36 mm

Movement: Caliber 9-90, rhodium-plated, fausses côtes decoration, mirror-polished screws, shaped movement, 18 jewels, regulated in 8 positions

Remarks: rare early platinum watch in a stepped case; engraving "S.S. Magoffin" on case back

Estimated value: $26,000 ↗

Men's Watch — 1935

Case: 18-karat yellow gold, bipartite, push-down case back with hinge, leather strap, 24 x 40 mm

Movement: Caliber 9-90, rhodium-plated, fausses côtes decoration, mirror-polished screws, shaped movement

Remarks: extremely rare men's watch in a lavish rectangular case

Estimated value: $27,000 ↗

Men's Watch — 1929

Case: 18-karat yellow and white gold, bipartite, push-down case back with hinge, leather strap, 26 x 37 mm

Movement: 9 lines, gold-plated, frosted finish

Remarks: extremely rare men's watch in a two-tone case; this watch was offered with an 18-karat gold buckle and an excerpt from the Patek Philippe master registry

Estimated value: $23,000 →

Men's Watch — 1937

Reference number: 520

Case: 18-karat yellow gold, bipartite, push-down case back, leather strap, 24 x 40 mm

Movement: Caliber 9-90, rhodium-plated, fausses côtes decoration, mirror-polished screws, shaped movement

Remarks: elegant men's watch in a rectangular case; this watch was offered with an original Patek Philippe buckle and an excerpt from the master registry

Estimated value: $15,000 ↗

Men's Watch — 1936

Case: 18-karat yellow gold, push-down case back, leather strap, 22 x 36 mm

Movement: Caliber 9-90, rhodium-plated, côtes de Genève, 18 jewels, regulated in 8 positions, manual winding

Remarks: elegant men's watch in rectangular case

Estimated value: $9,500 ↗

Men's Watch — 1938

Case: stainless steel, push-down case back, leather strap, 23 x 40 mm

Movement: Caliber 9-90, rhodium-plated, côtes de Genève, 18 jewels, regulated in 8 positions, manual winding

Remarks: simple men's watch in rectangular stainless steel case

Estimated value: $27,000 ↗

Men's Watch — 1938

Case: 18-karat yellow gold, push-down case back, leather strap, 23 x 40 mm

Movement: Caliber 9-90, rhodium-plated, côtes de Genève, Seal of Geneva, 18 jewels, regulated in 8 positions, manual winding

Remarks: rare men's watch in a rectangular case; this watch bears a dedication engraved on the case back and was offered with a gold buckle

Estimated value: $19,000 ↗

Men's Watch — 1938

Reference number: 491

Case: 18-karat yellow gold, push-down case back, leather strap, 21 x 43 mm

Movement: Caliber 9-90, rhodium-plated, côtes de Genève, 18 jewels, regulated in 8 positions, manual winding

Remarks: elegant early men's watch in rectangular case; this watch was offered with an excerpt from the Patek Philippe master registry, a gold buckle, and in its original box

Estimated value: $24,500 ↗

Men's Watch — 1940

Case: 18-karat yellow gold/red gold, push-down case back, leather strap, 21 x 37 mm

Movement: Caliber 9-90, rhodium-plated, côtes de Genève, 18 jewels, regulated in 8 positions, manual winding

Remarks: extremely rare red and white gold men's watch; the watch was sold by Tiffany & Co. in New York

Estimated value: $20,500 ↗

Men's Watch — 1942

Reference number: 1559
Case: 18-karat yellow gold, push-down case back, leather strap, 22 x 39 mm
Movement: Caliber 9-90, nickel-plated, côtes de Genève, manual winding
Remarks: rectangular men's watch with subsidiary seconds
Estimated value: $6,750 →

Men's Watch — 1947

Case: 18-karat yellow gold, push-down case back, leather strap, 25 x 41 mm
Movement: Caliber 9-90, rhodium-plated, côtes de Genève, 18 jewels, regulated in 8 positions, manual winding
Remarks: men's watch with diamond-set dial
Estimated value: $11,000 ↗

Top Hat — 1937

Case: 18-karat red gold, push-down case back, gold link bracelet
Movement: Caliber 8L, nickel-plated, côtes de Genève, 18 jewels, regulated in 8 positions, manual winding
Remarks: rare rectangular men's watch whose shape is reminiscent of a top hat
Estimated value: $8,800 ↗

Top Hat — 1939

Case: 18-karat red gold, push-down case back, leather strap, 25 x 36 mm
Movement: Caliber 9-90, rhodium-plated, côtes de Genève, manual winding
Remarks: rare rectangular men's watch whose shape is reminiscent of a top hat
Estimated value: $8,100 ↗

Men's Watch — 1947

Case: 18-karat yellow gold, push-down case back, leather strap, 23 x 36 mm
Movement: Caliber 9-90, rhodium-plated, côtes de Genève, Seal of Geneva, manual winding
Remarks: elegant men's watch with subsidiary seconds in a rectangular case with rolling-pin shaped lugs
Estimated value: $6,100 →

Men's Watch — 1940

Case: 18-karat yellow gold, push-down case back, leather strap, 23 x 34 mm
Movement: Caliber 9-90, rhodium-plated, côtes de Genève, Seal of Geneva, 18 jewels, regulated in 8 positions, manual winding
Remarks: elegant men's watch with subsidiary seconds in a square case with rolling-pin shaped lugs
Estimated value: $6,100 ↗

Men's Watch — 1947

Case: 18-karat red gold, leather strap, 26 x 37 mm
Movement: Caliber 10-200, rhodium-plated, côtes de Genève, manual winding
Remarks: rare men's watch with patented dust and moisture-protected case; the case is opened by a slide on the side
Estimated value: $7,450 →

Shark — 1945

Reference number: 2554
Case: 18-karat white gold, bipartite, push-down case back, leather strap, 28 x 43 mm
Movement: Caliber 9-90, rhodium-plated, fausses côtes decoration, mirror-polished screws, shaped movement, 18 jewels, regulated in 8 positions
Remarks: extremely rare men's watch; Ref. 2554 served as the basis for Ref. 5100 with ten days' power reserve in 2000; this watch was offered with a Patek Philippe buckle and excerpt from the master registry and in its original box
Estimated value: $33,800 ↗

Men's Watch — 1940

Reference number: 1530

Case: 18-karat red gold, push-down case back, leather strap, 25 x 36 mm

Movement: Caliber 9-90, rhodium-plated, côtes de Genève, Seal of Geneva, 18 jewels, regulated in 8 positions, manual winding

Remarks: red gold men's watch in a rectangular case with double signature; this watch was sold by Tiffany & Co.

Estimated value: $6,500 →

Herrenuhr

Men's Watch — 1946

Reference number: 1445

Case: 18-karat yellow gold, push-down case back, leather strap, 21 x 39 mm

Movement: Caliber 9-90, rhodium-plated, côtes de Genève, 18 jewels, manual winding

Remarks: elegant men's watch in rectangular case; this watch was offered with excerpt from master registry, gold clasp, and in its original box

Estimated value: $6,800 →

Men's Watch — 1952

Reference number: 2404

Case: 18-karat yellow gold, push-down case back, leather strap, 24 x 37 mm

Movement: Caliber 9-90, rhodium-plated, côtes de Genève, Seal of Geneva, 18 jewels, regulated in 8 positions, manual winding

Remarks: men's watch with subsidiary seconds; this watch has an exceptional case with remarkable lugs and a strongly domed crystal

Estimated value: $8,800 →

Men's Watch — 1950

Reference number: 1560

Case: 18-karat yellow gold, push-down case back, leather strap, 22 x 38 mm

Movement: Caliber 9-90, rhodium-plated, côtes de Genève, Seal of Geneva, manual winding

Remarks: elegant men's watch in rectangular case

Estimated value: $6,100 →

Men's Watch — 1950

Reference number: 2476

Case: 18-karat red gold, push-down case back, leather strap, 26 x 39 mm

Movement: Caliber 9-90, rhodium-plated, côtes de Genève, Seal of Geneva, 18 jewels, regulated in 8 positions, manual winding

Remarks: elegant men's watch with subsidiary seconds; this watch has an exceptional case whose upper part is slightly domed, including the lug

Estimated value: $9,500 →

Men's Watch — 1960

Reference number: 2476

Case: 18-karat white gold, bipartite, push-down case back, leather strap, 26 x 39 mm

Movement: Caliber 9'''-90, rhodium-plated, fausses côtes decoration, mirror-polished screws, shaped movement

Remarks: fine elegant men's watch in white gold shaped case; this watch was offered with an excerpt from the Patek Philippe master registry

Estimated value: $43,000 ↗

Men's Watch — 1953

Reference number: 2529

Case: 18-karat yellow gold, bipartite, push-down case back, leather strap, 28 x 36 mm

Movement: Caliber 10-200, rhodium-plated, fausses côtes decoration, polished screws

Remarks: elegant men's watch with stepped center part; this watch was offered with an 18-karat gold buckle and an excerpt from the Patek Philippe master registry

Estimated value: $8,100 →

Asymmetric Men's Watch — 1938

Reference number: 1401

Case: 18-karat yellow gold, push-down case back, leather strap, 20 x 38 mm

Movement: Caliber 9-90, rhodium-plated, côtes de Genève, Seal of Geneva, 18 jewels, regulated in 8 positions, manual winding

Remarks: extremely rare men's watch with asymmetrical case that lays on the wrist in a slightly slanted manner

Estimated value: $34,000 ↗

Men's Watch — 1940

Reference number: 1480
Case: 18-karat rose gold, push-down case back, leather strap, 22 x 40 mm
Movement: Caliber 9-90, rhodium-plated, côtes de Genève, Seal of Geneva, 18 jewels, regulated in 8 positions, manual winding
Remarks: elegant men's watch with remarkably shaped, fluted lugs
Estimated value: $21,600 ↗

Hour Glass — 1955

Reference number: 1593
Case: 18-karat yellow gold, push-down case back, leather strap, 25 x 41 mm
Movement: Caliber 9-90, rhodium-plated, côtes de Genève, Seal of Geneva, 18 jewels, regulated in 8 positions, manual winding
Remarks: extremely rare men's watch with strongly fitted case reminiscent of an hourglass; this watch was offered in its original box and with a gold buckle
Estimated value: $21,000 ↗

Men's Wristwatch — 1951

Reference number: 2442
Case: 18-karat yellow gold, push-down case back, leather strap, 27 x 43 mm
Movement: Caliber 9-90, rhodium-plated, côtes de Genève, Seal of Geneva, manual winding
Remarks: extremely rare men's watch strongly fitted case; double signature of Patek Philippe and Gübelin on dial; this watch was offered with a Patek Philippe certificate
Estimated value: $54,000 ↗

Men's Watch — 1949

Reference number: 2456
Case: 18-karat yellow gold, push-down case back, leather strap, 23 x 39 mm
Movement: Caliber 9-90, rhodium-plated, côtes de Genève, 18 jewels, manual winding
Remarks: elegant men's watch in unusually designed rectangular case; this watch was offered with an excerpt from the master registry, a gold clasp, and in its original box
Estimated value: $18,000 ↗

Men's Watch — 1965

Reference number: 1588
Case: 18-karat yellow gold, push-down case back, leather strap, 23 x 37 mm
Movement: Caliber 9-90, rhodium-plated, côtes de Genève, manual winding
Remarks: simple men's watch in rectangular case
Estimated value: $11,500 ↗

Model — 1950

Reference number: 2434
Case: 18-karat yellow gold, push-down case back, leather strap, 25 x 40 mm
Movement: Caliber 9-90, rhodium-plated, côtes de Genève, 18 jewels, regulated in 8 positions, manual winding
Remarks: elegant men's watch in rectangular case; this watch was offered with an excerpt from the master registry
Estimated value: $6,750 →

Men's Watch — 1954

Reference number: 2472
Case: 18-karat yellow gold, push-down case back, leather strap, 27 x 36 mm
Movement: Caliber 10-200, rhodium-plated, côtes de Genève, manual winding
Remarks: fine red gold men's watch; this watch was offered in its original box
Estimated value: $9,500 →

Men's Watch — 1945

Case: 18-karat yellow gold, push-down case back, leather strap, 20 x 42 mm
Movement: Caliber 9-90, rhodium-plated, côtes de Genève, manual winding
Remarks: elegant men's watch in rectangular case
Estimated value: $12,200 ↗

Men's Watch — 1951

Reference number: 2493

Case: 18-karat yellow gold, push-down case back, leather strap, 31 x 40 mm

Movement: Caliber 10-200, rhodium-plated, côtes de Genève, Seal of Geneva, 18 jewels, regulated in 8 positions, manual winding

Remarks: elegant men's watch in square case; this watch was offered in its original box

Estimated value: $6,750 →

Men's Watch — 1955

Reference number: 2469

Case: 18-karat yellow gold, push-down case back, leather strap, 27 x 38 mm

Movement: Caliber 9-90, rhodium-plated, côtes de Genève, 18 jewels, regulated in 8 positions, manual winding

Remarks: men's watch in tonneau-shaped case with subsidiary seconds

Estimated value: $8,100 →

Model — 1957

Reference number: 2488

Case: 18-karat yellow gold, push-down case back, leather strap, 28 x 35 mm

Movement: Caliber 10-200, rhodium-plated, côtes de Genève, 18 jewels, regulated in 8 positions, manual winding

Remarks: elegant rectangular men's watch

Estimated value: $4,100 →

Men's Watch — 1950

Reference number: 2446

Case: 18-karat yellow gold, push-down case back, leather strap, 26 x 35 mm

Movement: Caliber 10-200, rhodium-plated, côtes de Genève, 18 jewels, regulated in 8 positions, manual winding

Remarks: this watch was offered with Patek Philippe gold buckle

Estimated value: $4,700 ↗

Men's watch — 1960

Reference number: 2540/2

Case: 18-karat rose gold, bipartite, push-down case back, leather strap, 31 x 41 mm

Movement: Caliber 27SC, rhodium-plated, fausses côtes decoration, mirror-polished screws, Seal of Geneva, 18 jewels, regulated in 8 positions

Remarks: extremely rare men's watch in rounded square (carré galbé) case; so-called TV watch; this watch was offered with an excerpt from the Patek Philippe master registry

Estimated value: $19,000 →

Men's Watch — 1976

Reference number: 3585

Case: 18-karat white gold, screw-down case back, leather strap, Ø 36 mm

Movement: Caliber 1-350, rhodium-plated, côtes de Genève, gold rotor, Seal of Geneva, 28 jewels, regulated in 8 positions, automatic winding

Remarks: elegant men's watch in a so-called TV screen case in white gold

Estimated value: $4,700 ↗

Jump Hour — 1989

Case: 18-karat red gold, push-down case back, leather strap, 28 x 38 mm

Movement: rhodium-plated, côtes de Genève, manual winding

Remarks: limited men's watch with jump digital display in a tonneau-shaped case; this watch was offered in its original box with papers

Estimated value: $40,500 ↗

Calatrava — 1965

Reference number: 570

Case: 18-karat white gold, push-down case back, leather strap, Ø 35 mm

Movement: Caliber 27SC, rhodium-plated, côtes de Genève, Seal of Geneva, 18 jewels, regulated in 8 positions, manual winding

Remarks: very fine Calatrava in white gold

Estimated value: $30,000 ↗

Calatrava — 1953

Reference number: 2509
Case: 18-karat yellow gold, screw-down case back, leather strap, Ø 35 mm
Movement: Caliber 12-400, rhodium-plated, côtes de Genève, Seal of Geneva, 18 jewels, regulated in 8 positions, manual winding
Remarks: large Calatrava in water-resistant case
Estimated value: $17,500 ↗

Calatrava — 1957

Reference number: 2508
Case: 18-karat yellow gold, screw-down case back, leather strap, Ø 35 mm
Movement: Caliber 27SC, rhodium-plated, côtes de Genève, Seal of Geneva, 18 jewels, regulated in 8 positions, manual winding
Remarks: elegant men's watch; this watch was offered with an excerpt from the Patek Philippe master registry
Estimated value: $12,200 ↗

Calatrava — 1960

Reference number: 570
Case: 18-karat white gold, tripartite, push-down case back, leather strap, Ø 35 mm
Movement: Caliber 27SC, rhodium-plated, with fausses côtes decoration, mirror-polished screws, Seal of Geneva, 18 jewels, regulated in 8 positions
Remarks: extremely rare large Calatrava in white gold; this watch was offered with a Patek Philippe white gold buckle
Estimated value: $30,000 ↗

Model — 1960

Reference number: 2509
Case: stainless steel, bipartite, screw-down case back, leather strap, Ø 35 mm
Movement: Caliber 12'''-400, rhodium-plated, fausses côtes decoration, mirror-polished screws, Seal of Geneva, 18 jewels, regulated in 8 positions
Remarks: important men's watch; additional movement protection cap; this watch was offered with an excerpt from the Patek Philippe master registry
Estimated value: $47,000 ↗

Calatrava — 1957

Reference number: 2462
Case: 18-karat yellow gold, push-down case back, leather strap, Ø 33 mm
Movement: rhodium-plated, côtes de Genève, manual winding
Remarks: elegant men's watch with subsidiary seconds
Estimated value: $5,400 →

Calatrava — 1949

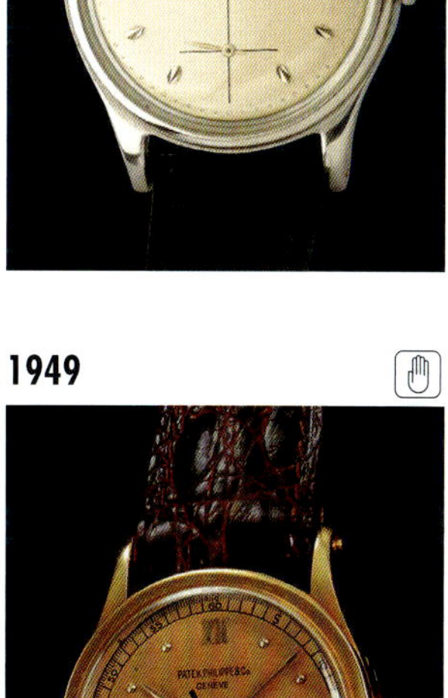

Case: 18-karat red gold, push-down case back, leather strap, Ø 30 mm
Movement: Caliber 12SC, rhodium-plated, côtes de Genève, manual winding
Remarks: rare men's watch
Estimated value: $7,500 ↗

Calatrava — 1938

Case: stainless steel, push-down case back, leather strap, Ø 30 mm
Movement: Caliber 12-120, rhodium-plated, côtes de Genève, 18 jewels, regulated in 8 positions, manual winding
Remarks: elegant men's watch with subsidiary seconds
Estimated value: $6,750 →

Calatrava — 1935

Reference number: 35
Case: stainless steel, tripartite, push-down case back, leather strap, Ø 31 mm
Movement: 12 Lines, rhodium-plated, fausses côtes decoration, polished screws, Lépine wolf-toothed winding wheels
Remarks: elegant Calatrava with subsidiary seconds in stainless steel case; this watch was offered with a Patek Philippe buckle
Estimated value: $6,750 ↗

Calatrava — 1950

Reference number: 1589
Case: 18-karat red gold, push-down case back, leather strap, Ø 36 mm
Movement: Caliber 12-400, rhodium-plated, côtes de Genève, Seal of Geneva, 18 jewels, regulated in 8 positions, manual winding
Remarks: this watch was a state gift
Estimated value: $8,100 ↗

Calatrava — 1938

Case: 18-karat yellow gold, push-down case back, leather strap, Ø 36 mm
Movement: Caliber 12-120, rhodium-plated, côtes de Genève, manual winding
Remarks: rare large Calatrava with subsidiary seconds
Estimated value: $10,800 ↗

Hooded Lugs — 1938

Case: 18-karat red gold/stainless steel, push-down case back, leather strap, Ø 33 mm
Movement: rhodium-plated, côtes de Genève, manual winding
Remarks: rare two-tone men's watch with hooded lugs
Estimated value: $12,200 ↗

Men's Watch — 1946

Reference number: 1461
Case: 18-karat yellow gold, push-down case back, leather strap, Ø 32 mm
Movement: Caliber 10-200, rhodium-plated, côtes de Genève, manual winding
Remarks: fine men's watch with subsidiary seconds and teardrop-shaped strap lugs
Estimated value: $4,750 ↗

Men's Watch — 1950

Reference number: 1578
Case: 18-karat rose gold, push-down case back, leather strap, Ø 35 mm
Movement: Caliber 12-120, rhodium-plated, côtes de Genève, 18 jewels, regulated in 8 positions, manual winding
Remarks: elegant men's watch with extremely rare black dial; this watch was offered with excerpt from the Patek Philippe master registry
Estimated value: $9,500 ↗

Men's Watch — 1950

Reference number: 1584
Case: 18-karat yellow gold, push-down case back, leather strap, Ø 34 mm
Movement: Caliber 12-120, rhodium-plated, côtes de Genève, 18 jewels, manual winding
Remarks: elegant men's watch; this watch was offered with Patek Philippe master registry excerpt and gold clasp
Estimated value: $12,900 ↗

Men's Watch — 1953

Reference number: 2453
Case: 18-karat red gold, push-down case back, leather strap, Ø 33 mm
Movement: Caliber 10-200, rhodium-plated, côtes de Genève, Seal of Geneva, 18 jewels, regulated in 8 positions, manual winding
Remarks: extremely rare men's watch
Estimated value: $10,800 ↗

Men's Watch — 1952

Reference number: 2459
Case: 18-karat yellow gold, push-down case back, leather strap, Ø 36 mm
Movement: Caliber 12-120, rhodium-plated, côtes de Genève, 18 jewels, manual winding
Remarks: fine men's watch with subsidiary seconds
Estimated value: $11,500 ↗

Snail — 1949

Reference number: 1491

Case: 18-karat yellow gold, tripartite, push-down case back, leather strap, Ø 34 mm

Movement: Caliber 27SC, rhodium-plated, fausses côtes decoration, mirror-polished screws, Seal of Geneva

Remarks: elegant men's watch with sweep seconds; this watch was delivered to Somazzi and also has that signature on the dial

Estimated value: $13,500 →

Snail — 1951

Reference number: 1491

Case: 18-karat red gold, push-down case back, leather strap, Ø 34 mm

Movement: Caliber 12-120, rhodium-plated, côtes de Genève, 18 jewels, regulated in 8 positions, manual winding

Remarks: red gold men's watch with curved strap lugs; this watch was offered with a Patek Philippe gold buckle and certificate

Estimated value: $15,000 ↗

Asymmétrique — 1935

Reference number: 497

Case: 18-karat yellow gold, push-down case back, leather strap, 25 x 37 mm

Movement: Caliber 91, rhodium-plated, côtes de Genève, Seal of Geneva, 18 jewels, regulated in 8 positions, manual winding

Remarks: rare men's watch with exceptional case; the design of the strap lugs dominate the shape of the case

Estimated value: $20,300 ↗

Men's Watch — 1955

Reference number: 2515

Case: 18-karat yellow gold, push-down case back, leather strap, Ø 36 mm

Movement: Caliber 12-400, nickel-plated, côtes de Genève, Seal of Geneva, 18 jewels, regulated in 8 positions, manual winding

Remarks: gold men's watch with subsidiary seconds

Estimated value: $5,400 ↗

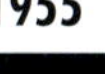

Men's Watch — 1942

Reference number: 1528

Case: 18-karat yellow gold, push-down case back, leather strap, Ø 34 mm

Movement: Caliber 12-120, rhodium-plated, côtes de Genève, manual winding

Remarks: extremely rare elegant men's watch with central, movable strap lugs

Estimated value: $7,500 →

Men's Watch — 1953

Reference number: 2533

Case: 18-karat yellow gold, screw-down case back, leather strap, Ø 34 mm

Movement: Caliber 27SC, rhodium-plated, côtes de Genève, Seal of Geneva, 18 jewels, regulated in 8 positions, manual winding

Remarks: elegant men's watch; this watch was offered with a Patek Philippe buckle

Estimated value: $10,800 ↗

Men's Watch — 1960

Reference number: 2568

Case: 18-karat yellow gold, push-down case back, leather strap, Ø 33 mm

Movement: Caliber 10-200, rhodium-plated, côtes de Genève, 18 jewels, regulated in 8 positions, manual winding

Remarks: elegant men's watch

Estimated value: $4,750 →

Men's Watch — 1957

Reference number: 2481

Case: 18-karat yellow gold, push-down case back, leather strap, Ø 37 mm

Movement: Caliber 27SC, rhodium-plated, côtes de Genève, Seal of Geneva, 18 jewels, regulated in 8 positions, manual winding

Remarks: elegant men's watch; this watch was offered with a Patek Philippe master registry excerpt

Estimated value: $10,800 ↗

Chronometer — 1949

Reference number: 2452

Case: 18-karat red gold, push-down case back, leather strap, Ø 35 mm

Movement: Caliber 10-200, rhodium-plated, côtes de Genève, manual winding

Remarks: nearly unworn red gold men's watch; this watch was offered in its original box and chronometer bulletin

Estimated value: $16,200 ↗

Discovolante — 1957

Reference number: 2594

Case: 18-karat white gold, bipartite, push-down case back, leather strap, Ø 32 mm

Movement: Caliber 23-300, rhodium-plated, fauses côtes decoration, polished screws, Seal of Geneva, 18 jewels, regulated in 8 positions

Remarks: fine, flat men's watch with wide bezel

Estimated value: $6,100 →

Men's Watch — 1954

Reference number: 2515

Case: 18-karat yellow gold, tripartite, push-down case back, leather strap, Ø 36 mm

Movement: Caliber 12-400, rhodium-plated, fausses côtes decoration, polished screws

Remarks: rare men's watch with subsidiary seconds and blue dial; stepped case

Estimated value: $8,100 ↗

Men's Watch — 1961

Reference number: 3430

Case: 18-karat yellow gold, bipartite, push-down case back, leather strap

Movement: Caliber 23-300, rhodium-plated, fausses côtes decoration, mirror-polished screws, Seal of Geneva, 18 jewels, regulated in 8 positions

Remarks: elegant men's watch; this watch was offered in its original box

Estimated value: $9,500 ↗

Men's Watch — 1960

Reference number: 3417

Case: stainless steel, screw-down case back, leather strap, Ø 35 mm

Movement: Caliber 12-400, rhodium-plated, côtes de Genève, gold escapement, Seal of Geneva, 18 jewels, regulated in 8 positions, manual winding

Remarks: rare anti-magnetic men's watch; soft-iron core to protect the movement from magnetic fields; this watch was offered with a Patek Philippe buckle

Estimated value: $27,000 ↗

Men's Watch — 1954

Reference number: 2484

Case: platinum, push-down case back, leather strap, Ø 33 mm

Movement: Caliber 10-200, rhodium-plated, côtes de Genève, 18 jewels, regulated in 8 positions, manual winding

Remarks: men's watch in platinum case with diamond-set dial

Estimated value: $20,300 →

Men's Watch — 1947

Reference number: 1569

Case: 18-karat yellow gold, push-down case back, leather strap, Ø 36 mm

Movement: Caliber 12-120, rhodium-plated, côtes de Genève, 18 jewels, regulated in 8 positions, manual winding

Remarks: elegant men's watch with Patek Philippe gold buckle; this watch was offered with an original certificate

Estimated value: $7,500 ↗

Men's Automatic Watch — 1954

Reference number: 2526

Case: platinum, screw-down case back, leather strap, Ø 35 mm

Movement: Caliber 12-600 AT, rhodium-plated, côtes de Genève, Seal of Geneva, 18-karat gold rotor, 30 jewels, regulated in 8 positions, automatic winding

Remarks: extremely rare automatic watch with diamond-set dial; only 600 pieces of this watch were manufactured, 20 of which were platinum

Estimated value: $81,000 ↗

Men's Automatic Watch — 1957

Reference number: 2526

Case: 18-karat red gold, screw-down case back, leather strap, Ø 35 mm

Movement: Caliber 12-600 AT, rhodium-plated, côtes de Genève, gold rotor, 30 jewels, regulated in 8 positions, automatic winding

Remarks: extremely rare men's watch with subsidiary seconds; only 30 of this watch were manufactured; enamel dial

Estimated value: $54,000 ↗

Men's Automatic Watch — 1963

Reference number: 3429

Case: 18-karat white gold, screw-down case back, leather strap, Ø 35 mm

Movement: Caliber 27-460, rhodium-plated, gold rotor, automatic winding

Remarks: extremely rare men's nearly new watch; only about 200 pieces of this watch were manufactured in white gold; this watch was offered with a Patek Philippe gold folding clasp and certificate

Estimated value: $16,200 ↗

Men's Watch — 1965

Reference number: 3429

Case: platinum, bipartite, screw-down case back, leather strap, Ø 35 mm

Movement: Caliber 27-460-200, rhodium-plated, fausses côtes decoration, mirror-polished screws, 18-karat gold rotor, Seal of Geneva, 37 jewels, regulated in 8 positions

Remarks: important men's watch with subsidiary seconds in platinum case

Estimated value: $40,500 ↗

Men's Watch — 1963

Reference number: 3419

Case: stainless steel, comprising several parts, screw-down case back, leather strap and stainless steel Milanaise bracelet, Ø 34 mm

Movement: Caliber 27AM-400, rhodium-plated, fausses côtes decoration, polished screws, Seal of Geneva

Remarks: specially shaped case with quick-change system for fast change of steel bracelet and leather strap; this system was protected by Swiss patent no. 340786; this watch was offered with a leather strap and a stainless steel Milanaise bracelet

Estimated value: $6,750 ↗

Men's Automatic Watch — 1960

Reference number: 3444

Case: 18-karat yellow gold, screw-down case back, leather strap, Ø 35 mm

Movement: Caliber 27-460, rhodium-plated, côtes de Genève, automatic winding

Remarks: automatic men's watch; 18-karat gold rotor

Estimated value: $10,800- ↗

Men's Automatic Watch — 1952

Reference number: 3514

Case: 18-karat yellow gold, screw-down case back, leather strap, Ø 34 mm

Movement: Caliber 27-460M, rhodium-plated, côtes de Genève, gold rotor, Seal of Geneva, 37 jewels, regulated in 8 positions, automatic winding

Remarks: elegant men's watch with subsidiary seconds and date at 3 o'clock

Estimated value: $10,800 ↗

Men's Automatic Watch — 1941

Reference number: 3425

Case: 18-karat red gold, screw-down case back, leather strap, Ø 33 mm

Movement: Caliber 27-460, rhodium-plated, côtes de Genève, gold rotor, automatic winding

Remarks: extremely rare men's watch, manufactured only about 100 times in red gold; this watch was offered with a Patek Philippe folding clasp and certificate

Estimated value: $15,000 ↗

Men's Automatic Watch — 1958

Reference number: 2584

Case: 18-karat rose gold, push-down case back, gold Milanaise bracelet, Ø 36 mm

Movement: Caliber 12-600AT, rhodium-plated, côtes de Genève, gold rotor, 30 jewels, regulated in 8 positions, automatic winding

Remarks: elegant men's watch in rose gold with subsidiary seconds

Estimated value: $12,200 ↗

Piaget

Georges Piaget made pocket watches in the solitary environment of a farming house in La Côte-aux-Fées in 1874. By the beginning of the twentieth century, twenty-five years later, the company had also begun making wristwatches. The success of the brand remained modest, however.

That was to change in the 1950s, when Piaget began producing its own calibers under the leadership of Gerald and Valentin Piaget. The company's profits inclined steeply.

Six years later, Piaget introduced its own manually wound movement. Caliber 9P was very flat and thus followed the fashion of the era. Such flat watch movements were to become Piaget's signature element in the ensuing years. The same was true of automatic Caliber 12P, introduced in 1959. To this day, it remains one of the thinnest automatic calibers in existence. Its full height of only 2.3 millimeters was only possible because Piaget's watchmakers chose to use a micro rotor. Its design was, however,

complicated: in order to guarantee a secure hold for the rotor despite the low height of the movement, the watchmakers used bearings on both sides. So that the small rotor had enough weight to wind the mainspring, they crafted it in 24-karat gold. Thus they achieved a new automatic movement only 0.2 millimeters higher than manually wound Caliber 9P.

Piaget's business continued to develop so positively that the brothers purchased Baume & Mercier in 1964. The family wanted to continue progressing in the area of flat automatic movements, however, and because competitor Lassalle was manufacturing an even thinner movement, in 1983 Piaget simply bought this company's complete stock of discontinued production. Super-thin Caliber 2000—despite being outfitted with a central rotor—was even flatter than Piaget Caliber 12P at 2.08 millimeters.

Piaget's watches can be basically divided into thin, elegant men's models and exceptional jeweled timepieces. Robust sports watches, on the other hand, were not and are not something one can expect to find in this company's collection.

In 1988, some of Piaget's stock was sold to the Vendôme Group (today called Richemont), to which Cartier also belonged. Then in 1993, Piaget was completely sold to this group. Ironically, just a few years previously, the firm would have been able to buy the ailing Cartier group itself—something that would have made Piaget the concern's flagship instead of only a member and movement supplier as it is today.

Automatic Calendar — 1947

Case: stainless steel, screw-down case back, leather strap, Ø 35 mm

Movement: Felsa Caliber 694, rhodium-plated, 25 jewels, automatic winding

Remarks: rare early automatic watch with manual date adjustment by pushing the button at 8 o'clock

Estimated value: $675 →

Men's Watch — 1955

Case: 18-karat yellow gold, push-down case back, leather strap, Ø 34 mm

Movement: ETA Caliber 2390, rhodium-plated, manual winding

Remarks: gold men's watch with portrait of Saudi king Ibn Saud on dial; coat of arms of royal house engraved on case back

Estimated value: $1,900 ↗

Men's Watch — 1957

Case: 18-karat white gold, push-down case back, leather strap

Movement: Piaget Caliber 9P, ultra flat (2mm), côtes de Genève, 18 jewels, regulated in five positions

Remarks: very fine men's watch with fitted, domed case; recessed crown

Estimated value: $2,300 →

Men's Watch Protocole — 1963

Case: 18-karat yellow gold, push-down case back, leather strap

Movement: Piaget Caliber 9P, ultra flat (2mm), côtes de Genève, 18 jewels, regulated in five positions

Remarks: very fine extra-flat men's watch with guilloché case and dial

Estimated value: $2,000 →

Men's Watch — 1960

Case: 18-karat white gold, push-down case back, leather strap

Movement: Piaget Caliber 9P, ultra flat (2mm), côtes de Genève, 18 jewels, regulated in five positions

Remarks: very fine extra-flat men's watch with clous de Paris guilloché decoration on bezel

Estimated value: $2,300 →

Men's Watch — 1967

Case: 18-karat white gold, push-down case back, leather strap

Movement: Piaget Caliber 9P, ultra flat (2mm), côtes de Genève, 18 jewels, regulated in five positions

Remarks: very fine extra-flat men's watch with clous de Paris guilloché decoration

Estimated value: $2,600 →

Men's Watch — 1963

Case: 18-karat yellow gold, push-down case back, covered strap lugs, leather strap

Movement: Piaget Caliber 9P, ultra flat (2mm), côtes de Genève, 18 jewels, regulated in five positions

Remarks: very fine extra flat men's watch

Estimated value: $2,300 →

Men's Automatic Watch — 1980

Case: 18-karat yellow gold, push-down case back, leather strap, Ø 35 mm

Movement: Piaget Caliber 12P1, rhodium-plated, côtes de Genève, micro rotor, 30 jewels, regulated in 6 positions, automatic winding

Remarks: very fine extra flat men's watch with gold buckle; the movement has a micro rotor and was regulated in six positions

Estimated value: $2,450 →

Pierce

In 1888, Léon Levi and his brothers founded the Manufacture des Montres & Chronographes Pierce SA in Biel. The Levi brothers' decision to dedicate themselves completely to making chronographs was courageous and forward-looking at the same time: chronographs were still relatively unimportant at that point. Their heyday began only with mass motorization and the introduction of motor sports. Pierce's chronographs, which were at first outfitted with purchased movements, quickly achieved high recognition. Since over time more and more companies began offering chronographs in their collections, the 1920s were characterized by a higher supply than demand. These watches were harder to sell, and a price war broke out. In order to stabilize the prices, the horological governing bodies fought back. The result was that the *établisseur* Pierce was no longer supplied with *ébauches*: the company had no other choice but to develop and manufacture its own movements in the early 1930s.

Well-known and popular among collectors are the 13-line Pierce chronograph calibers 130 and 134. These autonomous movements are interesting from a technical view since they are outfitted with a vertical clutch, allowing the movement to get along without a separate clutch wheel. Pierce in no way only manufactured chronographs. The creativity of the company's technicians was evident in other developments as well.

In the 1940s, Pierce introduced its own automatic movement, Caliber 861. Although pendulum and rotor windings were both already technically matured, Pierce made its own "shaking" automatic according to a patent from 1933. Here, the winding weight was led straight along two racks. In one direction, a small toothed rack wound the mainspring.

Another special development was the Correctomatic from the 1950s, which may have looked like a chronograph, but wasn't one. The little buttons at 2 and 4 o'clock were used for rate regulation instead. By pushing one of the two buttons, the index was moved. One of the buttons made the movement run faster, and the other slowed it down. This was made possible by a little mechanism that put the pressure on the index, allowing for fine adjustment of the watch. Another specialty was the Duofon: an alarm wristwatch that let its wearer adjust the volume of the alarm. The wearer could choose whether the Duoton should ring loudly or more discreetly, in which case it only rattled quietly. A small window at 6 o'clock displayed whether the watch was set to loud or quiet.

In the 1990s, Pierce was still introducing various models outfitted with different calibers made by other manufacturers. Among these was a small series of an automatic alarm wristwatches outfitted with Omega/Lémania Caliber 980. Like the Omega Memomatic, Pierce's timepiece could also be set precisely to the minute.

Chronograph — 1940

Case: 18-karat red gold, push-down case back, leather strap, Ø 37 mm
Movement: nickel-plated, côtes de Genève, column-wheel control of chronograph, manual winding
Remarks: gold chronograph with 60-minute counter
Estimated value: $1,900 →

Chronograph — 1950

Case: gold-plated, stainless steel push-down case back, leather strap, Ø 37 mm
Movement: rhodium-plated, decorated, column-wheel control of chronograph, manual winding
Remarks: chronograph with rare 60-minute counter
Estimated value: $675 →

Chronograph — 1945

Case: chrome-plated, stainless steel push-down case back, leather strap, Ø 36 mm
Movement: nickel-plated, column-wheel control of chronograph, manual winding
Remarks: chronograph with rare 60-minute counter
Estimated value: $1,100 →

Chronograph — 1940

Case: chrome-plated, stainless steel push-down case back, leather strap, Ø 34 mm
Movement: nickel-plated, côtes de Genève, column-wheel control of chronograph, manual winding
Remarks: unusual one-button chronograph with button at 4 o'clock
Estimated value: $550 →

Correctomatic — 1950

Case: gold-plated, stainless steel screw-down case back, leather strap, Ø 35 mm
Movement: nickel-plated, with regulating lever system via button, manual winding
Remarks: on the Correctomatic the watch's rate can be regulated forward or backward using a button on the case; Pierce's own regulating lever system makes this possible
Estimated value: $1,100 ↗

Duofon — 1965

Case: stainless steel, push-down case back, leather strap, Ø 33 mm
Movement: Caliber 135, nickel-plated, twin spring barrels, gong, manual winding
Remarks: alarm wristwatch with Pierce manufacture caliber; movement has integrated gong; second crown allows the alarm volume to be chosen
Estimated value: $1,100 ↗

Automatic — 1946

Reference number: 311199
Case: chrome-plated, stainless steel screw-down case back, leather strap, Ø 37.5 mm
Movement: Caliber 861, nickel-plated, 17 jewels, automatic winding
Remarks: rare early automatic watch by Pierce; Caliber 861 has a so-called "shaking" weight that tensions the mainspring via a toothed rack
Estimated value: $800 →

Alarm — 1976

Case: stainless steel, screw-down case back, leather strap
Movement: Caliber AS 5008, 17 jewels, automatic winding
Remarks: automatic wristwatch alarm with AS movement
Estimated value: $525 →

Record

Record's watches are only known among collectors these days. This company was founded in 1903 as Record Dreadnought Watch, a somewhat martial moniker. As the name suggests, these watches didn't need to shy away from their competitors: the highest rate precision possible was the uppermost goal of the small watch manufacturer. According to those in charge, this could only be achieved if the components were manufactured as precisely as possible. Manufacturing tolerances that were too great were, according to the company, one of the main elements negatively influencing the precise rate of a watch.

This concept displayed the desired success in the 1920s. At this time, Record Watch already entertained three production facilities where both pocket and wristwatches were manu-factured. Many timepieces by Record were delivered with an official chronometer certifi-cate. But even without a chronometer certificate, Record's watches achieved the best rates. This was certainly one of the reasons why Record Watch was allowed to provide various military outfits with service watches all over the world.

Alongside chronometers, Record is above all known for its calendar watches, the so-called Datofix models. Both three-handed watches and chronographs were outfitted with complete calendar mechanisms and an optional moon phase. Chronographs, among them some with split-seconds functions, were also something Record had in its program. It was here that mainly manually wound movements by Venus were used.

Most of the movements, however, came from the company's own production. Record's first movement with automatic winding was Caliber 161/162, presented in 1944, and then successor model 171/172. This was an automatic movement with winding according to the Harwood principle, using a weight on a central bearing that was not able to swing freely, but rather oscillated between two spring-loaded limiting bumpers. This hammering movement is the reason that the system is also called a hammer automatic.

The successor to the hammer automatics from 1952 was Caliber 174, a modern rotor automatic that was also available with date and power reserve displays.

In 1961, Record Watch Co. lost its independence and was sold to Longines in Saint-Imier. After that, watches were produced under the double signature "Record Longines." These watches were no longer outfitted with *manufacture* calibers, but mainly ETA technology. For Longines, this formerly reputable brand was only a subsidiary that manufactured reasonably priced watches, and it was later completely abandoned.

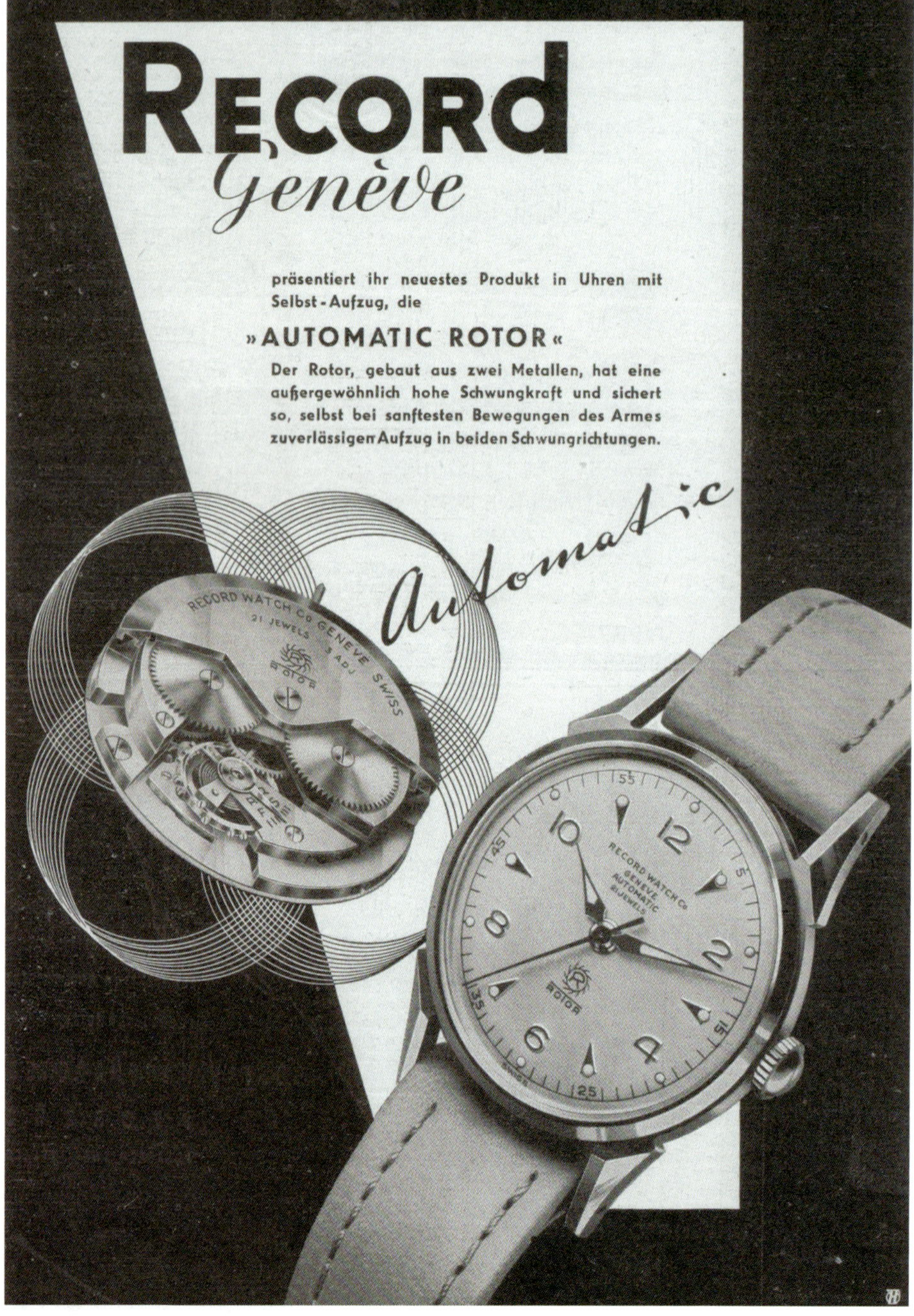

Automatic — 1950

Case: 14-karat red gold, screw-down case back, leather strap, Ø 33 mm

Movement: Caliber 172, rhodium-plated, 20 jewels, automatic winding

Remarks: red gold hammer automatic; this watch was offered in its original box

Estimated value: $550 →

Automatic — 1950

Case: 14-karat red gold, screw-down case back, leather strap, Ø 33 mm

Movement: Caliber 172, rhodium-plated, 20 jewels, automatic winding

Remarks: red gold hammer automatic; this watch was offered in its original box

Estimated value: $550 →

Rotor Automatic — 1953

Case: stainless steel, screw-down case back, leather strap

Movement: Caliber 174, rhodium-plated, automatic winding

Remarks: bilaterally winding automatic movement with unusual direction changer

Estimated value: $550 →

Rotor Automatic — 1956

Case: gold-plated, stainless steel push-down case back, leather strap

Movement: Caliber 174, rhodium-plated, 21 jewels, regulated in 3 positions

Remarks: large automatic outfitted with the rare Record automatic caliber 174

Estimated value: $550 →

Datofix — 1956

Case: 18-karat red gold, push-down case back, leather strap, Ø 32 mm

Movement: nickel-plated, côtes de Genève, jewels set in chatons, manual winding

Remarks: men's watch with complete calendar and moon phase

Estimated value: $1,350 →

Datofix — 1950

Case: stainless steel, screw-down case back, leather strap, Ø 34 mm

Movement: Caliber 1076, nickel-plated, manual winding

Remarks: men's watch with complete calendar and moon phase

Estimated value: $1,500 →

Datofix — 1945

Case: 18-karat red gold, push-down case back, leather strap, Ø 35 mm

Movement: Caliber 1066, nickel-plated, côtes de Genève, jewels set in chatons, manual winding

Remarks: men's watch with complete calendar and moon phase

Estimated value: $1,600 →

Calendar Watch with Moon Phase — 1945

Case: gold-plated, screw-down case back, leather strap, Ø 34 mm

Movement: Caliber 107C, nickel-plated, manual winding

Remarks: men's watch with complete calendar and moon phase

Estimated value: $1,100 →

Datofix — 1945

Case: 18-karat red gold, push-down case back, leather strap, Ø 35 mm

Movement: nickel-plated, manual winding

Remarks: red gold men's watch with complete calendar and moon phase

Estimated value: $1,600 →

Bidynator Automatic — 1955

Case: 18-karat yellow gold, screw-down case back, leather strap, Ø 37 mm

Movement: Felsa caliber, nickel-plated, automatic winding

Remarks: automatic men's watch with Felsa Bidynator automatic caliber; complete calendar and moon phase

Estimated value: $1,900 →

Chronograph — 1930

Case: stainless steel, push-down case back, leather strap, Ø 35 mm

Movement: silver-plated, côtes de Genève, column-wheel control of chronograph, manual winding

Remarks: chronograph with 45-minute counter and movable strap lugs

Estimated value: $800 →

Chronograph — 1950

Case: 18-karat yellow gold, push-down case back, leather strap, Ø 38 mm

Movement: nickel-plated, côtes de Genève, column-wheel control of chronograph, manual winding

Remarks: heavy gold chronograph with 45-minute counter

Estimated value: $2,000 →

Chronograph — 1950

Case: stainless steel, push-down case back, leather strap, Ø 37 mm

Movement: rhodium-plated, côtes de Genève, column-wheel control of chronograph, manual winding

Remarks: chronograph with 45-minute counter

Estimated value: $550 →

General Service Watch W.W.W. — 1948

Case: stainless steel, screw-down case back, textile strap, Ø 35 mm

Movement: Caliber 022K, rhodium-plated, manual winding

Remarks: men's watch of the British armed forces "W.W.W."

Estimated value: $550 →

Chronograph with Complete Calendar — 1945

Case: stainless steel, gold-plated, push-down case back, leather strap, Ø 35 mm

Movement: Caliber 88, nickel-plated, côtes de Genève, column-wheel control of chronograph, manual winding

Remarks: elegant chronograph with 30-minute and 12-hour counters; complete calendar and moon phase

Estimated value: $1,600 →

Calendar Watch with Moon Phase — 1955

Case: gold-plated, stainless steel push-down case back, leather strap, Ø 36 mm

Movement: Venus Caliber 206, nickel-plated, manual winding

Remarks: men's watch with complete calendar and moon phase

Estimated value: $1,100 →

By Amanda Triossi and
Daniela Mascetti
600 full-color illustrations
320 pages · 9⅝ x 13³/₁₆
ISBN-13: 978-7892-0945-0
$75.00 · Cloth

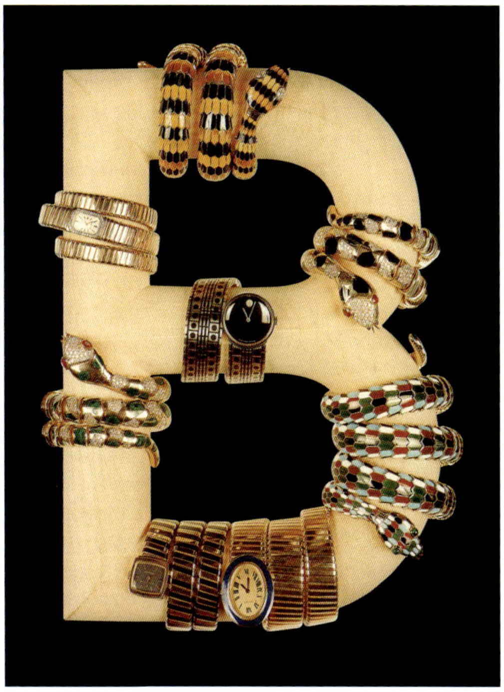

Bulgari

A dazzlingly illustrated history of Bulgari jewelry, this engaging book tells the story of the world's first family of jewelers, goldsmiths, and silversmiths, and the pieces that made their name.

Since its start in Rome in 1884, the Bulgari firm has succeeded in launching influential trends and revivals in jewelry design. In this captivating volume, new photography and archival pictures trace the development of the Bulgari style, a distinctive look that has enchanted royalty, movie stars, and others for more than a century.

Published by ABBEVILLE PRESS
137 Varick Street, New York, NY 10013
1-800-ARTBOOK (in U.S. only)
Also available wherever fine books are sold
Visit us at www.abbeville.com

Rolex

Rolex cannot be compared to any other company in the watch industry. This brand has long said good-bye to any of the usual standards, and its products are always preceded by a mythical reputation. Rolex stands for glamour and wealth, but also for precision and innovation. And there is one man is to thank for all of that: Hans Wilsdorf.

This self-made man—at the age of twelve he was orphaned and forced to find his way alone through the world—first learned everything about timekeepers when working at a large watch wholesaling outfit in La Chaux-de-Fonds. With this experience under his belt, the German later went to London to build up a watch wholesale business with a rich partner named Davis. He soon put all his money on wristwatches, for they were in demand among gentlemen since the Boer War in Africa had shown them to be so practical—they had a strong masculine image.

Wilsdorf focused on small 11-line calibers that he purchased from Swiss producer Aegler in Biel. They were even superior to many pocket watches in rate precision and robustness. The proof: Wilsdorf had one of his Aegler Caliber 1910s tested as a chronometer at a Swiss observatory, and it became the first wristwatch caliber to receive a chronometer certificate. In 1914, he repeated this experiment in Kew, England. This watch also did excellently and received a Class A certificate.

Wilsdorf had successfully introduced and maintained the Rolex brand name and the logo with the five-pointed crown for eleven years when he started having customs trouble in the British Empire in 1919 and had to move his business to Switzerland. In Geneva he founded Montres Rolex SA. Five years previously, Wilsdorf had won Aegler over as his exclusive movement supplier. He made Rolex Watch Co., Aegler SA out of this firm.

Rolex's success is based on two great inventions that helped wristwatches to their breakthrough, making them what they are today: water resistance and self-winding. Wilsdorf developed the first absolutely water-resistant Oyster case to house the Aegler movements. Because the constant winding of the movement threatened this water resistance, Wilsdorf developed the first serially mature rotor automatic with his technicians in 1931—and the Oyster Perpetual was born. From this point on, it was to be the standard, and to this day most automatic watches function according to its principle.

The Oyster remains the company's best-known model, especially the diver's watches and chronographs. The early Prince and Cellini models were not only reliable, they were also elegant timepieces.

Thanks to consistent development, the Oyster remained the measuring stick for robust sports watches. Modified as the Submariner, it became the first professional diver's watch. As the Oyster Sea Dweller it even received a helium valve and special gas mixtures for professional diving.

Rolex watches have also impressively proven their reliability on many expeditions. They have already been on top of Mount Everest, at both Poles, and at the deepest point of the earth, the Mariana Trench more than 11,000 meters down—and even in space.

As a senior citizen, Wilsdorf donated his shares of the company to the Wilsdorf Foundation he had established since he had no heirs. After his death in 1960, André J. Heiniger took the reins. In 1992, his son Patrick Heiniger followed him as president.

Oyster Chronograph Antimagnetic Jean-Claude Killy

1954

Reference number: 6036

Case: stainless steel, screw-down case back, leather strap, Ø 36 mm

Movement: Caliber 72C, rhodium-plated, column-wheel control of chronograph, manual winding

Remarks: rare chronograph with 30-minute and 12-hour counters; complete calendar with date, weekday, and month; model named for skiing race great of the same name

Estimated value: $81,000 →

Oyster Chronograph

1953

Reference number: 6236

Case: 18-karat yellow gold, tripartite, screw-down case back, leather strap, Ø 36 mm

Movement: Caliber 72C, rhodium-plated, finely finished, column-wheel control of chronograph, finely finished, beveled steel chronograph components, mirror-polished screws

Remarks: extremely rare chronograph with 30-minute and 12-hour counters; complete calendar; Ref. 6236 is the so-called Jean-Claudy Killy; only 170 pieces of this model in yellow gold were manufactured

Estimated value: $81,000 →

Chronograph Dato Compax

1949

Reference number: 4768

Case: stainless steel, tripartite, push-down case back, leather strap, Ø 35 mm

Movement: Caliber 72C, rhodium-plated, finely finished, column-wheel control of chronograph, finely finished, beveled steel chronograph components, mirror-polished screws, 17 jewels

Remarks: rare chronograph with 30-minute and 12-hour counters; complete calendar with date hand and window display of weekday and month; only 220 pieces of Ref. 4768 were manufactured

Estimated value: $81,000 ↗

Chronograph with Complete Calendar

1950

Reference number: 4768

Case: 18-karat rose gold, push-down case back, leather strap, Ø 35 mm

Movement: Valjoux Caliber 72C, rhodium-plated, column-wheel control of chronograph, manual winding

Remarks: rare rose gold chronograph with 30-minute and 12-hour counters; complete calendar and tachymeter scale

Estimated value: $61,000 →

Oyster Perpetual Chronometer Officially Certified

1953

Reference number: 6062

Case: stainless steel, screw-down case back, stainless steel link bracelet, Ø 36 mm

Movement: rhodium-plated, automatic winding

Remarks: extremely rare Oyster with complete calendar and moon phase; only 350 pieces of this model were manufactured in red gold, and just a few pieces in stainless steel between 1950 and 1953

Estimated value: $135,000 →

Oyster Perpetual Chronometer

1953

Reference number: 6062

Case: 18-karat yellow gold, bipartite, screw-down case back, leather strap, Ø 35 mm

Movement: rhodium-plated, polished screws, winding rotor

Remarks: extremely rare men's watch with complete calendar; date hand; window display of weekday and month; moon phase at 6 o'clock; only 350 pieces of this model were manufactured in red gold between 1950 and 1953

Estimated value: $74,300 ↗

Perpetual Chronometer Precision

1950

Reference number: 8171

Case: stainless steel, screw-down case back, leather strap, Ø 38 mm

Movement: rhodium-plated, automatic winding

Remarks: extremely rare Oyster with complete calendar, subsidiary seconds, and moon phase; this model was only manufactured in a small series and is difficult to find; this watch is number 279

Estimated value: $74,300 ↗

Perpetual Chronometer

1949

Reference number: 8171

Case: 18-karat red gold, push-down case back, leather strap, Ø 38 mm

Movement: rhodium-plated, automatic winding

Remarks: extremely rare men's watch manufactured in small series; this watch bears the number 202 and is nearly impossible to find in red gold; this watch was offered in its original box

Estimated value: $54,000 ↗

Military Antimagnetic Chronograph — 1932

Reference number: 2508

Case: stainless steel, tripartite, push-down case back, leather strap, Ø 35 mm

Movement: nickel-plated, finely finished, column-wheel control of chronograph, finely finished steel chronograph components, polished screws

Remarks: rare chronograph with 30-minute counter; this chronograph is one of the first chronograph models manufactured by Rolex

Estimated value: $40,500 ↗

Model — 1935

Reference number: 3371

Case: 18-karat yellow gold, tripartite, push-down case back, leather strap, Ø 35 mm

Movement: nickel-plated, finely finished, column-wheel control of chronograph, finely finished steel chronograph components, polished screws, 17 jewels

Remarks: rare very fine chronograph with 30-minute counter, tachymeter and blue telemeter scales; this watch was offered with a gold Rolex buckle

Estimated value: $27,000 →

Chronograph Antimagnétique — 1926

Reference number: 2057

Case: 18-karat yellow gold, tripartite, push-down case back, leather strap, 32 x 37 mm

Movement: nickel-plated, finely finished, column-wheel control of chronograph, finely finished, beveled steel chronograph components, polished screws

Remarks: very rare one-button chronograph with 30-minute counter; chronograph button integrated into crown

Estimated value: $47,500 →

Model — 1930

Reference number: 2919

Case: stainless steel, tripartite, push-down case back, leather strap, 33 x 44 mm

Movement: rhodium-plated, column-wheel control of chronograph, fine matte steel chronograph components

Remarks: very rare chronograph with 30-minute counter; tachymeter and telemeter scales; this watch was described in Paolo Gabbi's book *Rolex Chronographs*

Estimated value: $33,800 →

Chronograph Antimagnétique — 1946

Reference number: 2508

Case: stainless steel, push-down case back, leather strap, Ø 35 mm

Movement: rhodium-plated, column-wheel control of chronograph, manual winding

Remarks: automatic chronograph with 30-minute counter

Estimated value: $20,300 ↗

Chronograph Antimagnétique — 1950

Case: 18-karat yellow gold, push-down case back, leather strap, Ø 30 mm

Movement: nickel-plated, column-wheel control of chronograph, manual winding

Remarks: extremely rare chronograph with 30-minute counter and tachymeter scale

Estimated value: $16,000 →

Chronograph — 1948

Reference number: 4099

Case: stainless steel, push-down case back, leather strap, Ø 35 mm

Movement: rhodium-plated, column-wheel control of chronograph, manual winding

Remarks: rare chronograph in stainless steel with exceptional strap lugs

Estimated value: $17,500 ↗

Chronograph Antimagnetic — 1934

Reference number: 2508

Case: 18-karat yellow gold, push-down case back, leather strap, Ø 36 mm

Movement: nickel-plated, column-wheel control of chronograph, manual winding

Remarks: one of the first chronographs manufactured by Rolex with 30-minute counter and tachymeter scale

Estimated value: $21,600 ↗

Net2Watches

An Internet-Based Market

Exhibit Buy Sell Trade

Pre-owned, antique and collectible
wristwatches, pocket watches,
art and sculpture clocks

ONE MARKET, MANY EXHIBITORS

We put the world of watches in the palm of your hand!

www.Net2Watches.com
Email: Net2Watches@Net2Watches.com
Tel: 877-777-9771 • Tel: 516-317-7741 • Fax: 516-773-4297

Chronograph Antimagnétique

Reference number: 3834

Case: 18-karat yellow gold, push-down case back, leather strap, Ø 32 mm

Movement: rhodium-plated, manual winding

Remarks: extremely rare chronograph with 30-minute counter and tachymeter scale

Estimated value: $16,200 →

1934

Oyster Chronograph

Reference number: 4500

Case: stainless steel, screw-down case back, leather strap, Ø 36 mm

Movement: Caliber R23, rhodium-plated, column-wheel control of chronograph, manual winding

Remarks: rare Oyster chronograph with 30-minute counter and tachymeter scale

Estimated value: $21,600 ↗

1947

Chronograph Antimagnetic

Reference number: 3525

Case: 18-karat yellow gold, screw-down case back, leather strap, Ø 35 mm

Movement: rhodium-plated, column-wheel control of chronograph, manual winding

Remarks: one of the first Oyster chronographs manufactured by Rolex from 1945; 30-minute counter and telemeter scale; this watch was offered in its original box

Estimated value: $34,000 ↗

1945

Chronograph

Reference number: 3233

Case: 18-karat red gold, push-down case back, leather strap, Ø 31 mm

Movement: rhodium-plated, column-wheel control of chronograph, manual winding

Remarks: red gold chronograph with 30-minute counter

Estimated value: $9,500 →

1933

Oyster Chronograph

Reference number: 4500

Case: stainless steel, screw-down case back, gold bezel, leather strap, Ø 36 mm

Movement: rhodium-plated, column-wheel control of chronograph, manual winding

Remarks: Oyster chronograph with 30-minute counter; this watch was offered in its original box

Estimated value: $16,200 ↗

1949

Oyster Chronograph Antimagnetic

Reference number: 6234

Case: stainless steel, tripartite, screw-down case back, stainless steel link bracelet, Ø 36 mm

Movement: Valjoux Caliber 72, nickel-plated, finely finished, column-wheel control of chronograph, finely finished steel chronograph components, polished screws, 17 jewels

Remarks: rare chronograph with 30-minute and 12-hour counters; tachymeter and telemeter scales in Oyster case

Estimated value: $40,500 ↗

1962

Chronograph (Pre-Daytona)

Case: 14-karat yellow gold, screw-down case back, Ø 36 mm

Movement: rhodium-plated, column-wheel control of chronograph, manual winding

Remarks: blue tachymeter scale

Estimated value: $81,000 ↗

1965

Chronograph (Pre-Daytona)

Reference number: 6238

Case: stainless steel, screw-down case back, stainless steel link bracelet, Ø 36 mm

Movement: Caliber 722.1, rhodium-plated, column-wheel control of chronograph, 17 jewels, regulated in 3 positions, manual winding

Remarks: chronograph with 30-minute and 12-hour counters

Estimated value: $31,050 ↗

1966

Chronograph (Pre-Daytona)

1965

Reference number: 6238

Case: 14-karat yellow gold, screw-down case back, gold link bracelet, Ø 32 mm

Movement: Caliber 72B, rhodium-plated, column-wheel control of chronograph, manual winding

Remarks: chronograph with 30-minute and 12-hour counters

Estimated value: $59,400 ↗

Oyster Superlative Chronometer Cosmograph Daytona

1977

Reference number: 6263

Case: 18-karat yellow gold, tripartite, screw-down case back, yellow gold link bracelet, Ø 38 mm

Movement: Caliber 727/1531, rhodium-plated, finely finished, column-wheel control of chronograph, finely finished, beveled steel chronograph components, 17 jewels, regulated in 3 positions

Remarks: 30-minute and 12-hour counters; screw-in crown and buttons; this watch was offered in its original box and with a certificate

Estimated value: $31,000 ↗

Oyster Cosmograph Daytona

1968

Reference number: 6239/6263

Case: stainless steel, screw-down case back, stainless steel link bracelet, Ø 37 mm

Movement: Caliber 727, rhodium-plated, column-wheel control of chronograph, manual winding

Remarks: rare Cosmograph model with 30-minute and 12-hour counters; tachymeter scale on bezel

Estimated value: $28,400 ↗

Oyster Cosmograph Daytona

1979

Reference number: 6265/6263

Case: stainless steel, screw-down case back, stainless steel link bracelet, Ø 37 mm

Movement: Caliber 727, rhodium-plated, column-wheel control of chronograph, manual winding

Remarks: Daytona chronograph model with 30-minute and 12-hour counters; this watch was offered in its original box with a certificate, operation manual, and original invoice

Estimated value: $27,000 ↗

Oyster Cosmograph Daytona

1979

Reference number: 6265/6263

Case: stainless steel, screw-down case back, stainless steel link bracelet, Ø 37 mm

Movement: Caliber 727, rhodium-plated, column-wheel control of chronograph, manual winding

Remarks: Daytona chronograph model with 30-minute and 12-hour counters; this watch was offered in its original box and with certificate

Estimated value: $28,400 →

Oyster Cosmograph Daytona Paul Newman

1967

Reference number: 6239

Case: stainless steel, screw-down case back, stainless steel link bracelet, Ø 36 mm

Movement: column-wheel control of chronograph, manual winding

Remarks: Paul Newman Daytona chronograph model; this watch was offered in its original box and with a certificate

Estimated value: $54,000 ↗

Oyster Cosmograph Daytona Paul Newman

1960

Reference number: 6240

Case: stainless steel, screw-down case back, stainless steel link bracelet, Ø 37 mm

Movement: rhodium-plated, column-wheel control of chronograph, manual winding

Remarks: rare Daytona chronograph model with black tachymeter scale on bezel; this watch was offered with service chit and confirmation of authenticity

Estimated value: $54,000 ↗

Oyster Chronometer Cosmograph

1982

Reference number: 6263/6265

Case: 18-karat yellow gold, screw-down case back, gold link bracelet, Ø 37 mm

Movement: Caliber 727, rhodium-plated, column-wheel control of chronograph, manual winding

Remarks: rare Cosmograph model with 30-minute and 12 hour counters; tachymeter scale on bezel

Estimated value: $35,000 ↗

Oyster Chronometer Cosmograph

1957

Reference number: 6241

Case: 18-karat yellow gold, screw-down case back, leather strap, Ø 37 mm

Movement: Caliber 727, rhodium-plated, column-wheel control of chronograph, manual winding

Remarks: rare Cosmograph model with 30-minute and 12-hour counters; tachymeter scale on bezel

Estimated value: $40,500 ↗

Cosmograph

1980

Reference number: 6265

Case: 18-karat yellow gold, screw-down case back, leather strap, Ø 37 mm

Movement: Caliber 722, rhodium-plated, column-wheel control of chronograph, manual winding

Remarks: rare Cosmograph mode with 30-minute and 12-hour counters; tachymeter scale on bezel

Estimated value: $37,800 ↗

Men's Watch

1930

Reference number: 1017

Case: 9-karat yellow gold, push-down case back, leather strap, 27 x 27 mm

Movement: rhodium-plated, 17 jewels, regulated in 6 positions, manual winding

Remarks: early men's watch in gold case

Estimated value: $1,600 →

Men's Watch

1937

Reference number: 3139

Case: stainless steel, screw-down case back, leather strap, 29 x 37 mm

Movement: rhodium-plated, decorated, manual winding

Remarks: rare men's watch in cushion-shaped case

Estimated value: $2,700 →

Oyster Imperial Chronometer

1937

Reference number: 3116

Case: stainless steel, screw-down case back, leather strap, 30 x 38 mm

Movement: rhodium-plated, 18 jewels, regulated in 6 positions, manual winding

Remarks: rare Oyster Imperial chronograph model in tonneau-shaped case

Estimated value: $2,160 →

Oyster Chronometer Viceroy

1940

Reference number: 3359

Case: stainless steel/red gold, tripartite, screw-down case back, stainless steel/red gold link bracelet, 29 x 38 mm

Movement: nickel-plated, finely finished, polished screws, patented Super balance, 17 jewels, regulated in 7 positions

Remarks: extremely rare Oyster Viceroy model in a two-tone case; movement outfitted with patented Super Balance

Estimated value: $5,400 →

Oyster Channel Swimmer

1935

Reference number: 3224

Case: silver, screw-down case back, leather strap, Ø 33 mm

Movement: rhodium-plated, manual winding

Remarks: this watch, known as the Channel Swimmer, commemorates the swimming of the English Channel, which Mercedes Gleitze completed in 1927 wearing a Rolex Oyster—the most impressive test of robustness for a water-resistant wristwatch to that point

Estimated value: $2,700 →

Oyster Chronometer

1932

Reference number: 3474

Case: 9-karat yellow gold, screw-down case back, leather strap, 32 x 35 mm

Movement: rhodium-plated, manual winding

Remarks: early water-resistant Oyster

Estimated value: $4,050 →

Oyster For All Climates — 1924

Case: 9-karat yellow gold, screw-down case back, leather strap, 32 x 34 mm

Movement: rhodium-plated, regulated in 6 positions, manual winding

Remarks: with its predicate "for all climates," this rare Oyster model points out the fact that it was able to handle all climate difficulties

Estimated value: $2,700 →

Oyster — 1927

Reference number: 2136

Case: 9-karat yellow gold, screw-down case back, leather strap, Ø 32 mm

Movement: rhodium-plated, manual winding

Remarks: extremely rare early Oyster model in octagonal case with subsidiary seconds

Estimated value: $2,400 →

Oyster Observatory Ellsworth — 1938

Reference number: 3121

Case: gold-plated, stainless steel screw-down case back, leather strap, 29 x 35 mm

Movement: rhodium-plated, manual winding

Remarks: rare Oyster Ellsworth Observatory model

Estimated value: $1,350 →

Oyster Raleigh — 1941

Reference number: 3478

Case: stainless steel, screw-down case back, leather strap, 29 x 75 mm

Movement: rhodium-plated, manual winding

Remarks: rare Oyster Raleigh model

Estimated value: $1,900 →

Chronometer — 1928

Case: stainless steel/yellow gold, screw-down case back, leather strap, Ø 28 mm

Movement: rhodium-plated, manual winding

Remarks: rare two-tone men's watch in unusual case with covered strap lugs

Estimated value: $2,700 →

Oyster Junior Sport Extraprima — 1963

Reference number: 2784

Case: stainless steel, screw-down case back, leather strap, Ø 30 mm

Movement: rhodium-plated, manual winding

Remarks: rare Rolex Junior Sport Extraprima model

Estimated value: $2,700 →

Oyster Sport Aqua — 1940

Reference number: 3136

Case: stainless steel, screw-down case back, leather strap, 30 mm

Movement: rhodium-plated, automatic winding

Remarks: rare Oyster Sport Aqua model

Estimated value: $2,400 →

Oyster Perpetual Chronometer California Dial — 1949

Reference number: 5013

Case: stainless steel, screw-down case back, red gold bezel, 32 x 39 mm

Movement: rhodium-plated, automatic winding

Remarks: rare Oyster model with original California dial and subsidiary seconds

Estimated value: $4,700 ↗

Oyster Perpetual Chronometer

1939

Reference number: 3348

Case: stainless steel, screw-down case back, leather strap, Ø 29 mm

Movement: rhodium-plated, automatic winding

Remarks: extremely rare Oyster chronometer with very wide bezel

Estimated value: $2,700 ↗

Oyster Perpetual Chronometer
For Ronchi, Milan

1932

Reference number: 3347

Case: 18-karat red gold, screw-down case back, leather strap, Ø 29 mm

Movement: rhodium-plated, automatic winding

Remarks: extremely rare early Oyster model with double hour markers; III and IV hour markers are vertical on bezel, but lay flat on the dial; rare double signature "Ronchi Milano"

Estimated value: $13,500 ↗

Prince Chronometer

1935

Case: 18-karat yellow gold, push-down case back, leather strap, 20 x 40 mm

Movement: rhodium-plated, regulated in 8 positions, manual winding

Remarks: elegant Prince Classic model

Estimated value: $6,100 →

Prince 1/4 Century Club

1930

Reference number: 3937

Case: 14-karat yellow gold, push-down case back, leather strap, 22 x 44 mm

Movement: rhodium-plated, regulated in 6 positions, manual winding

Remarks: rare Rolex Prince as 1/4 Century Club model commemorating the company's 25th year as part of the Eaton Concern

Estimated value: $9,200 →

Prince Railway Observatory Quality

1936

Reference number: 1527M

Case: 18-karat white/yellow gold, push-down case back, leather strap, 22 x 42 mm

Movement: rhodium-plated, 15 jewels, regulated in 6 positions, manual winding

Remarks: rare Prince Railway model in perfect condition with observatory-quality movement

Estimated value: $16,000 ↗

Prince Railway Jump Hours
Observatory Quality

1930

Reference number: 1587HS

Case: 18-karat red/white gold, push-down case back, leather strap, 23 x 42 mm

Movement: rhodium-plated, regulated in 6 positions, manual winding

Remarks: rare men's watch in a stepped rectangular case with jump, digital hours and subsidiary seconds

Estimated value: $27,000 ↗

Prince Aerodynamic Chronometer

1950

Reference number: 3361

Case: 18-karat rose gold, bipartite, push-down case back, leather strap, 19 x 46 mm

Movement: Caliber 310, rhodium-plated, finely finished, polished screws, Ultra Prima quality, 18 jewels, regulated in 6 positions

Remarks: asymmetric Prince Aerodynamic model; introduced in 1939; Caliber 310 was manufactured from 1932 to 1938, but was also housed in later Prince models of Ultra Prima quality; this watch was offered with an 18-karat Rolex buckle

Estimated value: $13,500 →

Prince Brancard Chronometer
Extraprima

1934

Reference number: 971

Case: 18-karat yellow gold, push-down case back, leather strap, 25 x 43 mm

Movement: rhodium-plated, regulated in 8 positions, manual winding

Remarks: rare Prince chronometer in Art Deco style

Estimated value: $16,900 ↗

Prince Brancard Chronometer
Extraprima Observatory Quality

1935

Reference number: 971U

Case: silver/red gold, push-down case back, leather strap, 26 x 43 mm

Movement: rhodium-plated, 15 jewels, regulated in 6 positions, manual winding

Remarks: elegant men's watch in Brancard case; observatory-quality movement, regulated in six positions

Estimated value: $19,000 ↗

Prince Brancard Chronometer
Observatory Quality

1935

Case: 16-karat white/yellow gold, push-down case back, leather strap, 26 x 43 mm

Movement: Caliber 971, rhodium-plated, regulated in 6 positions, manual winding

Remarks: rare Prince Brancard chronometer with an observatory-quality movement

Estimated value: $30,000 ↗

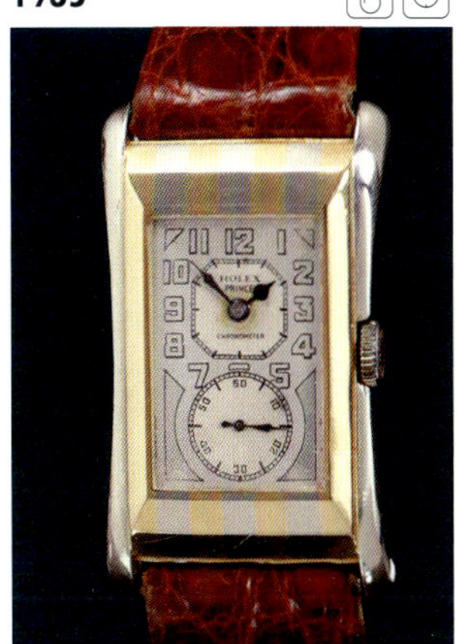

Prince Brancard Chronometer
Jump Hours Extra Prima
Observatory Quality

1945

Reference number: 1491

Case: 9-karat white gold, push-down case back, leather strap, 25 x 43 mm

Movement: rhodium-plated, regulated in 6 positions, manual winding

Remarks: rare chronometer with digital jump hour display; this watch was offered in its original box and with an original rate certificate from the observatory in Biel

Estimated value: $40,500 ↗

Oyster Perpetual Super Precision

1932

Reference number: 3353

Case: stainless steel/gold, screw-down case back, stainless steel link bracelet, Ø 29 mm

Movement: rhodium-plated, automatic winding

Remarks: extremely rare early automatic Oyster model with subsidiary seconds

Estimated value: $10,800 ↗

Oyster Perpetual Chronometer
Bubble Back Hooded Lugs

1982

Case: stainless steel/gold, screw-down case back, leather strap, Ø 32 mm

Movement: rhodium-plated, automatic winding

Remarks: Oyster Perpetual model with Roman numerals and hooded lugs

Estimated value: $6,100 →

Oyster Perpetual Chronometer
Bubble Back

1948

Reference number: 3372

Case: stainless steel, screw-down case back, leather strap, Ø 32 mm

Movement: rhodium-plated, automatic winding

Remarks: so-called Oyster Bubble Back

Estimated value: $4,100 →

Oyster Precision California Dial

1966

Reference number: 6424

Case: stainless steel, screw-down case back, leather strap, Ø 36 mm

Movement: rhodium-plated, manual winding

Remarks: extremely rare Oyster model with California dial; this watch was offered in its original box and with certificate

Estimated value: $4,700 ↗

Oyster Perpetual Chronometer with
Mickey Mouse Dial

1949

Reference number: 3131

Case: 14-karat rose gold, screw-down case back, leather strap, Ø 32 mm

Movement: rhodium-plated, automatic winding

Remarks: rare Oyster Perpetual model with original Mickey Mouse dial; this watch was offered in its original box and with a Rolex buckle

Estimated value: $13,500 →

Oyster Perpetual Chronometer Bubble Back

1940

Reference number: 3131

Case: 14-karat red gold, screw-down case back, leather strap, 32 x 39 mm

Movement: rhodium-plated, automatic winding

Remarks: rare red gold Bubble Back

Estimated value: $6,100 →

Oyster Perpetual Bubble Back

1948

Reference number: 3133

Case: stainless steel, screw-down case back, gold bezel, stainless steel/gold link bracelet, Ø 32 mm

Movement: rhodium-plated, automatic winding

Remarks: Oyster Bubble Back model with legible, large, luminous numerals

Estimated value: $8,800 ↗

Oyster Perpetual Chronometer Bubble Back Hooded Lugs

1949

Reference number: 3065

Case: stainless steel/gold, screw-down case back, two-tone link bracelet, 32 x 40 mm

Movement: rhodium-plated, automatic winding

Remarks: extremely rare Bubble Back model with hooded strap lugs and original California dial; this watch was offered in original box

Estimated value: $16,000 ↗

Oyster Peropetual Chronometer Bubble Back

1940

Reference number: 3131

Case: 14-karat rose gold, tripartite, screw-down case back, leather strap, Ø 32 mm

Movement: rhodium-plated, polished screws, winding rotor

Remarks: so-called Bubble Back chronometer in a rose gold case; this watch was offered with a Rolex gold buckle

Estimated value: $6,800 ↗

Oyster Perpetual Chronometer

1949

Reference number: 3131

Case: 18-karat yellow gold, tripartite, screw-down case back, 18-karat Oyster gold link bracelet, Ø 32 mm

Movement: rhodium-plated, polished screws, winding rotor

Remarks: rare Oyster chronometer with green enamel dial; this watch was offered in its original box

Estimated value: $54,000 ↗

Oyster Perpetual Chronometer

1948

Reference number: 3131

Case: 18-karat yellow gold, tripartite, screw-down case back, 18-karat Oyster gold link bracelet, Ø 32 mm

Movement: rhodium-plated, polished screws, winding rotor

Remarks: rare automatic Bubble Back chronometer with blue enamel dial; this watch was offered in its original box

Estimated value: $54,000 ↗

Oyster Perpetual Chronometer

1948

Reference number: 3327

Case: 18-karat yellow gold, tripartite, screw-down case back, 18-karat Oyster gold link bracelet, Ø 32 mm

Movement: rhodium-plated, polished screws, winding rotor

Remarks: rare Oyster Bubble Back chronometer with lavender-colored enamel dial and bezel index; this watch was offered in its original box; the trio pictured here was manufactured upon the request of an Indian customer

Estimated value: $54,000 ↗

Star Dial

1954

Reference number: 6098

Case: 18-karat yellow gold, bipartite, screw-down case back, leather strap, Ø 35 mm

Movement: red gold-plated, polished screws, winding rotor, 25 jewels

Remarks: big Bubble Back model in an unusual combination including a honeycomb-structured dial; dial displays extremely rare applied gold hour markers; this watch was offered with a gold 18-karat Rolex buckle in its original box

Estimated value: $27,000 ↗

Oyster Perpetual Day-Date

1960

Case: 18-karat rose gold, tripartite, screw-down case back, leather strap, Ø 35 mm
Movement: rhodium-plated, finely finished, polished screws, winding rotor
Remarks: rose gold Oyster Day-Date model with display of date and weekday
Estimated value: $6,700 ↗

Oyster Perpetual Datejust Chronometer

1952

Reference number: 6105
Case: 18-karat yellow gold, screw-down case back, leather strap, Ø 35 mm
Movement: rhodium-plated, automatic winding
Remarks: elegant Oyster Datejust model in gold; this watch was offered with an original testing certificate from the Biel observatory
Estimated value: $8,800 ↗

Oyster Perpetual Datejust Superlative Chronometer Serpico y Laino

1955

Reference number: 6605
Case: 18-karat yellow gold, screw-down case back, leather strap, Ø 36 mm
Movement: Caliber 1065, rhodium-plated, 25 jewels, regulated in 6 positions, automatic winding
Remarks: Oyster with extremely rare printing on dial: "Superlative Chronometer by official test, 50 m = 165 ft"; double signature "Serpico y Laino"
Estimated value: $7,500 ↗

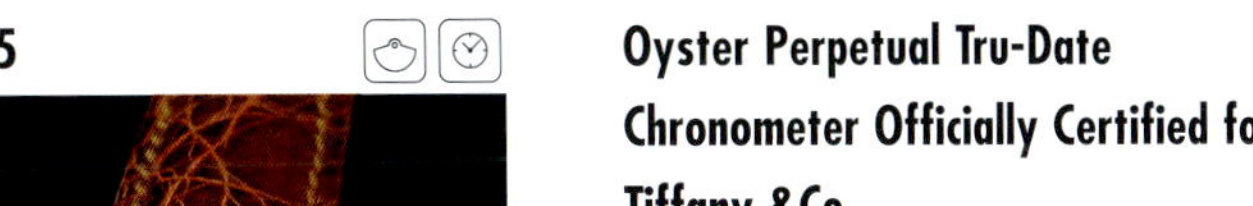

Oyster Perpetual Tru-Date Chronometer Officially Certified for Tiffany &Co.

1960

Reference number: 6534
Case: stainless steel, screw-down case back, leather strap, Ø 34 mm
Movement: Caliber 1065, rhodium-plated, 25 jewels, regulated in 6 positions, automatic winding
Remarks: Oyster Tru-Date model with rare printing on dial; watch delivered with double signature with Tiffany & Co.
Estimated value: $4,100 →

Oyster Perpetual Chronometer

1945

Reference number: 4467
Case: 18-karat yellow gold, screw-down case back, leather strap, Ø 36 mm
Movement: rhodium-plated, automatic winding
Remarks: elegant Oyster model in gold case
Estimated value: $10,800 ↗

Datejust Chronometer

1955

Reference number: 6305/1
Case: stainless steel, screw-down case back, stainless steel link bracelet, Ø 36 mm
Movement: Caliber 745, rhodium-plated, automatic winding
Remarks: rare Datejust model with guilloché dial; black/red date; white gold bezel; this model was manufactured only from 1953 to 1955
Estimated value: $5,400 ↗

Oyster Perpetual Day-Date Chronometer

1972

Reference number: 1803
Case: 18-karat yellow gold, screw-down case back, leather strap, Ø 35 mm
Movement: Caliber 1556, rhodium-plated, decorated, 26 jewels, regulated in 6 positions, automatic winding
Remarks: Oyster Perpetual Day-Date model in gold
Estimated value: $4,700 →

Date Chronometer

1956

Reference number: 1503
Case: 18-karat yellow gold, screw-down case back, Milanaise bracelet, Ø 34 mm
Movement: Caliber 1560, rhodium-plated, decorated, 26 jewels, regulated in 6 positions, automatic winding
Remarks: Rolex Date model with double signature Rolex and "Serpico y Laino"
Estimated value: $6,100 ↗

Oyster Perpetual Day-Date Chronometer

Reference number: 1803

Case: 18-karat yellow gold, screw-down case back, leather strap, Ø 36 mm

Movement: Caliber 1555, rhodium-plated, decorated, 26 jewels, regulated in 6 positions, automatic winding

Remarks: men's watch with display of day and date

Estimated value: $7,500 ↗

1961

Oyster Perpetual Chronometer

Reference number: 6084

Case: 18-karat yellow gold, bipartite, screw-down case back, 18-karat yellow gold link bracelet

Movement: nickel-plated, decorated, polished screws, winding rotor

Remarks: gold Bubble Back model with original Oyster gold link bracelet and index bezel; this watch was offered in its original box

Estimated value: $5,400 ↗

1953

Presidential Seal

Reference number: 6085

Case: 14-karat yellow gold, bipartite, screw-down case back, leather strap, Ø 33 mm

Movement: nickel-plated, decorated, polished screws, winding rotor

Remarks: important Oyster model with enameled dial of United States seal in cloisonné technique by C. Poluzzi; due to the great deal of work done by hand, this watch is considered unique

Estimated value: $175,500 ↗

1946

Oyster Perpetual Chronometer

Reference number: 6320

Case: stainless steel, screw-down case back, stainless steel link bracelet, Ø 33 mm

Movement: rhodium-plated, automatic winding

Remarks: rare Oyster Explorer model; this watch was offered in its original box

Estimated value: $4,100 ↗

1954

Oyster Perpetual Precision Explorer Date

Reference number: 5700

Case: stainless steel, screw-down case back, gold bezel, stainless steel link bracelet, Ø 35 mm

Movement: Caliber 1530, rhodium-plated, 25 jewels, automatic winding

Remarks: extremely rare Oyster Explorer Date for the Canadian market

Estimated value: $5,400 →

1960

Oyster Precision

Reference number: 6426

Case: stainless steel, screw-down case back, leather strap, Ø 35 mm

Movement: Caliber 1225, rhodium-plated, manual winding

Remarks: rare Oyster Precision model with dragon motif on dial

Estimated value: $4,100 ↗

1972

Star Dial

Reference number: 6427

Case: stainless steel, screw-down case back, stainless steel link bracelet, Ø 35 mm

Movement: Caliber 1210, rhodium-plated, manual winding

Remarks: rare Precision with star-shaped hour markers

Estimated value: $5,400 ↗

1965

Oyster Perpetual Tru-Beat Superlative Chronometer

Reference number: 6556

Case: stainless steel, screw-down case back, stainless steel link bracelet, Ø 35 mm

Movement: Caliber 1040, rhodium-plated, 26 jewels, regulated in 6 positions, automatic winding

Remarks: extremely rare Oyster model with jumping sweep seconds; the dial is printed with the rare and very unusual words "by official test"

Estimated value: $19,000 ↗

1956

Oyster Perpetual Tru-Beat Superlative Chronometer "officially certified"

1956

Reference number: 6556

Case: 18-karat yellow gold, screw-down case back, leather strap, Ø 34 mm

Movement: Caliber 1040, rhodium-plated, 26 jewels, regulated in 6 positions, automatic

Remarks: extremely rare Tru-Beat with jumping sweep seconds, a characteristic of the most sought-after models; only a few units of this model execution were manufactured in gold

Estimated value: $34,000 ↗

Oyster Perpetual Explorer Super Precision

1958

Reference number: 5500

Case: stainless steel, screw-down case back, leather strap, Ø 34 mm

Movement: Caliber 1530, rhodium-plated, automatic winding

Remarks: rare early Explorer model

Estimated value: $4,100 →

Oyster Perpetual Explorer

1954

Reference number: 6298

Case: stainless steel, screw-down case back, gold bezel, leather strap, Ø 35 mm

Movement: rhodium-plated, automatic winding

Remarks: extremely rare early Explorer model with additional printed words on dial "Rotor Self-Winding"

Estimated value: $6,100 →

Oyster Explorer Officially Certified Chronometer

1956

Reference number: 6610

Case: stainless steel, tripartite, screw-down case back, leather strap, Ø 36 mm

Movement: Caliber 11030, rhodium-plated, finely finished, polished screws, winding rotor, 25 jewels, regulated in 6 positions

Remarks: rare Oyster Perpetual chronometer with white dial

Estimated value: $30,000 →

Oyster Perpetual Precision Explorer

1953

Reference number: 6150

Case: stainless steel, screw-down case back, leather strap, Ø 35 mm

Movement: rhodium-plated, automatic winding

Remarks: early Explorer model

Estimated value: $8,100 ↗

Oyster Perpetual Explorer Super Precision

1958

Reference number: 5500

Case: stainless steel, screw-down case back, stainless steel link bracelet, Ø 34 mm

Movement: Caliber 1530, rhodium-plated, automatic winding

Remarks: rare Explorer model

Estimated value: $5,400 ↗

Oyster Perpetual Explorer

1953

Reference number: 6350

Case: stainless steel, screw-down case back, stainless steel link bracelet, Ø 35 mm

Movement: rhodium-plated, automatic winding

Remarks: rare Rolex Explorer model

Estimated value: $8,100 ↗

Oyster Perpetual Chronometer Explorer

1953

Reference number: 6350

Case: stainless steel, screw-down case back, leather strap, Ø 35 mm

Movement: rhodium-plated, automatic winding

Remarks: rare early Explorer model with three-dimensional structure on dial

Estimated value: $9,500 ↗

Explorer II

1984

Reference number: 16550

Case: stainless steel, tripartite, screw-down case back, stainless steel link bracelet, Ø 39 mm

Movement: Caliber 3085, rhodium-plated, finely finished, mirror-polished screws, winding rotor, 27 jewels, regulated in 6 positions

Remarks: Explorer II model with rare cream-colored dial; this watch was offered with guarantee

Estimated value: $8,900 →

Oyster Perpetual Milgauss

1958

Superlative Officially Certified Chronometer

Reference number: 6541

Case: stainless steel, screw-down case back, rotating bezel, stainless steel link bracelet, Ø 36 mm

Movement: Caliber 1066M, rhodium-plated, 25 jewels, regulated in 6 positions, automatic winding

Remarks: extremely rare first-edition Milgauss without foudroyante hand

Estimated value: $74,250 ↗

Oyster Perpetual Milgauss

1966

Reference number: 1019

Case: stainless steel, screw-down case back, stainless steel link bracelet, Ø 37 mm

Movement: rhodium-plated, automatic winding

Remarks: rare early Milgauss model; the movement is protected by a soft iron core and thus protected from magnetic fields to 1,000 Gauss

Estimated value: $27,000 ↗

Radiomir Panerai

1943

Reference number: 3646

Case: stainless steel, screw-down case back, leather strap, Ø 47 mm

Movement: rhodium-plated, côtes de Genève, jewels set in chatons, signed: "Rolex 17 rubis," 17 jewels, manual winding

Remarks: important combat diver's watch of the Italian navy; this watch was offered with its original leather strap

Estimated value: $54,000 ↗

Officine Panerai Brevettato
Combat Diver's Prototype

1938

Reference number: 3646

Case: stainless steel, screw-down case back, leather strap, Ø 47 mm

Movement: rhodium-plated, côtes de Genève, jewels set in chatons, manual winding

Remarks: important combat diver's watch of the Italian navy; this watch is a prototype that was only made for presentation; the case back is signed "Oyster Watch Geneva Swiss"

Estimated value: $94,500 ↗

Oyster Perpetual Datejust
Chronometer Thunderbird

1972

Reference number: 1625

Case: 18-karat yellow gold, screw-down case back, leather strap, Ø 36 mm

Movement: Caliber 1570, rhodium-plated, automatic winding

Remarks: early Thunderbird model in gold

Estimated value: $6,750 ↗

Oyster Perpetual Datejust
Chronometer Thunderbird

1977

Reference number: 1625

Case: stainless steel, screw-down case back, 18-karat gold bezel, Ø 36 mm

Movement: rhodium-plated, automatic winding

Remarks: rare Oyster Thunderbird model with black dial

Estimated value: $4,100 →

Oyster Perpetual Turn-O-Graph

1954

Reference number: 6202

Case: stainless steel, tripartite, screw-down case back, rotating bezel, leather strap

Movement: nickel-plated, finely finished, polished screws, winding rotor

Remarks: early Oyster Turn-O-Graph model with rotating black bezel with markers

Estimated value: $7,425 ↗

Oyster Perpetual Turn-O-Graph

1953

Reference number: 6202

Case: stainless steel, screw-down case back, stainless steel link bracelet, Ø 36 mm

Movement: Caliber A296, rhodium-plated, automatic winding

Remarks: rare Turn-O-Graph model with riveted Rolex steel bracelet

Estimated value: $8,100 →

Oyster Perpetual GMT-Master Officially Certified Chronometer

1956

Reference number: 6542

Case: stainless steel, screw-down case back, rotating bezel, stainless steel link bracelet, Ø 38 mm

Movement: Caliber 1030, rhodium-plated, 25 jewels, regulated in 6 positions, automatic winding

Remarks: original acrylic rotating bezel; second time zone set by 24-hour hand in conjunction with bezel

Estimated value: $9,500 ↗

Oyster Perpetual GMT-Master

1966

Reference number: 1675

Case: 18-karat yellow gold, screw-down case back, rotating bezel, gold link bracelet, Ø 39 mm

Movement: rhodium-plated, automatic winding

Remarks: gold GMT-Master model with 24-hour display; a second time zone can be set by the rotating bezel

Estimated value: $20,250 ↗

Oyster Perpetual GMT-Master PanAm Officially Certified Chronometer

1958

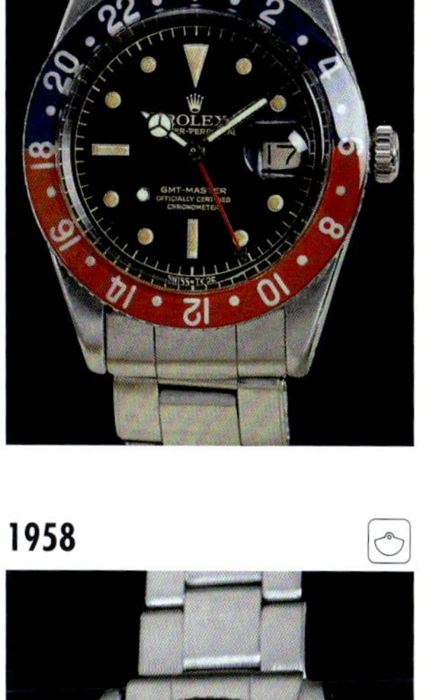

Reference number: 6542

Case: stainless steel, screw-down case back, rotating bezel, stainless steel link bracelet, Ø 38 mm

Movement: Caliber 1035, rhodium-plated, 25 jewels, regulated in 6 positions, automatic winding

Remarks: extremely rare GMT-Master model manufactured as a special series for PanAm; less than 200 pieces were made for this special series

Estimated value: $21,600 ↗

Oyster Perpetual GMT-Master

1960

Reference number: 1675

Case: stainless steel, screw-down case back, rotating bezel, stainless steel link bracelet, Ø 39 mm

Movement: rhodium-plated, automatic winding

Remarks: a second time zone can be set using the 24-hour hand and the rotating, two-tone bezel; the blue and red colors guarantee quick differentiation of day and night

Estimated value: $4,100 →

Oyster Perpetual Submariner James Bond

1955

Reference number: 6205

Case: stainless steel, screw-down case back, stainless steel link bracelet, Ø 36 mm

Movement: Caliber A260, rhodium-plated, automatic winding

Remarks: this watch got its nickname by appearing in several early James Bond films

Estimated value: $15,000 →

Oyster Perpetual Submariner 200 m/660 ft James Bond

1958

Reference number: 6538

Case: stainless steel, screw-down case back, stainless steel link bracelet, Ø 37 mm

Movement: Caliber 1030, rhodium-plated, 25 jewels, automatic winding

Remarks: this watch got its nickname by appearing in several early James Bond films

Estimated value: $27,000 ↗

Oyster Perpetual Submariner 100 m/330 ft

1961

Reference number: 5508

Case: stainless steel, screw-down case back, stainless steel link bracelet, Ø 37 mm

Movement: Caliber 1530M, rhodium-plated, 25 jewels, regulated in 6 positions, automatic winding

Remarks: unique Submariner model with Explorer dial and remarkable engraving on case back: "Casma Lima Peru 4/2/63"

Estimated value: $30,000 ↗

Tissot

Watch collectors—especially those who are interested in progressive technology—can't escape Tissot. This brand, which today belongs to the Swatch Group, made a name for itself in the past again and again with technical innovation. In the 1930s, Tissot was already offering an antimagnetic wristwatch. And in 1944, the Swiss company introduced a movement that many of its competitors oriented their own technology on: Caliber 28.5 was conceived as a module movement, so that without any great effort it would later be able to accommodate additional functions like date or weekday displays. The so-called Autolub caliber also belonged to the technical avant-garde in watchmaking.

Tissot was founded in 1853 by Charles-Félicien Tissot and his son Charles-Emile in Le Locle. Unlike most family histories, in this case it was the son who had the initiative to found his own company. Charles-Emile lived for many years with his uncle in New York after finishing his watchmaker apprenticeship, during which time he gained much experience with the most diverse types of watches. The untiring Charles-Emile did what we might call active distribution today: his many trips soon made Tissot well-known in many countries spanning the globe. Tissot watches were especially popular in Russia—Charles-Emile's son Charles lived in Moscow for many years and built up a subsidiary there. Special regiment watches were created for Russian officers, the backs of which were engraved with the coat of arms of each of the commanders. The October Revolution wiped out Charles's work with Tissot in one fell swoop, and Tissot's important Russian market broke down.

In 1883, Charles took over the management of Tissot, a company that was now based on quality and progress: up to the end of the nineteenth century, Tissot had won several gold medals and first prizes in watchmaking. In 1917, the Swiss firm launched its first wristwatch, and in 1920 it became a *manufacture*, beginning with large series production of wristwatches. In 1930, it merged with Omega and founded the SSIH (Société Suisse de l'Industrie Horlogère). Within this relationship, Omega received the role of premium brand while Tissot had to satisfy itself in the role of younger brother, covering the mid-priced segment. In 1932, the cooperative company bought movement maker Lémania, after which Tissot also purchased chronograph calibers from Lémania.

How creative Tissot still was in the area of movement technology was something the *manufacture* proved with the development of the above-mentioned Autolub caliber in the 1970s. Autolub stood for "self-lubricating" and was an important milestone: Tissot had developed a movement made of plastic that did not need to be oiled. This is a conceptual advantage, for old, hardened oil has been proven to be disadvantageous to a watch's rate. This

movement did not immediately become a great success, however, for the plastics that existed at that point in time were not robust enough and the cheaper prices of quartz movements represented more than enough competition for mechanical watches.

Tissot used quartz technology in the 1980s for avant-garde styled watches such as the Rock Watch whose case was created from natural stone. Each of these watches was unique. Tissot used granite, gneiss, and numerous exotic stones, and later even mother-of-pearl and briar wood, to make the watch cases. These watches were chiefly purchased by people interested in fashion. Today's collector concentrates above all on the brand's mechanical classics such as the Navigator with world time display, where a button at 2 o'clock moves a disk upon which the world reference cities are found.

Men's Watch

1935

Case: stainless steel, push-down case back, leather strap, 23 x 38 mm
Movement: Caliber 20, nickel-plated, manual winding
Remarks: early men's watch
Estimated value: $200 ↘

Chronograph

1935

Case: stainless steel, push-down case back, leather strap, Ø 38 mm
Movement: gold-plated, frosted finish, column-wheel control of chronograph, manual winding
Remarks: chronograph with 30-minute counter
Estimated value: $1,350 →

Chronograph

1935

Case: stainless steel, leather strap, Ø 37 mm
Movement: gold-plated, frosted finish, column-wheel control of chronograph, manual winding
Remarks: fine chronograph with enamel dial and movable strap lugs
Estimated value: $2,500 →

German Army Service Watch

1940

Case: plated, stainless steel push-down case back, leather strap, Ø 34 mm
Movement: nickel-plated, manual winding
Remarks: service watch of the Germany army, numbered "DH35427"
Estimated value: $550 →

Chronograph

1940

Case: stainless steel, push-down case back, leather strap, Ø 33 mm
Movement: nickel-plated, côtes de Genève, column-wheel control of chronograph, manual winding
Remarks: chronograph with 30-minute counter
Estimated value: $1,100 →

Chronograph

1945

Case: stainless steel, push-down case back, leather strap, Ø 37 mm
Movement: nickel-plated, column-wheel control of chronograph, manual winding
Remarks: chronograph with 30-minute counter
Estimated value: $1,350 →

Chronograph

1945

Case: 18-karat red gold, push-down case back, leather strap, Ø 35 mm
Movement: Caliber 27-41H, nickel-plated, column-wheel control of chronograph, manual winding
Remarks: red gold chronograph with 30-minute and 12-hour counters
Estimated value: $1,900 →

Chronograph

1950

Case: stainless steel, push-down case back, leather strap, Ø 35 mm
Movement: nickel-plated, column-wheel control of chronograph, manual winding
Remarks: chronograph with 30-minute and 12-hour counters
Estimated value: $1,500 →

Chronograph · 1940

Case: stainless steel, push-down case back, leather strap, Ø 37 mm

Movement: gold-plated, frosted finish, column-wheel control of chronograph, manual winding

Remarks: one-button chronograph with 30-minute counter

Estimated value: $1,600 →

Chronograph · 1945

Case: stainless steel, push-down case back, leather strap, Ø 32 mm

Movement: nickel-plated, column-wheel control of chronograph, manual winding

Remarks: early chronograph with 30-minute counter

Estimated value: $1,100 →

Chronograph · 1950

Case: 18-karat yellow gold, push-down case back, leather strap, Ø 35 mm

Movement: Caliber C27-41, nickel-plated, column-wheel control of chronograph, manual winding

Remarks: heavy gold chronograph with 30-minute and 12-hour counters

Estimated value: $1,600 →

Chronograph · 1940

Case: 14-karat yellow gold, push-down case back, leather strap, Ø 36 mm

Movement: gold-plated, frosted finish, column-wheel control of chronograph, manual winding

Remarks: one-button chronograph with 30-minute counter

Estimated value: $1,350 →

Calendar Watch with Moon Phase · 1945

Case: 14-karat yellow gold, push-down case back, leather strap, Ø 34 mm

Movement: nickel-plated, manual winding

Remarks: gold men's watch with complete calendar and moon phase

Estimated value: $800 →

World Time Watch · 1945

Case: 14-karat red gold, push-down case back, leather strap, Ø 36 mm

Movement: Caliber 28.5N-21, red gold-plated, automatic winding

Remarks: gold hammer automatic watch; rotating disk with world reference city names (24-hour indication)

Estimated value: $3,400 ↗

Sonorus T12 · 1971

Case: stainless steel, push-down case back, stainless steel link bracelet

Movement: Caliber AS 1930, nickel-plated, 17 jewels, manual winding

Remarks: rare alarm diver's watch in a heavy stainless steel case; tripartite case back with second case back to withstand great pressure in great depths; diving time is set by the third crown at 11 o'clock

Estimated value: $1,100 ↗

Sonorus PR516 · 1969

Case: stainless steel, screw-down case back, stainless steel link bracelet

Movement: Caliber AS 1930, nickel-plated, 17 jewels, manual winding

Remarks: alarm wristwatch in diver's watch look with rotating bezel

Estimated value: $950 →

Navigator Seastar T12 Automatic

1975

Case: stainless steel, screw-down case back, leather strap, Ø 42 mm

Movement: Caliber 798, gold-plated, automatic winding

Remarks: large men's watch with two-tone 24-hour dial; rotating bezel on the inside (flange) with world time display

Estimated value: $400 →

Seastar T12

1970

Case: stainless steel, push-down case back, leather strap, Ø 42 mm

Movement: Lémania Caliber LWO 1281, nickel-plated, manual winding

Remarks: stately chronograph with 30-minute and 12-hour counters

Estimated value: $400 →

Seastar T12

1975

Case: stainless steel, push-down case back, leather strap, 42 x 50 mm

Movement: Lémania Caliber LWO 1281, nickel-plated, manual winding

Remarks: stately chronograph with 30-minute and 12-hour counters

Estimated value: $400 →

Visodate Seamaster T12

1975

Case: stainless steel, screw-down case back, leather strap, 42 x 50 mm

Movement: Caliber 784-2, rhodium-plated, automatic winding

Remarks: diver's watch with rotating inner bezel (flange)

Estimated value: $350 →

Navigator Automatic Chronograph

1970

Case: stainless steel, screw-down case back, leather strap, Ø 38 mm

Movement: Lémania Caliber LWO 1341, nickel-plated, 17 jewels, automatic winding

Remarks: automatic chronograph with sweep minute and subsidiary 12-hour counters

Estimated value: $350 →

Navigator Automatic Chronograph

1970

Case: stainless steel, screw-down case back, leather strap, 42 x 46 mm

Movement: Lémania Caliber LWO 1343, rhodium-plated, automatic winding

Remarks: unworn chronograph with sweep 60-minute counter

Estimated value: $350 →

Navigator Automatic Chronograph

1975

Case: stainless steel, screw-down case back, stainless steel link bracelet, Ø 40 mm

Movement: Lémania Caliber LWO 1341, rhodium-plated, 17 jewels, automatic winding

Remarks: chronograph with sweep 60-minute and subsidiary 12-hour counters

Estimated value: $475 →

T12 Chronograph

1975

Case: stainless steel, push-down case back, stainless steel link bracelet, Ø 44 mm

Movement: Lémania Caliber LWO 1873, nickel-plated, 17 jewels, manual winding

Remarks: chronograph with 30-minute and 12-hour counters

Estimated value: $475 →

Tudor

Tudor has always languished in the shadow of its elder sibling Rolex. Regardless, this brand has been able to secure a loyal and enthusiastic following for itself over the decades. It is the hidden qualities of the watches that are so convincing, the special Rolex features that are practically free at Tudor—without the famous crown logo, of course, but also without the surcharge of being a Rolex.

In exchange, the Tudors carry the title of crown prince in their model names: Oyster Prince, Oyster Prince Day-Date, and Oyster Prince Submariner.

Hans Wilsdorf had registered many brand names during the course of the decades, but didn't end up using all of them. Tudor is the only one remaining active to the present day aside from Rolex. The company's founder had to wait a long time to get his name: when he went to register Tudor, he realized that it had been given out and used since 1906 and that there actually already were watches sold under that name. Only in the 1940s did Wilsdorf get rights to Tudor. Naturally, it made little sense to purposely undercut the Rolex quality that had been created and maintained for decades for a second brand. And so all Tudor watches literally profit from the technical achievements of the company's lead-ing brand. They don't always have to be the newest and most current developments—with regard to sports watch

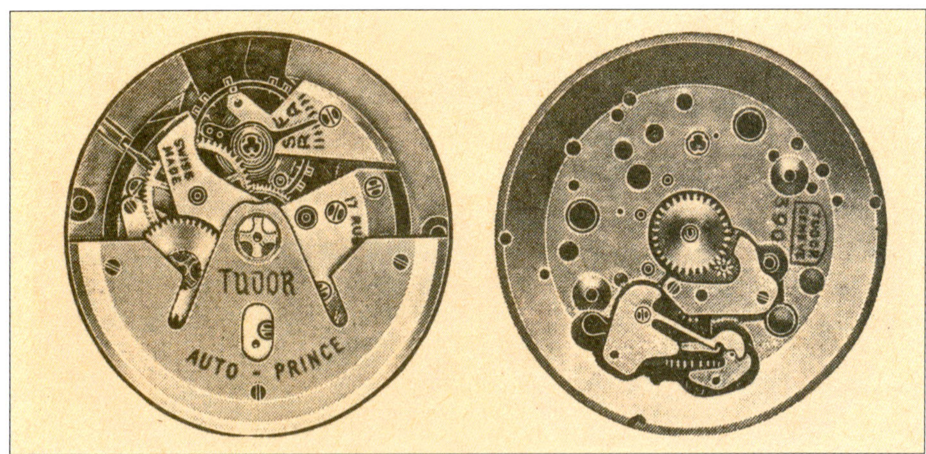

quality, the Rolex models were always ahead of their time anyway.

The company only "saved" on the movement: instead of a Rolex *manufacture* caliber, the Tudor models were chiefly outfitted with AS and ETA calibers, which were minutely regulated before being encased.

There is no rule without an exception, and the Tudor brand eventually did get its own movement: in the 1950s, the Tudor Prince Rotor was powered by Tudor Caliber 390. This movement couldn't hide its origins, which derived from a typical Rolex automatic caliber: various components were very close to Rolex Caliber 1030,

which was manufactured at the same time. Parts of the automatic winding technically corresponded to older rotor automatics, though. As Caliber 395, it was outfitted with an additional date display.

In all Tudor chronographs—as in Rolex's chronographs—it was Valjoux column-wheel calibers that did the work, usually the simpler versions without 12-hour counters. This model policy resulted in Tudor watches being misused for counterfeit Rolex watches. Alongside various Oyster models, Tudor also offered an alarm watch with its Advisor.

Oyster Prince

1963

Case: stainless steel, screw-down case back, stainless steel link bracelet, Ø 35mm
Movement: nickel-plated, automatic winding
Remarks: sporty men's watch
Estimated value: $1,100 →

Oyster Prince Ranger

1975

Reference: 9050
Case: stainless steel, screw-down case back, leather strap, Ø 34 mm
Movement: rhodium-plated, automatic winding
Remarks: rare Tudor Ranger model with large luminous numerals
Estimated value: $1,500 ↗

Oyster

1949

Case: 18-karat yellow gold, push-down case back, leather strap, Ø 32 mm
Movement: nickel-plated, 17 jewels, manual winding
Remarks: rare early gold men's watch
Estimated value: $1,100 →

Oyster Prince Submariner

1965

Reference: 7928
Case: stainless steel, screw-down case back, rotating bezel, leather strap, Ø 39 mm
Movement: gold-plated, automatic winding
Remarks: heavy diver's watch
Estimated value: $2,200 ↗

Submariner

1970

Case: stainless steel, screw-down case back, rotating bezel, stainless steel link bracelet, Ø 39 mm
Movement: Caliber 2484, nickel-plated, automatic winding
Remarks: diver's watch with rotating bezel
Estimated value: $2,100 ↗

Prince Oyster Date

1975

Reference: 90814
Case: stainless steel, screw-down case back, rotating bezel, leather strap, Ø 40 mm
Movement: rhodium-plated, decorated, automatic winding
Remarks: large automatic men's watch
Estimated value: $1,600 →

Oyster Date Chronograph

1980

Case: stainless steel, screw-down case back, stainless steel link bracelet, Ø 41 mm
Movement: Valjoux Caliber 234, rhodium-plated, column-wheel control of chronograph, manual winding
Remarks: chronograph with 45-minute counter
Estimated value: $4,700 →

Auto Chrono Time

1980

Case: stainless steel, screw-down case back, leather strap, Ø 40 mm
Movement: Valjoux Caliber 7750, nickel-plated, automatic winding
Remarks: large chronograph with 30-minute and 12-hour counters
Estimated value: $5,400 ↗

Universal Genève

Like many brands that specialize in precise chronographs, Universal Genève's roots can be traced back to Le Locle. There in 1894 Numa Emile Descombes and Georges Perret together founded the company Descombes & Perret. The goal of their company was the development of high-quality watches with complications. The pair not only wanted to stick with the design and manufacture of movements, but they also wanted to produce cases and dials themselves.

In the year of the company's founding, they applied for a patent for a watch with a combined 12- and 24-hour display. The additional 24-hour indication was actually a jump hour displayed in a window. That same year, the owners registered the brand Universal Watch.

The partnership came to an abrupt end when Descombes died in 1897. Perret had to look around for a new partner, whom he finally found in the young watchmaker Louis Berthoud.

In 1917, Universal Watch produced a large wrist chronograph with a 17-line movement already outfitted with an additional hour counter. This chronograph served at the front during World War I.

After the war, to make opening new markets a little easier, the owners moved their headquarters from Le Locle to Geneva, for in the big city there were much better travel options. Consequently, they changed the name of their company to Universal Genève.

One of the greatest achievements of the company was a patented hammer automatic from 1925, which was quite similar to Harwood's. Back then, Universal Genève specialized in chronographs whose excellent quality paid off in the 1930s when the company—like many others—was hit by the economic crisis. Because of the good quality of the Universal watches, they found financial backers, who secured the company's continued existence. Thus, in 1941 they founded an additional company in Les Ponts-de-Martel called Martel Watch. Universal Genève was successful back then because the watchmakers had put their money on chronographs with two buttons early on. Only in this way could one perform addition stopping. In the 1930s, the model families Compur and Compax joined the existing Standard line.

Universal Genève introduced its best-known model in 1944: the Tri-Compax Chronograph whose movement was additionally outfitted with a complete calendar and a moon phase display.

Universal Genève wrote aviation history with the Polerouter. SAS pilots wore them on their wrists when they opened lines from Scandinavia to Alaska and California by crossing the North Pole starting in 1954. To make sure that the Polerouter also worked correctly above the North Pole with its strong magnetic field, the watchmakers protected the movement with a soft iron core inside the case.

After 1967, Universal Genève partnered with Bulova and manufactured a watch using the Accutron Caliber 218. The cooperative venture ended with a takeover by Bulova. In 1977, Universal Genève once again became independent through a management buyout, but was sold to the Stelux Group nine years later. Today, Universal Genève still manufactures a flat micro rotor caliber, striking in its excellent rate performance.

8 Days

1935

Case: chrome-plated, push-down case back, leather strap, 26 x 43 mm

Movement: gold-plated, frosted finish, manual winding

Remarks: rare men's watch with eight-day shaped movement; twin spring barrels

Estimated value: $3,400 ↗

Polerouter Automatic

1965

Case: stainless steel, screw-down case back, leather strap, Ø 34 mm

Movement: Caliber 215, nickel-plated, côtes de Genève, micro rotor, 28 jewels, automatic winding

Remarks: sporty men's watch with fine micro rotor automatic movement

Estimated value: $675 →

Polerouter SUB Automatic

1965

Case: stainless steel, screw-down case back, rotating bezel, leather strap, Ø 37 mm

Movement: Caliber 69, nickel-plated, côtes de Genève, micro rotor, 28 jewels, automatic winding

Remarks: automatic men's watch in a solid case with rotating bezel and screw-in crown

Estimated value: $800 →

Automatic with Enamel Dial

1955

Reference number: 100105 3

Case: 18-karat rose gold, hipartite, screw-down case back, leather strap, Ø 36 mm

Movement: Caliber 138 C, rhodium-plated, finely finished, pendulum oscillating weight, polished screws

Remarks: extremely rare gold watch with enamel dial in cloisonné technique; this watch was made for Saud ibn Abd al-Aziz, who was king of Saudi Arabia from 1953 to 1964

Estimated value: $8,800 →

Compax

1948

Case: 18-karat rose gold, tripartite, push-down case back, leather strap, Ø 45 mm

Movement: Caliber 292, gold-plated, frosted finish, column-wheel control of chronograph, finely finished steel chronograph components, mirror-polished screws

Remarks: extremely rare very large chronograph with 30-minute and 12-hour counters; tachymeter scale; dial with luminous counters and luminous substance on hands

Estimated value: $13,500 →

Compax

1945

Reference number: 22430

Case: stainless steel, tripartite, push-down case back, leather strap, Ø 46 mm

Movement: Caliber 292, rhodium-plated, finely finished, column-wheel control of chronograph, finely finished steel chronograph components, polished screws, 17 jewels

Remarks: rare extra-large chronograph with 30-minute and 12-hour counters; case made of so-called Enver steel

Estimated value: $10,800 →

Calendar Watch with Moon Phase

1948

Case: 18-karat red gold, push-down case back, leather strap, Ø 34 mm

Movement: Caliber 291, nickel-plated, manual winding

Remarks: red gold men's watch with complete calendar and moon phase; date at 3 o'clock; window display of weekday at 12 o'clock; moon phase and month at 6 o'clock; subsidiary seconds

Estimated value: $13,500 →

Calendar Watch with Moon Phase

1945

Case: 18-karat white gold, push-down case back, leather strap, Ø 34 mm

Movement: Caliber 291, rhodium-plated, manual winding

Remarks: men's watch with complete calendar and moon phase; date at 3 o'clock; window display of weekday at 12 o'clock; moon phase and month at 6 o'clock; subsidiary seconds

Estimated value: $2,700 ↗

Compur
1940

Case: 18-karat red gold, push-down case back, leather strap, 26 x 34 mm

Movement: gold-plated, frosted finish, column-wheel control of chronograph, manual winding

Remarks: rare square chronograph with 30-minute counter; reference number 7396

Estimated value: $4,700 →

Chronograph
1940

Case: stainless steel, push-down case back, leather strap, 26 x 35 mm

Movement: Caliber 270, gold-plated, frosted finish, column-wheel control of chronograph, manual winding

Remarks: rare rectangular steel chronograph with 30-minute counter and tachymeter scale

Estimated value: $3,000 →

Uni-Compax
1945

Case: 14-karat yellow gold, push-down case back, leather strap, 26 x 35 mm

Movement: Caliber 289, nickel-plated, column-wheel control of chronograph, manual winding

Remarks: rare chronograph in square case

Estimated value: $4,100 ↗

Chonograph
1945

Case: stainless steel, push-down case back, leather strap, 26 x 35 mm

Movement: gold-plated, frosted finish, column-wheel control of chronograph, manual winding

Remarks: simple chronograph in square case

Estimated value: $3,000 →

Chronograph Extra
1930

Case: silver, hinged case back, leather strap, Ø 38 mm

Movement: Caliber 289, nickel-plated, column-wheel control of chronograph, manual winding

Remarks: very early crown-button chronograph with 30-minute counter and enamel dial; two flat pocket watch bows serve as strap lugs

Estimated value: $2,300→

Chronograph
1925

Case: silver, push-down case back, leather strap, Ø 40 mm

Movement: gold-plated, frosted finish, column-wheel control of chronograph, manual winding

Remarks: very early crown-button chronograph with 30-minute counter and enamel dial; two pocket watch bows serve as strap lugs

Estimated value: $16,500 →

Compax
1940

Case: 18-karat red gold, push-down case back, leather strap, Ø 36 mm

Movement: Caliber 287, gold-plated, frosted finish, column-wheel control of chronograph, manual winding

Remarks: rare red gold chronograph with 30-minute and 12-hour counters

Estimated value: $3,400 →

Chronograph
1925

Case: 18-karat yellow gold, push-down case back, leather strap, Ø 39 mm

Movement: gold-plated, frosted finish, column-wheel control of chronograph, manual winding

Remarks: very early crown-button chronograph with 30-minute counter and enamel dial; two pocket watch bows serve as strap lugs

Estimated value: $3,000 →

Aero-Compax — 1945

Case: stainless steel, push-down case back, leather strap, Ø 55 mm

Movement: Caliber 287, gold-plated, frosted finish, column-wheel control of chronograph, manual winding

Remarks: exceptionally large pilot's chronograph with 30-minute and 12-hour counters; settable control time in subdial at 12 o'clock

Estimated value: $10,800 ↗

Aero-Compax — 1945

Case: stainless steel, push-down case back, leather strap, Ø 37 mm

Movement: nickel-plated, column-wheel control of chronograph, manual winding

Remarks: pilot's chronograph with 30-minute and 12-hour counters; settable control time in subdial at 12 o'clock

Estimated value: $2,700 →

Split-Seconds Pilot's Chronograph for A. Cairelli — 1940

Case: stainless steel, push-down case back, leather strap, Ø 44 mm

Movement: rhodium-plated, double column-wheel control of chronograph, manual winding

Remarks: one-button pilot's chronograph with 24-hour dial, split-seconds function, and 16-minute counter for astronavigation; case back engraved with "AMI, Chronometro per Navigaz. Astronom. HA-I, N. Categ. 19620, MM. 200033"

Estimated value: $20,250 ↗

Aero-Compax — 1948

Case: 14-karat yellow gold, push-down case back, leather strap, Ø 32 mm

Movement: Caliber 283, nickel-plated, column-wheel control of chronograph, manual winding

Remarks: small pilot's chronograph with 30-minute and 12-hour counters; settable control time in subdial at 12 o'clock

Estimated value: $3,400 →

Aero-Compax — 1950

Case: 14-karat red gold, push-down case back, leather strap, Ø 37 mm

Movement: Caliber 287, gold-plated, column-wheel control of chronograph, manual winding

Remarks: red gold chronograph with 30-minute and 12-hour counters; settable control time in subdial at 12 o'clock; unusually shaped strap lugs

Estimated value: $3,800 →

Dato-Compax — 1948

Case: 18-karat yellow gold, push-down case back, leather strap, Ø 35 mm

Movement: Caliber 285, gold-plated, frosted finish, column-wheel control of chronograph, manual winding

Remarks: gold Dato-Compax chronograph with 30-minute and 12-hour counters; date at 12 o'clock

Estimated value: $3,400 ↗

Aero-Compax — 1945

Case: stainless steel, screw-down case back, leather strap, Ø 35 mm

Movement: Caliber 281, nickel-plated, column-wheel control of chronograph, manual winding

Remarks: pilot's chronograph with 30-minute and 12-hour counters; settable control time in subdial at 12 o'clock

Estimated value: $3,100 →

Compax 30 — 1950

Case: stainless steel, push-down case back, leather strap, Ø 38 mm

Movement: Caliber 285, gold-plated, frosted finish, column-wheel control of chronograph, manual winding

Remarks: simple chronograph with 30-minute and 12-hour counters

Estimated value: $2,000 →

Compur

1945

Case: stainless steel, push-down case back, leather strap, Ø 37 mm
Movement: Caliber 285, gold-plated, frosted finish, column-wheel control of chronograph, manual winding
Remarks: simple chronograph with 45-minute counter
Estimated value: $1,600 →

Uni-Compax Chronometer

1948

Case: red gold, push-down case back, leather strap, Ø 36 mm
Movement: Caliber 287, nickel-plated, column-wheel control of chronograph, manual winding
Remarks: very rare chronograph with 45-minute counter; chronometer certificate
Estimated value: $3,000 →

Compur

1950

Case: 18-karat yellow gold, screw-down case back, leather strap, Ø 38 mm
Movement: Caliber 285, gold-plated, frosted finish, column-wheel control of chronograph, manual winding
Remarks: simple chronograph with 45-minute counter; luminous numerals
Estimated value: $2,700 →

Chronograph

1945

Case: stainless steel, push-down case back, leather strap, Ø 32 mm
Movement: Caliber 283, gold-plated, column-wheel control of chronograph, manual winding
Remarks: simple chronograph with 30-minute counter
Estimated value: $1,900 →

Compax

1945

Case: stainless steel, push-down case back, leather strap, Ø 34 mm
Movement: Caliber 285, gold-plated, frosted finish, column-wheel control of chronograph, manual winding
Remarks: chronograph with 30-minute and 12-hour counters
Estimated value: $1,900 →

Uni-Compax

1950

Case: stainless steel, push-down case back, leather strap, Ø 35 mm
Movement: Caliber 285, gold-plated, column-wheel control of chronograph, manual winding
Remarks: sporty elegant chronograph with 45-minute counter
Estimated value: $1,600 →

Filmcompax

1940

Case: stainless steel, push-down case back, leather strap, Ø 37 mm
Movement: Caliber 287, nickel-plated, column-wheel control of chronograph, manual winding
Remarks: chronograph with 30-minute and 12-hour counters; additional special measuring possibility for directors and camera people on inner rotating bezel (flange)
Estimated value: $3,400 ↗

Compax

1950

Case: 18-karat yellow gold, push-down case back, leather strap, Ø 34 mm
Movement: Caliber 281, nickel-plated, frosted finish, column-wheel control of chronograph, manual winding
Remarks: rare gold chronograph with 30-minute and 12 hour counters
Estimated value: $2,700 →

Compax

1945

Case: 18-karat yellow gold, push-down case back, leather strap, Ø 33 mm

Movement: Caliber 283, gold-plated, frosted finish, column-wheel control of chronograph, manual winding

Remarks: simple gold chronograph with 30-minute and 12-hour counters

Estimated value: $2,500 →

Compax Climate Proof

1950

Case: 18-karat red gold, push-down case back, leather strap, Ø 34 mm

Movement: Caliber 481, nickel-plated, column-wheel control of chronograph, manual winding

Remarks: rare red gold Compax chronograph with 30-minute and 12-hour counters

Estimated value: $3,800 →

Compax

1950

Case: 18-karat yellow gold, push-down case back, leather strap, Ø 34 mm

Movement: Caliber 285, rhodium-plated, column-wheel control of chronograph, manual winding

Remarks: simple gold chronograph with 30-minute and 12-hour counters

Estimated value: $2,700 →

Chronograph

1950

Case: 18-karat red gold, push-down case back, leather strap, Ø 37 mm

Movement: Caliber 285, nickel-plated, column-wheel control of chronograph, 17 jowols, manual winding

Remarks: large chronograph with 30-mintue counter in red gold case

Estimated value: $3,000 →

Chronograph

1950

Case: stainless steel, push-down case back, leather strap, Ø 33 mm

Movement: Caliber 283, gold-plated, frosted finish, column-wheel control of chronograph, manual winding

Remarks: chronograph with 30-minute and 12-hour counters

Estimated value: $1,600 →

Compax

1945

Case: 18-karat red gold, push-down case back, leather strap, Ø 32 mm

Movement: Caliber 281, gold-plated, frosted finish, column-wheel control of chronograph, manual winding

Remarks: fine red gold chronograph with 30-minute and 12-hour counters; this watch was offered in its original box; remarkable teardrop-shaped strap lugs

Estimated value: $4,000 ↗

Chronograph

1970

Case: gold-plated, push-down case back, leather strap, Ø 38 mm

Movement: Venus Caliber 178, gold-plated, column-wheel control of chronograph, manual winding

Remarks: simple chronograph with 30-minute and 12-hour counters

Estimated value: $1,100 ↗

Aero-Compax

1968

Case: stainless steel, screw-down case back, leather strap, Ø 40 mm

Movement: Caliber 130, nickel-plated, column-wheel control of chronograph, manual winding

Remarks: rare large chronograph in solid stainless steel case with 30-minute and 12-hour counters; rotating bezel

Estimated value: $2,700 ↗

Tri-Compax — 1950

Case: 18-karat yellow gold, push-down case back, leather strap, Ø 35 mm

Movement: Caliber 481, rhodium-plated, column-wheel control of chronograph, manual winding

Remarks: chronograph with 30-minute and 12-hour counters; complete calendar; date and moon phase are displayed on subdial at 12 o'clock; window display of weekday and month

Estimated value: $4,700 →

Tri-Compax — 1945

Case: 18-karat red gold, push-down case back, leather strap, Ø 38 mm

Movement: Caliber 287, gold-plated, frosted finish, column-wheel control of chronograph, manual winding

Remarks: rare red gold chronograph with 30-minute and 12-hour counters; complete calendar; date and moon phase are displayed on subdial at 12 o'clock; window display of weekday and month

Estimated value: $5,400 →

Tri-Compax — 1955

Case: stainless steel, screw-down case back, leather strap, Ø 35 mm

Movement: Caliber 281, nickel-plated, column-wheel control of chronograph, manual winding

Remarks: chronograph with 30-minute and 12-hour counters; complete calendar; date and moon phase are displayed on subdial at 12 o'clock; window display of weekday and month

Estimated value: $4,000 ↗

Tri-Compax — 1945

Case: 18-karat yellow gold, push-down case back, leather strap, Ø 37 mm

Movement: Caliber 287, gold-plated, frosted finish, column-wheel control of chronograph, manual winding

Remarks: gold chronograph with 30-minute and 12-hour counters; complete calendar; date and moon phase are displayed on subdial at 12 o'clock; window display of weekday and month

Estimated value: $4,900 →

Tri-Compax — 1948

Case: 14-karat yellow gold, screw-down case back, leather strap, Ø 35 mm

Movement: Caliber 281, nickel-plated, column-wheel control of chronograph, manual winding

Remarks: gold chronograph with 30-minute and 12-hour counters; complete calendar; date and moon phase are displayed on subdial at 12 o'clock; window display of weekday and month

Estimated value: $6,100 →

Tri-Compax — 1948

Case: 18-karat yellow gold, push-down case back, leather strap, Ø 37 mm

Movement: Caliber 287, gold-plated, frosted finish, column-wheel control of chronograph, manual winding

Remarks: gold chronograph with 30-minute and 12-hour counters; complete calendar; date and moon phase are displayed on subdial at 12 o'clock; window display of weekday and month

Estimated value: $4,700 →

Tri-Compax — 1968

Case: stainless steel, screw-down case back, leather strap, Ø 37 mm

Movement: Caliber 281, nickel-plated, column-wheel control of chronograph, manual winding

Remarks: sporty Tri-Compax chronograph with 30-minute and 12-hour counters; complete calendar; date and moon phase are displayed on subdial at 12 o'clock; window display of weekday and month; tachymeter scale on the bezel

Estimated value: $4,900 →

Tri-Compax — 1950

Case: stainless steel, screw-down case back, leather strap, Ø 31 mm

Movement: Caliber 281, rhodium-plated, column-wheel control of chronograph, manual winding

Remarks: sporty Tri-Compax chronograph with 30-minute and 12-hour counters; complete calendar; date and moon phase are displayed on subdial at 12 o'clock; window display of weekday and month

Estimated value: $4,100 →

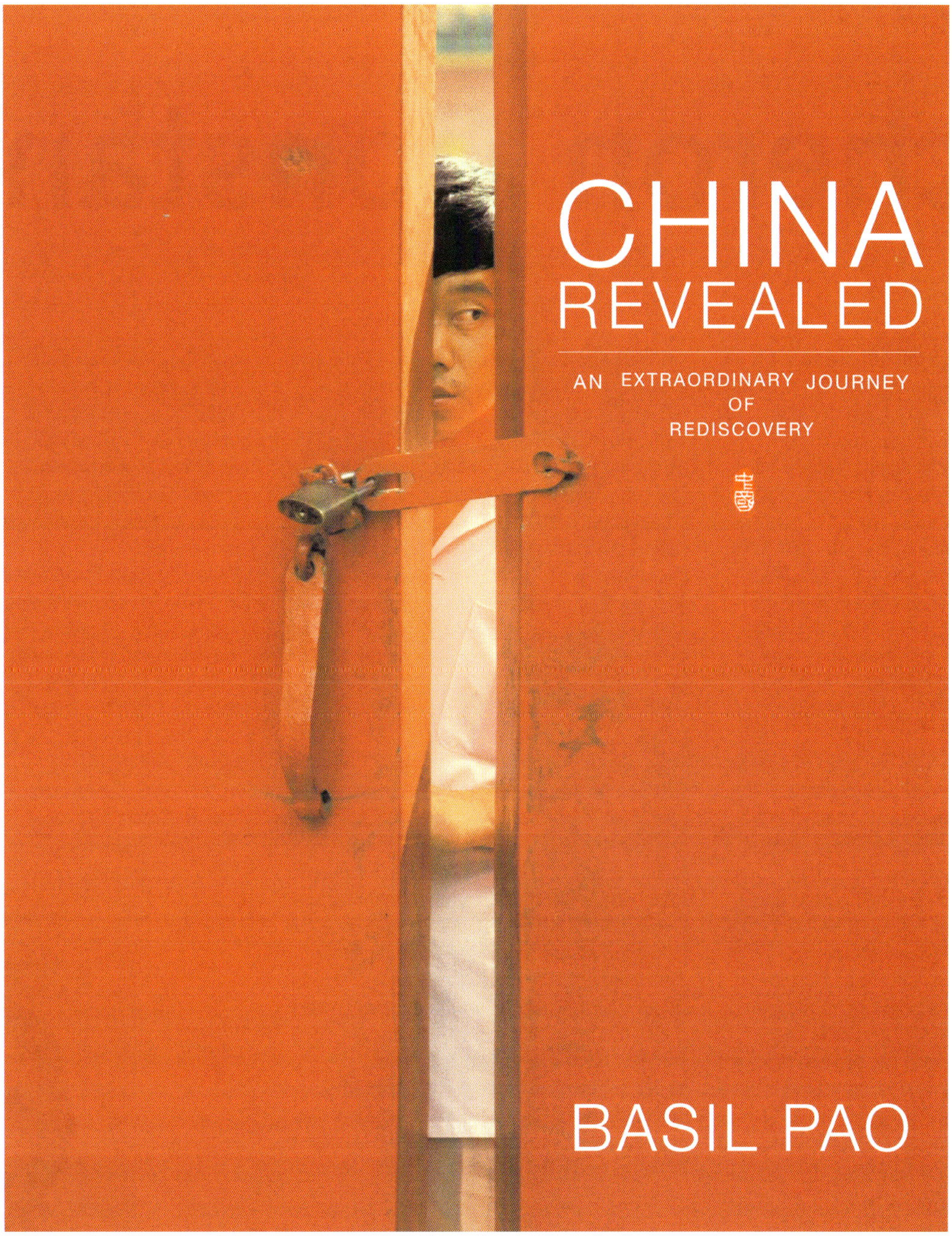

China Revealed

This richly illustrated travel guidebook portrays China's must-see places as well as regions visitors rarely discover. Basil Pao's spectacular photojourney highlights China's dramatic landscape and is accompanied by a personal and informative text, resulting in a fascinating volume that reveals China in the twenty-first century.

Text and photography by Basil Pao
381 full-color illustrations
384 pages · 11 5/8 x 9 5/8 · Cloth
ISBN-13: 978-0-7892-0947-4
$60.00

Published by ABBEVILLE PRESS
137 Varick Street, New York, NY 10013
1-800-Artbook (in U.S. only)
Also available wherever fine books are sold
Visit us at www.abbeville.com

Vacheron Constantin

Vacheron Constantin can rest assured: it is the oldest *manufacture* in the history of the Swiss watch industry. Unlike many companies with old names that have been founded in recent years, this firm has uninterruptedly manufactured timepieces since its founding 250 years ago.

Its history began in 1755 when Jean-Marc Constantin founded his company in Geneva. The customers for his demanding watches were mainly located in France. That such an important market had developed there lay in that country's spoiled and splendor-craving noble class—Louis XIV himself was an enthusiastic watch collector.

In 1789, this market literally fell apart overnight. The French Revolution had broken out, and the nobility was more occupied with simply saving itself. Watches were no longer a topic, at least for the time being.

Constantin had trouble keeping his head above water. When he died in 1805 and his heirs took over the company, they saw no other chance but to search out a new, solvent partner. In 1819, they found just the right person in François Vacheron, the son of a rich textile and wheat dealer. He took over the business side of the company that was now called Vacheron & Constantin.

The company's greatest success can be attributed to watchmaker George-Auguste Leschot, who designed a machine in 1839 that allowed a precision movement to be manufactured in a more cost-saving manner. This first step toward machine production was a small revolution for the watchmaking industry.

The company added wristwatches to its collection in about 1910 with movements that mainly came from LeCoultre. Right from the beginning, this company had a soft spot for jeweled watches, and along with elegant timepieces for daily use, the watchmakers also created models with a more avant-garde design: in the 1920s Vacheron & Constantin already had a design watch whose dial could be covered by a small Venetian blind.

Since the 1930s, there has also been a great selection of chronographs in the company's collection. Additionally, Vacheron & Constantin had a wristwatch with a minute repeater, though it was only manufactured in small series. Although Vacheron & Constantin manufactured high-quality watches, the owners were not able to keep the company financially independent. After they got into trouble once again thanks to World War II, Charles Constantin had no other choice but to sell the majority of stock in 1940. The new owner was Georges Ketterer.

Under Ketterer's management, Vacheron & Constantin was able to secure its position as a manufacturer of luxury watches. The lion's share of the movements utilized were not of the company's own production, but were purchased from Jaeger-LeCoultre in Le Sentier.

In 1955, in celebration of the company's 200th anniversary, Vacheron & Constantin introduced an ultra-flat wristwatch: its movement was a mere 1.64 millimeters high. This caliber continues to be one of the world's thinnest watch movements.

When the brand introduced its first sports watch in 1974, this seemed almost contrary to the image of the otherwise discreet gold watches it was famous for. The design of Model 222 was reminiscent of a porthole, and the stylized Maltese cross that the company had registered in 1880 as its logo could be found in numerous details on the case.

In the 1980s, an investor group headed by Arab sheikh Yamani purchased the company, until the Vendôme Group made him a lucrative offer in 1996 that he could not refuse.

Chronograph — 1947

Case: 18-karat yellow gold, push-down case back, leather strap, Ø 34 mm
Movement: Caliber V434, rhodium-plated, côtes de Genève, column-wheel control of chronograph, manual winding
Remarks: fine chronograph with 30-minute counter at 3 o'clock; this watch was offered with Vacheron Constantin certificate in its original box
Estimated value: $30,000 ↗

Chronograph — 1942

Case: 18-karat red gold, push-down case back, leather strap, Ø 34 mm
Movement: Caliber V434, nickel-plated, côtes de Genève, column-wheel control of chronograph, manual winding
Remarks: fine chronograph with 30-minute counter at 3 o'clock
Estimated value: $33,800 ↗

Chronograph — 1948

Case: 18-karat red gold, push-down case back, leather strap, Ø 36 mm
Movement: Caliber V492, nickel-plated, côtes de Genève, column-wheel control of chronograph, manual winding
Remarks: fine chronograph with 30-minute counter at 3 o'clock
Estimated value: $32,500 ↗

Chronograph — 1938

Case: 18-karat red gold, push-down case back, leather strap, Ø 36 mm
Movement: Caliber V434, rhodium-plated, côtes de Genève, column-wheel control of chronograph, manual winding
Remarks: fine chronograph with 30-minute counter at 3 o'clock; this watch was offered with Vacheron Constantin certificate in its original box
Estimated value: $32,500 ↗

Calendar Watch with Moon Phase — 1943

Case: 18-karat red gold, push-down case back, leather strap, Ø 35 mm
Movement: Caliber V485, nickel-plated, côtes de Genève, mirror-polished screws, manual winding
Remarks: men's watch with complete calendar and moon phase; date hand; window display of weekday and month; subsidiary seconds and moon phase at 6 o'clock
Estimated value: $20,250 ↗

Men's Watch — 1940

Case: stainless steel, tripartite, push-down case back, leather strap, Ø 35 mm
Movement: Caliber V455, rhodium-plated, fausses côtes decoration, polished screws
Remarks: extremely rare men's watch with subsidiary seconds and complete calendar; date hand; window display of weekday and month
Estimated value: $13,500 →

Calendar Watch — 1943

Case: 18-karat yellow gold, push-down case back, leather strap, Ø 35 mm
Movement: Caliber V455, nickel-plated, côtes de Genève, mirror-polished screws, manual winding
Remarks: men's watch with complete calendar; date hand; window display of weekday and month; subsidiary seconds at 6 o'clock
Estimated value: $16,000 ↗

Calendar Watch — 1943

Case: 18-karat yellow gold, push-down case back, leather strap, Ø 35 mm
Movement: Caliber V455A, rhodium-plated, côtes de Genève, manual winding
Remarks: rare gold men's watch with subsidiary seconds and complete calendar; date hand
Estimated value: $16,000 ↗

Chronograph
1945

Case: stainless steel, tripartite, push-down case back, leather strap, Ø 34 mm

Movement: Caliber V492, rhodium-plated, fausses côtes decoration, column-wheel control of chronograph, finely finished and beveled steel chronograph components, polished screws, 19 jewels, regulated in one position

Remarks: extremely rare sporty chronograph with 30-minute counter; telemeter and tachymeter scales

Estimated value: $40,500 →

Men's Watch
1933

Case: 18-karat yellow gold, push-down case back, leather strap, 22 x 38 mm

Movement: rhodium-plated, 15 jewels, regulated in 4 positions, manual winding

Remarks: extremely rare rectangular men's wristwatch with original black dial; movement regulated in four positions

Estimated value: $5,400 ↗

Men's Watch
1939

Case: 18-karat yellow gold, push-down case back, leather strap, Ø 34 mm

Movement: Caliber V203, rhodium-plated, côtes de Genève, manual winding

Remarks: extremely rare rectangular men's wristwatch with original strap lugs; this watch was offered in its original box and an excerpt from Vacheron Constantin's master registry

Estimated value: $13,500 ↗

Men's Watch
1935

Case: 14-karat yellow gold, push-down case back, leather strap, 21 x 35 mm

Movement: rhodium-plated, côtes de Genève, manual winding

Remarks: elegant men's 14-karat yellow gold watch with movable pin-shaped strap lugs

Estimated value: $4,750 ↗

Men's Watch
ca. 1935

Case: stainless steel, push-down case back, leather strap, 22 x 40 mm

Movement: nickel-plated, manual winding

Remarks: rare early men's watch in Art Deco design

Estimated value: $4,100 →

Men's Watch
1933

Case: 18-karat red gold, push-down case back, leather strap, 22 x 38 mm

Movement: nickel-plated, manual winding

Remarks: rare men's watch in a rectangular red gold case from the 1930s

Estimated value: $4,750 ↗

Men's Wristwatch
1945

Case: 18-karat red gold, push-down case back, leather strap, 23 x 39 mm

Movement: Caliber V435/3C, rhodium-plated, côtes de Genève, manual winding

Remarks: rare men's watch in a fitted rectangular case with a Vacheron & Constantin gold buckle; this watch was offered in its original box

Estimated value: $8,800 ↗

Men's Watch
1946

Case: 18-karat yellow gold, push-down case back, leather strap, 25 x 39 mm

Movement: Caliber V435/3C, rhodium-plated, côtes de Genève, manual winding

Remarks: rare men's watch in a shaped rectangular case

Estimated value: $6,800 ↗

Men's Watch — 1936

Case: platinum, bipartite, hinged push-down case back, leather strap, 22 x 44 mm

Movement: shaped movement, rhodium-plated, finely finished, polished screws, 17 jewels, regulated in 4 positions

Remarks: extremely rare men's watch in an elongated tonneau-shaped platinum case; Art Deco dial with minute scale on perimeter of dial; this watch was offered with a Patek Philippe white gold buckle

Estimated value: $27,000 ↗

Men's Watch — 1935

Case: stainless steel, bipartite, push-down case back, leather strap, 22 x 38 mm

Movement: shaped movement, rhodium-plated, fausses côtes decoration, polished screws

Remarks: men's watch in rectangular stainless steel case

Estimated value: $5,400 →

Men's Watch — 1955

Reference number: 4890

Case: 18-karat yellow gold, bipartite, push-down case back, leather strap, 30 x 34 mm

Movement: Caliber 1002, rhodium-plated, fausses côtes decoration, polished screws, 17 jewels, regulated in one position

Remarks: fine men's watch in a square case with remarkable, applied strap lugs

Estimated value: $4,750 →

Men's Watch — 1960

Reference number: 4108

Case: 18-karat rose gold, bipartite, push-down case back, gold link bracelet, 25 x 33 mm

Movement: Caliber 1001, rhodium-plated, fausses côtes decoration, polished screws, 18 jewels, regulated in 8 positions

Remarks: rare men's watch in a delicate square case; this watch was offered with an original Vacheron & Constantin yellow gold bracelet

Estimated value: $5,400 →

Montre à volets — 1930

Case: 18-karat white gold and yellow gold, leather strap, 26 x 33 mm

Movement: rhodium-plated, regulated in 5 positions, manual winding

Remarks: extremely rare men's watch with Venetian blind technology in front of the dial activated by a second crown at 9 o'clock; this watch was offered in its original box and with certificate

Estimated value: $47,250 ↗

Automatic Men's Watch — 1952

Reference number: 4737

Case: 18-karat yellow gold, push-down case back, leather strap, 36 x 44 mm

Movement: Caliber P499, rhodium-plated, côtes de Genève, automatic winding

Remarks: rare men's watch in a square case

Estimated value: $5,400 ↗

Men's Watch — 1947

Case: 18-karat yellow gold, push-down case back, leather strap, 27 x 36 mm

Movement: Caliber V458, rhodium-plated, côtes de Genève, 17 jewels, manual winding

Remarks: rare gold men's watch in a square case; remarkably shaped strap lugs

Estimated value: $3,400 →

Men's Watch — 1915

Case: 18-karat yellow gold, tripartite, hinged push-down case back, gold cuvette, leather strap, Ø 36 mm

Movement: gold-plated, frosted finish, blued screws

Remarks: rare early wristwatch whose case is clearly reminiscent of a pocket watch

Estimated value: $5,400 →

Men's Watch — 1947

Case: 18-karat red gold, push-down case back, leather strap, Ø 31 mm
Movement: Caliber V458, nickel-plated, côtes de Genève, 17 jewels, manual winding
Remarks: simple men's watch with remarkable strap lugs
Estimated value: $4,100 →

Men's Watch — 1945

Case: 18-karat yellow gold, push-down case back, leather strap, Ø 33 mm
Movement: Caliber 458/2B, rhodium-plated, côtes de Genève, manual winding
Remarks: very fine gold men's watch; this watch was offered in its original box
Estimated value: $6,800 ↗

Men's Watch — 1922

Case: 18-karat yellow gold, push-down case back, leather strap, 31 x 37 mm
Movement: gold-plated, frosted finish, manual winding
Remarks: early gold men's wristwatch in a cushion-shaped case; the subsidiary seconds dial is recessed into the dial
Estimated value: $3,400 →

Men's Watch — 1944

Case: 18-karat yellow gold, bipartite, push-down case back, leather strap
Movement: Caliber 466/3B, rhodium-plated, fausses côtes decoration, polished screws, 17 jewels, regulated in one position
Remarks: elegant men's watch with remarkable strap logs
Estimated value: $3,000 →

Model — 1955

Case: 18-karat red gold, bipartite, push-down case back, 18-karat red gold link bracelet, Ø 38 mm
Movement: Caliber P453/3B, rhodium-plated, fausses côtes decoration, polished screws, 17 jewels, regulated in one position
Remarks: rare large men's watch with solid gold link bracelet
Estimated value: $5,400 →

Men's Watch — 1940

Case: stainless steel, bipartite, screw-down case back, leather strap
Movement: rhodium-plated, fausses côtes decoration, polished screws, 17 jewels, regulated in one position
Remarks: sporty men's watch with luminous markers and hands inlaid with luminous substance
Estimated value: $4,750 ↗

Men's Watch — 1952

Case: 18-karat yellow gold, push-down case back, leather strap, Ø 35 mm
Movement: Caliber P454/5B, rhodium-plated, côtes de Genève, 17 jewels, manual winding
Remarks: unusual and rare men's watch with remarkably shaped strap lugs
Estimated value: $4,750 ↗

Men's Watch — 1943

Case: 18-karat red gold, push-down case back, leather strap, Ø 33 mm
Movement: Caliber V454, nickel-plated, côtes de Genève, manual winding
Remarks: rare red gold men's watch with lavish cloisonné enamel dial; gold buckle
Estimated value: $27,000 ↗

Men's Watch — 1948

Case: 18-karat red gold, push-down case back, leather strap, Ø 33 mm
Movement: Caliber V453, rhodium-plated, côtes de Genève, manual winding
Remarks: elegant men's watch
Estimated value: $3,800 →

Men's Watch — 1943

Case: 18-karat yellow gold, push-down case back, leather strap, Ø 34 mm
Movement: Caliber P453/3C, rhodium-plated, côtes de Genève, manual winding
Remarks: discrete men's wristwatch with subsidiary seconds
Estimated value: $4,200 ↗

Men's Watch — 1940

Case: stainless steel, tripartite, push-down case back, leather strap, Ø 34 mm
Movement: Caliber 453, rhodium-plated, fausses côtes decoration, polished screws
Remarks: elegant men's watch with subsidiary seconds and two-tone dial
Estimated value: $4,750 →

Men's Watch — 1940

Case: 18-karat red gold, push-down case back, leather strap, Ø 33 mm
Movement: Caliber 453, nickel-plated, côtes de Genève, manual winding
Remarks: rare red gold men's watch in simple case with subsidiary seconds
Estimated value: $4,750 ↗

Men's Watch — 1948

Case: 18-karat yellow gold, push-down case back, leather strap, Ø 36 mm
Movement: Caliber P453/36, rhodium-plated, côtes de Genève, manual winding
Remarks: simple men's watch with subsidiary seconds
Estimated value: $3,400 →

Men's Watch — 1947

Case: 18-karat yellow gold, push-down case back, leather strap, Ø 33 mm
Movement: Caliber P453/3B, rhodium-plated, côtes de Genève, manual winding
Remarks: simple gold men's watch with subsidiary seconds
Estimated value: $3,400 →

Men's Watch — 1944

Case: 18-karat yellow gold, push-down case back, leather strap, Ø 36 mm
Movement: Caliber P453/36, rhodium-plated, côtes de Genève, manual winding
Remarks: simple men's watch with subsidiary seconds
Estimated value: $3,400 →

Automatic Men's Watch — 1963

(Unique Piece)

Reference number: 2517
Case: 18-karat red gold, screw-down case back, leather strap, Ø 36 mm
Movement: Caliber 1072, nickel-plated, côtes de Genève, automatic winding
Remarks: extremely rare men's wristwatch; unique piece; movement has an 18-karat gold roller on ruby bearings
Estimated value: $5,400 ↗

Men's Watch

Reference number: 6454

Case: 18-karat yellow gold, tripartite, push-down case back, leather strap, Ø 33 mm

Movement: Caliber 1002, rhodium-plated, fausses côtes decoration, polished screws, Seal of Geneva, 18 jewels, regulated in 8 positions

Remarks: small men's watch with guilloché bezel

Estimated value: $3,000 →

1970

Men's Watch

Reference number: 4711

Case: 18-karat yellow gold, tripartite, push-down case back, leather strap, Ø 36 mm

Movement: Caliber P453/3B, rhodium-plated, fausses côtes decoration, polished screws, 17 jewels, regulated in one position

Remarks: elegant gold men's watch; this watch was offered with an 18-karat gold buckle

Estimated value: $6,750 →

1955

Men's Watch

Case: 18-karat red gold, push-down case back, leather strap, Ø 33 mm

Movement: rhodium-plated, côtes de Genève, manual winding

Remarks: simple red gold wristwatch with gold buckle

Estimated value: $3,400 →

1943

Men's Watch

Case: 18-karat yellow gold, push-down case back, leather strap, Ø 31 mm

Movement: Caliber 466/3B, rhodium-plated, côtes de Genève, manual winding

Remarks: discrete men's watch with indirect sweep seconds

Estimated value: $3,400 →

1947

Men's Watch

Case: 18-karat yellow gold, push-down case back, leather strap, Ø 37 mm

Movement: Caliber P454/5B, rhodium-plated, côtes de Genève, manual winding

Remarks: elegant men's watch in heavy gold case

Estimated value: $6,100 →

1951

Men's Watch

Reference number: 4413

Case: 18-karat red gold, push-down case back, leather strap, Ø 35 mm

Movement: Caliber P454/5B, nickel-plated, côtes de Genève, manual winding

Remarks: simple men's watch; this watch was offered with original gold buckle

Estimated value: $3,650 →

1952

Men's Watch

Case: 18-karat yellow gold, push-down case back, leather strap, Ø 34 mm

Movement: Caliber P453/3B, rhodium-plated, côtes de Genève, manual winding

Remarks: simple men's watch with subsidiary seconds

Estimated value: $4,100 →

1952

Men's Watch

Reference number: 20

Case: stainless steel, push-down case back, leather strap, Ø 30 mm

Movement: rhodium-plated, côtes de Genève, manual winding

Remarks: rare men's wristwatch with large crown partially recessed into case

Estimated value: $4,750 →

1938

Men's Watch — 1972

Reference number: 6486

Case: 18-karat yellow gold, push-down case back, yellow gold Milanaise bracelet, Ø 34 mm

Movement: Caliber K101/2, rhodium-plated, côtes de Genève, Seal of Geneva, 18 jewels, regulated in 8 positions, manual winding

Remarks: fine men's watch with Milanaise bracelet; the movement was adjusted in eight positions

Estimated value: $2,700 →

Men's Watch — 1969

Case: 18-karat yellow gold, push-down case back, leather strap, Ø 34 mm

Movement: Caliber K1001, rhodium-plated, côtes de Genève, manual winding

Remarks: elegant men's watch

Estimated value: $2,700 →

Men's Watch — 1956

Case: 18-karat yellow gold, push-down case back, leather strap, Ø 33 mm

Movement: Caliber 1001, rhodium-plated, côtes de Genève, manual winding

Remarks: elegant men's wristwatch in a fine gold case

Estimated value: $2,700 →

Men's Watch — 1970

Case: 18-karat yellow gold, push-down case back, leather strap, Ø 33 mm

Movement: Caliber K1014, rhodium-plated, côtes de Genève, manual winding

Remarks: elegant men's watch in a fine gold case

Estimated value: $2,450 →

Men's Watch with Stop-Seconds — 1952

Case: 18-karat red gold, push-down case back, leather strap, Ø 33 mm

Movement: Caliber P1008/BS, nickel-plated, côtes de Genève, Seal of Geneva, 19 jewels, manual winding

Remarks: rare men's wristwatch with hacking seconds, which makes setting the precise time easier; the movement was adjusted in eight positions

Estimated value: $3,800 ↗

Chronomètre Royal — 1954

Case: 18-karat yellow gold, push-down case back, leather strap, Ø 35 mm

Movement: Caliber P1008/BS, rhodium-plated, côtes de Genève, Seal of Geneva, 19 jewels, manual winding

Remarks: rare chronometer in a simple gold case

Estimated value: $11,500 ↗

Extra Flat — 1973

Reference number: 6352

Case: 18-karat white gold, push-down case back, white gold Milanaise bracelet, Ø 32 mm

Movement: Caliber 1003, rhodium-plated, côtes de Genève, 17 jewels, regulated in 8 positions, manual winding

Remarks: rare extra-flat men's wristwatch in white gold; the movement was adjusted in eight positions

Estimated value: $2,700 →

Chronomètre Royal — 1960

Reference number: 6694

Case: 18-karat yellow gold, screw-down case back, leather strap and gold link bracelet, 35 x 40 mm

Movement: Caliber 1072/1, rhodium-plated, côtes de Genève, Seal of Geneva, 29 jewels, regulated in 8 positions, automatic winding

Remarks: chronometer with date window at 3 o'clock; this watch was offered with an additional original yellow gold link bracelet; the movement was adjusted in eight positions and has a gold rotor with jewel bearings

Estimated value: $9,500 ↗

Chronomètre Royal

1952

Case: 18-karat yellow gold, push-down case back, leather strap, Ø 34 mm

Movement: Caliber P1008/BS, rhodium-plated, côtes de Genève, Seal of Geneva, manual winding

Remarks: rare chronometer with subsidiary seconds; the movement hacks for easier setting of the precise time

Estimated value: $11,500 →

Men's Watch

1952

Case: 18-karat yellow gold, push-down case back, leather strap, Ø 38 mm

Movement: Caliber P454/5B, rhodium-plated, côtes de Genève, 17 jewels, manual winding

Remarks: simple large men's watch

Estimated value: $4,100 →

Automatic Men's Watch

1952

Case: 18-karat yellow gold, screw-down case back, leather strap, Ø 35 mm

Movement: Caliber P1019, rhodium-plated, côtes de Genève, automatic winding

Remarks: simple gold men's watch

Estimated value: $4,750 →

Men's Watch

1969

Reference number: 6562

Case: stainless steel, bipartite, screw-down case back, leather strap, Ø 35 mm

Movement: Caliber K1072, rhodium-plated, fausses côtes decoration, 18-karat gold rotor in jeweled bearings, polished screws, Seal of Geneva, 29 jewels, regulated in 8 positions

Remarks: elegant men's watch with date at 3 o'clock

Estimated value: $6,100 →

Automatic Men's Watch

1961

Reference number: 6426

Case: 18-karat red gold, screw-down case back, leather strap, Ø 35 mm

Movement: Caliber 1071, nickel-plated, côtes de Genève, automatic winding

Remarks: extremely rare men's watch, only 20 of which exist with this dial version; this watch was offered with its original gold buckle

Estimated value: $6,800 ↗

Automatic Men's Watch

1943

Case: 18-karat yellow gold, screw-down case back, leather strap, Ø 35 mm

Movement: Caliber V477, nickel-plated, côtes de Genève, automatic winding

Remarks: extremely rare men's watch in 18-karat gold; the movement has a jewel-bearing hammer for the automatic winding

Estimated value: $5,400 ↗

Automatic Men's Watch

1951

Case: 18-karat yellow gold, screw-down case back, leather strap, Ø 36 mm

Movement: Caliber P1019, rhodium-plated, côtes de Genève, automatic winding

Remarks: elegant automatic men's watch

Estimated value: $5,000 →

Automatic Men's Watch

1962

Reference number: 6378

Case: 18-karat yellow gold, screw-down case back, leather strap, Ø 35 mm

Movement: Caliber K1071, rhodium-plated, côtes de Genève, 29 jewels, regulated in 8 positions, automatic winding

Remarks: discrete automatic men's watch with gold rotor and jewel bearings; the movement was regulated in eight positions

Estimated value: $5,400 ↗

Automatic Men's Watch — 1967

Reference number: 6782

Case: 18-karat yellow gold, screw-down case back, rotating bezel, leather strap, Ø 36 mm

Movement: Caliber K1072, rhodium-plated, côtes de Genève, Seal of Geneva, 29 jewels, regulated in 8 positions, automatic winding

Remarks: extremely rare men's watch with rotating bezel and window date display at 3 o'clock; the movement was regulated in eight positions

Estimated value: $9,500 →

Automatic Men's Watch — 1960

Reference number: 6038

Case: 18-karat yellow gold, screw-down case back, leather strap, Ø 35 mm

Movement: Caliber P1019, rhodium-plated, côtes de Genève, 21 jewels, regulated in 8 positions, automatic winding

Remarks: discrete automatic men's wristwatch with 18-karat gold rotor on jewel bearings; the movement was regulated in eight positions

Estimated value: $6,100 →

Automatic Men's Watch — 1969

Reference number: 6394

Case: 18-karat white gold, screw-down case back, leather strap, Ø 35 mm

Movement: Caliber 1072/1, nickel-plated, côtes de Genève, automatic winding

Remarks: automatic men's watch in a classic white gold case with date display at 3 o'clock; gold rotor on jewel bearings; this watch was originally sold in Okinawa

Estimated value: $6,800 →

Automatic Men's Watch — 1969

Reference number: 7397

Case: 18-karat white gold, screw-down case back, leather strap, Ø 35 mm

Movement: Caliber 1072/1, nickel-plated, côtes de Genève, automatic winding

Remarks: men's watch in white gold case with date display at 3 o'clock; gold rotor on jewel bearings; this watch was offered with its original gold buckle, sales tag, certificate, and instruction booklet; originally sold in Okinawa

Estimated value: $7,500 →

Automatic Men's Watch — 1963

Reference number: 6727

Case: 18-karat yellow gold, screw-down case back, leather strap, Ø 36 mm

Movement: Caliber 1071, nickel-plated, côtes de Genève, automatic winding

Remarks: very rare men's watch of which an estimated 500 pieces were made; gold rotor and jewel bearings; this watch was offered with its original gold buckle

Estimated value: $6,100 →

Automatic Men's Watch — 1969

Reference number: 6731

Case: 18-karat yellow gold, screw-down case back, leather strap, Ø 35 mm

Movement: Caliber 1072/1, nickel-plated, côtes de Genève, automatic winding

Remarks: men's watch in gold case with date window at 3 o'clock; gold rotor on jewel bearings; this watch was offered with its original gold buckle

Estimated value: $5,400 ↗

Automatic — 1960

Reference number: 6394

Case: 18-karat yellow gold, screw-down case back, leather strap, Ø 35 mm

Movement: Caliber 1071, nickel-plated, côtes de Genève, automatic winding

Remarks: rare fine men's watch; gold rotor on jewel bearings; this watch was offered with its original gold buckle

Estimated value: $6,800 ↗

Automatic Men's Watch — 1965

Reference number: 6592

Case: 18-karat yellow gold, screw-down case back, leather strap, Ø 35 mm

Movement: Caliber 1072, nickel-plated, côtes de Genève, automatic winding

Remarks: extremely rare men's watch of which only 50 pieces were made; date window at 3 o'clock; gold rotor and jewel bearings; this watch was offered with original gold folding clasp

Estimated value: $6,800 ↗

Automatic Men's Watch — 1965

Reference number: 6378

Case: 18-karat yellow gold, screw-down case back, leather strap, Ø 35 mm

Movement: Caliber 1072, nickel-plated, côtes de Genève, automatic winding

Remarks: rare men's watch with date window at 3 o'clock; gold rotor with jewel bearings; this watch was offered with original gold folding clasp

Estimated value: $5,400 ↗

Automatic Men's Watch — 1961

Case: 18-karat yellow gold, push-down case back, leather strap, 34 x 39 mm

Movement: Caliber K1120, rhodium-plated, côtes de Genève, automatic winding

Remarks: elegant men's watch in cushion-shaped case

Estimated value: $2,700 →

Automatic Men's Watch — 1963

Reference number: 6592

Case: 18-karat yellow gold, screw-down case back, leather strap, Ø 36 mm

Movement: Caliber 1071, nickel-plated, côtes de Genève, 29 jewels, regulated in 8 positions, automatic winding

Remarks: men's watch in yellow gold case; gold rotor with jewel bearings; the movement was adjusted in eight positions

Estimated value: $6,100 →

Automatic Men's Watch — 1958

Reference number: 6073

Case: 18-karat yellow gold, screw-down case back, leather strap, Ø 35 mm

Movement: Caliber P1019/2, rhodium-plated, côtes de Genève, 21 jewels, regulated in 8 positions, automatic winding

Remarks: simple men's automatic watch; regulated in 8 positions

Estimated value: $6,800 →

Alpina
Bellport Time Group, LLC
112 South Country Road, Suite 101
Bellport, NY 11713
Tel.: 631-776-1135
Fax: 631-776-1136
www.alpina-watches.com

Audemars Piguet (North America) Inc.
40 East 57th Street
New York, NY 10022
Tel.: 212-758-8400
Fax: 212-758-8538
www.audemarspiguet.com

Baume & Mercier
Richemont North America
Fifth Avenue and 52nd Street
New York, NY 10022
Tel.: 212-753-0111
Fax: 212-753-7250
www.baume-et-mercier.com

Breitling U.S.A. Inc.
206 Danbury Road
Stamford, CT 06897
Tel.: 800-641-7343
Fax: 203-327-2537
www.breitling.com

Cartier Inc.
Fifth Avenue and 52nd Street
New York, NY 10022
Tel.: 1-800-CARTIER
Fax: 212-753-7250
www.cartier.com

Certina
The Swatch Group (U.S.), Inc.
1200 Harbor Boulevard
Weehawken, NJ 07087
Tel.: 201-271-1400
Fax: 201-271-4633
www.certina.com

Chronoswiss
Bellport Time Group, LLC
112 South Country Road, Suite 101
Bellport, NY 11713
Tel.: 631-776-1135
Fax: 631-776-1136
www.chronoswiss.com

Doxa Watches USA
5847 San Felipe, 17th Floor
Houston, TX 77057
Tel.: 877-255-5017
Fax: 866-230-2922
www.doxawatches.com

Eberhard & Co.
DOMUSHora
1784 West Avenue Bay 3
Miami Beach, FL 33139
Tel.: 305-538-9300
Fax: 305-534-1952
info@domushora.com
www.eberhard-co-watches.ch

Eterna SA
Schützengasse 46
2540 Grenchen, Switzerland
Tel.: 011-41-32-654 72 11
Fax: 011-41-32-654 72 12
www.eterna.ch

Fortis
LWR Time Ltd.
15 South Franklin Street, Suite 214
Wilkes-Barre, PA 18711
Tel.: 570-408-1640
Fax: 570-408-1657
www.fortis-watch.com

Girard-Perregaux
Tradema of America, Inc.
201 Route 17 North
Rutherford, NJ 07070
Tel.: 1-877-846-3447
Fax: 201-507-1553
gpwebmaster@girard-perregaux-usa.com
www.girard-perregaux-usa.com

Glashütte Original
The Swatch Group (U.S.), Inc.
1200 Harbor Boulevard
Weehawken, NJ 07087
Tel.: 201-271-1400
Fax: 201-271-4633
www.glashuette-original.com

Hamilton
The Swatch Group (U.S.), Inc.
1200 Harbor Boulevard
Weehawken, NJ 07087
Tel.: 201-271-1400
Fax: 201-271-4633
www.hamilton-watch.com

Hanhart
Eric Armin, Inc.
Fine Watch Division
118 Bauer Drive, P.O. Box 7046
Oakland, NJ 07436-7046
Tel.: 800-272-0272
www.hanhartusa.com

IWC North America
645 Fifth Avenue, 6th Floor
New York, NY 10022
Tel.: 1-800-432-9330
Fax: 212-872-1312
www.iwc.ch

Jaeger-LeCoultre
645 Fifth Avenue
New York, NY 10022
Tel.: 800-JLC-TIME
www.jaeger-lecoultre.com

Lange Uhren GmbH
Altenberger Str. 15
01768 Glashütte, Germany
Tel.: 011-49-35053-44 0
Fax: 011-49-35053-44 100
info@lange-soehne.com
www.lange-soehne.com

Longines
The Swatch Group (U.S.), Inc.
1200 Harbor Boulevard
Weehawken, NJ 07087
Tel.: 201-271-1400
Fax: 201-271-4633
www.longines.com

Mido
The Swatch Group (U.S.), Inc.
1200 Harbor Boulevard
Weehawken, NJ 07087
Tel.: 201-271-1400
Fax: 201-271-4633
www.mido.ch

Movado Group, Inc.
650 From Road
Paramus, NJ 07652
Tel.: 201-267-8115
Fax: 201-267-8020
www.movado.com

Ulysse Nardin Inc.
2101 NW Corporate Boulevard, Suite 101
Boca Raton, FL 33431
Tel.: 561-988-6400
Fax: 561-988-0123
usa@ulysse-nardin.com
www.ulysse-nardin.com

Omega
The Swatch Group (U.S.), Inc.
1200 Harbor Boulevard
Weehawken, NJ 07087
Tel.: 201-271-1400
Fax: 201-271-4633
www.omegawatches.com

Officine Panerai
645 Fifth Avenue
New York, NY 10022
Tel.: 1-877-PANERAI
Fax: 212-891-2315
www.panerai.com

Patek Philippe
1 Rockefeller Plaza, #930
New York, NY 10020
Tel.: 212-581-0870
Fax: 212-956-6399
info@patek.com
www.patek.com

Piaget
663 Fifth Avenue, 7th Floor
New York, NY 10022
Tel.: 212-355-6444
Fax: 212-909-4332
www.piaget.com

Rolex Watch U.S.A., Inc.
Rolex Building, 665 Fifth Avenue
New York, NY 10022-5358
Tel.: 212-758-7700
Fax: 212-826-8617
www.rolex.com

TAG Heuer
LVMH Watch & Jewelry USA
960 S. Springfield Avenue
Springfield, NJ 07081
Tel.: 973-467-1890
www.tagheuer.com

Tissot
The Swatch Group (U.S.), Inc.
1200 Harbor Boulevard
Weehawken, NJ 07087
Tel.: 201-271-1400
Fax: 201-271-4633
www.tissot.ch

Tudor
Rolex Watch U.S.A., Inc.
Rolex Building, 665 Fifth Avenue
New York, NY 10022-5358
Tel.: 212-758-7700
Fax: 212-826-8617
www.rolex.com

Tutima USA, Inc.
P.O. Box 983
Torrance, CA 90508
Tel.: 1-TUTIMA-USA-1
Fax: 310-378-7843
www.tutima.com

Vacheron Constantin
Richemont North America
Fifth Avenue and 52nd Street
New York, NY 10022
Tel.: 212-753-0111
Fax: 212-753-7250
www.vacheron-constantin.com

Zenith
LVMH Watch & Jewelry USA
960 S. Springfield Avenue
Springfield, NJ 07081
Tel.: 973-467-1890
Fax: 973-467-5495
www.zenith-watches.com

Not all of the watch brands listed in this publication are still in existence today, and even if they are it may not be so easy to get information on vintage models from them via telephone, fax, or e-mail. However, contacting these brands may still be your best bet in obtaining a piece of information you desire.

Vulcain

Vulcan, the Roman god of fire, is described in mythology as an artistic smith—a fitting name giver for a watch company.
The company had to go through a number of renaming processes until it finally got this moniker, though: in 1858 it was registered in La Chaux-de-Fonds as Maurice Ditisheim. Almost forty years later, the owners added the name "Fabrique Vulcain" to what was essentially the last name of the company's founder. From 1900 on, it was briefly called Vulcain—to be renamed a decade later as Ditisheim & Cie. In 1911, it finally received the predicate "Fabrique Vulcain & Volta."

Hardly another watch brand is so strongly associated with one single product as Vulcain with its Cricket. In 1947, Vulcain introduced its first alarm wristwatch. Despite its smaller case dimensions, it was as loud as a cricket thanks to the doubly thick membrane case back, which is what gave it its name.

The Cricket sold so well through the decades that over the course of time, it became a synonym for the Vulcain brand. Its most famous wearers were in the United States where it remained "time minister" for many decades on the wrist of the president. Alongside the Cricket, Vulcain also had other watches in its line—most of which were outfitted with the brand's own calibers.

In 1961, restructuring took place once again: Vulcain SA became a founding member of MSR Holding (Manufactures Suisses Réunies), whose main stockholder was the company Revue. At the end of the 1970s, it was decided that from then on all watches of the MSR Group would only be distributed under the brand name Revue Thommen—except the Cricket. It remained the Vulcain Cricket until 1986, but had to bow to the Revue Thommen brand name then as well.

Revue sold the rights to the brand name Vulcain SA around the turn of the millennium, but the new Vulcain was bankrupt after about a year. Restructuring occurred yet again, and in the fall of 2001 all rights to the name were purchased by PMH with the goal of resuscitating the old Vulcain name and relaunching the Cricket. The fire has thus not yet gone out.

Men's Watch — 1925

Case: silver, push-down case back, leather strap, 25 x 40 mm
Movement: rhodium-plated, côtes de Genève, manual winding
Remarks: fine men's watch in unusual oval case
Estimated value: $800 →

Chronomètre — 1925

Case: silver, push-down case back, leather strap, 25 x 33 mm
Movement: rhodium-plated, jewels set in chatons, regulated in 5 positions, manual winding
Remarks: fine unworn wristwatch chronometer; regulated in 5 positions
Estimated value: $270 →

Chronomètre — 1930

Case: 18-karat yellow gold, push-down case back, leather strap, 35 x 36 mm
Movement: nickel-plated, jewels set in chatons, manual winding
Remarks: gold chronometer wristwatch
Estimated value: $550 ↗

Régulateur — 1940

Case: stainless steel, push-down case back, rotating bezel, leather strap, Ø 32 mm
Movement: rhodium-plated, manual winding
Remarks: men's watch with regulator dial
Estimated value: $400 →

Cricket — 1960

Case: 18-karat red gold, double push-down case back, leather strap, Ø 38 mm
Movement: Vulcain Caliber 120, nickel-plated, twin spring barrels, 17 jewels, manual winding
Remarks: gold alarm wristwatch with double sounding case back; this watch was offered in its original box
Estimated value: $1,900 ↗

Cricket — 1950

Case: gold-plated, double stainless steel push-down case back, leather strap, Ø 33 mm
Movement: Vulcain Caliber 120, rhodium-plated, twin spring barrels, 17 jewels, manual winding
Remarks: alarm wristwatch with double sounding case back
Estimated value: $1,100 →

Cricket Calendar — 1958

Case: stainless steel, double push-down case back, leather strap, Ø 34 mm
Movement: Vulcain Caliber 402 (S1), nickel-plated, 17 jewels, manual winding
Remarks: alarm wristwatch with subsidiary seconds and date; movement with spring barrel for movement and alarm
Estimated value: $1,100 ↗

Cricket Calendar — 1954

Case: gold-plated, stainless steel push-down case back, leather strap
Movement: Vulcain Caliber 401, rhodium-plated, 17 jewels, manual winding
Remarks: alarm wristwatch with subsidiary seconds and date; Caliber 401 only has one spring barrel, while the alarm is controlled by the strike train wheel
Estimated value: $950 →

Chronograph with Complete Calendar — 1965

Case: chrome-plated, stainless steel screw-down case back, leather strap, Ø 39 mm

Movement: Vulcain Caliber 730, rhodium-plated, column-wheel control of chronograph, manual winding

Remarks: chronograph with 30-minute and 12-hour counters; complete calendar

Estimated value: $800 →

Cricket — 1970

Case: gold-plated, double stainless steel push-down case back, leather strap, Ø 37 mm

Movement: Caliber MRS S2, nickel-plated, côtes de Genève, twin spring barrels, 17 jewels, manual winding

Remarks: alarm wristwatch with double sounding case back

Estimated value: $270 →

Cricket Nautical — 1961

Case: stainless steel, double push-down case back, Tropic plastic strap, Ø 42 mm

Movement: Vulcain Caliber 120, nickel-plated, twin spring barrels, 17 jewels, manual winding

Remarks: extremely rare professional diver's alarm wristwatch; water-resistant to 300 meters; using length and depth of dive, the decompression time necessary can be seen in a cutaway in the dial

Estimated value: $5,400 ↗

Cricket — 1970

Case: gold-plated, double push-down case back, leather strap, 38 x 42 mm

Movement: Caliber MSR S2, rhodium-plated, côtes de Genève, twin spring barrels, 17 jewels, manual winding

Remarks: alarm wristwatch with double sounding case back

Estimated value: $675 →

Cricket Nautical — 1966

Case: stainless steel, push-down case back, leather strap, Ø 42 mm

Movement: Vulcain Caliber 120, rhodium-plated, Exactomatic, 17 jewels, manual winding

Remarks: extremely rare variation of the Vulcain Cricket Nautical from 1966 with display of decompression times; case almost identical to Jaeger-LeCoultre Memovox Polaris

Estimated value: $7,450 ↗

Cricket Nautical — 1969

Case: stainless steel, push-down case back, plastic strap, Ø 42 mm

Movement: Vulcain Caliber MSR S2, rhodium-plated, côtes de Genève, Exactomatic, 17 jewels, manual winding

Remarks: rare Cricket Nautical; the colorful rings on the dial display the various decompression times

Estimated value: $1,600 →

Cricket Golden Voice — 1956

Case: gold-plated, stainless steel push-down case back, leather strap

Movement: Vulcain Caliber 406, rhodium-plated, Exactomatic, 17 jewels, manual winding

Remarks: small ladies' alarm in an early case version

Estimated value: $1,100 ↗

Cricket Golden Voice — 1957

Case: stainless steel, push-down case back, Milanaise bracelet

Movement: Vulcain Caliber 406, rhodium-plated, Exactomatic, 17 jewels, manual winding

Remarks: small ladies' alarm in stainless steel case

Estimated value: $800 →

Wakmann / Gigandet

What might seem like a double name for a venerable brand is in reality the double signature of two independent companies separated by the Atlantic Ocean.

Wakmann Watch Co., founded in New York, was the importer of various brands for the North American market. The most famous brand that it distributed was Breitling. Some of these watches even got a double signature and were known as Breitling Wakmann. Breitling's leading models were never offered under this double signature, however. Parallel to its distribution business after World War II, Wakmann began to produce—or have produced—watches under its own name.

Since the distribution of Breitling watches forced them to deal mainly with chronographs, it comes as no surprise that Wakmann also chiefly created chronographs under its own brand name. These were not produced in the United States, however, but completely purchased from suppliers in Switzerland. The company Charles

Gigandet SA in Tramelan was the largest supplier for Wakmann Watch Co. Behind this company name, however, were hidden three different, independent manufacturers. Alongside the company in Tramelan, there were also Gigandet-Rieder & Cie., which began its career in Langendorf, but later moved to Solothurn, and the Gigandet & Chopard workshop, which was also located in Tramelan, high in the hills above Neuchâtel.

The watches that Gigandet made for Wakmann and itself under its own brand name were, not surprisingly, similar to Breitling models of the day. Some of the dials and cases were certainly consciously designed in the same vein, and possibly even purchased from the same suppliers.

Although Wakmann's watches were strictly "only" products of a trade name, their aesthetic and technical quality fulfilled the highest demands. Above all, nothing was spared on the technical side, and thus Wakmann watches

were outfitted with movements that are sought after today—leading the pack were various Valjoux chronograph movements with column-wheel control such as calibers 72, 88, and 730 as well as the rare Valjoux Caliber 92.

Alongside the previously mentioned models offered under the double signature "Breitling Wakmann," there were also individual models on the American market signed Wakmann Gigandet even though these watches were normally exported to the United States only as Wakmann. Mainly, there were identical models in Europe and on other markets with Gigandet printed on the dial.

Alongside wristwatches, Wakmann also supplied the U.S. military with board clocks. These were also not made in the company's own workshop, but rather purchased from various manufacturers who then added the Wakmann name. Despite this, the mere fact that Wakmann supplied the army is proof of the quality of the company's private label watches.

Chronograph — 1950

Case: 18-karat yellow gold, push-down case back, leather strap, Ø 38 mm

Movement: Landeron Caliber 248, rhodium-plated, manual winding

Remarks: chronograph with 45-minute counter

Estimated value: $1,350 →

Chronograph — 1975

Case: gold-plated, double stainless steel push-down case back, leather strap, Ø 38 mm

Movement: Valjoux Caliber 726, rhodium-plated, column-wheel control of chronograph, manual winding

Remarks: chronograph with 30-minute and 12-hour counters

Estimated value: $675 →

Chronograph — 1960

Case: stainless steel, screw-down case back, leather strap, Ø 37 mm

Movement: nickel-plated, decorated, manual winding

Remarks: chronograph with 30-minute counter

Estimated value: $550 →

Chronograph — 1975

Case: stainless steel, screw-down case back, leather strap, Ø 37 mm

Movement: Valjoux Caliber 726, rhodium-plated, column-wheel control of chronograph, manual winding

Remarks: chronograph with 30-minute and 12-hour counters

Estimated value: $675 →

Chronograph with Complete Calendar — 1975

Case: stainless steel, screw-down case back, leather strap, Ø 37 mm

Movement: Valjoux Caliber 730, gold-plated, column-wheel control of chronograph, manual winding

Remarks: chronograph with 30-minute and 12-hour counters; complete calendar

Estimated value: $1,900 →

Chronograph — 1950

Case: 18-karat yellow gold, push-down case back, leather strap, Ø 38 mm

Movement: Landeron Caliber 248, rhodium-plated, manual winding

Remarks: elegant chronograph with 45-minute counter

Estimated value: $1,700 →

Chronograph Olympic Games — 1965

Case: gold-plated, stainless steel screw-down case back, leather strap, Ø 37 mm

Movement: Valjoux Caliber 7733, nickel-plated, 17 jewels, manual winding

Remarks: chronograph with 30-minute counter in a special edition for the Olympic Games

Estimated value: $400 →

Chronograph with Complete Calendar — ca. 1970

Case: black anodized, stainless steel screw-down case back, plastic strap

Movement: Valjoux Caliber 730, gold-plated, column-wheel control of chronograph, 17 jewels, manual winding

Remarks: chronograph with 30-minute and 12-hour counters complete calendar

Estimated value: $1,100 →

Chronograph with Complete Calendar — 1965

Case: stainless steel, screw-down case back, leather strap, Ø 37 mm

Movement: Valjoux Caliber 723, gold-plated, column-wheel control of chronograph, manual winding

Remarks: chronograph with 30-minute and 12-hour counters; complete calendar

Estimated value: $1,900 →

Chronograph with Complete Calendar — 1965

Case: stainless steel, screw-down case back, leather strap, Ø 37 mm

Movement: Valjoux Caliber 730, gold-plated, column-wheel control of chronograph, manual winding

Remarks: chronograph with 30-minute and 12-hour counters; complete calendar

Estimated value: $1,600 →

Chronograph with Complete Calendar — 1965

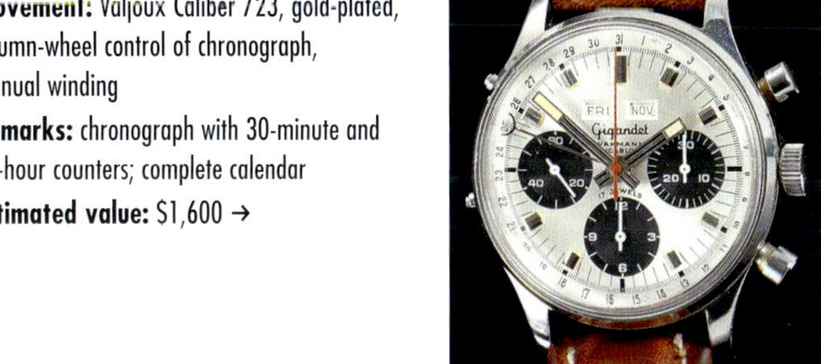

Case: stainless steel, screw-down case back, leather strap, Ø 37 mm

Movement: Valjoux Caliber 723, gold-plated, column-wheel control of chronograph, manual winding

Remarks: chronograph with 30-minute and 12-hour counters; complete calendar

Estimated value: $1,600 →

Chronograph with Complete Calendar — 1965

Case: stainless steel, screw-down case back, leather strap, Ø 38 mm

Movement: Valjoux Caliber 726, red gold-plated, column-wheel control of chronograph, manual winding

Remarks: chronograph with 30-minute and 12-hour counters; and complete calendar

Estimated value: $2,000 →

Chronograph signed Breitling — 1975

Case: gold-plated, screw-down case back, leather strap, Ø 39 mm

Movement: Valjoux Caliber 236, rhodium-plated, column-wheel control of chronograph, manual winding

Remarks: chronograph with 30-minute and 12-hour counters; complete calendar; rare double signature: Wakmann/Breitling

Estimated value: $550- →

Chronograph — 1969

Case: stainless steel, screw-down case back, rotating bezel, leather strap, Ø 38 mm

Movement: Landeron Caliber 51, nickel-plated, manual winding

Remarks: chronograph with 45-minute counter

Estimated value: $400 →

Automatic Chronograph Complete Calendar — 1975

Case: stainless steel, push-down case back, leather strap, Ø 42 mm

Movement: Landeron Caliber LWO 1341, nickel-plated, automatic winding

Remarks: automatic chronograph with sweep 60-minute and off-center 12-hour counters; date, weekday; additional regatta scale

Estimated value: $675 →

Automatic Chronograph Complete Calendar — 1975

Reference number: 9804

Case: gold-plated, stainless steel push-down case back, leather strap, Ø 42 mm

Movement: Lemania Caliber LWO 1341, nickel-plated, automatic winding

Remarks: automatic chronograph with sweep 60-minute and off-center 12-hour counters; date, weekday; additional regatta scale; case still bears original protective lacquer

Estimated value: $675 →

Zenith

This company grew large with its production of watches according to "American" standards, but it was really the introduction of the world's first automatic chronograph caliber that secured Zenith a special place in the history of Swiss watchmaking.

In 1865, twenty-two-year-old Georges Favre-Jacot founded his own workshop in Le Locle. He wanted to establish a more reasonable, rational production for precise pocket watches. Favre-Jacot had recognized that it was impossible to meet the growing demand for export using the usual production methods. Until then, machine-produced components still needed to be individually fit by hand. The effort was too great and the quality he achieved—at least on standard movements—was too poor to compete on the international market.

In the main export country, the United States, manufacturers like Waltham and Elgin produced better watches than the Swiss even at the lowest quality level. But that was precisely where Favre-Jacot saw his big chance: if he were to

manufacture according to American methods, he would logically also find success with his watches. And he was right: just ten years later

he employed more than a third of all workers in Le Locle, and his little operation had long become a factory.

The watchmaker impressively proved the quality of his watches when he won the first gold medal at the Swiss national exhibition in Geneva in 1896. Numerous other awards and many wins at chronometer competitions followed. Thanks to the precision of his watches, Favre-Jacot was also able to stand up to his competition when the Italian railway sought bids for a large contract for watches for its employees in 1909.

One of Favre-Jacot's movements was especially sought-after. Its name was Zenith. This moniker was soon to advance to become the name of the company.

In 1911, Favre-Jacot retired, leaving Zenith in the hands of his descendants who recognized the wristwatch trend in time and developed their own *manufacture* movements. After World War II, the first automatic watches arrived, still outfitted with hammer automatic winding. Zenith had begun with the manufacture of chronographs in the 1920s. At first the company used pocket watch calibers, but later they put movements by chronograph specialist Excelsior Park into their cases. Zenith only began its own movement production in 1960 when it took over Martel Watch-Universal Genève's production workshop. Universal Caliber 285 became Zenith Caliber 146, which the company used to outfit pilot's chronographs in the early 1970s. The company manufactured these watches, called Chronometro Tipo CP2, exclusively for A. Cairelli in Rome.

In 1969, Zenith once again captured the industry's attention, introducing the first chronograph movement with automatic winding to the world. They just beat out the developmental group comprising Heuer, Breitling, Hamilton-Büren, and Dubois Dépraz and thus proudly named their chronograph El Primero. "The first" was not only outfitted with a classic column wheel but also an extremely fast oscillation rate of 36,000 vibrations per hour.

That this caliber is still in production today is due to the insight of one visionary employee: in the late 1970s he did not sell off the tools for this meanwhile unprofitable mechanical caliber, but stored them in the attic of the *manufacture*. The watch company Zenith was taken over by the American Zenith Radio Company, which later sold it to Swiss machine maker Dixi. Thanks to its movement know-how, today Zenith is the crown jewel in the watch division of luxury goods concern Louis Vuitton, Moët & Hennessy (LVMH).

Chronograph — 1920

Case: sterling silver, push-down case back, leather strap, Ø 34 mm
Movement: rhodium-plated, côtes de Genève, column-wheel control of chronograph, manual winding
Remarks: early crown-button chronograph with 30-minute counter; enamel dial
Estimated value: $2,000 →

Chronograph Compax — 1950

Case: 18-karat yellow gold, push down case back, leather strap, Ø 34 mm
Movement: Caliber 146, rhodium-plated, côtes de Genève, column-wheel control of chronograph, manual winding
Remarks: chronograph with 30-minute and 12-hour counters
Estimated value: $1,800 →

Chronograph — 1945

Case: stainless steel, screw-down case back, leather strap, Ø 37 mm
Movement: Caliber 143-6, nickel-plated, column-wheel control of chronograph, manual winding
Remarks: chronograph with 45-minute counter
Estimated value: $1,100 →

Chronograph — 1960

Case: stainless steel, screw-down case back, leather strap, Ø 38 mm
Movement: Caliber 146HP, nickel-plated, column-wheel control of chronograph, manual winding
Remarks: sporty steel chronograph with 30-minute and 12-hour counters
Estimated value: $800 →

Chronograph El Primero — 1975

Case: stainless steel, screw-down case back, stainless steel link bracelet, 42 x 44 mm
Movement: Caliber 3019PHC, nickel-plated, column-wheel control of chronograph, 31 jewels, automatic winding
Remarks: former leading model of the early El Primero chronograph line; a sketch of this model long graced Zenith's stationery; remarkable rocking buttons
Estimated value: $2,000 ↗

Pilot's Chronograph El Primero — 1972

Case: stainless steel, screw-down case back, rotating bezel, leather strap, Ø 44 mm
Movement: Caliber 3019PHC, rhodium-plated, column-wheel control of chronograph, automatic winding
Remarks: rare pilot's chronograph of which only 2,700 were made
Estimated value: $1,600 →

Chronograph El Primero — 1975

Case: stainless steel, screw-down case back, stainless steel link bracelet, 38 x 41 mm
Movement: Caliber 3019PHC, nickel-plated, column-wheel control of chronograph, automatic winding
Remarks: chronograph with 30-minute and 12-hour counters; El Primero stands for the first automatic chronograph manufactured in series
Estimated value: $550 →

Chronograph El Primero — 1975

Case: stainless steel, push-down case back, stainless steel link bracelet, 38 x 41 mm
Movement: Caliber 3019PHC, nickel-plated, column-wheel control of chronograph, 31 jewels, automatic winding
Remarks: chronograph with 30-minute and 12-hour counters; El Primero stands for the first automatic chronograph manufactured in series
Estimated value: $675 →

Pilot's Chronograph Tipo CP-2 — 1970

Case: stainless steel, screw-down case back, rotating bezel, leather strap, Ø 43 mm
Movement: Caliber 146DP, nickel-plated, column-wheel control of chronograph, manual winding
Remarks: pilot's chronograph with 30-minute counter; this watch bears the additional signature of the contractor: "A. Cairelli Roma Tipo CP-2"
Estimated value: $1,900 ↗

Chronograph signed Türler — 1975

Case: stainless steel, screw-down case back, rotating bezel, leather strap, Ø 40 mm
Movement: Caliber 146HP, nickel-plated, column-wheel control of chronograph, manual winding
Remarks: chronograph with 30-minute and 12-hour counters; this watch was made for Türler in Switzerland and printed with the jeweler's logo
Estimated value: $950- →

Port Royal Chronometer Cal. 135 — 1965

Case: stainless steel, push-down case back, leather strap, Ø 36 mm
Movement: Caliber 135, rhodium-plated, côtes de Genève, beveled, 19 jewels, manual winding
Remarks: chronometer wristwatch with unusual dial design
Estimated value: $5,400 →

Chronometer Cal. 135 — 1965

Case: stainless steel, screw-down case back, leather strap, Ø 36 mm
Movement: Caliber 135, rhodium-plated, with côtes de Genève, beveled, 19 jewels, manual winding
Remarks: rare chronometer wristwatch
Estimated value: $5,400 ↗

Chronometer 2000 Cal. 135 — 1965

Case: stainless steel, screw-down case back, leather strap, Ø 35 mm
Movement: Caliber 135, rhodium-plated, with côtes de Genève, beveled, 19 jewels, manual winding
Remarks: chronometer wristwatch
Estimated value: $2,700 →

Chronometer — 1965

Case: stainless steel, screw-down case back, leather strap, Ø 334 mm
Movement: Caliber 40-T, rhodium-plated, beveled, manual winding
Remarks: rare chronometer wristwatch
Estimated value: $1,100 →

Chronomètre Captain de Luxe — 1965

Case: 18-karat yellow gold, screw-down case back, leather strap, Ø 37 mm
Movement: Caliber 2562PC, nickel-plated, automatic winding
Remarks: rare gold automatic chronometer
Estimated value: $2,000 →

Chronomètre Captain Automatic — 1966

Case: red gold, screw-down case back, leather strap, Ø 35 mm
Movement: Caliber 133.8, nickel-plated, côtes de Genève, automatic winding
Remarks: chronometer wristwatch with hammer automatic winding, manufactured in an estimated edition of 200 pieces; red gold buckle
Estimated value: $3,000 →

Collector's Topic:
Pilot's Watches

On the following pages we have chosen some professional pilot's watches and pilot's chronographs from our catalogue data and have displayed them here in alphabetical order according to brand. In individual cases, these particular watches will not be listed in their brand chapters.

Michael Ph. Horlbeck

Replica of a Laco pilot's watch outfitted with historical Durowe Caliber V2/5 with indirect sweep seconds.

The pilot's watch is almost as old as the airplane itself. In 1906, Louis Cartier developed the first "pilot's watch" for his friend, Brazilian aviation pioneer Alberto Santos-Dumont. Santos-Dumont had complained that while flying it was not entirely safe to read the time from a pocket watch. Thus, Cartier created a watch that could be worn on the wrist and so read easily at any time.

The path from this to a professional pilot's watch—which above all serves as a navigational instrument—did not turn out to be that long. As soon as airplanes were able to reach higher altitudes and fly longer stretches, a reliable wristwatch to calculate the course and oversee one's position became more and more important. It was theoretically possible to put classic ship's chronometers into an airplane's cockpit, but in a situation where every ounce of weight is of importance, these timepieces were simply too heavy.

Rate precision was also the main focus of pilot's watches, and thus the first pilot's watches were quite large, not because it was easier to read the time on them, but because the only movements that could fulfill the precision requirements at the time were pocket watch movements. The clunky cases were outfitted with soldered strap lugs holding extra-long straps—and were even often worn around the pilot's thigh.

From the late 1930s on, new materials and production methods led to more precise and robust wristwatch movements, and as a result the dimensions of the pilot's watch shrank down to a "wearable" size.

Alongside normal three-handed watches, timepieces were also developed early on that displayed important additional functions for the pilot. One of the first of these was the Weems Watch, named for its inventor, American navigation teacher Philip van Horn Weems. To synchronize the seconds with a time signal, Weems created a mechanism at the end of the 1920s that made it possible to reset the running second hand back to zero using a rotating subdial. This was not only faster than manually resetting the hand, it also hindered one from accidentally changing the time when pulling out the crown.

Heavenly Navigation

The Hour Angle Watch, introduced a little later, was an invention of Atlantic crossing pioneer Charles A. Lindbergh and utilized a rotating bezel with engraved angle degree numerals for navigation. The so-called hour angle gives the position of a celestial body in relation to a meridian, and via the deviation of the local time at the place of departure or arrival the pilot could quickly and reliably determine his or her current latitudinal position.

Alongside the normal time, professional navigation watches were often regulated by so-called sidereal time, which was directly based on the rotation of the earth's axis—the foundation of which is the sidereal day, which is about four minutes shorter than the solar day normally used as the basis of timekeeping. However, navigation according to sidereal time demands much more talent of a pilot or navigator than the otherwise usual status of the sun or hour angle. Thus, these watches were really something special for experienced navigators, and correspondingly rare.

The Trick with the Rotation

A rotating bezel with legible reference markers quickly became the recognizable characteristic of a pilot's watch. It could be used with simple chronograph timekeeping if the marking, for example, was directed at the current position of the hand at the beginning of a chronograph measurement—or adjusted to the desired end point of the measurement.

One critical disruptive factor for the rate of a pilot's watch is and always was magnetism, brought about, for example, by the strong starting magnets of a turbine or motor, some of which were positioned close to the cockpit. Once a movement is magnetized—even slightly—the rate for a mechanical movement clearly deviates. In order to avoid this danger, pilot's watches were designed more and more to include an extra core made of slightly magnetically affected soft iron. This soft iron core attracted the disruptive magnetic rays, keeping them away from the movement.

The use of a chronograph movement in a pilot's watch was the next developmental step, basically the logical progression of the rotating bezel with one reference marker. On a chronograph, one push of the button is enough to begin the measurement of a time interval—while the main time continues to be displayed unchanged.

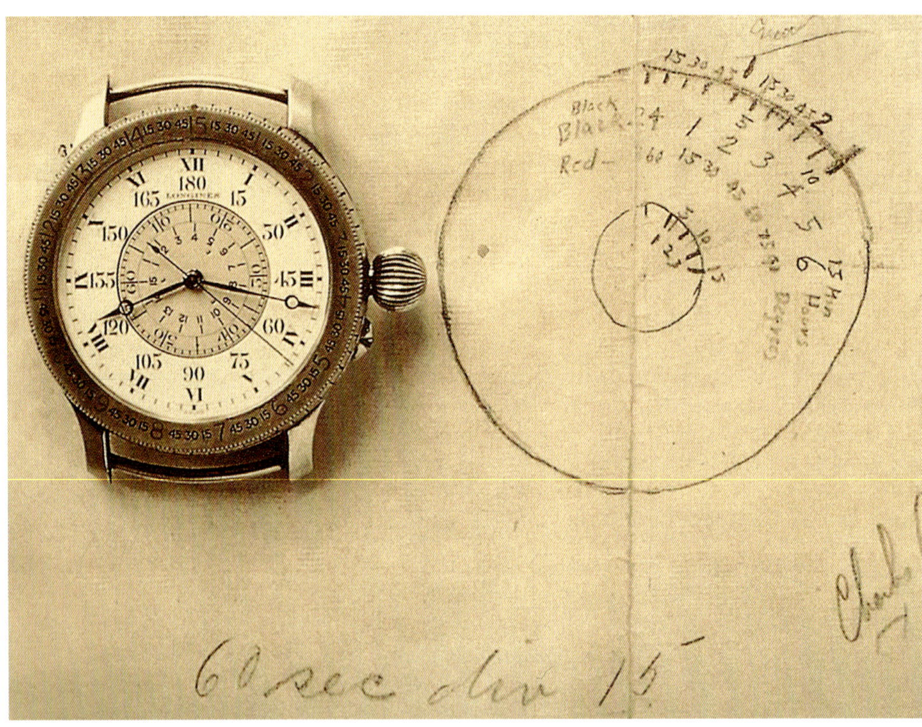

Photo: Lange Uhren

There is no doubt: the chronograph truly made being a pilot a little bit easier.

Flyback—
More Than Just a Toy

When Longines introduced Caliber 132N, its first chronograph caliber with flyback function, it was immediately recognized as perfect for the pilot. Thanks to a number of additional components, the Longines movement made it possible to interrupt a time interval measurement with just a push of a button, reset the counters to zero, and immediately begin the measurement again by letting the reset button go. The quick restart allowed for minimal deviation from the course during in-flight navigation. The pilot no longer had to move his or her fingers around to push three buttons—once to interrupt the measurement, once to reset, and then a third time to start a new measurement.

Breguet

Type 20

1945

Case: stainless steel, tripartite, screw-down case back, rotating bezel, leather strap, Ø 38 mm

Movement: Valjoux Caliber 222, rhodium-plated, column-wheel control of chronograph functions, fine matte steel chronograph components

Remarks: rare pilot's chronograph with 30-minute counter and flyback function

Estimated value: $8,000 →

Breguet

Pilot's Chronograph

1940

Case: stainless steel, tripartite, screw-down case back, rotating bezel, leather strap, Ø 37 mm

Movement: Valjoux Caliber 222, rhodium-plated, column-wheel control of chronograph functions, fine matte steel chronograph components

Remarks: rare pilot's chronograph for the French air force with 30-minute counter and flyback function

Estimated value: $8,000 →

Breitling

Chronograph

1967

Reference number: 765 CP

Case: stainless steel, tripartite, screw-down case back, rotating bezel, leather strap, Ø 41 mm

Movement: Venus Caliber 178, red gold-plated, column-wheel control of chronograph functions, fine matte steel chronograph components, 17 jewels

Remarks: large chronograph with 15-minute and 12-hour counters; hour scale printed on black rotating bezel; this watch was offered in its original box

Estimated value: $2,050 ↗

Breitling

Navitimer Automatic

1977

Reference number: 1806

Case: stainless steel, tripartite, screw-down case back, rotating bezel, leather strap, Ø 48 mm

Movement: Caliber 12, red gold-plated, fine matte steel chronograph components, micro rotor, fine adjustment

Remarks: large navigational chronograph for the Iraqi air force with 30-minute and 12-hour counters; date window at 6 o'clock; slide rule function on rotating bezel

Estimated value: $2,700 →

Breitling

Navitimer

1968

Reference number: 1860

Case: stainless steel, screw-down case back, rotating bezel, Ø 48 mm

Movement: Caliber 12, fine matte steel components, micro rotor, eccentric fine adjustment, automatic winding

Remarks: automatic chronograph with 30-minute and 12-hour counters; date window at 6 o'clock

Estimated value: $2,700 →

Dodane

Pilot's Chronograph

1968

Case: stainless steel, comprising several parts, screw-down case back, rotating bezel, leather strap, Ø 38 mm

Movement: Valjoux Caliber 222, nickel-plated, column-wheel control of chronograph functions, finely finished steel chronograph components, 17 jewels

Remarks: pilot's chronograph for the French air force; inscribed with "Force Aerienne Française - FG 14-11-68"; 30-minute counter and flyback function

Estimated value: $1,900 →

Doxa

Pilot's Chronograph

1940

Case: stainless steel, screw-down case back, leather strap, Ø 38 mm

Movement: rhodium-plated, côtes de Genève, column-wheel control of chronograph functions, manual winding

Remarks: rare pilot's chronograph for the German air force

Estimated value: $1,600 →

Eterna

Manually Wound Service Watch

1935

Case: stainless steel, leather strap, 38 x 48 mm

Movement: Caliber 852S, nickel-plated, manual winding

Remarks: early pilot's watch for the German air force

Estimated value: $800 →

Hamilton

1973

General Service Watch

Case: stainless steel, leather strap, 35 x 41 mm

Movement: rhodium-plated, manual winding

Remarks: service wristwatch for the British armed forces

Estimated value: $475 →

Hamilton

1965

Service Watch of the Royal Air Force

Case: stainless steel, screw-down case back, leather strap, Ø 36 mm

Movement: Caliber H 75, rhodium-plated, manual winding

Remarks: pilot's wristwatch for the British Royal Air Force

Estimated value: $800 ↗

Hamilton

1969

Chronograph for the Royal Air Force

Case: stainless steel, screw-down case back, leather strap, Ø 39 mm

Movement: Valjoux Caliber 7733, nickel-plated, manual winding

Remarks: pilot's chronograph with 30-minute counter for the British Royal Air Force; the right side of the case is integrated crown and button protection

Estimated value: $950 ↗

Hanhart

1935

German Air Force Chronograph

Case: stainless steel, screw-down case back, leather strap, Ø 41 mm

Movement: nickel-plated, column-wheel control of chronograph functions, manual winding

Remarks: rare German pilot's chronograph with unusual dial

Estimated value: $3,400 →

Hanhart

1936

German Air Force Chronograph

Case: nickel-plated, screw-down case back, rotating bezel, leather strap, Ø 39 mm

Movement: nickel-plated, column-wheel control of chronograph functions, manual winding

Remarks: one-button chronograph for an early version of the German air force

Estimated value: $2,450 →

Hanhart

1935

German Air Force Chronograph

Case: chrome-plated, screw-down case back, leather strap, Ø 41 mm

Movement: nickel-plated, with column-wheel control, manual winding

Remarks: one-button pilot's chronograph for an early version of the German air force with 30-minute counter

Estimated value: $2,000 →

Hanhart

1940

German Navy Chronograph

Case: nickel-plated, screw-down case back, rotating bezel, leather strap, Ø 39 mm

Movement: nickel-plated, with column-wheel control, manual winding

Remarks: rare one-button chronograph for the German navy with stamped eagle and number (KM185)

Estimated value: $4,050 →

Hanhart

1942

German Air Force Chronograph

Case: nickel-plated, screw-down case back, leather strap, Ø 39 mm

Movement: nickel-plated, with column-wheel control, manual winding

Remarks: rare one-button chronograph for the German air force with rotating bezel

Estimated value: $2,400 →

Hanhart

1945

German Air Force Chronograph

Case: stainless steel, screw-down case back, rotating bezel, leather strap, Ø 38 mm

Movement: nickel-plated, column-wheel control of chronograph functions, manual winding

Remarks: stainless steel pilot's chronograph with 30-minute counter

Estimated value: $2,000 →

Heuer

1945

German Air Force Pilot's Watch

Case: stainless steel, made of several parts, push-down case back, rotating bezel, leather strap, Ø 38 mm

Movement: nickel-plated, finely finished, column-wheel control of chronograph functions, finely finished steel chronograph components, polished screws

Remarks: rare pilot's chronograph for the German air force with 30-minute counter and military engraving on case back: "Kampfgeschwader 53, 10. Staffel"; fluted rotating bezel with reference marker

Estimated value: $4,050 ↗

Heuer

1975

Pilot's Chronograph

Case: stainless steel, screw-down case back, rotating bezel, leather strap, Ø 39 mm

Movement: Valjoux Caliber 7733, nickel-plated, manual winding

Remarks: pilot's chronograph for the Argentinean air force (Fuerza Aerea Argentina) with 30-minute counter

Estimated value: $2,300→

Heuer

1991

German Army Chronograph

Case: stainless steel, tripartite, screw-down case back, rotating bezel, leather strap, Ø 43 mm

Movement: Valjoux Caliber 230, rhodium-plated, column-wheel control of chronograph functions, hacking seconds, polished steel chronograph components, 17 jewels

Remarks: pilot's chronograph with 30-minute counter; the movement is regulated according to sidereal time for navigational purposes; engraving on case back "6645-12-146-5018"; this watch was offered with leather pouch and accessories

Estimated value: $1,350 →

Heuer

1970

German Army Pilot's Chronograph

Case: stainless steel, screw-down case back, rotating bezel, leather strap, Ø 43 mm

Movement: Valjoux Caliber 230, nickel-plated, column-wheel control of chronograph functions, manual winding

Remarks: Germany army pilot's chronograph with 30-minute counter and flyback function; degree of luminosity printed on dial (3H); number 6645-12463774

Estimated value: $1,900 →

IWC

1940

German Air Force Pilot's Watch

Case: stainless steel, lacquered, push-down case back, leather strap, Ø 55 mm

Movement: Caliber IWC 52, gold-plated, frosted finish, jewels set in chatons, manual winding

Remarks: extremely rare pilot's watch for the German air force; this watch was offered with original leather strap and box

Estimated value: $33,750 ↗

IWC

1940

Large Pilot's Watch

Case: matte gray, four parts, push-down case back, soft iron core, leather strap, Ø 55 mm

Movement: gold-plated, frosted finish, jewels set in chatons

Remarks: nearly new navigational bomber pilot's watch for the German army

Estimated value: $27,000 →

IWC

1940

Large Pilot's Watch

Case: matte gray, four parts, push-down case back, soft iron core, leather strap, Ø 55 mm

Movement: Caliber 52, gold-plated, frosted finish, jewels set in chatons

Remarks: extremely rare pilot's observation and navigational watch for the German army

Estimated value: $8,100 →

IWC — 1941

Mark IX

Case: stainless steel, several parts, push-down case back, rotating bezel, pilot-style textile strap, Ø 37 mm

Movement: Caliber 83, rhodium-plated, fausses côtes decoration, jewels set in chatons, polished screws

Remarks: extremely rare "special watch for pilots" as IWC describes the Mark IX; a reference time can be set with the rotating bezel

Estimated value: $16,000 ↗

IWC — 1944

Mark X

Case: stainless steel, push-down case back, leather strap, Ø 35 mm

Movement: Caliber IWC 83, nickel-plated, côtes de Genève, jewels set in chatons, manual winding

Remarks: Mark X pilot's watch for the Royal Air Force with case back engraving "W.W.W.M14177"

Estimated value: $4,600 →

IWC — 1944

Mark X

Case: stainless steel, bipartite, push-down case back, leather strap, Ø 35 mm

Movement: Caliber 83, rhodium-plated, jewels set in chatons, fausses côtes decoration, polished screws

Remarks: early pilot's watch for the British Royal Air Force with military case back engraving "W.W.W.M17417"; this watch was offered with an IWC buckle

Estimated value: $4,050 →

IWC — 1943

Mark X

Case: stainless steel, bipartite, push-down case back, leather strap, Ø 35 mm

Movement: Caliber 83, rhodium-plated, jewels set in chatons, fausses côtes decoration, polished screws

Remarks: early pilot's watch for the British Royal Air Force with military case back engraving "W.W.W.M14198"; the watch was offered with an IWC buckle

Estimated value: $4,700 →

IWC — 1951

Mark XI

Case: stainless steel, screw-down case back, leather strap, Ø 36 mm

Movement: Caliber IWC 89, nickel-plated, côtes de Genève, manual winding

Remarks: pilot's watch for the Royal Air Force; this watch has an additional magnetic soft iron core

Estimated value: $4,700 ↗

IWC — 1951

Mark XI Royal Air Force/BOAC

Case: stainless steel, screw-down case back, leather strap, Ø 36 mm

Movement: Caliber IWC 89, nickel-plated, côtes de Genève, manual winding

Remarks: extremely rare pilot's watch for the Royal Air Force; after World War II, this watch was used by the British Overseas Aircraft Cooperation (BOAC); the BOAC logo is engraved on the case back

Estimated value: $5,400 ↗

IWC — 1952

Mark XI

Case: stainless steel, tripartite, screw-down case back, rotating bezel, leather strap, Ø 36 mm

Movement: Caliber 89, rhodium-plated, fausses côtes, jewels set in chatons, polished screws

Remarks: pilot's watch for the Royal Air Force with a rare white dial

Estimated value: $2,400 →

IWC — 1963

Mark XI (civilian model)

Case: stainless steel, screw-down case back, leather strap, Ø 36 mm

Movement: IWC Caliber 89, nickel-plated, côtes de Genève, manual winding

Remarks: this watch was offered with its original box and papers

Estimated value: $4,050 ↗

Junghans — 1950

German Army Pilot's Chronograph

Case: chrome-plated, screw-down case back, leather strap, Ø 38 mm

Movement: Caliber 88, gold-plated, frosted finish, column-wheel control of chronograph functions, manual winding

Remarks: rare first edition of the pilot's chronograph for the German army with a fluted bezel; engraved with "Luftwaffe Nr. 6645-12-120-9351/88-0110"

Estimated value: $3,000 ↗

Junghans — 1955

German Army Pilot's Chronograph

Case: matte finish, stainless steel screw-down case back, rotating bezel, leather strap, Ø 38 mm

Movement: Caliber 88, gold-plated, frosted finish, column-wheel control of chronograph functions, manual winding

Remarks: pilot's chronograph for the German army; engraved with "Bundeseigentum Nr.12-124-8591"

Estimated value: $1,900 ↗

Laco — 1940

Pilot's Watch

Case: matte grey, tripartite, push-down case back, leather strap, Ø 55 mm

Movement: Durowe caliber, gold-plated, frosted finish, polished screws, 22 jewels

Remarks: pilot's watch for the German air force; assembled by Wempe in Hamburg

Estimated value: $3,400 ↗

A. Lange & Söhne — 1936

Observation Watch for the German Air Force

Case: nickel, push-down case back, leather strap, Ø 58 mm

Movement: gold-plated, frosted finish, jewels set in chatons, Glashütte gold pallets, gold escape wheel, manual winding

Remarks: exceptionally rare air force observation watch; according to shipping records, this watch was delivered to the minister for air travel in Berlin on March 31, 1936; only a few pieces of this model were made with optimal rate

Estimated value: $20,250 ↗

A. Lange & Söhne — 1938

Pilot's Watch with Special Dial

Case: silver, Ø 55 mm

Movement: Caliber 45, gold-plated, frosted finish, Glashütte gold pallets, manual winding

Remarks: extremely rare pilot's observation watch; sold on November 29, 1938 to the minister for air travel and the head of the air force; rare pre-series of the war version of Lange's pilot's watches (Caliber 45 was a small series of 10 pieces)

Estimated value: $27,000 ↗

A. Lange & Söhne — 1939

Observation Watch for the German Air Force

Case: silver, push-down case back, Ø 55mm

Movement: gold-plated, frosted finish, Glashütte gold pallets, manual winding

Remarks: exceptionally rare air force observation watch; according to shipping records, this watch was delivered to the minister for air travel in Berlin on September 5, 1939; only nine pieces of this model were made that included a movement with an optimal rate

Estimated value: $20,250 ↗

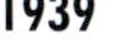

A. Lange & Söhne — 1940

Pilot's Watch

Case: matte grey, push-down case back, leather strap, Ø 55 mm

Movement: Caliber 48.1, gold-plated, frosted finish, manual winding

Remarks: pilot's watch for the German air force with military engraving

Estimated value: $6,100 ↗

A. Lange & Söhne — 1940

Case: matte grey, push-down case back, Ø 55 mm

Movement: Caliber 45, gold-plated, frosted finish, Glashütte gold pallets, manual winding

Remarks: exceptionally rare air force observation watch; according to shipping records, this watch was delivered to the minister for air travel in Berlin on January 18, 1940; rare pre-series of the war version of Lange's pilot's watches (Caliber 45 was a small series of 17 pieces)

Estimated value: $16,000 →

A. Lange & Söhne — 1941

Fighter Pilot's Watch for Hermann Goering

Case: silver, push-down case back, leather strap, Ø 55 mm

Movement: gold-plated, frosted finish, manual winding

Remarks: important, unique silver fighter pilot's observation watch; special order for federal minister of air travel Hermann Goering; sent to Berlin on March 5, 1941; this watch was offered with an excerpt from Lange's master registry and an extra-long pilot's leather strap

Estimated value: $94,500 ↗

A. Lange & Söhne — 1943

Pilot's Watch

Case: painted, push-down case back, leather strap, Ø 55 mm

Movement: gold-plated, frosted finish, manual winding

Remarks: pilot's watch for the German air force

Estimated value: $6,100 ↗

Lémania — 1920

Chronograph

Case: nickel, push-down case back, leather strap, Ø 32 mm

Movement: nickel-plated, côtes de Genève, column-wheel control of chronograph functions, manual winding

Remarks: early one-button chronograph with enamel dial

Estimated value: $1,900 →

Lémania — 1935

German Air Force Pilot's Watch

Case: stainless steel, leather strap, 38 x 50 mm

Movement: nickel-plated, manual winding

Remarks: early pilot's watch for the German air force

Estimated value: $950 →

Lémania — 1938

German Air Force Chronograph

Case: stainless steel, screw-down case back, leather strap, Ø 38 mm

Movement: gold-plated, frosted finish, column-wheel control of chronograph functions, manual winding

Remarks: pilot's chronograph for the German air force, RLM-NAV 5130 (stands for "Reichsluftfahrtministerium Navigation" or Federal Air Travel Ministry Navigation)

Estimated value: $2,400 ↗

Lémania — 1950

Royal Air Force Chronograph

Case: stainless steel, screw-down case back, leather strap, Ø 40mm

Movement: Caliber 2220, nickel-plated, column-wheel control of chronograph functions, manual winding

Remarks: pilot's chronograph for the Royal Air Force with 30-minute counter

Estimated value: $1,350 ↗

Lémania — 1960

Swedish Air Force Pilot's Watch

Case: stainless steel, screw-down case back, leather strap, Ø 40 mm

Movement: Lémania Caliber LWO 2225, nickel-plated, manual winding

Remarks: pilot's watch for the Swedish air force (57/2461-TG195) with reset device for the second hand

Estimated value: $1,900 ↗

Lémania — 1965

Royal Air Force Chronograph

Case: stainless steel, bipartite, screw-down case back, leather strap, Ø 40 mm

Movement: Caliber LWO 2220, nickel-plated, column-wheel control of chronograph functions, matte steel chronograph components

Remarks: one-button pilot's chronograph for the British Royal Air Force (6BB/924-3306-2141/65) with 30-minute counter; asymmetrical case to protect the crown and buttons

Estimated value: $1,350 →

Longines — 1938

Weems

Case: stainless steel, push-down case back, rotating bezel, leather strap, Ø 33 mm

Movement: Caliber 12.68N, gold-plated, frosted finish, jewels set in chatons, manual winding

Remarks: rare navigational pilot's watch for the Royal Air Force; AM (Air Ministry) engraved on military case back

Estimated value: $2,700 ↗

Longines — 1941

Pilot's Watch with Hacking Seconds

Case: gold-plated, push-down case back, leather strap, Ø 31 mm

Movement: rhodium-plated, jewels set in chatons, manual winding

Remarks: early pilot's watch according to a Longines patent with resettable sweep second and minute counters

Estimated value: $2,000 ↗

Longines — 1939

Weems

Case: stainless steel, push-down case back, rotating bezel, leather strap, Ø 34 mm

Movement: Caliber 12.68N, gold-plated, frosted finish, manual winding

Remarks: early pilot's watch with rotating bezel according to the Weems principle

Estimated value: $1,350 ↗

Longines — 1942

Weems

Case: stainless steel, push-down case back, rotating bezel, leather strap, Ø 27 mm

Movement: Caliber 10L, rhodium-plated, jewels set in chatons, manual winding

Remarks: early navigational pilot's watch with rotating and locking bezel according to the Weems principle

Estimated value: $1,350 ↗

Longines — 1946

Weems

Case: 14-karat yellow gold, push-down case back, rotating bezel, leather strap, Ø 33 mm

Movement: Caliber 10L, rhodium-plated, jewels set in chatons, manual winding

Remarks: early navigational pilot's watch with rotating and locking bezel according to the Weems principle

Estimated value: $2,400 ↗

Longines — 1946

Weems Chronograph

Case: stainless steel, push-down case back, rotating bezel, leather strap, Ø 47 mm

Movement: rhodium-plated, côtes de Genève, manual winding

Remarks: pilot's watch with resettable sweep second and minute counters; rotating bezel with reference markings

Estimated value: $12,150 ↗

Longines — 1936

Weems

Case: sterling silver, push-down case back, leather strap, Ø 47 mm

Movement: Caliber 18-69N, rhodium-plated, côtes de Genève, manual winding

Remarks: early navigational pilot's watch

Estimated value: $12,150 ↗

Longines — 1937

Lindbergh

Case: stainless steel, push-down case back, rotating bezel, leather strap, Ø 47 mm

Movement: Caliber 18.69N, gold-plated, frosted finish, manual winding

Remarks: rare, early large pilot's watch with sweep seconds and enamel dial

Estimated value: $16,000 ↗

Longines

Lindbergh

1934 

Case: stainless steel, several parts, hinged push-down case back, stainless steel cuvette, rotating bezel, leather strap, Ø 47 mm

Movement: Caliber 18.69N, rhodium-plated, côtes de Genève, polished screws, fine adjustment, 15 jewels

Remarks: extremely rare nearly new Hour Angle pilot's navigational watch; this watch was offered with a nearly unworn original leather strap; the Hour Angle concept came from Charles Lindbergh, the first to cross the Atlantic alone

Estimated value: $16,000 ↗

Longines

Lindbergh Hour Angle Watch

1938

Case: stainless steel, push-down case back, rotating silver bezel, leather strap, Ø 33 mm

Movement: Caliber 10L, rhodium-plated, jewels set in chatons, manual winding

Remarks: early, rare Hour Angle navigational watch with rotating bezel and rotating inner disk

Estimated value: $2,300 ↗

Longines

Lindbergh

1940

Case: 10-karat yellow gold, tripartite, push-down case back, leather strap, Ø 33 mm

Movement: Caliber 10L, rhodium-plated, finely finished, polished screws, 15 jewels

Remarks: early, small Hour Angle navigational watch in gold case

Estimated value: $2,700 →

Longines

Lindbergh

1943

Case: gold-plated, tripartite, push-down case back, rotating bezel, leather strap, Ø 33 mm

Movement: Caliber 12L, rhodium-plated, finely finished, polished screws, 15 jewels

Remarks: early, small Hour Angle navigational watch in gold case

Estimated value: $2,100 →

Longines

Lindbergh Hour Angle Watch

1947

Case: stainless steel, push-down case back, rotating bezel, leather strap, Ø 33 mm

Movement: Caliber 12L, rhodium-plated, jewels set in chatons, manual winding

Remarks: early, extremely rare Hour Angle navigational watch with rotating and locking bezel; this watch was offered with its original leather strap and silver buckle

Estimated value: $9,500 ↗

Longines

Astro Navigation

1954

Case: stainless steel, push-down case back, leather strap, Ø 47 mm

Movement: Caliber 37.9S, rhodium-plated, jewels set in chatons, manual winding

Remarks: extremely rare pilot's watch for Swissair with 24-hour display for astronavigation

Estimated value: $8,100 ↗

Longines

German Air Force Pilot's Watch

1936

Case: stainless steel, push-down case back, rotating bezel, leather strap, 40 x 51 mm

Movement: Caliber 15.94, gold-plated, frosted finish, manual winding

Remarks: pilot's watch for the early German air force

Estimated value: $1,600 →

Longines

Royal Serbian Air Force Pilot's Watch

1939

Case: stainless steel, push-down case back, leather strap, Ø 37 mm

Movement: Caliber 15.26, gold-plated, frosted finish, manual winding

Remarks: rare pilot's watch for the Royal Serbian air force with military engraving on the case back

Estimated value: $3,400 →

Longines
Royal Air Force

1940

Case: stainless steel, bipartite, screw-down case back, textile strap, Ø 36 mm

Movement: Caliber 12.68Z, gold-plated, frosted finish, jewels set in chatons, blued screws, 15 jewels

Remarks: rare pilot's navigation watch for the Royal Army with subsidiary seconds; military engraving "W.W.W. F4780" on case back

Estimated value: $3,400 →

Longines
Service Watch

1940

Case: stainless steel, bipartite, screw-down case back, rotating bezel, textile strap, Ø 36 mm

Movement: Caliber 12.68N, gold-plated, frosted finish, jewels set in chatons, blued screws, 18 jewels

Remarks: rare pilot's navigational watch for the British Royal Air Force engraved with "AM" (Air Ministry); sweep seconds; military engraving "AM 6B/159" on case back

Estimated value: $1,200 →

Longines
Royal Air Force Pilot's Watch

1944

Case: stainless steel, screw-down case back, leather strap, Ø 37 mm

Movement: Caliber 2.68Z, gold-plated, frosted finish, jewels set in chatons, manual winding

Remarks: pilot's watch for the British air force; engraved with "WWW-F5833"

Estimated value: $2,000 ↗

Longines
Royal Air Force Pilot's Watch

1951

Case: stainless steel, screw-down case back, leather strap, Ø 44 mm

Movement: Caliber 14.68N, gold-plated, frosted finish, jewels set in chatons, manual winding

Remarks: rare pilot's for of the Royal Air Force

Estimated value: $3,400 ↗

Longines
Military Chronograph

1941

Case: stainless steel, screw-down case back, leather strap, Ø 37 mm

Movement: Caliber 13ZN, gold-plated, frosted finish, column-wheel control of chronograph functions, manual winding

Remarks: rare military pilot's chronograph with 30-minute counter

Estimated value: $10,800 ↗

Longines
Military Chronograph

1968

Reference number: 8226-2

Case: stainless steel, tripartite, screw-down case back, rotating bezel, leather strap, Ø 38 mm

Movement: Caliber 332, rhodium-plated, finely finished, column-wheel control of chronograph functions, finely finished steel chronograph components, 17 jewels

Remarks: pilot's chronograph with 30-minute and 12-hour counters; a second time zone can be set with the knurled rotating bezel

Estimated value: $3,800 ↗

Marvin
Pilot's Watch

1935

Case: chrome-plated, bipartite, stainless steel push-down case back, leather strap, Ø 40 mm

Movement: Caliber 810, rhodium-plated, finely finished, jewels set in chatons, 15 jewels, regulated in 3 positions

Remarks: pilot's watch with rotating bezel

Estimated value: $1,100 →

Minerva
German Air Force Chronograph

1940

Case: stainless steel, screw-down case back, leather strap

Movement: gold-plated, frosted finish, column-wheel control of chronograph functions, manual winding

Remarks: rare pilot's chronograph for the German air force with 30-minute counter and snail tachymeter scale

Estimated value: $ 2, 500 ↗

Movado

1935

Pilot's Chronomètre

Case: stainless steel, push-down case back, rotating bezel, Ø 38 mm

Movement: Caliber Movado 75, rhodium-plated, jewels set in chatons, 15 jewels, manual winding

Remarks: extremely rare early pilot's watch with certified chronometer movement, which explains the fact that the movement was regulated in four positions

Estimated value: $2,000 →

Natalis

1930

Pilot's Watch

Case: chrome-plated, tripartite, screw-down case back, rotating bezel, leather strap, Ø 41 mm

Movement: gold-plated, frosted finish, polished screws, cylinder escapement

Remarks: early rare pilot's watch for the German air force; inner rotating inner bezel with marker

Estimated value: $3,400 →

Omega

1944

Royal Air Force Pilot's Watch

Case: stainless steel, screw-down case back, leather strap, Ø 32 mm

Movement: Caliber 30 T2, nickel-plated, manual winding

Remarks: rare pilot's watch for the Royal Air Force

Estimated value: $1,900 →

Omega

1953

Royal Air Force Pilot's Watch

Reference number: 2777-1SC

Case: stainless steel, screw-down case back, leather strap, Ø 37 mm

Movement: Caliber 283, red gold-plated, manual winding

Remarks: pilot's watch for the Royal Air Force, engraved with "6645/101000/6B/5425432/53"; this watch has an anti-magnetic soft iron core

Estimated value: $2,700 →

Omega

1927

German Air Force

Case: stainless steel, several parts, push-down case back, rotating bezel, leather strap, Ø 40 mm

Movement: Caliber 26.5 SOB, rhodium-plated, fausses côtes decoration

Remarks: rare early pilot's watch with fluted rotating bezel and large crown; this watch still has its original crystal

Estimated value: $6,750 ↗

Omega

1944

Royal Air Force Pilot's Watch

Case: stainless steel, several parts, push-down case back, rotating bezel, leather strap, Ø 33 mm

Movement: Caliber 23.4 SC, nickel-plated, polished screws; 15 jewels

Remarks: rare early pilot's watch with locking rotating bezel and engraved minute scale

Estimated value: $4,700 ↗

Omega

1935

Pilot's Watch

Case: stainless steel, push-down case back, rotating bezel, leather strap, Ø 40 mm

Movement: Caliber 26.5 SOB, rhodium-plated, manual winding

Remarks: rare early pilot's watch with rotating bezel

Estimated value: $10,800 ↗

Omega

1940

Royal Air Force Air Ministry

Case: stainless steel, push-down case back, rotating bezel, leather strap

Movement: Caliber 23.4 SC, nickel-plated, manual winding

Remarks: pilot's watch for the English Air Ministry, rotating bezel with locking according to the Weems principle; this watch was offered with an additional stainless steel link bracelet

Estimated value: $2,160 ↗

Record
1948

General Service Watch W.W.W.

Case: stainless steel, screw-down case back, textile strap, Ø 33 mm

Movement: Caliber 022K, rhodium-plated, manual winding

Remarks: men's watch for the W.W.W. British armed forces

Estimated value: $550 →

Sita
1927

Pilot's Watch

Case: chrome-plated, several parts, push-down case back, rotating bezel, leather strap, Ø 41 mm

Movement: nickel-plated, decorated

Remarks: rare early pilot's watch with rhodium-plated rotating bezel and outer five-minute scale

Estimated value: $1,350 →

Tutima
1940

Case: nickel-plated, tripartite, screw-down steel case back, rotating bezel, leather strap, Ø 39 mm

Movement: gold-plated, frosted finish, column-wheel control of chronograph functions, fine matte steel chronograph components, shock protection

Remarks: pilot's chronograph for the German air force with 30-minute counter

Estimated value: $5,400 →

Wempe
1944

Large Pilot's Watch

Case: matte grey, tripartite, push-down case back, leather strap, Ø 55 mm

Movement: gold-plated, frosted finish, polished screws

Remarks: pilot's watch for the German air force; this watch has the following engraved on its case back: "RLM Nav. B.-Uhr 1484"

Estimated value: $3,400 →

Wempe
1942

Large Pilot's Watch

Case: matte grey, tripartite, push-down case back, leather strap, Ø 55 mm

Movement: Caliber 31, gold-plated, frosted finish, polished screws

Remarks: large pilot's observation and navigational watch for the German air force

Estimated value: $4,050 →

Wittnauer
1940

Weems

Case: stainless steel, made of several parts, hinged push-down case back, steel cuvette, leather strap, Ø 48 mm

Movement: Caliber 137.9, rhodium-plated, finely finished, jewels set in chatons, polished screws, 16 jewels

Remarks: large pilot's watch according to the Weems patent for quick synchronization of the time without resetting the hands

Estimated value: $12,900 →

Universal Genève
1940

Split-Seconds Chrono for A. Cairelli

Case: stainless steel, push-down case back, leather strap, Ø 44 mm

Movement: rhodium-plated, with double column wheel control of chronograph functions, manual winding

Remarks: one-button pilot's chronograph with 24-hour dial; split-seconds function; 16-minute counter for astronavigation; case back engraved with "AMI, Chronometro per Navigaz. Astronom. TIPO HA-I, N. Categ. 19620, MM"

Estimated value: $20,250 ↗

Zenith
1970

Pilot's Chronograph Tipo CP-2

Case: stainless steel, screw-down case back, rotating bezel, leather strap, Ø 43 mm

Movement: Caliber 146DP, nickel-plated, column-wheel control of chronograph functions, manual winding

Remarks: pilot's chronograph with 30-minute counter; this watch bears additional signature of A. Cairelli Roma Tipo CP-2

Estimated value: $1,900 ↗

ISBN-13: 978-0-7892-0935-1
ISBN-10: 0-7892-0935-7
U.S. $35.00
53500
EAN
9 780789 209351